The Clear Lake Mirror-Reporter

ME 90   CLEAR LAKE, IOWA, THURSDAY, FEBRUARY 1959   NUMBER 2

EATH OF SINGERS HERE SHOCKS NATION

ck 'n Rollers, Pilot Die in Tragic Plane Crash

rock-and-roll headlines: Buddy Holly's plane crash, the day the music died.

North Iowa's Daily Newspaper
Edited for the Home

MASON CITY GLOBE-GAZETTE

HOME EDITION

"The Newspaper That Makes All North Iowans Neighbors"

Copyright© 1981 Lee Enterprises, Inc.

VOL. 97   Associated Press and United Press International Full Lease Wires   MASON CITY, IOWA TUESDAY, FEBRUARY 3, 1959   No. 99

Four Killed in Clear Lake Plane Crash

Pioneer Buddy Holly dies way too soon. Who knows what he might have gotten up to? (S.K.R./London Features International)

Clear Lake, Iowa. Rock-and-roll tragedy in the snow. Buddy Holly, Richie Valens, and the Big Bopper paid thirty-five dollars each for their fateful plane ride. (Elwin Musser, *Globe Gazette*)

e Big Bopper's forte s rock-and-roll com- (BMI/Michael Ochs hives, Venice, Calif.)

La Bamba's Richie Valens. He made it to the age of seventeen. (Michael Ochs Archives, Venice, Calif.)

The late, great Otis Redding strutting his stuff. (S.K.R./London Features International)

Jimi in full regalia. (Henry Diltz)

Chuck Berry onstage—his number-one song, "My Ding-a-Ling," says it all. (Copyright © 1994 Michael Jacobs/MJP)

Jim Gordon and Chris Hillman—those pesky voices told him to kill his mother. (Henry Diltz)

Jerry Lee Lewis being fed a few peas by his thirteen-year-old cousin/bride. (AP/Wide World Photos)

Kiss man Gene Simmons. He's seen it all before.
(Richard Creamer)

ROCK BOTTOM

■

**Other Books by
Pamela Des Barres**

I'm with the Band

*Take Another Little Piece of My Heart:
A Groupie Grows Up*

■

■

St. Martin's Press

❋

New York

■

PAMELA DES BARRES

■

Dark Moments

in

Music

Babylon

■

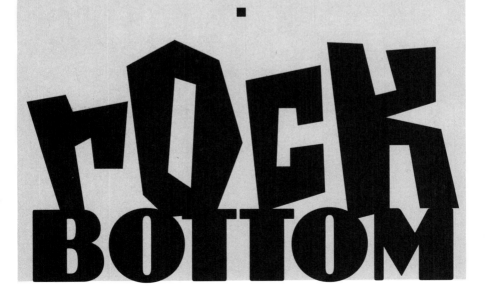

ROCK BOTTOM

■

This tome is dedicated

to my soul sister

MARY MAGDALENE—

the first groupie

■

ROCK BOTTOM: DARK MOMENTS IN MUSIC BABYLON. Copyright © 1996 by Pamela Des Barres. All rights reserved. Printed in the United States of America. No part of this book may be used or reproduced in any manner whatsoever without written permission except in the case of brief quotations embodied in critical articles or reviews. For information, address St. Martin's Press, 175 Fifth Avenue, New York, N.Y. 10010.

Design by Songhee Kim

Library of Congress Cataloging-in-Publication Data

Des Barres, Pamela.
    Rock bottom : dark moments in music Babylon / Pamela Des Barres.
        p.   cm.
    ISBN 0-312-14853-4
    1. Rock musicians—Biography.   2. Rock music—History and criticism.   I. Title.
ML394.D48   1996
781.66'092'2—dc20
[B]   96-22453
                                                                                                        CIP
                                                                                                        MN

First Edition: October 1996
10 9 8 7 6 5 4 3 2 1

CONTENTS

ACKNOWLEDGMENTS

First, I want to thank all the souls who gave up their earthly lives to rock and roll. I love you, Elvis. Jim, Moonie, Bonzo, Gram. But I also want to graciously thank those who didn't find it necessary to split the scene—Lou Reed, David Bowie, Iggy Pop, Joan Jett, Pete Townshend, James Brown, Ray Davies, Jimmy Page, Robert Plant, Elvis Costello, Robbie Robertson, the remaining Beatles, Ray Charles, Van Morrison, Neil Young, Keith Richards, Tina Turner, Ozzy Osbourne, Brian Wilson, Elton John, David Crosby, the Everly Brothers, Al Greene, Little Richard—who still live the life, but have managed somehow to hang on to their bodies and keep on rocking.

Thank you to my friend Gene Simmons, who gave me the idea for this book. He may have a very long majestic tongue, but he still thinks in dollar signs. Many thanks to Frankie Gaye, Eddie Cochran's family, Johnny Thunders's sister Marion, Sharon Sheeley, Richard Cole, the late Monika Danneman, Jan and Gertie Berry, Linda Alderetti, "Legs" Larry Smith, Sam Andrew, the Nelson family, Karen Lamm, Paul Ferrara, Todd Schifman, Nina Antonio,

Mr. Super Freak himself, Rick James, Nancy Parsons, Carol Clerk, Kathy Etchingham, B. P. Fallon, Merle Allin, and Miss Mercy, for opening hearts full of memories for me to poke into. Bravo to my editor, Jim Fitzgerald, for braving the rock-and-roll storm with me. Special thanks to Adam Wolf, David Portnow, Carol Clerk, and Chris Marlowe for much-needed assistance. And deep gratitude to those who carry the blazing rock torch into the twenty-first century: Terence Trent D'Arby, Oasis, Shirley Manson, Perry Farrell, the Red Hot Chili Peppers, Dwight Yoakam, Beck, Rage Against the Machine, Supergrass, Courtney Love, Prince, Eddie Vedder, Springsteen (always), Kim Gordon, and Sean Lennon. And I bow to Bob Dylan. Thank you for being on the planet the same time as I am. Your presence has blessed my uproarious life.

■

God let me come along at this time.
—ELVIS PRESLEY

■

■

INTRODUCTION

■

Rock and roll is over four decades old. Frightening but true. When Etta James belted out "Roll with Me, Henry" in 1955, she was boldly begging for some all-night-long S-E-X. "Insistent savagery" is how the 1956 *Encyclopaedia Britannica* described the fearsome "youth" music. Swivel-hipped god Elvis, with a face full of pancake makeup and eyes rimmed with dark blue eye shadow, was chopped at waist level on "The Ed Sullivan Show" for inciting a steamy sexual riot among pubescent girls all over America. I was one of them, though still in a state of prepubescent curiosity. But when the Beatles made it onto the "Sullivan Show" a few years later, my hormones were dribbling out of my ears as I slobbered all over the screen. Their first album was called *Meet the Beatles*. And that's just what I wanted to do.

Rock-and-roll panic grew and grew to unbelievable proportions while alarmed and bemused parents shook their heads in dismay. Huge stars were created almost overnight (and uncreated just as quickly). Suddenly an important group of humanity—teenagers—were ready to shake, rattle, and roll, idolizing and emulating the rockers who inspired such instant, hard-hitting, high-flying sexual and social rebellion.

I am a daughter of rock and roll. My very first records were Elvis's "Jailhouse Rock"/"Treat Me Nice" and Jerry Lee Lewis's "Great Balls of Fire." I was nine years old. I've got to admit those two hunks of vinyl set the tone for the rest of my life. All was calm in suburbia until Elvis told me that when he walked through the door, I had better be polite, and Jerry Lee broke my will, but what a thrill. I wanted to kiss the asses of those who inspired my soul and made me hot. And nothing was going to stop me. Armed with this awestruck determination, I eventually incited my own kind of infamy, becoming a rock courtesan supreme, being carted across the country by various rock gods, forming my own all-girl band, the GTOs (Girls Together Outrageously), with the late avant-genius Frank Zappa at the helm. He produced our record, *Permanent Damage,* in 1970, and Jeff Beck was a guest guitarist. Roderick "the Mod" Stewart (as he was called then) sang some backup vocals. I was in my element. I needed to be near what moved me so deeply that I wanted to climb inside Jimmy Page's guitar, hold Keith Moon's drumsticks, be in the room with Hendrix when he dropped a handful of acid and spewed fantastic cosmic wisdom. It was a heady existence, full of tightrope tension with a backbeat.

Rock stardom can be outrageously rewarding, but along with the onerous fame, massive amounts of money, and way too much backstage naughtiness of every description come the stresses and strains of chronic mass adulation. Sheltered, isolated, and protected, with every absurd whim catered to, rock stars are often the sacrificial lambs of their own success—and excess. Inspiring their fans to tortured, worshipful frenzy, rock stars often come to believe that they are above (or below) most of the laws that apply to the rest of us, taking madcap chances, teetering majestically on that invisible ragged edge in a tattered velvet cloak, while half the world watches. Jimi Hendrix set his guitar on fire and the keening wail freed the soul of rock and roll. Anything went. Anything goes. And it's not always pretty.

Little Frankie Lymon was not quite fourteen when he had his first smash hit with the Teenagers in 1955, "Why Do Fools Fall in Love?," written for a schoolgirl he had a crush on. A few more hits followed in those early sweet-beat years of rock and roll, and then Frankie went solo with "Goody Goody." But by the time little Frankie Lymon was twenty years old, his high-pitched angel voice had deepened and he had a heroin habit. Nobody cared about him anymore. He got a few lip-synching dates, played some record hops, and tried to clean up, but just couldn't seem to do it. Frankie got married and had to pimp out his young wife to keep up his habit. Dreaming of a comeback, he moved to Hollywood and rekindled a relationship with the Platters' Zola Taylor. He married her, even though he was married already. He messed with

Zola's life and she wanted an annulment, telling the papers that her marriage to Frankie had been "a joke." ("He ain't my stick," she said.) Back with wife number one, Frankie was arrested for theft and heroin possession. After a brief stint in the army (he was dishonorably discharged), Frankie married wife number three in 1967. On February 28, 1968, he was found on the bathroom floor of his grandmother's Harlem apartment, dead from an overdose of heroin. No longer a teenager, Frankie had made it to the ripe old age of twenty-six. Years later the three Mrs. Lymons and their lawyers became involved in a heated battle over massive back royalties for "Why Do Fools Fall in Love?" The legal wranglings continued for years. Finally, in 1992, a federal court proclaimed the winner. It wasn't a Mrs. Lymon at all, but the two Teenagers—Jimmy Merchant and Herman Santiago. The court found that they were the song's authors and awarded them royalties going back to 1969.

He wasn't called the Killer for nothing. When Jerry Lee Lewis married his thirteen-year-old cousin Myra, the Killer's career all but stopped in mid-strut as headlines blared CRADLE SNATCHER! After thirteen years of wedded hell, Myra finally filed for divorce on the grounds of adultery and abuse. In 1971 Jerry Lee married Jaren Gunn, but wife number four actually had the nerve to sue him for divorce, seeking piles of money. Having just plea-bargained to a pot possession misdemeanor charge, Jerry must not have been too happy when Jaren's divorce lawyers filed charges accusing Jerry of telling Jaren, "If you don't get off my back and leave me alone, you will end up in the bottom of a lake." Jaren was found dead at the bottom of a pool on June 8, 1982, weeks before her settlement was supposed to come through. The death was ruled an accident. Jerry Lee's next wife, twenty-three-year-old Shawn Stephens, didn't live long either. After a few stormy months of marriage, Shawn told her mother she was going to leave the Killer, but was found dead in her bed the next morning. An investigation by local law enforcement followed. No charges were ever brought against Jerry Lee or anyone else. Jerry Lee tied the knot with the sixth Mrs. Lewis in 1984. She's still alive.

In 1959, when Danny Rapp of Danny and the Juniors sang his joyous ode to the music he loved, "Rock and Roll Is Here to Stay," he hadn't planned on the endless empty years of obscurity that would follow his happy hit records. Finally in 1983 he locked himself in an Arizona motel room and blew his brains out. Depressed over his failing marriage and drug and alcohol problems, Temptations singer Paul Williams shot himself in a parked car in 1973. In 1990 Del Shannon, who hit number one in 1961 with "Runaway," blew his head off with a shotgun. An old friend of mine, Tommy Boyce of the successful songwriting duo Boyce and Hart (forty-two million records sold!), shot himself in the head just last year. Unable to kick his heroin habit, so did Nirvana's Kurt Cobain.

Skinny little Stiv Bators, founder of the Dead Boys and gothic punk supergroup Lords of the New Church, has to qualify for the most unusual rock death: On his way home from a club in the middle of the night, Stiv was run over by a car in Paris, but because he was so stoned, he found his way home, fell into bed comatose, and later died of his injuries.

What comes first, the addiction or the rock and roll? Are addictive people attracted to the high-wire lifestyle, or does the madness create the addict? I think the tendency has to be there, but rock stars have endless opportunities to fulfill this compulsion. They were (and are) expected to shoot, hit, sniff, snort, inhale, imbibe, drop, pop, and slop up all sorts of lethal substances in the name of rock and roll.

It seems that heroin has always had a comfy little niche in the rock world. In 1988, the original inspired guitarist of the Red Hot Chili Peppers, Hillel Slovak, OD'd on heroin shortly after the release of the Peppers' third album, *The Uplift Mofo Party Plan,* missing out on the massive success that followed. Mother Love Bone's singer/songwriter Andrew Wood cleaned up his habit to record their debut album, *Apple,* for Polydor, but a month before the release date, March 1990, he wanted one more bite, and died from an overdose. Twenty-two-year-old spiky-haired Darby Crash, punk frontman for the Germs, committed heroin suicide in 1980 after only one album on Slash Records. It was rumored that he was having a difficult time with his sexuality. He and one of his few girlfriends planned to leave the planet together, but Darby made sure that his dose was lethal and hers wasn't. In October 1995, Blind Melon singer Shannon Hoon was discovered in the back of the tour bus, slumped in his seat, dead from a heroin overdose. More recently, the Stone Temple Pilots had to cancel a slew of tour dates due to singer Scott Wellands's admitted heroin addiction, which was followed by a long stint in rehab.

If you don't count the pioneers—bluesman Robert Johnson, who was poisoned by a jealous husband when he was just twenty-seven, or "white man's blues" country gold Hank Williams, who died in 1953 of drug and alcohol poisoning at age twenty-nine—the first apparent rock-and-roll death occurred on Christmas Eve 1954, when Johnny Ace, a smooth-crooning R&B rocker, blew his head off in between shows in a game of Russian roulette. Twenty-four years later Chicago singer Terry Kath played the same game. There are several versions of the story—he was alone, he was at a party, he shot himself through the head at the breakfast table in front of his family. One thing is sure—Terry Kath played Russian roulette with one of his own guns and he lost the game.

They say the music died on February 3, 1959, when the four-seater plane carrying Buddy Holly, the Big Bopper (J. P. Richardson), and seventeen-year-old Ritchie Valens crashed in an Iowa cornfield, instantly killing the three famous rockers. The seemingly geeky, bespectacled Buddy Holly was the first rock star to become involved in all aspects of his chosen profession. He performed, wrote, arranged, and played guitar. He had plans to build his own recording studio in his hometown of Lubbock, Texas. He wanted to produce—himself, as well as new artists. He had a unique vision.

The Winter Dance Party Tour had become an exhausting grind, and Buddy booked the plane for himself and the Crickets, Tommy Allsup, and Waylon Jennings (who, years later, went on to shake up the country world as an "outlaw"), due to the freezing cold and their mechanically challenged tour bus. Image conscious, Buddy was also concerned about his rumpled stage clothes and wanted to have time to do his laundry. At the last minute the Crickets gave their seats to Valens, who flipped a coin for the prized seat on the plane, and to the Big Bopper, who was suffering from a bad cold.

Buddy sang most of his hit singles that night—"Peggy Sue," "Maybe Baby," "Rave On." Ritchie Valens had a double-sided hit record with "Donna" and "La Bamba"—the high-school kid from the San Fernando Valley was number two on the Top Ten and a bit overwhelmed by his success. The Big Bopper's "Chantilly Lace" had been on the charts for six months, but he was ill, his wife was pregnant again, and he couldn't wait to get home. After playing for fifteen hundred teenagers that night, the musicians paid their thirty-six-dollar fees to Dwyer Flying Service, climbed into the Beechcraft Bonanza, and headed into stormy weather. The next morning Buddy Holly's mother turned on the radio, pleased to hear a string of her son's hits, then learned about his death from the anguished disc jockey.

Some of the music definitely died that day, but the music has died over and over again. One of the great soul singers of all time, Otis Redding, was poised for crossover success after a kick-ass set at the Monterey Pop Festival and a scintillating rendition of the Stones' "Satisfaction." He wrote the sweet ballad "Dock of the Bay" to thank his Monterey audience, but it wasn't released until two weeks after his plane crashed in Wisconsin's frozen Lake Monona on December 10, 1967, killing Otis and four members of his band, the Bar-Kays. Otis was twenty-six. For months afterward my band mate Miss Mercy carried around a photo of Otis torn out of *Jet* magazine, frozen stiff in the seat of the plane.

On New Year's Eve 1985 Rick Nelson and his band died in a small plane once owned by Jerry Lee Lewis, who had sold it due to its constant mechanical problems. The rumor started that Rick had been freebasing on the plane, thereby causing the fiery accident, and though absolutely untrue, the rumor has become the stuff of rock legend. When I interviewed his kids, they said people still ask them how their father could have done such a horrible thing. It breaks them up.

When "Sweet Home Alabama" boogie band Lynyrd Skynyrd lost singer Ronnie Van Zant, guitarist Steve Gaines, and backup singer Cassie Gaines in a plane crash on October 20, 1977, it seemed they were cursed. Their final tour had been called "Tour of the Survivors," promoting the album *Street Survivors,* which featured "That Smell," a song about death. The cover of the album, a photo of the band engulfed in flames, was yanked by the record company after the accident.

I'm sorry to say that I wasn't as familiar as I should have been with the brilliant soul of Stevie Ray Vaughan until I listened to all his records while writing his chapter for this book. I'm not big on regrets, but I wish I had seen Stevie play live before his helicopter went down on August 27, 1990.

I've experienced my own rock casualties. Three members of my all-girl band, the GTOs, are no longer with me. Twenty-three years ago, Miss Christine mysteriously OD'd in a hotel room after mixing up a prescription-drug cocktail; Miss Sandra died of breast cancer, leaving four children; and Miss Lucy died of AIDS three years ago. I miss them a lot. In 1979 my friend Lowell George, who combined boogie funk with R&B in Little Feat, died at thirty-four from just too much booze and coke abuse. He was so talented and so damn sweet. I knew Badfinger's Tommy Evans, who hung himself in his backyard eight years after his partner, Pete Ham, hanged himself in his garage. I spoke to Tommy's wife, Marianne, and she told me such a sad tale. Signed to Apple and guided by the Beatles, Badfinger had several lilting pop hits before the music business ate them whole. Apple dissolved, the band was in litigation with Warner Bros., and there were horrendous management problems. When Pete Ham hanged himself in 1975, he left behind a suicide note calling Badfinger's manager a "soulless bastard." Tommy gamely tried to carry on, but it proved too much for him. "Tommy had throat problems," Marianne told me, "spitting out blood, he couldn't eat. . . . He was being sued for four million dollars." Tommy's son Stephen, six years old at the time, found his father hanging from a tree in the backyard.

Along with the death of Gram Parsons, I lost two friends from the Byrds— Gene Clark, who passed away on May 24, 1991, from "natural causes" stemming from decades of substance abuse, and drummer Mike Clarke, who died of liver failure in his mother's arms on December 19, 1993. I wrote complete chapters on my friends Gram Parsons, Keith Moon, John Bonham, and Jim Morrison, all of whom died from drug and alcohol abuse. In fact, every one of the chapter subjects no longer alive abused alcohol or drugs at one time.

It's been quite a humdinger experience writing this book. Whenever possible I looked up brothers, sisters, parents, girlfriends, wives, roadies, and band mates and took them out to breakfast, lunch, or dinner to reminisce about lost (dead or alive) loved ones. I went to Seattle to visit Jimi Hendrix's sweet father. I took trains in rainstorms to the English countryside, spending the day with the lady who claimed she was Jimi's fiancée (and the evening with Marc Bolan's witty PR man). I went to a suburban fifties tract house and watched old black-and-white footage of Eddie Cochran with his teary-eyed sister and nephew while holding his precious guitar in my arms. I whiled away the day in jail with superfunky felon Rick James and—guess what?!—was totally charmed by him. I spent the afternoon with Dennis Wilson's ex-wife while she tried to explain how the only Beach Boy who actually surfed could have drowned. I took Marvin Gaye's brother, Frankie, out to dinner and tried to avoid asking why in the world his father had shot and killed his big brother. It wasn't an easy gig.

Rap-a-tat-tat! Drugs and alcohol seem to be most rockers' ammo of choice, but gangsta rap has created a whole new world where aggro can thrive. Guns and violence have replaced pills and needles. The first rapper to get in severe trouble with the law was Ricky Walters, a.k.a. Slick Rick, whose debut album sold over a million copies. Rick is now serving time in New York for attempted murder after shooting his cousin. In 1991 Flavor Flav (William Drayton) spent twenty days in jail for punching his girlfriend and, in 1993, was sentenced to three months in prison for firing a gun at his neighbor. Flav, who has had his driver's license suspended forty-three times, was arrested again in November 1995 when police found an automatic weapon in his belt and three vials of crack. N.W.A.'s Dr. Dre was first arrested in January 1991 when he slugged and kicked TV hostess Dee Barnes because she included a segment on Ice Cube in her piece on N.W.A. He received twenty-four months' probation. Charged with assault and battery for breaking producer Damon Thomas's jaw in New Orleans in 1992, Dre was sentenced to house arrest in June 1993. In February 1995 Da Mob's J-Dee (Dasean Cooper) was convicted of murdering his girlfriend's roommate and sentenced to twenty-nine years to life.

After presenting an award at the MTV Music Awards in September 1993, Snoop Doggy Dogg (Calvin Broadus), charged with being an accomplice to murder, surrendered to police detectives. Snoop was sitting in the driver's seat of his jeep on August 25 when, according to witnesses, an argument broke out between Snoop's friend Shawn Abrams and his bodyguard, McKinley Lee, and another man, Philip Woldermarian. According to police, the rapper and his team chased Woldermarian to Woodbine Park three blocks away, where Lee fired the fatal shot. Lee insisted that the victim had been pointing a gun at the jeep and he fired in self-defense. On February 20, 1996, Snoop and his bodyguard were aquitted of first- and second-degree murder charges after the jury listened to testimony supporting Lee's statement that Woldermarian had indeed reached for his gun before Lee fired the fatal shot. Under lengthy questioning, two of Woldermarian's friends admitted taking the gun from him in order to improve the chances that the rapper and his bodyguard would be convicted of murder. The following day the judge declared a mistrial on charges of manslaughter. (Later the L.A. prosecutors decided not to retry Snoop and his bodyguard on the remaining manslaughter charges, which the court then dismissed.) Said an exuberant Snoop, "Victory is on. . . . The media made us guilty. But by the grace of God, the jury found us not guilty." When the judge ruled that Snoop had to stand trial in the murder case, the rapper told the press, "I will continue to make good music and keep my faith in God."

"I was in jail as a fetus," claims Tupac Shakur. The rapper's mother was a Black Panther who, while pregnant with Tupac, spent time in prison, awaiting trial. Tupac's first album, *2Pacalypse Now,* came under attack when a teenage car thief insisted the album's lyrics incited him to kill a Texas state trooper in April 1992. Arrested in March 1993 for carrying a concealed weapon, two days later Tupac was charged with assaulting a limo driver on the set of the Fox TV show "In Living Color." In March 1993 he allegedly attacked director Allen Hughes with a lead pipe after being axed from Hughes's film *Menace II Society,* and spent fifteen days in jail. Seven months later Tupac was arrested again, accused of shooting two off-duty policemen. The charges were later dropped when witnesses said one of the officers shot first. One month later, however, Tupac was arrested for sodomizing and sexually abusing a twenty-year-old woman in his Manhattan hotel room. (The victim, who admitted giving Tupac head in a nightclub, told police that Tupac later held her down while three other men repeated the act.)

While awaiting trial, Tupac was arrested for carrying a loaded 9mm pistol and half a gram of marijuana. In New York to stand trial, Tupac was headed to a recording studio in Times Square when he was robbed by three gunmen. Tupac, of course, put up a fight and was shot four times. Two bullets grazed his head, another punctured his left palm, and one went through the back of his right thigh and slit his scrotum. Against doctor's wishes Tupac checked himself out of the hospital and charged into court. Found guilty of sexual abuse (but not the more serious sodomy charges), Tupac was sentenced to up to four and a half years in prison. On October 12, 1995, Death Row Records posted $1.4 million bail to spring the rapper from Rikers Island's maximum-security prison, pending his appeal of his conviction. The headline in the *L.A. Times* upon Tupac's early release: I AM NOT A GANGSTER.

Uh-oh. Tupac's troubles with the law continued. In early April 1996, an L.A. municipal judge ordered Tupac to serve 120 days in jail due to his failure to do court-ordered Caltrans work, which violated his probation on two misdemeanor battery cases. Tupac's attorneys filed an appeal. He still faces felony charges in L.A. for alleged possession of a loaded firearm. After the hearing, the twenty-four-year-old said, "They can put me in jail for a hundred and twenty years, but I'll still be richer than all of them."

Rock and roll will always make headlines:

December '84—ROCK SINGER [Vince Neil] ARRESTED IN FATAL CAR CRASH
January '85—ROCK SINGER FACES MANSLAUGHTER CHARGE

September '85—HEAVY METAL STAR GETS $2.6 MILLION SENTENCE

September '88—SINGER JAMES BROWN CHARGED IN GUN INCIDENT AND
POLICE CHASE

November '88—JAMES BROWN ADDICTED TO PCP

January '89—BROWN GETS SIX YEARS IN GEORGIA SENTENCE

February '91—GODFATHER OF SOUL PAROLED AFTER TWO YEARS OF SENTENCE

September '93—DID MICHAEL DO IT?

April '94—EX-WIFE SUES AXL ROSE, ALLEGING YEARS OF ABUSE

June '94—BASSIST FOR BAND HOLE FOUND DEAD

August '94—ROCK STAR BILLY IDOL RELEASED AFTER POSSIBLE OVERDOSE
HOSPITALIZES HIM

February '95—BLIND MELON SINGER CHARGED

February '95—RAP STAR EAZY-E SAYS HE HAS AIDS

March '95—RAP SINGER EASY-E DIES OF AIDS AT 31

October '95—DEPECHE MODE'S LEAD SINGER BACK HOME AFTER SUICIDE TRY

October '95—BOBBY BROWN CHECKS INTO REHAB IN DESPERATE BID TO WIN
BACK WHITNEY

October '95—BLIND MELON'S SHANNON HOON FOUND DEAD

November '95—LOVE IN COURT. "Courtney Love was in the mood to play
games as her assault trial began in Orlando, Fla. Wearing a
black ruffled suit, the rock star whispered from the defense
table Thursday: 'Hey, prosecutors. Pssssst. . . . Can I be O.J.
and you be Christopher Darden?'"

June '96—MILLI VANILLI FIGURE FLEES DRUG CENTER

July '96—MUSICIAN TOURING WITH SMASHING PUMPKINS DIES

■

I feel so alone sometimes.
The night is quiet for me.
I'd love to be able to sleep.
I am glad that everyone is
gone now. I'll probably
not rest. I have no need
for all this. Help me Lord.

—a note written by ELVIS PRESLEY,
December 1976

■

LAUGHING SYD BARRETT

■

Scream

Thy

Last

Scream

■

Nobody seems to be able to pinpoint when Pink Floyd's founder, Syd Barrett, began his slide into legendary madness. Like most poetic, gifted artists, Syd was wildly sensitive, difficult to understand, and headed down a decidedly precarious path that few would dare follow. After his highly creative, tumultuous period with the Floyd, the mischievous twinkle in Syd's eyes got flat and foreboding, then blinked out completely. Over twenty years have passed since Syd graced the rock world with his starlit piper's heart, but his mythic legend continues to grow. His rabid cult following flourishes, his few records are released over and over again, but unlike Hendrix, Lennon, and Morrison, Syd Barrett is still alive.

Roger Keith Barrett was a gorgeous, happy kid with a wicked sense of humor, adored by his parents and siblings, admired by his peers and teachers. Though his father, a prominent doctor, passed away when Syd was fifteen, his mother lavished attention on her talented son, encouraging his keen interest in art and music. At fourteen Syd briefly played guitar in a band he called The

Hollerin' Blues, and soon had major status in his hometown of Cambridge, where the local girls were entranced by his dark, wavy bangs and the unique way he decked himself out. (It was during this time that he picked up the nickname Syd at a local pub.) During his two-year stint at Cambridge Technical Art College Syd was so preoccupied with his guitar that his girlfriend Libby Gausden often felt left out. "He was totally lost," she recalled. "I used to loathe that guitar, like every girlfriend did." When Syd took her to see a new, unsigned band, the Rolling Stones, Libby was once again left on the sidelines as Syd had a long musical chat with singer Mick Jagger.

Syd continued to paint and was accepted at a prestigious London art college, but found that playing music with fellow students Nick Mason, Richard Wright, Roger Waters, and Bob Klose held more fascination and promise than the classroom. Syd had started singing and writing songs, setting his sights on pop stardom. A hardcore fan of rhythm and blues, he called the fledgling band Pink Floyd after two Georgia bluesmen, Pink Anderson and Floyd Council, and proudly painted the new moniker on their banged-up old van in bright pink letters, though the band did little more than play pubs and parties for the next year and a half. Musical tastes of the band members were diverging, and Syd was getting a little too far out for Bob Klose, so Klose called it quits early in 1965. (Syd was already experimenting with feedback and echo boxes.) Klose recalled Syd as a gifted artist. "He had almost too much talent, if such a thing is possible. But there were definitely no signs of what was to come. . . . The music business is so full of cheats and exploiters that a true artist is always going to be vulnerable."

In the summer of '65 nineteen-year-old Syd was getting as far out as possible, gobbling pure LSD and becoming involved in Sant Mat (Path of the Masters), a Sikh sect, with much reverence and excitement. When he was turned down by the Maharaji Charan Singh Ji and told instead to pursue his studies, Syd was crushed and humiliated, and began his own spiritual training by using vast quantities of psychedelics, which he quickly channeled into music.

After garnering a substantial following, in February 1966 Pink Floyd made their debut at London's oh-so-trendy Marquee Club, sending out invitations that read: "Who will be there? Poets, pop singers, hoods, Americans, homosexuals (because they make up ten percent of the population), twenty clowns, jazz musicians, one murderer, sculptors, politicians, and some girls who defy description are among those invited."

Also among those invited was Peter Jenner, one half of a rock managing team, who was impressed enough to promise the group that he would make them "bigger than the Beatles." Jenner and Andrew King bought the band new equipment, and Syd embarked on a staggering period of creativity, combining all his far-reaching influences—the *I Ching,* Tolkien's Middle Earth tales, Dylan, Chicago blues, the Byrds, English folk ballads, the Beatles, the

Stones, avant-electronics—into a psychedelic stew uniquely his own. He was the group's leader and inspiration, coming up with bass lines and drum rolls, as well as the motivating vision—a vision that would last for decades. When the Floyd played the Roundhouse in October 1966 in front of a mind-altering light show, it was an "event." Paul McCartney arrived in white robes and a headdress, and Marianne Faithfull won the "Shortest and Barest" prize for her very naughty nun's habit. Soon after, Pink Floyd became the house band at UFO, a dark and damp underground den of iniquity where nothing was forbidden and everything was encouraged. The show revolved around Syd, and the rest of the band were hard pressed to keep up with his "No Rules!!" law, keeping their eyes on their whimsical leader at all times. And he *looked* so cool in his King's Road popped-out regalia—a disarming, unruly velvet-and-satin showcase.

Syd lived with an attractive model, Lyndsay Korner, in a flat with a purple door, and his days were spent high and productive. He considered himself a "progressive" artist, taking his inspiration from Handel's *Messiah,* William Blake, and acid guru Timothy Leary. With several labels showing interest, Jenner and King chose EMI for Pink Floyd, and when the band's first single, Syd's outrageous "Arnold Layne" (about a fellow who enjoyed cross-dressing), was released in March 1967, it was banned on London's pirate radio. With the help of the ensuing controversy, the single managed to crack the Top Twenty and is now regarded as a classic of megaproportions. "Arnold Layne just happens to dig dressing up in women's clothing," said Syd. "A lot of people do, so let's face up to reality!"

In that 1967 Spring of Love the original Pink Floyd began their brief period of glory, playing on "Top of the Pops," headlining huge venues in front of flying-high fans, grabbing rave reviews, creating musical and visual milestones for bands to live up to for years to come.

The original Pink Floyd before Syd Barrett *(second from right)* took the low road (after he took the high road). (MICHAEL OCHS ARCHIVES/ VENICE, CALIF.)

The follow-up single, "See Emily Play," was written by Syd after he "slept under the stars" and encountered a naked girl dancing in the woods. No one knows if this incident truly took place because Syd was almost always in the grip of an intense acid trip, his eyes glittering from someplace far away and ultimately unreachable. But who wanted to burst the Summer of Love bubble by coming down on somebody's groovy trip? Already quite eccentric, Syd was starting to show signs of extremely bent behavior—he once fried an egg over a small camp stove in the middle of a Floyd set at the UFO club. It was a sure sign of sad things to come, but I certainly wish I could have been there.

In the studio, however, Syd was a miracle. Pink Floyd's album, *The Piper at the Gates of Dawn*—the title of chapter seven in the children's book *The Wind in the Willows* (one of Syd's favorites)—is a stunning accomplishment, full of innocent fairy-tale imagery gone mad ("Lazing in the boggy dew, sitting on a unicorn"), singsong vocals, and trippy-hippie psycho-delic enchantment. We get to meander through Syd's personal dreamscape, where he was barely balancing on the edge of bewitched, beleaguered reality. Years later Roger Waters told *Q* magazine, "What enabled Syd to see things the way he did? It's like why is an artist an artist? Artists simply do, see and feel things in a different way than other people. In a way it's a blessing but it can also be a terrible curse." By the time Syd's masterpiece reached number six on the charts, he had more pressing things on his mind.

When gigs had to be canceled, the management labeled Syd's problem as "nervous exhaustion." For weeks at a time the twenty-two-year-old seemed in complete control, and then he would snap—once keeping his girlfriend locked in a room for three days, shoving crackers under the door while she begged to be let out. When the badly shaken girl was discovered by friends and released, Syd promptly locked himself in the same room for an entire week. Besides the blasts of acid that Syd bestowed upon himself, sycophantic friends would dose his drinks just to watch him shatter into interesting fragments.

There was pressure from the rest of the band to conform to some sort of commercial "pop star" ideal that the increasingly fragile Syd couldn't even comprehend. Demands were made for a third Barrett single. It must have been difficult for the band to realize the full extent of how Syd was losing his grip. They didn't spend much time with their elusive leader, and even playing music together became virtually impossible. At a gig in July with the Animals, it became excruciatingly clear that Syd was slowly switching off. He just stood onstage with his guitar dangling around his neck, staring at the audience, catatonic. When the Floyd started their first tour of the United States, they soon realized it would be Syd's last. In between brief moments of dissonant brilliance and frenzied sexual encounters with eager, adoring girls, Syd unraveled. The look on his face was one of horrified paranoia. He had gotten a bad perm and his hair frizzed out from his head like a fright wig, the blazingly bright colors he wore giving his ashen features a dreadful glow. In San Francisco Syd bought a pink Cadillac, only to give it away to a total stranger a few days later. During a record-company tour of Hollywood, upon reaching the corner of

Sunset and Vine, Syd piped up, "It's great to be in Las Vegas!" On Dick Clark's "American Bandstand" Syd refused to lip-synch to "See Emily Play," and on Pat Boone's TV show he stared blankly as a flustered Pat asked an array of dumb questions. He just walked off the set of a third television show. Finally the disastrous tour was halted, with the East Coast never getting the opportunity to see Syd Barrett's Pink Floyd.

Recording sessions for the second album proved to be madness, with Syd insisting that a Salvation Army band be brought in for "Jugband Blues." The lyrics are telling: "I'm not here/And I'm wondering who could be writing this song." In another tune, "Vegetable Man," Syd describes what he is wearing, tossing in the chorus, "Vegetable man, where are you?" Good question. Onstage he would either not play at all, play an entirely different song than the rest of the band, or strum the same chord endlessly, sitting cross-legged and staring flatly at the audience. When the Floyd toured with the Jimi Hendrix Experience, Jimi nicknamed Syd "Laughing Syd Barrett." Maybe the guitar god witnessed something in the dark-ringed eyes that nobody else could see.

Syd let his hair get matted and grungy, beat up his girlfriend (once smashing her repeatedly with a mandolin), and dropped endless tabs of LSD (once tripping for three solid months), becoming more and more withdrawn. The band never knew what would happen when he finally made it to the stage. "We staggered on thinking we couldn't manage without Syd," said Nick Mason, "so we put up with what can only be described as a fucking maniac. We didn't choose to use those words, but I think he was." At this point, an old friend of Syd's, David Gilmour, was brought in to pick up Syd's formidable slack onstage.

The most notorious Syd Barrett tale seems like a verification of Mason's assessment. Weary of waiting for Syd to pull himself out of his backstage mirror-trance, the band went onstage without him. Fifteen minutes later he appeared with a mixture of his favorite downer-drug, Mandrax, and a full jar of greasy Brylcreem rubbed into his frizzed-out hair. The hot lights soon turned Syd's head into an oily, dripping, monstrous display of insanity. On a night soon after this fearsome demonstration, the band just didn't pick Syd up for a gig.

Jonathon Green interviewed Syd for *Rolling Stone,* hoping to share in the Piper's spiritual revelations, but the article was scrapped after the subject spent most of the time staring at the top corner of the room. "Now look up there," an awestruck Syd told Green. "Can you see the people on the ceiling?"

After a harrowing band meeting, it was put to Syd that perhaps he could become to Pink Floyd what Brian Wilson was to the Beach Boys—he could write and record but not perform live. Did Syd realize he was being excised from his own band? The split wasn't announced until April 6, but after more disastrous sessions, a haunted Syd stood around in EMI's Abbey Road lobby with his guitar for two days, waiting to fulfill his Brian Wilson role. He never got the chance.

A month later the doomed yet still eerily exotic Syd Barrett went back into the studio to attempt a solo record. It was an uneven, chaotic, and ultimately abortive experience that left Syd teetering more precariously than ever. He spent some time in a hospital, moved from place to place, spent days and weeks in bed, and turned up at Floyd gigs, staring a deep, dark hole into the eyes of David Gilmour, his replacement.

March of '69 found Syd back in the studio due to the determination of Malcolm Jones, the youthful boss of EMI's progressive Harvest label. Jones was ecstatic with the first session, in which Syd completed six guitar and vocal tracks. The drummer on *The Madcap Laughs* sessions was Jerry Shirley. "Syd had a terrible habit of looking at you and laughing in a way that made you feel really stupid," he recalled. "He gave the impression he knew something you didn't." The sessions proved to be maddening and tedious for the musicians. Soft Machine were brought in for overdubs and soon realized the tracks they thought were rehearsal tapes were actually the final takes. Said Robert Wyatt, "We'd say, 'What key is that in, Syd?' and he would simply reply, 'Yeah!' or 'That's funny!'" David Gilmour, who always took a concerned interest in Syd's life, came in to finish the record. (Guilt, perhaps?) But by the time the final session took place, Syd's deterioration was blatant and shocking. Accompanied by the sound of his lyric pages being turned, Syd stops and starts, singing in an agonized, strangled voice. It hurts to listen to it. *Melody Maker* described *The Madcap Laughs* as "the mayhem and madness representing the Barrett mind unleashed."

Record sales were respectable, which prompted Gilmour to produce Syd's second album, *Barrett,* released in November 1970. Though Syd's looming madness was laced with touches of former magic, especially on "Baby Lemonade" and "Gigolo Aunt," the sessions were torture. Syd's directions came out of faraway left field: "Perhaps we could make the middle darker and maybe the end a bit middle afternoonish," he'd tell the confused musicians. "At the moment it's too windy and icy." The lyrics told of a desolate place where Syd was spending most of his time: "Cold iron hands clap the party of clowns outside," and even more revealing, "Inside me I feel so alone and unreal." The Madcap wept.

Syd was still surrounded by doting groupie girls, hangers-on, and drug dealers who haunted his London flat, soaking up the Piper's sad/mad sheen. He continued to paint, locking himself in his room, slowly becoming even more reclusive and incommunicative. In the summer of 1970 Floyd's Roger Waters saw Syd carrying two large bags in Harrods department store, but when Syd spotted Roger, he dropped the bags and ran crazily from the store. Curious, Roger peeked into the abandoned Harrods bags and found several pounds of candy.

Somehow Syd managed an on-again, off-again schizophrenic relationship with a Cambridge girl, Gayla Pinion, and when he tired of London's mayhem, dragged her back to his mother's house in Cambridge with promises of marriage. The release of his second solo album held no interest for Syd, who told friends that he was going back to school to become a doctor. Needless to say, the good Doctor Barrett never materialized.

During a celebratory family meal for Syd and Gayla's engagement, Syd had a coughing fit at the table, disappeared upstairs, and came back with all of his hair chopped off. "No one batted an eyelid," said Gayla. "They just carried on with the meal as if nothing had happened—didn't say a word. I thought, Are they mad, or is it me?" The couple's brief engagement was shattered by Syd's increasing violent jealousy, and Gayla had to give up on life with the Madcap, leaving him alone in his mother's cellar.

In 1971 another *Rolling Stone* writer and huge Barrett fan, Mick Rock, hunted Syd down, reporting that he looked "hollow-cheeked and pale . . . his eyes reflect a permanent state of shock. He has a ghostly beauty which one normally associates with the poets of old." Syd told the reporter that he walked a lot, painted, wasted time, and feared getting old. He said that he felt "full of dust and guitars."

Cajoled out of his musical exile by a drummer called Twink (formerly with the Pink Fairies), Syd gave some appalling performances with a band called "Stars" before crawling back to the comfort of his dark cellar-world. An attempt at a third solo album was a pathetic misfortune. As Pink Floyd found massive success, their founder thrashed around in his cellar, tearing himself and the place apart—an incident that landed him in the hospital once again. But back in the real world, a cult was forming around Syd Barrett. A publication called *The Terrapin,* sponsored by the "Syd Barrett Appreciation Society," brought together Syd freaks from all over the world. Even the pop weeklies reported "Syd sightings." One such sighting had him trying on three different sizes of trousers at a trendy boutique, announcing that they all fit him perfectly.

In the mid-seventies Syd moved back to London, where he spent the next eight years in two rooms at Chelsea Cloisters watching a TV suspended from the ceiling, drinking Guinness, and making constant treks to his refrigerator (fascinated with televisions, Syd once had half a dozen). Within a year the once-skinny pop star would weigh over two hundred pounds and shave himself bald—perhaps Syd's way of remaining in exile.

Due to David Bowie's cover of "See Emily Play" and the repackaging of Pink Floyd's first two LPs, Syd had plenty of money and found assorted eccentric ways to rid himself of it. He bought things and threw them away, he bought things and *gave* them away—clothes, TVs, stereo equipment, guitars. He gave massive tips to porters and delivery people, inviting them in and offering more gifts, which they gladly carried away.

EMI repackaged *The Madcap Laughs* and *Barrett,* hoping to cash in on Syd's cult legend, and Peter Jenner gave it one more try in the studio with Floyd's founder. Syd *did* show up at the studio—with no strings on his guitar—and when somebody gave him some typed lyrics, Syd promptly bit the person's hand, thinking he was being handed a bill. If Syd turned right upon leaving the studio, he would return; if he turned left, he was gone. Jenner gave up after three days, and Syd Barrett never recorded again.

On June 5, 1975, during one of Pink Floyd's *Wish You Were Here* sessions, David Gilmour spotted a chubby fellow with a shaved head toddling around Abbey Road's Studio Three wearing a short-sleeved sport shirt. When he wandered into the control room, nobody knew who he was. "We were all whispering, 'Who the fuck's this funny geezer?'" Gilmour recalled. "I think I was the first to recognize him." Even though Syd said a few words, he wasn't really there. He showed up for Gilmour's wedding reception later that day, chuckling under his breath. No one in Pink Floyd has seen him since.

Disc jockey Nicky Horne turned up at Cloisters, hoping for a Syd Barrett interview, and was greeted by a huge, fat man with shaved eyebrows, wearing only pajama bottoms. "Syd can't talk," the fat man said and closed the door.

In 1988 EMI brought Syd's solo efforts out on CD, which sell consistently. Numerous bootlegs are available. EMI also released a "new" Syd collection called *Opel,* and had hoped to include "Vegetable Man" and "Scream Thy Last Scream," but Pink Floyd wouldn't grant permission. We can only imagine how the Madcap Piper's last scream might have sounded. In April 1992 Atlantic Records offered half a million dollars for any type of Syd Barrett recording. The family sent a polite refusal.

Syd Barrett is back in Cambridge in his own basement flat at the end of a dead-end street, by all accounts leading a normal life. His brother-in-law Paul Breen says Syd doesn't play music anymore, prefers his own company to the company of others, likes good wine, has started to paint again ("surprisingly traditional, a country cottage, a vase of flowers"), watches a lot of television, and is a reasonably content man—despite rumors reported in *News of the World* that he has been heard "shrieking like a lunatic" and "barking like a dog."

The haunted gaze of the madcap piper. (BARRY PLUMMER)

I met with journalist Mike Watkinson, who cowrote Syd's biography, and he told me about his only encounter with the "increasingly insular" Syd. "The Syd Barrett of '69 is dead," he insists. "I liken it to David Bowie burying Ziggy Stardust. It's that dramatic. I knew what I was going to see but it still gave me a hell of a shock. We had a degree of cooperation with the family; it had been set up. We were driving in the outskirts of Cambridge, it was very tense in the car, and I happened to glance out the window and I saw this familiar figure walking by. One of his old friends had told me about Syd's distinctive walk—limping on the front of his feet. He must have weighed fifteen stone [210 pounds]. He looked straight in my face. It was very disconcerting. I felt like a private detective and just froze. We set out after this retreating figure and he disappeared. I watched him walk down the street in a classic Charlie Chaplin fadeout. We went to the address, knocked on the door, I explained who we were and what we were doing, and a look of such incredible fear crossed his face. I can remember what he said, it was quite peculiar—'No, I'm not Syd Barrett, I'm only staying here. I don't live here.'"

It was once reported that Syd had "expired in a shop doorway," but like the never-ending fascination surrounding him, Syd Barrett is very much alive behind the closed doors of his own madcap design.

JAN BERRY

■

Riding the

Wild Surf to

Dead Man's

Curve

■

Jan Berry, young, brilliant, and beautiful—the sky was the limit.
(THE JAN BERRY COLLECTION)

On a golden, sunny Southern California afternoon when I was fourteen years old, I got a ride to the beach where Jan and Dean were performing on some short-lived sun 'n' fun TV show. Glorious summer of '62—way before Bob Dylan's warnings and the war in Vietnam. I squeezed through the surfer dudes and beach bunnies to get a much closer look at the bronzed dolls steaming up the sand, and bouncing around in front of them, absolutely agog, I realized I was a worshiper of rock and roll and could never, *ever* be close enough. The handsome blonds were wearing matching silver sharkskin suits and little ties, miming the words to one of their massive hits, "Heart and Soul." I had always thought of Dean as the goofy sidekick and Jan as the cute heartthrob, so I swooned into the cute one's twinkly eyes, but he didn't notice me. Bummer in the summer.

Not only was Jan the obvious object of teen passion, he was an original, one of the main forces behind the "California sound"—composer, musician, producer, innovator, very cute hunk-of-stuff.

Jan began his career as half of the duo Jan and Arnie, two teenagers from L.A.'s University High who wanted to make a record. "It was 1958. I was working at Western Recorders," Joe Lubin, one of rock's forerunning producers, told me, "and I heard some music through these thick metal doors—four bars that kept playing over and over intrigued me. I knew the engineer, so I went in and saw two young kids, sixteen, seventeen, dressed in jeans and full of sand. They even had their surfboards with them!" The "kids" were making an acetate and Joe expressed a keen interest. He heard something special. "I asked where they recorded the song and Jan told me he did it at his house on an Ampex recorder that his dad bought him. It had some echo, and I said, 'Great! Let's go up there!' I wanted to reproduce this sound all the way. There was some mad banging going on that I loved."

Joe jumped into Jan's convertible and was surprised to wind up in Bel Air. "That's where the stories came along about recording in garages. I think we were the first ones," he says modestly. "I'm sure we were. You never knew you were making history." Jan played an old out-of-tune upright piano and he and Arnie (Ginsberg) sang. "I wanted to lay down the track of Jan singing and Arnie answering," Joe continues enthusiastically, "but there was something missing—that metallic sound. How did they get that sound?" Neither Jan nor Arnie could remember how the "mad banging" came about, but when Jan's mother came in with some snacks, she reminded the boys that Arnie had been hitting the top of an old metallic toy high chair, and it was retrieved from the back of the garage. "Arnie was hitting the piano stool like a backbeat of a drum, and the metallic chair gave it a raw sound. Along with the out-of-tune piano, to my stupid ear it was all wonderful."

Joe's ear was not so stupid after all. "I come into my office the next morning," Joe remembers with a smile. "My secretary tells me that the phone is going off the hook, they all want that song by those two kids!" Jan and Arnie had sneaked into Joe's office, stolen the tape, and convinced a disc jockey at a local station to play "Jennie Lee"—lots of echo and overdubs, tons of "bomp-bomps," and excessive amounts of teen joy. After quickly getting Jan and Arnie under contract, Joe got them a deal with Doris Day's label, Arwin Records, "and the rest is history. People wanted to copy that sound, but nobody knew how we got the sound." Joe laughs before getting serious. "The Beach Boys copied our sound. Jan and Dean were known as *the* West Coast sound. I got a call from Dick Clark saying, 'I want those guys!' They played the Hollywood Bowl in Bermuda shorts—sun-tanned, beautiful-looking guys. There was so much screaming you couldn't even hear them, twenty thousand people standing up. It was uncontrolled."

The single "Jennie Lee" (written about a local stripper of the same name—

the "bomp-bomps" were inspired by her bouncing breasts) went to number eight on the national charts, but after two more forty-fives, the pressure proved too much for Arnie. While Jan got in the swing of his newfound hot-shot status—getting into trouble for drag-racing down Venice Boulevard, bringing booze to school in a plastic lemon-squeezer, sticking his cute bare ass out of car windows (he was arrested for indecent exposure three times), and cherry-bombing trash cans—Arnie quietly left the duo to pursue a career as an architect. Jan corraled former Uni High football buddy Dean Torrence into taking his place, and not a "bomp-bomp" was wasted. Jan and Arnie became Jan and Dean and cut another echo-filled record in Jan's garage—"Baby Talk," which jumped straight into the Top Ten. It was the bright and shining Hula-Hoop America of 1959.

"Jan and I stayed in school," Dean Torrence tells me as we chat in his Hunt-ington Beach home while he keeps a daddy's eye on five-year-old Katie, who is busy with her Legos. "I kept two jobs, and I heard 'Baby Talk' on the radio by the pool at my lifeguard job. A little light went on and I said, 'Maybe I won't have to do this lifeguard thing anymore, even though it's kinda fun.'" Dean is in his mid-fifties—tanned, blond, and tousled. Youthful in his de-meanor, he punctuates his stories with wry laughter. Like Arnie, Dean was planning to be an architect and Jan a surgeon when pop success struck. "We didn't let the business rule us, we kind of ruled the business!" he says with in-tensity. "We thought about the consequences a lot more than those who were completely dominated by their record company. We had something else to fall back on. Jan would get out his pathology book and say, 'Oh, I gotta read an-other five hundred pages anyway. I don't care, I'm gonna be a surgeon. I'm not even gonna know you guys!' We just didn't get intimidated."

I can sense in Dean a real admiration for Jan. Since Jan had been the driving force and always spoke his mind, did Dean ever feel jealous or envious of his partner? "Jan was *allowed* to speak his mind," he says adamantly. "He was light-years ahead of the rest of us. Even at eighteen or nineteen, Jan would tell al-most anybody what to do. Some people considered him obnoxious, but he was just knowledgeable. Arrogant? Yeah, he might have been. But I don't think I was jealous—as long as I was benefiting from it." Dean laughs. "If I had just been a classmate, an observer, and hadn't gotten anything out of it, I might have been jealous. But again, he was so far beyond the rest of us, so bright, so full of vision and ambition and so much drive. The way I looked at it, he deserved it. He had a God-given talent, a huge IQ, and he put it all to-gether. Jan would love to sit and take notes," Dean reminisces. "He wrote mu-sic, so he would take the first four bars on take thirteen, the second six bars of take two—he was down to the notes. On 'Baby Talk' there was one 'bomp' that he loved. It had a certain resonance to it, and he moved it to another take. When I'd come back in a day or two, the tape would be solid white splicing on the back."

Thirty-five years later Dean still seems amazed. I've heard that Jan was a genious in the studio. Does Dean think so? "Oh yeah! Unlike when you call Brian Wilson or Lennon/McCartney geniuses. Maybe they're brilliant makers of music—they can't figure out how to keep their checkbook straight—but in this one arena they're very talented. Jan was literally a genius, his 170 IQ proved it. His major was biology and his minor was music. Most other guys minored in something that had to do with their studies, but Jan got grades for producing Jan and Dean records." A lot of *gold* Jan and Dean records.

Since the boys were in school, rock-and-roll road trips took place on weekends, Christmas vacation, and all summer long. Big fans of Laurel and Hardy, the duo interspersed goofy repartee into their stage antics and pulled mischievous pranks on touring companions. (Jan and Dean got to know Stan Laurel and spent time with him before his death.) My friend Dick St. John (from the pop duo Dick and Dee Dee) recalls Jan as quite a ladies' man, often turning up on the bus with last night's nylons proudly wrapped around his neck. "Spastic jokes were popular," Dick says, then goes on to tell me how Jan or Dean would fake seizures in roadside restaurants to shock Midwestern patrons. They once conned Dick into faking one of his own, then scurried from the restaurant, leaving a mortified Dick alone on the floor. "Jan took my fold-up suitcase somewhere in Wisconsin," Dick recalls, shaking his head. "I look over and see Jan going down the mountain on a surfboard or something, and I realize, 'Oh my God! That's my suitcase he's opened up!' It was destroyed."

Jan hired Lou Adler and Herb Alpert as the duo's managers after meeting them with Sam Cooke, and the boys' garage tracks were arranged and overdubbed in a two-track studio. Instead of using the same overused studio musicians as a backup band, Jan pulled together an incredible lineup including Glen Campbell, Leon Russell, and Hal Blaine. In 1962 Jan and Dean played a teen hop with a new group, the Beach Boys, and Jan started writing songs with Brian Wilson, which resulted in Jan and Dean's first number-one record, "Surf City," about a young man's fantasy spot where there are two girls for every boy. "Honolulu Lulu" followed, then came the car songs—"Dead Man's Curve," "Little Old Lady from Pasadena," "Drag City"—and then "Sidewalk Surfin'," which capitalized on (created?) the skateboard craze. Now in a real live studio, Jan produced and arranged (and mostly wrote) everything. He wanted the sound to be hard and filled out, and was the first to use dual drums. Some say he was hardheaded, bossy, and belligerent, but according to Dean, he deserved to be that way.

I ask Dean if they had many fans or groupies following them around. "We had 'steadies' then." He smiles wryly. "It was early for groupies. There was no birth control, an innocent time. They'd come around but would giggle and drool, put your name on their school notebook." Jan had a steady, Jill Gibson, on and off for years, but still managed to date a bevy of Hollywood debs, including Ann-Margret and Yvette Mimieux. Jill finally left Jan when she woke up one morning and found him frolicking in the raw with two girls he had picked up on the beach. (Just an innocent frolic, mind you.)

Naturals in front of the camera, Jan and Dean got signed to Paramount, but on the first day of shooting on their first film, during the first take of a train wreck sequence, Jan was badly injured, breaking his leg. Already in his second year at UCLA Medical School, he fashioned a makeshift tourniquet, dragged himself a quarter of a mile to the highway, and was taken by a passing car to the closest hospital. His leg was saved and he recovered. The next time he wouldn't be so lucky.

In late 1965 Jan and Dean were offered their own weekly TV series, "Jan and Dean on the Road," sort of a Route 66 rock-and-roll travelogue. "There would have been a bit of music onstage, then we'd get in our Corvette and go get in trouble!" Dean tells me, grinning. "Two blond guys in their car who really *did* have hit records!" During the taping of the zany pilot, Jan studied medicine as well as his script, cramming his photographic memory full of medical data in between madcap takes and tunes. Finals were coming up and he had to think about an internship, but the pilot was very well received and the series was a go. How could Jan do both?

"I was driving across the Golden Gate Bridge after a gig with Jan," Dean says quietly. "I was trying to bring up a picture of where Jan would be in a couple of years, but I couldn't see it. I couldn't see him dealing with the music on a long-term basis because he was real stubborn and would eventually come to loggerheads with the record company. And we would have to make that choice between school, our degrees—he would have to think about internship. You can't do that part-time. I could kind of figure me out a little bit, but I couldn't get a picture of what was going to happen to him, and it just didn't feel right. I kept thinking, Something bad is gonna happen. I didn't see it happening to me. I just couldn't see any future for Jan. I looked out and saw Alcatraz, and I felt it was something like that—like jail, something that would confine him so he wouldn't be able to fulfill his promise. I didn't see him dead, but I knew he wouldn't be able to fulfill all those dreams he had. He's always been so stubborn and so antiestablishment, and I thought, The system is going to catch up with him and take care of him in one way or another."

Having just completed the TV pilot, Jan was back in the studio recording half the night and taking finals all day. Hopped up with ambition, he pushed himself insanely, always trying to cram too many things into twenty-four hours.

"He was always in a hurry," declares Dean. "He had lots of stuff to do, lots of things on his mind. He liked to do the driving, he wanted that control. He'd get an idea, he'd want to write a piece of music and he'd say, 'Hand me a pencil!' I'd steer the car and he'd be working on our charts from the night before. I actually got good driving with my left hand. He always had so many things going on in his mind. He could work on bunches of things, and that's eventually what got him in trouble. He was driving down this side street that we'd driven many, many times before, and the way he drove was just *flat out*. There are signs up all over this street that runs from Sunset to Wilshire, saying 'Twenty-five Miles an Hour,' and you get within a couple of blocks from the school and it's five miles an hour!" Dean remarks with horror. "The way Jan thought was, 'That doesn't apply to me. I'm in a hurry. That applies to other people who don't have a Corvette, who don't have an IQ of 170.' I don't know why he hit that truck, he shouldn't have hit it. The bottom line is, if he had been going the speed limit, a little bit of rubbing compound would have fixed it. But his car was totaled. It looked like it was dropped out of an airplane."

On his way to a business meeting on April 12, 1966, his recently received draft notice on his mind (among many other things, I'm certain), Jan careened around Whittier Boulevard at high speed, hit a curb, lost a tire, went out of control, and rammed into the rear of a parked Ford pickup. Whittier Boulevard became Dead Man's Curve for a horrible split second.

"I saw the car after the accident," Dean continues sadly. "There's a windshield frame from the inside and it's attached in the middle. This piece popped off and the frame hit Jan in the head. Other than that he didn't have any broken bones, hardly anything happened except for a whap in the head." Yeah, but what a whap.

In 1972 I was walking up Woodrow Wilson Drive on my way to visit the Zappa family when a sports car slowed down beside me and a guy asked if I'd like a ride. Why not? I climbed into the passenger seat and this smiling fellow looked familiar. "Hi," he said, awkwardly holding out his left hand. "I'm Jan Berry of Jan and Dean." I instantly recalled the Dead Man's Curve tragedy, and marveled at Jan's ability to drive a car again. When I commended him for his bravery, he said to me with a crooked grin, "I'm stubborn."

Jan was pronounced dead at the scene, but when the paramedics pulled him out of the top of the crushed silver Stingray, they found weak signs of life and rushed him to UCLA Medical Center—the same place Jan studied five days a week. After extensive brain surgery, the doctors said he might never come out of his coma and, if he did, would never walk or talk again. But thirty days later stubborn Jan Berry woke up and said, "Hi, Mom!" Then the work began.

Jan's former girlfriend, Jill Gibson, came to see Jan at the hospital and he said, "Jill, let's go home." He had lost a lot of time and didn't remember that they had broken up. Jan's massive head injury left him with his entire right side paralyzed—his arm, his leg, even his eye. He also had aphasia, a severe communication disorder, and had to relearn how to move his tongue to form words. The man in a hurry who always had had too many things on his mind could now handle only one or two ideas at a time—with much difficulty. A therapist moved into his home and taught Jan how to tell time, add, and subtract. He had to relearn the alphabet. Jan's music and medical knowledge were gone. The prankster who had faked funny seizures was now having them for real.

His right hand was useless and his right foot pointed upward, which caused him to drag his leg, but against all the doctor's odds, Jan walked and drove a car. Then the music started coming back to him. He was Jan Berry, musician, not somebody to be pitied.

Jan parents, Bill and Clara Berry, have known their share of grief, having lost a daughter in a swimming pool tragedy and a son in a mountain climbing

Police survey the wreckage of Jan's Corvette. Some joker stuck a photo of Jan and Dean in the twisted metal. (THE JAN BERRY COLLECTION)

accident before Jan's crack-up. They spent almost all of their time by Jan's side as he struggled to recuperate. I met with the Berrys at their sprawling yet cozy house in Bel Air. "The doctor said that the brain stem was injured," Mrs. Berry tells me. "After the accident what Jan wanted was to be independent. No grown man likes to come home and be dependent again, so he went through numerous episodes of renting places and having people live with him. Most of them took advantage of him. While he was still in the hospital two young kids broke into his house and took all his hi-fi equipment," she recalls sadly. Since Jan insisted on living in his own place, the Berrys hired various people to look after his needs. "One time Jan's brother caught this fellow putting Jan's clothes into the trunk of his car. We worried because we knew how vulnerable he was," she continues. "One of the episodes up at his Mulholland house, his maid called and said, 'You'd better get up here. There are some people in Jan's office putting cocaine into little packages and he's not aware of what's going on.'"

Jan was frustrated, trapped, lonely. He didn't see Dean much anymore. He started taking drugs. The Berrys recount several more tales of users and abusers. More than once Jan trusted so-called friends to invest his money, says his mother. "Con men will paint flowers all over you, and that's exactly what they did to Jan." Besides losing a ton of money in bad investments, Jan went on gambling benders. "I flew up to Las Vegas twice to stop Jan from gambling," Mr. Berry explains. "You hate to deprive him of everything, so we went to the cashier and got him three thousand dollars. He doesn't see to his right, so we decided to stay to see what happened, and in less than fifteen minutes the three thousand was gone." Dean told me Jan has lost close to two hundred thousand dollars in Las Vegas.

The Berrys' stories often don't jibe with Dean's. They don't think Dean's 1978 TV movie, *Dead Man's Curve,* was very accurate. "In the movie Dean comes in with Laurel and Hardy movies to cheer Jan up," Mrs. Berry tells me. "But we were there—I remember Lou Adler coming in with the projector."

Jan called his father from Hawaii a few years ago, saying he was going to kill himself, and his father went to bring his son back home. More than once, Jan Berry has contemplated suicide—what a trial for his parents. "It hasn't been easy," Mrs. Berry concedes. But when they recall the days before the accident, it's a different story. "One of Jan's professors took a real liking to him and told us that Jan would be working and before long they'd all be watching him work on a cadaver. It was a big loss," Mrs. Berry recalls. "He had beautiful artistic hands. All of his professors said he was a born surgeon." Mrs. Berry adds, "If you look at his left hand today . . ." Her voice trails off as she thinks about what could have been. "When he lived alone after the accident, I want you to know that he scrambled his own eggs and fried his own bacon," she then says with some pride. "Sometimes when he calls me on the phone, he'll say, 'Hi, Mom, how are you? Are you sitting with your feet up?' I have varicose veins.

He was always generous and always sweet, but sneaky in one way." She smiles. "If I told him, 'You're not to do that,' he'd say, 'Okay, Mom,' then find a way to do it." Mr. Berry chuckles and adds, "He still does."

I stop to pick up Chinese food on my way to have dinner with Jan Berry and his wife, Gertie, at their home in Brentwood. Jan met Gertie four years ago on tour in Ontario, Canada, where she was a waitress at Lulu's Roadhouse, the longest bar in the world (according to the *Guinness Book of World Records*). They got married onstage in Las Vegas in August 1991 during a Jan and Dean concert. When the minister asked Jan, "Do you take this woman. . . ," Jan shouted joyously, "Yes, sir!" The wedding cake was covered in blue-icing waves, with the little plastic groom on a surfboard carrying the bride.

I arrive with my steaming cartons and Gertie greets me warmly. She's a young, bright-eyed blonde who shows me around the former bachelor pad she has cheered with countrified homey touches. "Jan will be out in a minute," she tells me as she sets the table. "He fell down today and isn't feeling too well." I hear Jan shuffling into the room, and as I turn around I'm greeted with that sweet, crooked smile. "Hello, I'm Jan Berry." Of Jan and Dean. He's a bit heavier, his hair's fuller and longer, but he's wearing a Hawaiian surfer's shirt and seems pleased to meet me. I remind him that he once picked me up hitchhiking. "I picked up a lot of girls," he says with his boyish grin, "but it's different when you're married."

Throughout the interview Jan has a lot of trouble finding the right words to say. I think he *knows* what he wants to say, but the damage to his brain won't allow the words to come forth. He sometimes seems frustrated, and other times pretty happy. He has a naive, childlike quality, an innocence that I'm sure betrays a torrent of jilted high hopes. What comes up a lot in conversation are his feelings about his partner, Dean Torrence. When Jan fumbles for a word or an idea, Gertie lovingly helps him out.

PAMELA: What's your relationship with Dean like?

JAN: Dean is in the past and he loves the past. It's all wrong but he's believing it now.

GERTIE: He wasn't on the original "Surf City," he didn't show up for the session, but he went in and remixed it later. Dean never came to see Jan in the hospital, not once. In the TV movie he did, he remembered it differently. I just want everything to be true. The truth is important to Jan. He used to drink and take drugs, but he quit nine years ago. Dean won't let him forget it.

PAMELA: Did you go to AA?

JAN: Yeah. I just quit.

GERTIE: Didn't you quit because Dean threatened to leave the show?

JAN: In Long Island we finished and he told me, "That's it, we're through." So, uh, jeez, you know, he has beer and alcohol, but you can get them overbalanced somehow.

GERTIE: He's saying that Dean still drank.

JAN: A long time ago I remember I had alcohol and drugs, cocaine. I was driving along the freeway on the 101 and it was just beautiful. I can remember that. A lot of times I can't remember, but this time was just so beautiful. It was hard for me to quit, so I had to have a UCLA doctor who deals with drugs and we were having appointments two, three times a week. I was off for about a year and a half and then . . . It was Christmastime. I slipped, you know, so I had to start all over.

PAMELA: Were you getting high in the early days?

JAN: Before I had my accident, I used pills, maybe. I don't remember.

PAMELA: Where were you headed the day of the accident?

JAN: I had a letter from the draft board. I was thinking all the time, What's happening? Twenty-five was my age when I had the accident. Before that I was in medicine.

GERTIE: He was six months away from his internship.

JAN: I had an appointment, but I was never there because that was the accident, but we were planning to open a Jan and Dean label. Yeah.

PAMELA: Did you have to learn to do everything again?

JAN: Reading, writing, walking, learning the ABCs. I didn't want to work all the time, but I did have to because my mind said, "Gee, it's so flustering!" Still I would want to do it. The mind is more brain damaged. It will never be the same since I had the accident.

GERTIE: Jan can read now, but he can't read for too long because his mind has to work so hard, he sweats. It seems to be an effort for his brain. If he can't say the words, he'll spell things out for me. He's always had a photographic memory.

JAN: Gee, it's too bad I fell down this morning . . .

GERTIE: Jan has only use of one side. Even though he does walk, he balances himself and the one arm just hangs. When he loses his balance, there's nothing to save him. The one foot gets caught, and he falls hard when he falls.

JAN: It's hard on the brain.

GERTIE: He can't see to his right. Many times he's passed me and not seen me.

PAMELA: When did you start performing again?

JAN: Uh . . . uh . . . about '85.

GERTIE: Jan went on the road by himself. Dean didn't want to go out with Jan.

JAN: No, no, because the movie came on at that time. That's what happened. *[Much, much effort.]* There were little frictions with me and Dean.

PAMELA: Did you have anything to do with the movie?

GERTIE: [Dean] came to Jan and took him out to lunch to see how he acted, how he moved his arm. When the movie came out they gave Mr. Berry

[Jan's dad] five thousand dollars. I wish they wouldn't have. It meant he accepted how the movie was done.

PAMELA: So Dean didn't stay in touch with Jan?

GERTIE: No. Jan's mom was telling me that Dean was always jealous of Jan because Dean had to study hard and all Jan had to do was look at a book and pass his grades. Jan also wrote the music and produced.

JAN: But for Dean still photography was the business . . .

GERTIE: He wasn't making it, is what Jan means. When somebody asked Jan and Dean to be at a show, they gave Dean half the money that Jan made. He saw this big crowd and saw dollar signs.

PAMELA: When did you start in music?

JAN: Young. Glen Campbell released a book. I played with him.

GERTIE: Ann-Margret wrote a book but it doesn't say anything about Jan Berry. I thought it would. He dated Ann-Margret. *[Laughing.]* Jan said she probably wouldn't say anything about being in the backseat of his car in the garage!

PAMELA: What's the first thing you remember after the accident?

JAN: At the UCLA hospital bed, you know.

PAMELA: Where you were going to school, right?

JAN: That was rough. Lou Adler came to the hospital bed and he wanted to have a screening of a movie, he set the whole thing up, and I was really happy because he played Laurel and Hardy.

GERTIE: In the movie it was Dean who came in with the movies.

JAN: I was stubborn and bullheaded. I didn't behave.

GERTIE: The doctor told me that if he hadn't had that stubbornness, he wouldn't be as far as he is.

PAMELA: How did you meet Dean?

JAN: In high school. I don't know how we met. *[Reads his fortune cookie.]* "You have a natural . . ." What's that word? ". . . grace and . . ."

GERTIE: Sound it out, you know what this is. . . .

JAN: It's too hard. "C-o-n . . ."

GERTIE: ". . . grace and great consideration of others." That's a nice one, Jan.

PAMELA: It's great that you got right back in a car after the accident.

GERTIE: He's smacked a lot of cars up. Jan's not afraid of anything. Sometimes he stands at the edge of the stage. New Year's Eve three years ago he fell offstage and this man caught him! You're lucky somebody caught you, Jan! You're a big man. You're not easy to catch!

PAMELA: Why didn't Dean come see you in the hospital?

JAN: Somebody said that when I was still unconscious that he was there, but I think that was it.

PAMELA: A handsome and talented man like you must have had a lot of girlfriends.

GERTIE: *[Smiling.]* Too much for one man. One time he went to the beach and came back with two girls and I guess the alarm went off and woke up his girlfriend.

JAN: It was a big room, the dining room, and I figured, "Well, gee, we can make out and all this stuff."

GERTIE: Are you sure it wasn't the living room, Jan? He gets the couch and table mixed up.

JAN: It was a large house and I figured Jill was sleeping. I said, "See ya later!" and I figured, "That's it!" No dice. *[Sighs.]* You know, it's kinda getting me down, but do you want to continue with this interview?

Jan is weary and goes to bed. I stay for a little while with Gertie and look through Jan's bright and shining memorabilia. She gives me a photo of the demolished Corvette. She's a devoted wife, but it's a difficult situation.

A few days later I take some pictures with Jan in his front yard. Gracious and agreeable, he poses with a surfboard before getting into his car and driving down the street to pick up his dry cleaning. It makes me nervous. I invite Jan and Gertie to my birthday party, but Jan's going to be back East, doing another gig with Dean.

I call Dean to tell him Jan feels hurt that he didn't come to see him in the hospital so long ago, and he heaves a sigh. "I think that's what he was told. I was there a couple of times with his parents, but he doesn't remember, so what good does it do? I went once when he was awake—he was in the wheelchair; we did show Laurel and Hardy. He started falling in with some drug people, people I didn't relate to. There was a period of time when we didn't have anything in common. There was probably a period of time when I didn't talk to him that much," he finally admits. "He was so stubborn, it didn't help to talk to him. He probably never understood why I couldn't sit with him for ten or twelve hours a day. I tried to get him to understand. I would invite him to my graphics office, but *I* have to schedule taking a leak and there isn't much for him to do. He just didn't understand."

Over time Jan found that his precious music was still locked in his brain cells. He started writing songs and did some recording, eventually booking himself into Holiday Inns, but after ABC aired *Dead Man's Curve,* yesterday's sun 'n' fun duo was back in demand, playing to huge, appreciative audi-

Jan and me in his front yard, posing with one of his surfboards. (ADAM W. WOLF)

ences at state fairs and theme parks. Everybody was amazed that Jan Berry was back onstage. He was a downright inspiration, as the review of the Butte County Fairgrounds gig proves: "If your trip is to focus on Jan Berry's half-beat-late and tortured vocals during the haunting 'Dead Man's Curve,'" states the *Chico Record,* "rather than embrace the miracle that this incredible man is able to even perform, well, I guess that's too bad."

I ask Dean how long the duo will continue to play. "Jan has said to me that it would be okay for him to go out onstage in a wheelchair," he tells me, "but I don't want to do that. On the other hand I don't want him to panic that it's almost over." I mention that Jan is still feisty and determined—and still getting behind the wheel to pick up his dry cleaning! "He shouldn't be. He could be out the driveway right now—one more bang in the head—and I'd have to really, for the first time, go out and look for a job!" Dean laughs in a sad and tragic way. "You know," he says finally, "Jan and Dean haven't been inducted into the Rock and Roll Hall of Fame. It's not so much for me, but for Jan. Who else could have done what he did? He wrote and arranged and produced all those hit records—what a sound! He got together the most incredible musicians. He pretty much discovered Lou Adler and Herb Alpert. Lesser people have been inducted—I'm not going to name names. Jan Berry should be honored—before it's too late."

I agree with Dean. But who brought the Laurel and Hardy movie to the hospital? Lou Adler or Dean Torrence? One of rock and roll's mysteries, I suppose. At least it made Jan Berry happy.

MARC BOLAN

■

Twentieth-Century Boy

■

The usually loudmouthed, raging young crowd at Thee Experience Club was hushed and expectant. I had already taken my place on the grimy floor, folding my ostrich feathers around me, waiting breathlessly for Tyrannosaurus Rex to turn me into a "Child Star." When Steve "Peregrine" Took and the ringleted boy/girl beauty Marc Bolan joined us, cross-legged on the club floor, the audience and the musicians became one big beating hippie heart for almost an hour. It was 1969, and along with the marijuana and musk in the air, there was a smidge of leftover peace-and-love hope that briefly united the wilting flower children. We floated along, enraptured by the gentle acoustic unicorn-speak of these mystical poets. Two years later Marc Bolan would explode onto the pop scene, strewing it with sequins and sparkling flash. How did this androgynous Tolkien elf with the rosebud mouth become the Lurex-clad, glitter-god pioneer of glam rock?

Even as a young child growing up in the borough of Hackney, brash and cheeky Mark Feld demanded constant attention from his parents and older brother, Harry. Quite a bit smaller than his brother, Mark invented heroic fantasy personas to build up his short stature, hoping to stir up an air of importance and originality. It seemed he was never satisfied with the status quo, always wanting to create something *more* in his life. While his peers slogged over their homework, Mark was up in his room rocking out to Bill Haley records.

The week that Elvis Presley's "Hound Dog" hit the British charts, nine-year-old birthday boy Mark Feld got his first guitar. But instead of actually *playing* the coveted instrument, Mark was much more interested in how it looked on him, perfecting his Elvis and Bill Haley moves in front of the mirror—already outrageously image-conscious. He put a band together of neighborhood kids who couldn't really play music, called it Susie and the Hula Hoops, and did a few gigs at local schools.

Britain's first pop television show, "Oh Boy," was filmed in Hackney, and Mark often took the bus to see acts like Billy Fury and Adam Faith. He proudly claimed to have met one of his absolute heroes, American rocker Eddie Cochran, at one of these shows, insisting that he carried Eddie's guitar into the studio for him. Nobody has been able to verify this fantastic report, but if young Mark actually got his hands on the legendary axe, it would have been in the spring of 1960, right before Cochran's death in a British taxicab accident.

Besides rock and roll, the only thing eleven-year-old Mark Feld seemed to care about was his image. He begged his mother to take him to the local tailor to have an Italian-style suit made to his unusual specifications, eventually branching out farther and farther on the bus, desperately seeking affordable fashion. Years later he confessed to stealing motorbikes to pay for his early clothes habit. Looking sharp was all that mattered, *staying* sharp, the ultimate goal. His brother, Harry, said that Mark wasn't able to pass a mirror without stopping for a quick (or lengthy) preen.

By the summer of 1962 the snappily dressed fourteen-year-old had become a Mod "face" and, along with two of his natty gang, was featured in the British men's lifestyle magazine *Town*. In the article, entitled "The Young Take the Wheel," Mark said, "You got to be different from the other kids. I mean, you got to be two steps ahead. The stuff that half the haddocks you see around are wearing, I was wearing two years ago. . . . I brought a jacket back from Paris—I was in Paris with my parents but I didn't like it much—and this jacket was just rubbish over there but it's great here. Great shoulders." Harry says the family never even went to Paris.

It was obvious that young Mark Feld wanted to be noticed. He wanted to be important. He wanted to be famous for *something*.

The teenage fashion plate started frequenting the Soho clubs and boutiques, "making the scene" with his friend Jeff Dexter. After seeing the Cliff Richard movie *Summer Holiday* in 1963, Mark excitedly told Jeff he was going to sing and become a big star like Cliff Richard. Would Jeff be interested in managing him? The fact that Mark couldn't really play or sing didn't seem to matter.

When he started tuning in to the "Pop Goes the Beatles" shows on BBC radio, Mark's determination to succeed in the pop world started taking precedence over his appearance.

When Mark felt that Mod fashion was becoming commonplace, he sought a new way to climb out of the pit of conformity. Wandering through a secondhand bookstore, he stumbled upon the English romantic poets—Keats, Shelley, Byron—before glomming on to French bard Arthur Rimbaud, whose mystical opaqueness seemed to jolt Mark's vivid imagination. "When I first read him," Mark said later, "I felt like my feet were on fire."

Mark may have been in the subtle process of mixing up his varied influences, but his parents were concerned about his seeming lack of initiative, so when Mark expressed an interest in modeling, his mother put up her savings so he could attend a fancy West End modeling school. His success was minimal, perhaps because of his height, but years later, at the peak of his fame, Mark claimed to have once been the cardboard cutout in every John Temple menswear store in England. With some of his catalog earnings, Mark bought himself a new acoustic guitar.

The brief modeling career over, Mark took his new guitar and moved to a friend's flat in London, where he spent hours playing, trancelike, to Bob Dylan records. He considered Dylan a poet with a conscience, a genius with vision—not unlike himself—and in January 1965 recorded his own wispy high-pitched version of "Blowin' in the Wind," along with two more songs, for his very first demo. Calling himself "Toby Tyler," Mark made the record-company rounds, but there were no takers.

Mark's first sexual encounter had taken place in Hackney with a dark-haired girl named Terry, but he had never gotten entangled romantically— probably because he was so wrapped up in himself! Allan Warren, a friend from his early days in London, claims that Mark was bisexual. "He went to bed with anyone, because everyone did in those days. It was nothing new. Rather than go to bed alone, if someone was pretty—irrespective of whether they were a girl or a boy— you'd go to bed with them. . . . Mark loved the girls, but I think in the be-

The enchanting Marc Bolan, who reigned briefly as king of glam rock. (PAUL CANTY/ LONDON FEATURES INTERNATIONAL)

ginning he was very shy with them. He was much more at ease with the boys. Boys took the lead if they fancied him, whereas if he fancied a girl, he'd have to chase her. It was really an ego thing, because he loved himself and he loved to be worshiped." Many years later Mark would confirm Warren's theory. "When I was fifteen I wasn't very sure of myself," he said. "I wanted to find out, so I went with a bloke. It was so that I'd never have to look back and wonder what I'd missed out on."

On a trip to Paris Mark supposedly met up with an older American man at the Louvre, and this chance encounter took on such epic proportions that he would refer to the incident for years to come. Mark spoke about his host's many books on magic and marveled as the mysterious American conjured up spirits, read people's minds, levitated, and cast white spells in Mark's presence. In some of the tellings Mark spent months in the forest with "the wizard" learning his secrets, but his future manager, Simon Napier-Bell, later said the truth was that Mark had met the strange fellow in a gay bar, spent one night with him, and invented the entire scenario, altering reality—and, as usual, creating something fantastic and poetic out of the mundane. Whether it happened in real life or in his head, the encounter with "the wizard" had a potent impact on Mark, because he became even more dreamy—writing stacks of cosmic prose about dragons and young gods, calling it his "art"—eventually changing his name from Mark Feld to Marc Bolan (originally with an umlaut over the "o").

His immense self-belief, constant hustling, and efforts to make certain he was always in the right places paid off for Marc, and he was finally offered a deal at Decca Records in the summer of 1965. But since Decca was unsure how to market their curious solo wonder, Marc's first single, "The Wizard," failed to sell. After a second single bombed, despite TV appearances on "Ready, Steady, Go!" and "Thank Your Lucky Stars," Marc was cut loose. Entirely undeterred, and drunk with the bittersweet lure of thwarted fame, Marc relentlessly pursued his dream, calling manager Simon Napier-Bell and arranging to drop off a tape of his songs. Arriving only with his guitar, Marc charmed the Yardbirds' manager, serenading him for close to an hour. "I thought he was a Charles Dickens urchin," Napier-Bell said, commenting on Marc's unique assortment of mismatched clothes. "It's now become very fashionable to wear old clothes—two jackets on top of one another, that sort of thing. Back then it was pretty unique." As Marc went through his repertoire, Napier-Bell was taken with Marc's strange, quavering voice and pseudo-enchanted slang-bang lyrics—impressed enough, in fact, to book him into a studio that same evening to cut some demos.

Marc's new manager took on many roles: counselor, friend, partner, confidant, lover. "How can you manage anybody and not have a relationship with them?" Napier-Bell said. "The sexual borders had completely collapsed by that time. Straight people thought they shouldn't be straight. In fact, in the sixties it was pretty difficult to have any sort of relationship with someone without it being sexual."

Record companies didn't find Marc's urchin charm compelling enough to sign him, and only after Napier-Bell threw his weight around did he finally secure a deal for Marc on Parlophone. *The Beginning of Doves,* which included "Hippy Gumbo" and the whimsical "Perfumed Garden of Gulliver Smith," failed to dent the charts, but Napier-Bell had faith in his new protégé and teamed him up with John's Children, a loud post-Mod band he was managing at the time. It was a fairly disastrous union, with Marc never really committing to the band due to his high solo hopes. After a debacle German tour with the Who and a failed single, Marc was back on his own in June 1967, placing a classified ad in *Melody Maker* for lead and bass guitarists and a drummer for his new group, as well as "any other astral flyers like with cars, amplification and that which never grows in window boxes."

Marc did one gig with a few of the freaky players who responded to the ad, and according to music paper reports, it was a mind-boggling disaster. What would the determined elf conjure up next? A few months earlier he had happened upon a Ravi Shankar concert, and the Indian sitar player—seated on a carpet, floating in incense—left an indelible impression on Marc. Could he incorporate this mellow hippie ethic into his own music to attain his ultimate goal of stardom?

One of the *Melody Maker* applicants, Steve "Peregrine" Took, seemed to share Marc's fanciful vision (his name was taken from Tolkien's *Lord of the Rings*) and decided to grab his bongos and go along with Marc for the carpet ride. Took had naturally gravitated to the gentle, nonthreatening hippie scene, having been a high-strung child who was taunted mercilessly because of his asthma and chronic eczema. The pair got into Eastern religion and mysticism—both on a heady romantic quest.

Not wanting to seem meek-mouthed and overly folky like British troubadour Donovan, Marc chose the name Tyrannosaurus Rex, hoping to give the trippy duo a hard-assed edge. They took their gongs, bells and panpipes into the studio to cut some demos, which Marc promptly gave to pacesetter pirate deejay John Peel. The songs became a staple on his radio show, which led to a deal for Tyrannosaurus Rex on EMI.

Producer Tony Visconti caught the duo at the UFO Club and was mesmerized by "the very precious, very powerful, and powerfully charismatic exotic gypsy" and approached Marc Bolan about working with Tyrannosaurus Rex. The album that came from that fortuitous meeting, *My People Were Fair and Had Sky in Their Hair But Now They're Content to Wear Stars on Their Brows,* went on that year to outsell albums by Pink Floyd and Hendrix. Marc Bolan's most fervent wish was about to be granted.

His fleeting bisexual skirmishes behind him, Marc was involved with another girl named Terry and in January 1968 sent her one of many flowery notes describing her "Torquay smile" and "ballerina body" and calling her the "unique Theresa of the childhood dancing nights." But by spring Marc was writing romantic odes to June Child, a blond and beautiful, intelligent public-relations woman five years his senior. They left their respective partners and moved into an attic flat in Ladbroke Grove.

I spoke to the notorious B. P. "Beep" Fallon, Marc's publicist during this period, and he told me that June was the most important person in Marc's life. "She instructed Marc in a lot of the ways of the world. When they met he couldn't drive a car. He never learned really. One time they went for a driving lesson down in Sussex, no one on the road, but Marc just freaked! His mind would wander off into a B-minor instead of into third gear. She was instructive in terms of the machinery of the material world." With June taking care of the day-to-day activities, Marc was free to wrap himself up in the second Tyrannosaurus Rex album, *Prophets, Seers and Sages, the Angels of the Ages,* which invoked his latest inspiration, Kahlil Gibran, whose mystic work *The Prophet* had become the peacenik bible.

Marc may have seen himself as spokesperson for his love-minded flower-children followers, but despite his unique, uncanny way with words, Marc had to wait in the hall to get into the BBC bar during a "Top of the Pops" taping. "There was nobody to sign us in," B.P. recalled. "We were all sitting in the corridor with people stepping over us, and Marc says, 'What do they want us to do? Drink dewdrops out of rose petals?'"

Even though Marc was getting a lot of press with his highly active rosebud mouth, the second album didn't sell as well as the first, partly due to the winding down of the wide-eyed peace-dream scene. After his fairy-tale book of poetry, *Warlock of Love,* failed to stir up sales, Marc found he could no longer rely on good karma alone. When the third Tyrannosaurus album, *Unicorn,* fared poorly, he was forced to reinvent himself once again.

During an extended tour of the United States, Marc and Steve Took's relationship began to break down. Marc's power trip pretty much relegated Steve to a glorified sideman, and the frustrated musician started taking a lot of acid, more than once stripping naked onstage and generally wreaking tortured havoc with the music. After a drug bust in which Marc and June came to his aid, hiring a high-priced lawyer, Took was relieved of his bongo duties.

His replacement was Mickey Finn, a gentle ex-model/artist who slid right into Took's place without a ripple. The new duo went to Wales to rehearse and Marc was briefly entranced with living the simple life. He chopped wood and sang to the sheep. On a postcard to a friend dated June 1969, Marc enthused about people wearing "deep green peace as a halo here."

Marc was entranced by the flamboyant American star of *Hair,* Marsha Hunt (who later had a daughter with Mick Jagger), and had a wild fling with her before, full of remorse, suddenly making the decision to marry June Child. The cosmic couple took their vows at Kensington Registry Office on January 30,

1970. Marc was later quoted as saying, "It seemed like a funky thing to do at the time."

While most of his rock compatriots were flying on various substances, Marc was relatively careful at this point in his career. He admits to taking acid only a few times, and once having a drink spiked with STP, a vicious hallucinogen. At a party for *Rolling Stone* magazine, when June came to fetch her husband, she found him confused and stumbling around, wailing about "eating himself." When she got him home, a very terrified Marc had to be pried from the car and sedated by a doctor.

Marc plowed back into his fifties records, strapped on a white Stratocaster, changed his band name to the abbreviated T. Rex, and came up with the poppy commercial smash "Ride a White Swan" for the *Beard of Stars* album. Despite press complaints about his bleating, high-pitched tremolo, a successful British tour followed, and after some blazing TV appearances, the "bopping elf" started getting mobbed. It became clear that a bass player was needed to fill out T. Rex's sound.

Steve Currie answered another *Melody Maker* ad and left his band, the Meteors, to join T. Rex, playing his first gig at London's Roundhouse ten days after the announcement to the press. Soon after, Marc brought drummer Bill Legend aboard. Some mourned the passing of the cross-legged carpet-and-incense scene, but Marc had waited too long for this chance to shine—he was unstoppable. He made himself very accessible to the rock press, his ego barely contained, and enjoyed shaking up the old guard, who felt he was betraying his mellow hippie ethics with his plugged-in Strat. He reveled in the attention and soon became the most visible, quotable, controversial musician in England. "It's just cock-rock, man, which is a groove," he announced. "I mean, if you see a chick and she's got nice breasts, you've got to go up to her and say, 'You've got good tits!' Right? I do it all the time. It doesn't have to be a sordid number. Chick's got good tits. The end." Oh yes.

T. Rex's second single, "Hot Love," was number one on the British charts for six weeks, and Marc was determined to take the group even further. He succeeded with the catchy "Bang a Gong (Get It On)," recorded for the *Electric Warrior* album, which features one of my fave lines of all time: "You're dirty-sweet and you're my girl." Oh yes.

Before a performance on "Top of the Pops," Marc suddenly decided to throw some glitter on his face, and that three-second act turned into an entire movement! The former Mod "face" fashion plate, Cliff Richard wannabe Marc Bolan taught people how to shimmer and glimmer—wrapping his small frame in velvet and gold lamé and brilliant skintight satins, slipping his small feet into women's tap shoes, painting silver stars under his eyes. It wasn't just the T. Rex audience that glommed on to the glamour. It wouldn't be long before acts like Rod Stewart and the Faces, Slade, the Sweet, Gary Glitter, and David Bowie became successful glam rockers, but for a moment in time, Marc

Bolan stood alone in his very own giant pile of glistening glitter—a lustrous blur of spontaneous innovative combustion.

"You had this so-called blues boom in England in the sixties—Fleetwood Mac, John Mayall—and people looked pretty denim-y and uninteresting," B. P. Fallon told me. "There was too much gray. What was needed after that was something flash and loud and vulgar and, to some people, annoying. Marc was very shiny. He brought that in, and it actually opened the door for Bowie. Suddenly men were checking their eye makeup. And the music was much more forthright and jumpin', much more below the belt." I asked Beep if shiny Marc enjoyed himself. "Oh, yes, he was a laugh, you see. It's all theater. He created his own stage. Marc wanted adulation and he didn't pretend that he didn't want it. Up until then it wasn't cool to let on that you wanted people to scream at you. People didn't scream at Jethro Tull."

Marc and June moved into a grand flat in upscale Maida Vale, bought a white Rolls-Royce, and spent time with rock's elite at trendy Tramps and the Speakeasy. With two British number ones under his sequined belt, Marc's T. Rex got a killer American record deal, and in January 1972, when "Get It On" went to number one in America, the Bolans celebrated by dropping fistfuls of dollar bills from their seventh-floor New York City hotel balcony.

For a short time "T. Rextasy" mania was rampant. Marc's crown of curls and haughty, wicked grin graced the covers of every teen magazine. But teenage fans are flighty, and Britain's rock press is notoriously fickle. After such a feverish storm of vainglorious vampy fame, could a Bolan backlash be far behind?

Already imbibing quite a bit of champagne and brandy, Marc started using cocaine, which slowly seemed to erode his acutely astute judgment calls. Mad for his own high-profile image (as usual), believing his own quixotically quotable hot air, he and June took over all the T. Rex business dealings, which turned into a disaster. As Marc climbed higher on his own personal pedestal, people began dropping away, including publicist B. P. Fallon, who paraphrased Dylan in his departing note: 'It's all right, Marc, I'm only leaving.'"

While Marc's increasingly younger androgynous fans ate him up whole, the venemous rock press jeered that "the Jeepster" had totally sold out. When *Slider* came out the end of July, after an initial one hundred thousand copies sold in four days, sales gradually slowed down. During an American tour when T. Rex's supporting act, the Doobie Brothers, began to headline the bill, Marc hired three black backup singers to fill out the sound. One of the singers was Gloria Jones. "Gloria was this wild rock-and-roll girl," Beep explained. "She wrote 'If I Was Your Woman' for Gladys Knight, but she didn't have June's *savoir faire* about the mechanicals." Though the Bolans had just bought a rural retreat on the Welsh border, Marc was soon flaunting his steamy, head-over-heels relationship with Gloria, and his five-and-a-half-year marriage was over. Without June's watchful eye and attention to detail, Marc's carefully constructed shiny universe began to collapse.

Tanx, the follow-up album to *Slider,* featured a suggestive shot of Marc (the tank between his legs), hiding bloated features behind his mop of hair and a strategically placed feather boa. Two singles, "Twentieth Century Boy" and "The Groover," reached the British Top Five, but Marc's number-one days were over. In the spring of 1974, the band's American label, Warner Bros., dropped T. Rex.

T. Rex continued to release records in England, but only hard-core fans were buying. Marc refused to believe he was failing, pretending he was still an adorable superstar even though his regular tequila breakfasts were making him fat. At a January 1974 gig in Glasgow, an out-of-control Marc stepped into one of his star-shaped stage props, fell onto his back, and had to be helped off-stage by Mickey Finn and two roadies. Flailing around in his tap shoes and feather boas, Marc was as close to self-parody as it gets.

Most of 1974 was spent plodding about in the sunshine. "He took time to go to Monte Carlo and that was like la-la-land, so he lost touch," Beep recalled sadly. "Hangin' out with Ringo, gambling every night, isn't going to tell you much about the music scene, is it?" The once-glossy idol was idle. He was bored—the sodden and swollen twenty-six-year-old looked forty. Ashamed of reality, he took to making up wild stories to bolster his trampled ego. He told anybody who would listen that he was going to be a great actor—in his first role he would play the part of a menacing drug dealer opposite David Niven.

Temporarily staving off Marc's decline, producer Mike Mansfield offered him a job on a teen pop show, "Supersonic," which Marc grabbed like a neon lifesaver, hoping to entice a new batch of teenybop viewers. During the taping of the first show, Marc got a call that he was about to be a daddy. Gloria gave birth to Rolan Bolan on September 26, 1975, which created a houseful of Librans, and Marc was delighted. (Rolan Bolan now attends Loyola Marymount College in Westchester, California, where he's a film major.) He took his parental responsibility seriously and his life took a gradual upswing. After another appearance on the TV show "Today," in which a witty Marc upstaged the host, he was offered a slot interviewing guests like the Who's Keith Moon and bluesman John Mayall. His records continued to bomb, but at least Marc was back in the public eye—a place he desperately needed to be. He was never a has-been in his own mind and he grabbed every opportunity to outrage. Said Keith Altham, his publicist, "He'd say things like 'What shall I be this week? Bisexual? Trisexual? Shall we say I take a gold bed with me on the road?' "

The punk scene, which shook the music world to its core, seemed to give Marc much-needed inspiration. Early in 1977 he told the *Sun* newspaper, "I've been sitting around waiting for the pop climate to change, for something like punk rock to come along. I consider myself to be the elder statesman of rock. The godfather of punk, if you like." He got excited again, cut out his lethal drinking, started an exercise program, began to eat healthy foods. Marc was slim again, but so were record sales. Regarded as a rock dinosaur (!), Marc continued to tour and began writing a monthly column for *Record Mirror*. The column featured a shot of Marc wearing a crown and holding a scepter—it seemed he still had a sense of humor about himself.

Marc met with Mike Mansfield, the former producer of "Supersonic," and they cooked up a six-week series for Marc to showcase new talent and perform his own hits. Initially announcing guests like Presley, Sinatra, and the Rolling Stones, Marc and his 4:15 in the afternoon kiddie time slot had to settle for acts like the Bay City Rollers and Mud. I rented a video of these shows, in which Marc prances, preens, and mimes halfheartedly to his double-tracked former-glory smashes, and felt sad and embarrassed for him. The camera closes in on him at the end of each show, and he purses his slicked lips and says, "Keep a little Marc in your heart. We'll be back at the same Marc time, the same Marc channel." For the final show Marc convinced his nemesis, David Bowie, to appear, and together they performed a song hastily written in the dressing room. It was a mess. Bowie missed his cue, and Marc tripped over the microphone and off the stage—a pitiful display for the glitter master's last televised appearance. In spite of Marc's refusal to admit failure, it must have hurt. "Marc used to say that success was a lot like riding the monster, riding the big Tyrannosaurus Rex," Beep said. "There you are, merrily galloping along, and if you're not careful it can turn around and bite your head off. A lot of people that we both know have been vulnerable-ized and fucked up by that happening. People have gotten hurt beyond redemption. People have gotten hurt beyond fixing."

A lock of Marc's hair tangled in the demolished hood of the Mini-Cooper. *(PA NEWS)*

The night of September 16, 1977, Marc went to the Speakeasy and then had dinner with Gloria and her brother Richard at Morton's, where much imbibing went on. After the meal Marc convinced Gloria to play the piano and sing love songs for him, and they left for home at four A.M.

Marc was thrown into the backseat of the purple Mini-Cooper and died instantly. *(PA NEWS)*

Gloria got behind the wheel of

her purple Mini 1275 GT with her brother Richard following behind. Just before five A.M., after crossing Putney Bridge, the Mini disappeared over the bridge along Queens Ride. When Richard neared the bridge, he saw rising steam. The Mini had crashed into a tree, the passenger's side taking the force of the impact. Gloria was unconscious but still breathing. Marc, who had always had a fear of and fascination with cars, had been thrown into the back of the Mini, lifeless in his orange glittery trousers and neon-green shirt. He looked like he had fallen asleep in a tumbled heap—only one small scratch marred his porcelain skin.

Marc often said in interviews that he wouldn't live to see his thirtieth birthday. He almost made it. He would have been thirty in two weeks.

"Eddie Cochran's death was always interesting to Marc—the car death," Beep said. "Cars are featured in a lot of his lyrics. . . . 'Hubcap driving star halo'. . . . There's tons of them—'I got a Rolls-Royce and it's good for my voice,' blah, blah, blah. . . . When Elvis died, we were talking about how Maria Callas died on the same day and she just got a little squirt in the corner of the newspaper. Marc said, 'I'm glad I didn't die today,' and a couple of weeks later he did. It was very sad. He was twenty-nine. He was looking good again. He'd been through his 'fat Elvis' period. He had credence with all the punk people. It wasn't like he died forgotten." I asked Beep if he thought Marc had made an important contribution to the mercurial world of rock and roll. "Oh yes," he says with no hesitation. "There are people who are very talented through practice and application, and then there are people who have a gift that goes beyond worldly definition. Marc had a lot of unworldly knowledge that can't be learned. It isn't born of study. It's like trying to explain 'soul.' Either you know what it is, or you don't."

Marc wasn't the only member of his bands to meet an untimely end.

After Steve "Peregrine" Took was booted out of Tyrannosaurus Rex, his life became a series of stoned-out mishaps and tragedies. Upon receiving a small royalty check, he bought some morphine and a bag of magic mushrooms, and in the middle of the night, October 27, 1980, he woke out of a bombed sleep and grabbed a cherry to eat. But the morphine had numbed his throat and Took choked to death on the cherry pit.

Bass player Steve Currie faded into obscurity and, disenchanted with the music scene, moved to Portugal in 1980. At midnight on April 28, 1981, on his way back home in the village of Val Da Perra, Currie swerved off the road and was killed.

The sad truth is, icons were made to be broken, but Beep was right—Marc Bolan didn't die forgotten.

The Marc Bolan Tree on Queens Ride is tied with ribbons and covered in flowers and love notes to this day.

"I don't think Marc is unhappy," said Gloria. "The only thing that is happening up there is that Marc is telling Elvis how to sing and Jimi how to play."

JOHN "BONZO" BONHAM

■

In

Through

the

Out Door

■

The Bonzo I remember was a wide-eyed, sweet-faced prankster, a simple, adoring family man caught up in the maniacal rock-and-roll maelstrom. During Zeppelin's slay-day, when I was a teenage nymphet hanging on the arm of Jimmy Page, Bonzo was actually protective of me, treating me with curious respect, and I saw him as an overgrown teddy bear, unaware of his gargantuan force, plowing through life with the unnatural grace only a rock drummer can summon up. Bonzo thrived in the comfort zone of his family, but when he was cut loose on the road for endless months, boredom and loneliness set in and his pranks became legend—TV sets tossed out of hotel windows, cars driven into pools, frightening things perpetrated on suspecting young girls all over the world. The only other musician who measured up to the level of Bonham's mayhem was fellow drummer and close friend Keith Moon of the Who. They both debauched themselves to death within two years of each other—Keith made it to thirty; Bonzo, the ripe old age of thirty-two.

John Henry Bonham, the sturdy son of a carpenter, grew up in the Worcestershire countryside, beating his mother's pots and pans, creating drum sets with coffee tins and other household doodads, making loads of unruly noise until his mother bought him a real live drum for his tenth birthday. A few years later his father brought home a complete set of drums, and even though the kit was a bit used and rusty, it was John's greatest prize. Every day John Bonham's crashing and bashing was heard throughout the quiet town of Kidderminster. At sixteen he left school to work at building sites with his father, which built up his stocky frame—all the better to beat the drums. His first band, Terry Webb and the Spiders, played locally, featuring a cheeky John wearing a purple jacket with velveteen lapels and a string tie. His family wasn't keen about their son trying to eke out a living as a musician, so John dutifully

ed Zeppelin's John "Bonzo" Bonham—
nnatural grace behind the drums. (MICHAEL
CHS ARCHIVES/VENICE, CALIF.)

worked as a builder during the day while spending nights playing drums with neighborhood bands like the Nicky James Movement, A Way of Life, and Steve Brett and the Mavericks.

At barely eighteen, when John made the decision to become a full-time musician, he also met his future wife, Pat, at a dance in Kidderminster. John knew right away that he needed Pat as much as he needed his music, and went about convincing her that one day he would be a hugely successful drummer and take care of her in grand style. After all the lofty promises, he moved his new bride into a fifteen-foot trailer where the newlyweds could barely afford to eat. John even had to give up cigarettes to pay the rent.

Some of the local bands wouldn't hire the brash John Bonham because he played too hard, too loud. He idolized Keith Moon and was awestruck by Ginger Baker, intent on imitating and outdoing the masters. His far-reaching goal was to be an equal member of an important rock band, not to be hidden away behind the front men. His reputation as a drummer to be reckoned with had begun.

John played a brief stint with Crawling King Snakes, featuring Robert Plant on vocals, but couldn't afford to keep making the trip to Birmingham. For a while he went back to playing with A Way of Life, closer to Kidderminster, but when Robert formed the Band of Joy, the young singer convinced John to join. It didn't last long. Early in 1968 John was offered a tour with singer Tim Rose and gratefully accepted the forty pounds a week it provided.

While John blissfully brought home the bacon, his friend Robert Plant was dancing on heady ground, being wooed by guitarist Jimmy Page. The former Yardbird and session man supreme was forming a new band, and after seeing Robert perform with his latest group, Hobbstweedle, had asked him to be the lead singer for this very important new project. Did Robert know any good drummers?

John hadn't heard from Robert in three months, and when his old friend excitedly told him about the "New Yardbirds," John wasn't interested. He was finally being well paid for playing the drums and had even gotten a mention in the music press for his most recent Tim Rose gig. He thought the New Yardbirds sounded like a rehash, and besides, there were other possibilities. He had been offered jobs with Chris Farlowe and Joe Cocker. Why get involved with something untested and untried?

But after Jimmy Page heard John play with Rose at the Country Club in North London, he could see the future of his new band and was determined to hire the no-holds-barred, energetic firebrand.

John still couldn't afford a phone and was stunned when the telegrams started to arrive at his local pub—eight from Robert Plant and *forty* from Jimmy Page's infamous, imposing manager, Peter Grant. (There were none from Jimmy, already a notorious skinflint, who would soon be dubbed "Led Wallet.") The drummer balked, weighing his options, finally deciding to take the job with the New Yardbirds. "I knew that Jimmy was a good guitarist and that Robert was a good singer," Bonham said years later, "so even if we didn't have any success, at least it would be a pleasure to play in a good group."

For the first rehearsal Jimmy, Robert, and John were joined by session player/bassist John Paul Jones, and after pumping out a couple hours of old R&B classics, the foursome knew they had struck rock gold. John was a bit intimidated by the quiet, mysterious Jimmy, but he also knew the music they created together was supernatural.

A few days later the New Yardbirds left for a tour of Scandinavia, where they got an inkling about their potential. The music they played was sheer, mad magic, and it demanded a new name. In Richard Cole's book, *Stairway to Heaven* (he would later be Zep's road manager and constant companion), he recalled how the band name came from a conversation he had with two members of the Who: "Moon and Entwistle were growing weary of the Who and were kidding about starting a new band with Jimmy Page. Moon joked, 'I've got a good name for it. Let's call it Lead Zeppelin 'cause it'll go over like a lead balloon!'" Despite being the butt of a good joke, Jimmy decided to use the name, changing it to "Led Zeppelin" so there would be no chance of mispronunciation. Wasting no time, Led Zeppelin went into the studio, where they cut their first record in thirty hours for a cost of less than five thousand dollars, including the cover art of the Hindenburg zeppelin sinking into the ocean. The album—full of forever-imitated raunchy riffs, Bonzo's frenzied, primal attack, and Robert's seductive caterwaul—sounds like it was recorded in a sweaty little club full of sweaty little girls. It's still one of my favorite hunks of rock and roll, despite the lambasting it took from the critics.

While they waited for the record release, Zeppelin played a few club dates in England, but Peter Grant had his huge sights set on America, the land of the almighty dollar. After signing his band to an unprecedented deal with Atlantic Records, he booked Zeppelin's American tour without the benefit of product in the stores. It was a risk that paid off beyond even Peter's grandiose expectations.

America knew they were coming. I could certainly feel it in the air when a new British band was about to hit town, and January 2, 1969, Zeppelin clobbered Los Angeles with transcendental force. The Whiskey-a-Go-Go was full of sweaty little girls, ready for mischief. Haughty Robert Plant shrieked and preened, totally at home in his glory. Enigmatic John Paul winked at the agog audience, and Bonzo's thrashing made us all thrillingly deaf. But even though his guitar raged, the frail darling Jimmy Page was ill with the flu. I can still see the damp ringlets clinging to his cheekbones as he was carried offstage by road manager Richard Cole. One of his red patent-leather slippers fell off and was quickly retrieved—one of those memorable rock-and-roll moments.

By the final date at the Fillmore in New York, the album was being played on the radio and the members of Led Zeppelin were amusing themselves with two-hour sets, setting new rock-and-roll standards. The show was so extraordinary that the headliner, Iron Butterfly, refused to follow them. But the bad press had started. *Rolling Stone* called Robert "a pretty soul belter who can do a good spade imitation," comparing Zeppelin to the Jeff Beck Group in "self-indulgence and restrictedness." Despite hundreds of protest letters, the press continued to slag off Led Zeppelin, creating such contempt within the band that they refused to do interviews for many years to come, which added to their burgeoning mystique.

Bonzo needed hours to unwind after one of his bombastic performances and, on that first tour, engaged Richard Cole in the first of many, many post-show antics. It all began innocently enough with raw eggs and half-eaten dinners sailing through hotel rooms, but soon degenerated to the lowest levels of rock-and-roll debauchery. From the outside, Zeppelin's naughty road hijinks seemed almost decadently glamorous. In reality, the band had too much pent-up energy and too many hours to fill.

Zeppelin spent only two months in England before their second trip to America, opening at the Fillmore West with a three-and-a-half-hour set. In May they hit the American Top Ten, and most of the next year was spent on the road. Bonzo was playing with the biggest bass drum made, and his solo was evolving into the highlight of the show, sometimes lasting over thirty minutes. When he threw away his sticks and played with his hands, the crowds went insane. The rest of the band took to ambling back to the dressing room during Bonzo's thrash fest, where Jimmy and Robert would do a bit of primping (and later a bit of boozing, popping, snorting, and sundry sexual favors).

Bonzo had a gigantic appetite for booze, often becoming belligerent, passing out, and sleeping it off in jail cells all over the world—and getting into reams of trouble in general. It was road manager Richard Cole, a mighty abuser himself, who was in charge of keeping Bonzo in line. Richard is a longtime friend of mine, and has been clean and sober for many years. He has plenty of tales about Bonzo dumping huge amounts of baked beans on Richard and his girl of the moment while they made love, then calling in Peter Grant, who doused them with champagne; trimming an adoring groupie's pubic hair with Robert's shaving gear; flooding John Paul's hotel room with a garden hose; punching out complete strangers; or relieving himself in the most unlikely places.

The hedonistic concept of "free love" peaked with Zeppelin's rise, freeing thousands of teenage girls to pursue these British cream-boats with rampant fervor. The band was besieged by packs of persistent dolls more than willing to sacrifice themselves to the hammer of the gods. "Percy" (as Robert was nicknamed), "Bonzo," and "Jonesy" were married men but couldn't always resist the teenage temptresses. In the middle of one night at the Chateau Marmont, Bonzo dressed himself up as a waiter and rolled a service cart featuring Jimmy Page as the main course into a roomful of underage girls the guitarist always fancied.

The Zeppelin "mudshark episode" at Seattle's Edgewater Inn has become a torrid slice of rock-and-roll folklore. Though Richard Cole admits to being the ringleader, Bonzo was front and center with his fishing pole dangling off the balcony. "It wasn't even a shark!" Richard asserts. "I caught this red snapper, and the chick was a redhead. It was still alive and I just pushed it in on her ginger pussy! Bonzo was in the room, but it was me that did it." I am amazed that Bonzo didn't assist. "No, he didn't, but he brought his wife in to have a look!"

And then there was the octopus incident. "We were doing two shows that night and it was Bonzo's birthday," Richard tells me with a gleam. "Bonzo had a four-foot-high bottle of champagne next to him onstage. A lot of times on that second tour we did two shows a night, but had to stop them because we got so drunk during the shows—especially Bonzo—that the second show was always a fiasco." After the mad second set, a friend took some of the boys back to a motel room where they were presented with four octopuses. "This guy had two girls in there, naked. There was all these mixed vegetables, fruit, turnips, and cucumbers in the bath, so we put the girls in there with the octopuses." Apparently Jimmy was goo-goo-eyed as one of the sea creatures discovered the joy of sex. When I mention to Richard that Jimmy had always told me he avoided those kinds of naughty displays, he roars, "Jimmy's always been full of shit. He was there. Bonzo was there. His wife, Pat, must have gone home. Jonesy would come and have a look, but that's about it. He would get up to his own devious things that we'd never see. The only one that was ever documented was when he woke up with a drag queen and the room caught on fire!" (Jonesy always insisted that he hadn't known he'd picked up a transvestite.)

The third tour of America was even more depraved. There was the "dog act," in which a lovely young thing had various forms of sex with her Great Dane while members of Zeppelin cheered her on. Richard admits to frying up a pan of bacon and shoving the charred stuff into the appropriate place so the boys could watch the hungry mutt chowing down.

During a pop festival at the Singer Bowl in New York, a ravenously drunk Bonzo wearied of a Ten Years After set and paced backstage until he finally snapped. "He was very sweet, Bonzo, except when he got to a certain point in drinking and then he would turn nasty," Richard says. "No one wanted to go near him except me. If he was drunk, the others would say 'Leave Bonzo here!' and I'd say 'Fuck off! I'm not leaving 'im here!' At least you knew where you stood with Bonzo." On this particular afternoon Bonzo drank plenty enough to turn quite nasty, throwing a carton of orange juice all over Alvin Lee, Ten Years After's front man, and his magic guitar, thoroughly ruining his eternal solo. For an encore, Bonzo dragged Jeff Beck's drummer from behind his drums and took over the duties. After pounding out a stripper's beat, Bonzo danced for the crowd, then peeled himself stark naked, and was hustled offstage by an enraged Peter Grant, narrowly avoiding the cops. Another time Bonzo saw fit to remove Chuck Berry's drummer from behind his kit and slam-banged along with "Sweet Little Sixteen." This time he received a compliment from the legendary Mr. Berry, who winked at Bonzo and said, "Now, *there's* a real drummer!"

The Hollywood club in 1969 was Thee Experience, where anything and everything went—times ten. The owner, Marshall Brevitz, enjoyed the notoriety of having the rock wunderkinds under his roof and actually encouraged Zeppelin's wickedness. I tried not to watch as Richard Cole carried a skinny, wailing girl around upside down, his face buried in her crotch, then had abandoned sex with her on the liquor-covered tabletop while the rest of the band observed like it was no big deal. In Richard's book, *Stairway to Heaven,* he recalls a raging night at Thee Experience. "While we were waiting for our third round of drinks, two girls volunteered to crawl under the table and perform oral sex on the band. They did it in record time."

In August Zeppelin had somehow managed to finish recording *Led Zeppelin II* in between all the madness. Featuring "Whole Lotta Love" and Bonzo's showcase number, "Moby Dick," *Led Zeppelin II* came out during the band's fourth tour of America, knocking the Beatles and the Stones out of the number-one spot. And their first album was still in the Top Twenty.

Due to Peter's unflagging faith and ferocity, and the lads' willingness to work ridiculously hard, Zeppelin had become one of the highest-paid rock acts in history in a very short time. It irked Jimmy Page that the critics took to calling their thunderous sound "heavy metal," but it couldn't be denied that Led Zeppelin had altered the course of rock and roll forever.

Jimmy, Robert, John Paul, and Bonzo all bought homes in the English countryside. Besides buying his old farmhouse, Bonzo spent a fortune on cars, acquiring eight of them, including his first Rolls-Royce, by the end of 1969. He was at his happiest riding a tractor around his property wearing overalls and a huge pair of goofy galoshes, but Bonzo had two distinctly different personalities. The right (or wrong) amount of alcohol could turn the gentle homebody into a raving, violent monster. At a chichi press reception Bonzo yanked an expensive painting off the wall and crashed it over a pontificating critic's head. I once saw him do the same humiliating thing to a photographer friend of mine before shoving a hot steak-and-kidney pie down his pants. I also witnessed Bonzo barrel through the door of the Rainbow Bar and Grill late one night, then haul off and slug my friend Michele Myer in the jaw before being wrestled to the ground by two huge bouncers. "Bonzo liked to drink and have fun," Richard says ruefully, "but he was a bad drunk, especially if his wife had just left and he was morose." Didn't all the female attention make up for it? I ask. "I don't think Bonzo was that interested in sleeping with the girls," Richard insists. "He just wanted the company."

While I was cavorting with Jimmy Page, Linda Alderetti was Bonzo's constant companion. She spent a whole lot of time on the road with Bonzo and concurs with Richard. "That was a strange thing. We slept together once or twice, but it wasn't about sex for him. He wanted someone who was savvy and good-looking, someone in the light who everybody knew." Linda was the cashier at the Rainbow Bar and Grill, Zeppelin's favorite Hollywood nest. One night, while waiting for Linda to get off work, Bonzo got pissed off at a good friend who was spending too much time with Linda. "By the end of the night John was choking Steve Mariott on the floor. Nobody could pull him off! Bonzo was a big, overgrown baby. I witnessed him beat up so many people. Zeppelin happened to get away with all that wild stuff because of the times. Not only did anything go—it was all covered up! The more money they made for people, the worse damage they could do. You and I got to see a side of rock and roll that will never be seen again," Linda says intently. "The insanity, the overindulgence of every whim, everything being catered to in every way—we literally lived with twenty-four-hour security to clean up the mess we left behind."

By the fifth American tour Zeppelin were getting bored with the same old hump and bump, the interminable travel, even the crush of the countless slavish girls. Richard was always looking for ways to keep his boys amused, once hiring several strippers to perform privately for Zep. After the girls frolicked, Richard put on a performance of his own by dressing in some of the strippers' clothes, doing his own striptease, and having sex with one of the girls while sixty screwdrivers were ingested. "There's nothing immoral in it," Richard insists. "It's just that most people wouldn't dream of doing it. That's the whole story of Led Zeppelin right there." The alcohol consumption was getting ridiculous. Richard swears that, one night in Frankfurt, he, Peter, and the boys put away 280 drinks in one sitting.

Peter Grant was getting a reputation as a dangerous man. He had supposedly been involved with the British Mafia, and since he weighed over three hundred pounds, people tended to take him seriously. Nobody crossed him more than once. Even though some of the tales of aggro are shocking, I admired Peter's sole devotion to his boys. He was always good to me. Sitting on his lap was one of the safest places in the world.

One night in Atlanta a couple of soldiers pointed a gun at Zeppelin, spouting off about their long hair, and Peter picked them both up off the ground, bellowing, "What's your fucking problem, Popeye?" But ask anything about those whispered stories of broken kneecaps, and people become strangely mum. Even Richard Cole. "I knocked a guy's kneecaps once because he wouldn't get out from under the revolving stage. The stage would have slid forward and the gear would have fallen off and crushed people. And I knocked three guys out in a hotel corridor," he admits. "One of them said he was Pagey's brother and his friend went for me, so I nailed all three of 'em. They called the police but they didn't know the police were working for us! They gave 'em another beating and threw 'em out!" I personally saw Richard kick a guy's teeth out when he got too close to Robert at the Rainbow. "You see someone coming over with their eyes bulging and their hands in their pockets, you're not going to take a chance," he explains. "If you're wrong, you're wrong, but if you're right . . ."

In May 1970 Zeppelin holed up in an old Hampshire country house with a mobile recording studio, and a few weeks later *Led Zeppelin III* was completed. In August they were back out on the road, hitting America for the sixth time in eighteen months. Thirty-six shows in seven weeks quickly became a blur. Fans were getting more demanding and unruly. Riots were becoming commonplace. Security had to be tightened. The boys spent more and more of their time sequestered in their rooms, getting royally bombed.

Led Zeppelin III went gold the day it came out, but the critics brutalized the band and their fans: The lyrics were meaningless drivel hidden by hollow, deafening bravado stolen from authentic bluesmen. *Rolling Stone* actually blamed Zeppelin for the acceleration of drug use among their audience members. Jimmy Page felt he was being personally attacked and took the band directly back to the studio, where they began work on their fourth album. Once again they used the mobile unit, staying at the country house in Hampshire, where Bonzo, dressed in his finest tweeds, would take full advantage of the local pub.

For the fourth album Robert dug even deeper into romantic Celtic mythology, coming up with the classic lyrics for "Stairway to Heaven" while the rest of the band ran through the newly composed music. Years later Robert recalled the moment: "I was holding a paper and pencil, and for some reason I was in a very bad mood. Then all of a sudden I was writing out words. . . . I just sat there and looked at the words and then I almost leaped out of my seat." With this song Jimmy believed that Robert had come into his own as a songwriter. Today "Stairway" is the most requested song all over the world.

Zeppelin shook up the record company when they demanded that the fourth album have no group name, no title, and no Atlantic logo. Instead Jimmy had each member of the band choose his own personal symbol from his *Book of Runes*. Robert chose the sign for peace. John Paul's represented self-confidence. Jimmy designed his own symbol, which appeared to spell "zoso," though he maintained it wasn't a word at all. Bonzo's three interlocking circles represented unity, but the band insisted it must have been inspired by the Ballantine beer insignia.

After five months of recording, Zeppelin wanted to thank their fans by playing small clubs around the British Isles. Richard tells me that Bonzo was not on his best behavior. "Unfortunately, I broke his nose twice. The first time was in Ireland. We had to go through the war zone, and the promoter had given us all a bottle of Jameson's Irish whiskey each! When we got to the hotel, Bonzo went to the kitchen to order some sandwiches, and the next thing we knew, our chauffeur is running for me. 'Bonzo is in the kitchen, and the chef has a knife!'" It seems that when Bonzo had been drinking, he became headstrong and refused to take no for an answer. The fact that the kitchen had been closed for half an hour made no difference to the hungry drummer. He was closing in on the chef, who was making threats with a huge carving knife. "Bonzo wouldn't shut up," Richard continues. "He wouldn't leave the kitchen, so I gave him a whack on the nose and broke it, which was a lot safer than the chef sticking a knife in him! He went up to Peter's room and said, 'Richard's broken my nose! I'm leaving the band!' and Peter says, 'Aww, fuck off, don't wake me up to tell me that kind of bullshit! Go to bed!'"

In the fall of 1971 Led Zeppelin were at their pinnacle. Jimmy and I had broken up by this time, but Robert sent a limo for me when Zep played the Forum, saying that he wouldn't go on until I got there. As I climbed from the plush den-on-wheels, Robert spotted me and bounded to the stage. It was a heady feeling. By this time the members of Zeppelin were making their own rules. "The doors had to open now," Richard said. "If they didn't we'd break them down. And that was it. We made our own laws. If you didn't want to fucking abide by them, don't get involved."

The charm of America had turned into a grind for the band, and boredom created all sorts of tawdry scenarios. In the middle of a nostalgic fish-and-chips dinner with Bonzo, Richard was interrupted by two girls who wanted to play. When Richard and his friends retired to the bedroom, Bonzo tried to watch TV but couldn't hear anything except orgasmic wails. "He picked up one of the girls' shoes by the front door. 'Let me really give her something to shout about!' and proceeded to drop his pants . . . and shit in the shoe!" A lovely Led Zeppelin memento.

Linda shakes her head, recalling the war stories. "John did not grow up with much sophistication, and he was not very bright. But he was a sweetheart with a soft, soft heart, and that was his weakness and he knew it, so he never showed that to anybody."

The members of the band tormented one another at every turn. On a tour of Japan, after splintering their own rooms with samurai swords, Richard and Bonzo hacked through Jonesy's door, found him comatose in bed, and dragged him into the hallway, where he woke up the next afternoon. Traveling on a Japanese train, Jimmy Page's geisha girl of the moment was stunned to find one of Bonzo's repulsive offerings in her purse. When the poor girl realized what had happened, Bonzo leaned over to Richard and said joyfully, "It looks like the shit hit the purse!"

The fourth album came out in November, followed by a brief tour of England. The show at Wembley Stadium featured acrobats, clowns, jugglers, and a pig bouncing up and down on a trampoline. And three hours of very loud music. "You feel your eardrums being pushed inward like sails full of wind," ranted *Melody Maker.* "It's painful, but it rips out an emotion common to most everyone in the hall. Excitement, and something rude, something so alive it smells. . . ."

While Jimmy wrote the soundtrack for Kenneth Anger's *Lucifer Rising,* the rest of the band spent time with their families. Bonzo loved his farm and took serious pride in his car collection, which now numbered twenty-one, including a Maserati, a Jensen, and an AC Cobra. He would eventually own dozens of vehicles, one of his prizes being a Model T bread van. At his local pub, Bonzo gave *Melody Maker's* Chris Welch a rare peek into his down-to-earth persona, admitting he never deliberately tried to be "one of the best drummers and I don't want to be. . . ." Claiming he wasn't "more exciting than Buddy Rich," Bonzo explained that he only played what he liked. "I'm a simple, straight-ahead drummer and I don't pretend to be anything better than I am." When asked about the future of Zeppelin, Bonzo announced, "We might be on top next year, or I might be back on the buildings!"

The fifth album was recorded at Stargroves, Mick Jagger's country home, and engineered by Eddie Kramer. Even though Bonzo's pranks included crashing into the room Kramer shared with his girlfriend, yanking open his huge raincoat, and giving them the rare treat of his nude body, Kramer has nothing but praise for Bonzo's brilliance. "His sound was so great it facilitated a *monumental* drum sound on record. You can't describe it; you have to hear it.

Bonzo sounded that way because he hit the drums harder than anyone I ever met. He had this bricklayer's ability to bang the drum immensely hard. Yet he had a very light touch. In many ways, he was the key to Led Zeppelin. . . . Once he mastered his part, everything else would fall into place."

Houses of the Holy, which includes my favorite raunchy ditty, "Dancing Days," wasn't released until almost a year later, March 1973, due to the usual cover-art hassles. The band geared up to tour again while Peter Grant entirely altered the business side of rock and roll, demanding 90 percent of the box-office receipts for his boys—and getting it.

With the exception of more money and a rented jet, Led Zeppelin's eighth North American tour was just like all the rest. Although Jimmy Page kept getting older, his girls remained in their early teens. Bonzo bought more cars and trashed more hotel rooms. The band toured Asia, Europe, and the British Isles, selling 120,000 tickets in one day. Their brief drop of downtime was spent with their families. Jimmy bought a manor in Plumpton with a moat, Robert renovated his three-acre sheep ranch, John Paul relished time with his daughters, and Bonzo set about rebuilding his one-hundred-acre Old Hyde Farm. He began breeding Hereford cattle, showing great warmth for the animals, and taking great pride in his new enterprise. But the road always beckoned.

On a tour of France in March 1973, a security guard nicknamed Bonzo "Le Bête" ("The Beast") after he totaled three dressing-room trailers with his symphonic gong mallet, and the name stuck. Bonzo was getting so blotto that he couldn't remember if he was supposed to be onstage, in bed, or on the jet. Even though it was up to Richard to make sure Bonzo got from point A to point B, he wasn't faring much better himself. "I don't think anyone took as many drugs or drank as much as we did. We were in a hotel in Atlanta and I said, 'What shall we drink?' Bonzo said, 'Brandy Alexanders.' They brought out a tray, and while the bill was being paid, we drank them all. I said, 'You'd better bring out a pitcher!' By the time he came back with that bill, Bonzo shouted out, 'You'd better bring four more pitchers!'"

At the request of the band, Richard procured a Boeing jet called the *Starship*, and Zeppelin traveled around the world in what Robert called "a floating palace." A floating den of iniquity.

On the band's next tour of America, Bonzo's twenty-fifth birthday was celebrated at a disc jockey's home in Hollywood. George Harrison recklessly slammed the top tier of the birthday cake into the face of the Beast, who promptly hurled the Beatle and his wife, Patti, into the pool along with all the other party guests—except for Peter Grant and Jimmy Page. Glowering Peter was much too large to deal with. Jimmy, the nonswimmer, walked elegantly into the shallow end before he could be hurled into deep waters.

The *Starship* helped ease the endless sameness of touring, but as Bonzo told Richard, "It does get to be a real drag after a while." Filming on the Zeppelin movie had begun with concert footage being shot for *Song Remains the Same.* Jimmy was weak and exhausted, and worried about all the strange death threats he was getting.

When Bonzo learned that individual segments of Zeppelin's movie would be shot in and around their homes, he suggested taking the director to a pub so he could film the band "getting blotted out of our minds." He got his wish. Bonzo's segment featured his beloved farm, the prize bulls, his remarkable car collection, and his local pub. Sessions for the sixth album, *Physical Graffiti,* were in progress, and Zeppelin had decided to start their own record label—Swan Song. My ex, Michael Des Barres, signed his band, Detective, to Zep's label. It seemed like a fabulous idea at the time. It turned out to be a nightmare.

On the flight to New York for the East Coast Swan Song inaugural wing-ding, a zonked-out Bonzo pissed in his first-class seat, then offered it to an innocent roadie, who was forced to suffer in damp humiliation while Bonzo snored comfortably back in coach. After the New York bash at the Four Seasons, Zeppelin hit L.A. for an absurdly lavish bash. Their first Swan Song single, Bad Company's "Can't Get Enough of Your Love," went to number one. It seemed Led Zeppelin could do no wrong.

The L.A. party coincided with Elvis playing the Forum, and Zeppelin were thrilled to be invited. When the King announced his "favorite band" was in the audience and the spotlight landed on Zeppelin, Bonzo was out cold, snoring, having spent the night snorting coke with Richard Cole. Still, Bonzo was ecstatic when Elvis later asked for *his* autograph for Presley's daughter, Lisa Marie.

The Pretty Things' *Silk Torpedo* was Swan Song's first album release in England, and the Halloween-night celebration featured fire-eaters, magicians, naked women gyrating in cherry Jell-O, and strippers dressed (briefly) as nuns and as virgins being sacrificed at Black Mass altars. At the end of the night, Bonzo and the roadies enjoyed a free-for-all Jell-O toss.

So much money was being made that Zeppelin had to go into tax exile at the beginning of 1975, spending the year abroad, most of it touring. All eight albums were still on the *Billboard* charts when the band's double album, *Physical Graffiti,* hit the number-one spot. In America seven hundred thousand seats sold out in one day. The Ticketron outlets were chaotic mob scenes. Again the *Starship* was rented, which now accommodated forty-four roadies and a doctor wielding two black bags full of medications of all kinds. This time out, Bonzo dressed himself in a white boiler suit and black derby like the demented "droogs" in *A Clockwork Orange.*

Seemingly on top of the universe, Led Zeppelin had become jaded and used to extravagant excess. The lovely females had long become pests. When Bonzo and Richard met up with Bad Company in Dallas, they actually traded sweet young things. "Too often we treated girls like just another commodity," Richard admits, "like exchanging one bottle of champagne for another."

Rousing from his comalike sleep on the *Starship* one fine day, Bonzo attacked one of the stewardesses, tore open his robe to reveal himself, and threatened to take her from behind before Peter and Richard could struggle him to the ground. There was plenty of press on the plane, but Richard demanded silence, and got it. On another flight Bonzo yanked a fellow's glasses from his face, broke them into smithereens, and squashed them into the carpet. He ordered a tour photographer to walk down the airplane aisle without the benefit of his clothing. The Plaza Hotel in New York insisted on a ten-thousand-dollar deposit before Bonzo checked in, but for some reason, the Hollywood Riot House always reserved several floors for Zeppelin, despite the incessant destruction. On the last day of the American tour, Bonzo hurled six TV sets to the ground and would have sent the piano sailing except it wouldn't fit through the window.

It wasn't fun anymore. There were too many dealers around, offering free merchandise just to breathe Zeppelin's rarefied air. Pot and psychedelics had been replaced on the scene with escalating amounts of cocaine and heroin. Zeppelin had gone as high up as possible. Things were about to change dramatically.

There had always been mumblings about Jimmy Page's supposed pact with the devil and about the members of Zeppelin trading their souls in exchange for mammoth success. I knew Jimmy was deeply enthralled with Aleister Crowley, "The Great Beast 666," the hedonistic magician who practiced "sex magick" and lived by his own credo, "Do what thou wilt shall be the whole of the law." Jimmy bought Boleskine House, Crowley's castle in Scotland, and wore his long black cloak. I even helped with his obsession by locating an annotated Crowley manuscript at Gilbert's bookstore on Hollywood Boulevard. A Southern Baptist minister claimed that when "Stairway to Heaven" was played at a very slow speed, the words "Here's to my sweet Satan" could be faintly heard, but I never believed Led Zeppelin had signed papers with Lucifer.

The devil wasn't around, but there were more and more drugs. "Everybody wanted to know Jimmy," Linda tells me. "Dealers wanted to be around him. It was getting crazy. Jimmy was *out there,* and he loved drag bars. We would lose him halfway through the night and find him in the women's bathroom, in the stall with three drag queens doing drugs." Linda explains that Jimmy's going to drag bars satisfied his curiosity about the scene. "That whole second-to-last tour was a nightmare," she continues. "Robert didn't want to be on the road. Jimmy was in his Nazi uniform, spending half his time at the drag clubs. John was withdrawn at the time—all he wanted to do was stay in and get loaded. He was drinking so much, shooting a lot of heroin."

There was finally relief from the lunacy: family holidays in Switzerland and France. And Bonzo became a father for the second time—a sister Zoe for young Jason. The plan was to tour America again in the fall, but on the fourth of August, on the Greek island of Rhodes, Robert's wife, Maureen, crashed their car into a tree, shattering Robert's right elbow and leg. The doctors told him he wouldn't be able to walk for at least six months. Everything was postponed while Robert took his healing process to Malibu.

Jimmy soon moved to Malibu Colony to write Zep's next record with Robert. Bonzo and Jonesy followed in October to begin rehearsals. Angry about having to leave his family, Bonzo stomped around L.A. on the lookout for big trouble . . . and he found plenty. He had grown a full beard and had gotten fat, his drinking completely out of control. He was like a belligerent child who could have anything he wanted but had been blessed (cursed?) with more than he could handle already.

Jimmy had promised to produce Detective's album, and they played a big-deal showcase for him at the Starwood. With much fanfare he arrived with Peter Grant and promptly nodded out. I sat there, mortified, attempting to rouse him to zero avail. When Detective turned up for their photo shoot with their errant, enigmatic producer, he was comatose. They sat in front of the rumpled bed and took the photos anyway.

Album number seven, *Presence,* was cut in Munich in eighteen days, despite the fact that Jimmy, Bonzo, and Richard were using heroin daily. After recording, Zeppelin finally completed the filming for *Song Remains the Same,* adding some footage of Bonzo race-car driving. In April 1976 *Presence* became the first album to go platinum on advance sales alone.

Another tax-exile summer for Bonzo was spent with his family in the South of France, followed by a little jaunt to Monte Carlo. "Pat had just gone home with Jason," Richard recalls. "We'd gone out to a casino and Bonzo had one of those gas guns in a shoulder holster and starts waving it about in front of all these wealthy people with their bodyguards! Before I could get the gun away from him, I half knocked him out, hit him on the nose, broke it for the second time, and then we got arrested. They took us down to the cells and I had all the fucking coke in my socks, and Bonzo says, 'Get the gear out! Get the gear out!' He wanted us to do the blow in the cell!"

The overgrown teddy bear taking a dip. (ROBERT KNIGHT)

Bonzo frolicking in the pool, with a view of Robert Plant's lovely backside. (ROBERT KNIGHT)

The eleventh tour of the United

States started on April Fool's Day 1977—a month late due to Robert's tonsillitis. Peter's wife had left him. Jimmy was weak and listless. He, Richard, and half the road crew were strung out on smack. Bonzo, Peter, and one of the roadies pummeled a security man in San Francisco and, along with Richard, who had stood lookout, were charged with assault. Bonzo turned his Chicago hotel room into so much firewood. After a concert in Houston, fans rampaged, causing half a million dollars in damages. Forty were arrested. When Zeppelin got to New Orleans, Robert got a call from Maureen, who told him that Karac, his five-year-old son, had just died of a respiratory virus. Bonzo flew back to England with Robert on a private jet and was the only other Zeppelin member to attend Karac's funeral.

Right from the beginning of the tour, Richard felt something was amiss. "It should never have happened. The whole thing just *went* then. That was it. It was never the same again. *Never.* The whole thing just erupted. It was like somebody said, 'Here, you fuckers, have *this!*'"

Two months later Bonzo was bombed out and crashed his Jensen on the way home from his local pub, breaking two ribs. Robert continued his mourning, holed up with his wife and daughter. Jimmy got more strung out on heroin. The band rarely spoke to each other.

"The last tour was fatal for everyone concerned," Linda tells me. "I left halfway through the tour because John and I got into this huge fight. We were all loaded, he was chasing me all over the hotel, he got me in the bedroom and pinned me down on the floor. I looked at him and said, 'I think it's time to go home. I'm leaving.' When I left, for Bonzo it got worse. The San Francisco disaster, Karac's death, and then it ended. John was left at home and it was the beginning of the end. He had only ever been at home for three or four months at a time. His wife got to see the insanity. His drug abuse had gotten really bad. You don't just go home and lose your drug habit."

It took Robert a long, long time to recover from his grief, and it was Bonzo who convinced him to come to a rehearsal, ten months after Karac's death. Several months later, in December 1978, the band went to Stockholm to record their next album, *In Through the Out Door.* The reviews were shockingly bad, but the album sold in the millions. They played their first show in two years in Copenhagen, followed by two concerts in England. At a rehearsal for these shows, Bonzo put his eleven-year-old son, Jason, behind his kit and the kid was so good, everyone was dumbfounded, especially his beaming father. Said Bonzo, "It was the first time I ever *saw* Led Zeppelin!"

There was another brief tour of Europe, but things were bad. In Nuremberg, Bonzo fell off his drum seat after the third song, and it was chalked up to "exhaustion." In late summer Zeppelin decided to settle in at Jimmy's new house (he moved to Windsor after a young man died of a drug overdose at his Sussex house) to begin rehearsals for the upcoming U.S. tour.

On September 24, 1980, Bonzo stopped at a pub and drank four quadruple vodkas, returned to Jimmy's house, where he continued his endless imbibing at the band's reunion bash, then passed out cold on the couch at midnight. A Zeppelin assistant dragged Bonzo to one of Jimmy's bedrooms so he could sleep it off. When Bonzo hadn't turned up by the next afternoon, he was discovered by a roadie, cold and blue, having died sometime that morning.

John Henry Bonham was cremated, then buried a few days later while eight local fans stood watching in the rain. A memorial was held at a church near Bonzo's precious farm. The coroner ruled the death accidental, caused by "pulmonary edema"—waterlogging of the lungs caused by inhaling vomit. Group members said it was hard to tell how drunk Bonzo had been because he was always drunk. On the last night of his life Bonzo had ingested "forty measures" (forty shots) of vodka.

Bonzo had been telling friends that he had kicked his heroin habit, but Linda feels differently. "He called me from Germany right before he died, asking me to come see him. I just couldn't. Bonzo absolutely died on heroin. When he died it was *credited* to heroin. He choked on his own vomit from an overdose. That is exactly how he died. You know they called him 'the Beast,'" she continues sadly. "If he was out of control, nobody wanted anything to do with him—and that was wrong. He died lonely, in that sense. Somebody could have helped him, he could have been okay, they could have woken him up, sent him home. . . ."

Richard Cole was in jail in Rome, having been wrongly arrested for "terrorism," when he got the news from his lawyer that one of "his boys" had died. At first he thought it had to be Jimmy. "I don't know what the true story about Bonzo's death was," he admits. "No one really knows. I heard all kinds of stories. The smack dealer told me that he sold stuff to one of the roadies that afternoon." Did he ever see any signs that Jimmy had coerced the band into signing a pact with Satan in return for their massive success? "I didn't see the black magic. Did you? The stuff about them making a pact with the devil is a load of old bollocks! It would have come out when one of 'em was drunk, I'm sure—'Oh, I should never have done that!' They had their fair share of tragedy, but it was all indulgence."

When I tell Linda that I think Bonzo had been in over his head, she agrees. "He was in over his head with everything. As his fame and wealth grew, he couldn't make the transition. He saw his friends more into stability, and he wanted that, but it eluded him. He wasn't educated enough, yet there was a side to him, the dreamer, who fantasized about it. In the end he took the insanity home with him—he didn't know how to get out of the madness, he didn't know how to stop."

On December 4, 1980, Led Zeppelin finally issued this puzzling statement: "The loss of our dear friend, and the deep sense of harmony felt by ourselves and our manager, have led us to decide that we could not continue as we were."

KURT COBAIN

∎

All Apologies

∎

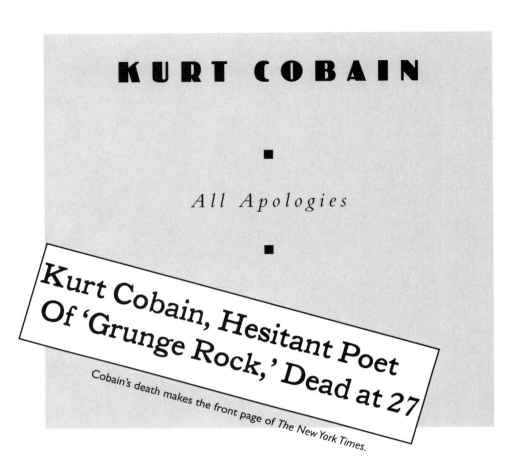

Kurt Cobain, Hesitant Poet Of 'Grunge Rock,' Dead at 27

Cobain's death makes the front page of *The New York Times.*

A few months before Kurt Cobain took his life, I had the strange pleasure of meeting him, oh so briefly. I was in Seattle on assignment for *Interview* magazine and my subject was Courtney Love. I was excited and jittery as my friend Victor drove me through the damp darkness while I pondered my questions for this dizzy, dangerous diva. I only knew to expect the unexpected.

The interview almost didn't happen. I had just gotten to Seattle and was on the phone when I was interrupted by an emergency call from Courtney, who nervously told me she wouldn't be able to do the interview the next day because Kurt had a few days off and she was taking him to "this life-enhancement thing." A journalist's nightmare for sure. To this day I wonder if they ever got there. A few minutes later she called and asked if I could come over "right now."

When I arrived I was met at the door by Cali, Frances Bean's male nanny, who ushered me into the messy living room where Kurt leaned against the wall—hovering, arms crossed in front of him, hunched, wary. His gaze was piercing, haunted, pointed. I felt like I was being sized up. He nodded to me. I was, as usual, all smiles. "It's *so* nice to meet you!" All he said was hello. Hello, hello, hello, hello, how low. Then he swooped his baby daughter into his arms and high up in the air, and tumbled with her on the floor, laughing.

The chat with Courtney was amazing. I was there for hours, drinking lots of red wine that Hole's guitarist, Eric Erlandson, had so graciously provided, getting tipsy, bonding with the outspoken blonde. She spoke often of Kurt, how lucky she was to be his wife, how much she loved him ("On a personal level, just in terms of his fidelity and that kind of stuff, he's amazing"), how talented he was ("I married one of the best songwriters of my generation"). I felt as if I'd met a kindred spirit grrrl and thought we would never lose contact. But I didn't see Courtney again until July, and by then everything had changed.

There was a serious drought, a dangerous apathetic lull in the world of rock before Nirvana stumbled out of Seattle. The Pistols were long gone. The airwaves were thick with torpid, droning leather metal, or sickly sweet Vegas showroom crooners, lugging around huge soulless voices. Where was the necessary angst? The prodding, provoking, pinching, and pointing that was rock and roll?

Kurt Cobain never wanted to lead that particular alternative parade. He tried to supply us with the questions, but seemed to know there would never be any answers. He condemned racists, homophobes, and sexists; he splayed his tortured heart because he had no choice. The "spokesperson of a generation" tag that was thrust on the frail, reclusive outcast became the cross he had to bear. Someone else might have been able to handle that heavy crown of thorns, thrive on it even, but Kurt was stunned and confused by his sudden importance—and ultimately crushed by the burden.

The suicide rate in the logging town of Aberdeen, Washington (pop. 17,000), is twice the national average. The town's incidence of unemployment, domestic violence, and alcohol and drug abuse is high, and the median household income is about $23,000. Once a thriving timberland, Aberdeen has become a ghost town full of boarded-up buildings and dotted with dismal trailer parks—and thriving bars.

Kurt Cobain was born in Hoquiam, Washington, raised in the flats of Aberdeen, and, by all accounts, the first few years of his life with his mother, Wendy, a homemaker, and his father, Donald, who worked at the local Chevron station, were warm and cozy—almost idyllic. There was music on Wendy's side of the family, and before the age of two, Kurt had his own toy guitar and, at seven, had started a record collection that included the Beatles, the Monkees, and his favorite, *Alice's Restaurant* by Arlo Guthrie. Perceptive, curious, and enthusiastic, Kurt was also diagnosed as hyperactive and dosed with the drug Ritalin, which kept him up all night and asleep at his school desk, until an allergy to sugar and red food dye was discovered. Seemingly always in some kind of mischief, Kurt blamed it all on a fictitious character he called "Boda." Sometimes Wendy even set a place for Boda at the dinner table, but Don wasn't so good-natured, and Kurt often got a belt-whipping. He ex-

Kurt in the air. When he wasn't onstage, he wanted to sleep. (CHARLES PETERSON)

celled in art, and even though a picture he drew graced the cover of the school newspaper, Kurt didn't think it was good enough. In third grade he started taking drum lessons, sometimes wanting to be a "rock star" when he grew up ("I wanted to be Ringo Starr," Kurt later said, "but I wanted to be John Lennon playing drums"), sometimes a stuntman like his hero, Evel Knievel.

Kurt's suburban bliss was shattered at eight years of age when his parents divorced. After work and on weekends, Don spent most of his time away from home, either playing sports or coaching. Bitter and resentful, Wendy even wondered if she had ever loved him. Since Kurt and his dad fought about his lack of interest in sports, he must have blamed himself for the split and the family upheaval that followed. Kurt was left-handed and Don had tried to get him to switch sides, but he couldn't do it (or *wouldn't* do it). Years later Kurt said that after the divorce, he "always felt ashamed." In the mortgaged house where Wendy still lives, Kurt's scrawl is still visible on his bedroom wall: "I hate Mom, I hate Dad, Dad hates Mom, Mom hates Dad. It simply wants to make you be sad."

"It just destroyed his life," said Wendy. "He changed completely. I think he was ashamed. And he became very inward—he just held everything in. He became real shy." He also became deeply angry and emotionally withdrawn, and his health problems escalated. He had regular bouts of chronic bronchitis and was diagnosed with a severe curvature of the spine, scoliosis.

Kurt lived with Wendy for a little over a year until she settled in with a guy Kurt called "a mean huge wifebeater." He then moved into his dad's prefab house until Don married a lady with two kids, after promising Kurt he would never remarry. At every opportunity Kurt lashed out at his stepsiblings, resenting every toy his dad bought for them. When Don talked him into joining the junior-high wrestling team, Kurt made sure that his dad saw him voluntarily lose an important championship. Don took him out hunting, but Kurt refused to shoot anything. His only solace was listening to Queen's "We Are the Champions" over and over on the eight-track in his dad's truck. Don had joined the Columbia House record and tape club, and at ten years old, Kurt glommed on to Led Zeppelin, Black Sabbath, and Kiss. Even when Don applied for legal custody and it was granted, Kurt wanted out of his dad's house. Wendy suggested that Kurt move in with his hip uncle Chuck, and he excitedly agreed.

For Kurt's fourteenth birthday, Uncle Chuck gave him a choice—a bicycle or a guitar. Guess which one he chose? Kurt took guitar lessons and started writing songs. Instead of hanging out with the kids at school, he holed up in his room and practiced for hours on his secondhand Sears guitar. *Creem* magazine became his bible, and the Sex Pistols and the whole punk scene, a fascinating new option. Kurt's early music was mean and nasty, and he turned his ten-watt amp up loud, annoying the neighbors. He also started smoking pot.

When Don insisted that Kurt join the Babe Ruth baseball team, he didn't make it up to bat very often. Instead, he sat on the bench with Matt Lukin, talking about music. Matt played in a local band, the Melvins, and Kurt told him that he was going to start his own punk band. In art class Kurt met the Melvins' leader, Buzz Osborne, and he was so thrilled to know people in a working band that he started humping the Melvins' equipment when they played gigs in Seattle. "When I first met Kurt Cobain," Buzz said, "he looked like a teenage runaway." Buzz made tapes for Kurt to listen to: Black Flag, the Buzzcocks, the Circle Jerks. Kurt spiked his hair and started spray-painting rude slogans on cars and buildings.

After bouncing around living with various relatives, Kurt finally convinced his mother to let him come back home. Wendy was about to dump another husband, longshoreman Pat O'Connor. After catching him cheating on her, Wendy threatened to shoot O'Connor with one of his own guns, then took his entire collection and hurled it into the Wishkah River. Kurt saw the whole thing, paid some kids to fish the guns out, then sold them to buy his first real amplifier. He started hanging out at Melvins rehearsals, where he met fellow guitarist Chris Novoselic and his girlfriend, Shelli. They started spending time together, drinking and listening to music. Kurt eventually dug up the courage to audition for the Melvins, which he screwed up bad. "I was so nervous that I forgot all the songs," Kurt told Michael Azzerad for his Nirvana bio, *The Story of Nirvana: Come As You Are.* "I literally couldn't play a note. I just stood there with my guitar and played feedback with a blushed face." But the Melvins were impressed that Kurt was already writing his own songs.

Kurt worked on his music instead of schoolwork, and by the eleventh grade, he was smoking a lot of marijuana and skipping classes. One of his best friends was gay and Kurt took a lot of flak from jocks in school who beat the crap out of him and called him a faggot. For a while Kurt seemed to enjoy the notoriety ("I was a *special* geek"), but it proved to be too much trouble and he ended the friendship. The only other person Kurt got close to his last year at Weatherwax High was a girl named Jackie. The night Kurt was about to lose his virginity, Wendy busted into his room in a fit, calling Jackie a slut. After dropping out of school a month before graduation, in June 1985 Kurt went back to his dad's house and seemingly went straight for a few weeks. He stopped smoking pot, pawned his guitar, and actually took the navy entrance exam, receiving one of the highest scores in the country. The navy recruiter came to the house two nights in a row, but when Kurt was supposed to sign on the dotted line, he went down to the basement, smoked a joint, came back upstairs, and said two words: "No thanks." Then he packed his things and left his father's house for the last time.

After spending a few months crashing with friends, Kurt finally got a place of his own, which he decorated with blood-spattered baby dolls hanging by their necks. "There was beer and puke and blood all over the carpet," Kurt later said. "Garbage stacked up for months. I never did do the dishes." He got a job as a busboy, then as a janitor at Aberdeen High, but never managed to pay his rent and was thrown out. Kurt then spent his days in the library, reading and writing poetry, sleeping in a cardboard box on a friend's porch, in Chris Novoselic's van, or under the North Aberdeen Bridge—usually after an evening of spray-painting the neighborhood with slogans like ABORT CHRIST, GOD IS GAY, and NIXON KILLED HENDRIX. He eventually landed with the Shillinger family after befriending one of their six kids and lived there eight months, doing his daily chores like everybody else in the family. Wendy was employing "tough love" techniques and never looked him up.

Kurt's first band was a trio he called Fecal Matter, but after playing a few gigs and recording a four-track demo ("Bambi Slaughter," "Territorial Pissings"), they split up because Kurt didn't feel the other two had enough dedication. While he honed his music, Kurt continued to rampage around town with his can of spray paint, finally getting arrested as he was painting the words HOMO SEX RULES. He was taken to the station, where the cops cleaned out his pockets and found a guitar pick, a can of beer, a mood ring, and a tape by a band called A Million Dead Cops. Fined $180, Kurt was given a thirty-day suspended sentence on the charge of vandalism. That summer of 1986 Kurt got briefly hooked on the opiate painkiller Percodan and shot heroin for the first time, knowing there wasn't enough of the drug in Aberdeen to get him into serious trouble. Kurt was high-strung and agitated, and started cracking his knuckles, scratching his face, and constantly tossing his hair. And he was getting paranoid. He thought everybody knew the savage thoughts going through his head. The opiates gave him relief from the hatred he had brewing down inside. Always looking for a new way to get wasted, Kurt discovered shaving cream propellant, which he inhaled for a buzz, joyously turning his friends on to the experience.

There was another short group stint with Brown Towel, but it wasn't until Chris Novoselic listened to the Fecal Matter tape that Kurt had given him almost a year earlier that the two started playing together. But it was short-lived because Chris and Shelli took off for Arizona to look for work.

Wendy shook off her tough-love training long enough to pay rent for a dilapidated dump on East Second Street that Kurt shared with a tank full of turtles. He started going to Olympia, checking out bands, and listened to the progressive Evergreen College radio station, KAOS, which had its own record label, K, distributing bands like Young Marble Giants and Vaseline. Kurt was so impressed that he got a tattoo of the K logo on his left forearm.

Chris Novoselic was back from Arizona and, after a couple of false starts, he and Kurt put a band together with drummer Aaron Burckhard, playing shows as Skid Row, Ted Ed Fred, Windowframe, and Bliss before deciding on Nirvana. Years later, when Kurt was asked what the name meant to him, he replied, "Total peace after death."

Kurt was driven, and the other two musicians had a difficult time matching his enthusiasm—especially Aaron, who preferred the mainstream to Kurt's "punk shit." But Kurt's zeal yanked them along, and their first gig—a house party in Raymond—confused all the guests when they refused to play cover songs. Slowly they started picking up real gigs, and in April 1987 played a live radio show on Evergreen's KAOS, which became their first demo.

Evicted from his turtle-filled dump, Kurt moved into Tracy Marander's studio apartment in Olympia, escaping Aberdeen once and for all. Tracy was Kurt's first real girlfriend, and they enjoyed thrift-store shopping together, filling their tiny apartment with a strange mixture of sixties kitsch and Kurt's art collages—tortured dolls, ruined religious artifacts, pictures of diseased vaginas from medical texts, dead insects. He played with Nirvana almost every night and cleaned dentists' offices by day, lifting enough nitrous oxide to pay for Nirvana's next recording session. But mostly he slept on the job and was fired after eight months. He hated working, being around what he called "average people." "They just get on my nerves so bad," he said. "I just cannot ignore them at all. I have to comfort them and tell them that I hate their guts."

During this time in his life, Kurt experienced his first bout of stomach pain, so severe that it almost disabled him. He started taking more drugs to dull the agony and even did heroin a few times. "You can feel it throbbing like you have a heart in your stomach," he said. "It just hurt really bad." The condition would torment Kurt for the rest of his life, confounding an endless stream of specialists.

The Nirvana demo was recorded in six hours and cost Kurt $152.44. He did all his vocals in one take and was very pleased with himself. Jack Endino engineered and was so touched by the raw power of Kurt's voice that he handed the tape over to Jonathan Poneman of the new underground Sub Pop label, who played it for his partner, Bruce Pavitt. They offered Nirvana five hours in the studio, where the band recorded four songs for the upcoming *Sub Pop 200* sampler. They were also asked to contribute to a compilation EP for the C/Z label. Nirvana's "Mexican Seafood" was included on the *Teriyaki Asthma* EP, and because they weren't sure how to spell Kurt's name, decided on "Kurdt," which he glommed on to for a short time.

Aaron Burckhard was fired after an embarrassed Chris had to pick him up at the local jail, where he had called a black cop "a fucking nigger." When he was "too hung over" to come to the next rehearsal, Kurt let Aaron go. He was replaced with Chad Channing, who played his first Nirvana show in May 1988 at Seattle's Vogue club. This was when the "Seattle sound" was really brewing. Soundgarden had just gotten a major deal at A&M, Mudhoney was doing local gigs, and Mother Love Bone was starting up. In June Nirvana recorded a single, "Love Buzz," for Sub Pop, and Kurt handwrote the bio, which closed with: "Willing to compromise on material (some of this shit is pretty old). Tour any time forever. Hopefully the music will speak for itself."

The Sub Pop catalog claimed that Nirvana's single was "Heavy pop sludge," but only printed a thousand copies, which sold out instantly. When Kurt heard himself on the radio for the first time, he was thrilled but didn't expect more than playing clubs—and maybe even paying his rent.

Nirvana ended 1989 with intensive rehearsals for their Sub Pop album, *Bleach,* recording the basic tracks in five hours on Christmas Eve. Kurt either hastily scribbled lyrics on the way to the studio or during the sessions, later saying that he hadn't put much thought into the words. But songs like "Negative Creep" and "Scoff" are pretty telling. *Bleach* was completed by the end of January at a cost of $606.17, paid for by fan and friend Jason Everman, who joined Nirvana just in time for a two-week tour of the West Coast.

Once again Kurt wrote Nirvana's bio beginning: "Greetings, Nirvana is a three piece spawned from the bowels of a redneck loser town called Aberdeen," after listing Nirvana's musical influences, including such widely different groups as the Knack, Black Flag, Led Zeppelin, the Stooges and the Bay City Rollers. Influences also included "H. R. Puffnstuf [sic], . . . divorces, drugs, . . . the Beatles, . . . Slayer, Leadbelly, [and] Iggy." Kurt proudly proclaimed that the underground music scene had become stagnant. Nirvana didn't want to rock the scene, Kurt explained kiddingly. "We want to cash in and suck butt up to the bigwigs in hopes that we too can get high and fuck wax figures hot babes, who will be required to have a certified AIDS test two weeks prior to the day of handing out backstage passes." Someday soon, Kurt said, the band would "need chick spray repellent" and "do encores of 'Gloria' and 'Louie Louie' at benfit [sic] concerts with all our celebrity friends."

In one of his first interviews, Kurt said that Nirvana had a "gloomy, vengeful element based on hatred," adding "I'd like to live off the band. I can't handle work."

When *Bleach* came out in June, Nirvana didn't think it sounded "heavy" enough, but were still happy to slog around America on a very low-budget promo tour. Playing the sleaze circuit, the band rarely made over a hundred bucks a night and often had to sleep in the van, but spirits were buoyant. Audiences were eating them up. And the record was selling. In Chicago Kurt dragged a huge yard-sale crucifix onstage. Excitement was so high in Pittsburgh that Kurt smashed his favorite guitar. It really pissed Jason off. That's when Kurt and Chris realized that he wasn't right for the band. Canceling the final seven shows, Nirvana drove home in silence, and Jason was fired when they got to Seattle. He never got his $606.17 back.

A "three piece" again, Nirvana drew ecstatic crowds in Seattle, then went on a two-week Midwestern tour, but it started out badly. Kurt was sick. He was rushed to the hospital after collapsing in Minneapolis, but the doctors could do nothing for his horrendous stomach pain.

Right after recording the *Blew* EP, Nirvana headed for Europe with the band TAD, playing thirty-six shows in forty-two days. Though the tour was difficult due to Chris's escalating drinking, Nirvana's falling-apart equipment, and the shocking workload, Kurt was amazed to discover that Nirvana were getting raves in the rock press and had masses of devoted fans. All the shows were sold out, and the pressures enormous. By the time they got to Rome, Kurt was frazzled and exhausted, totaling his guitar five songs into the show and climbing onto the speaker stacks and threatening to jump. "He had a nervous breakdown onstage," said Sub Pop's Bruce Pavitt, who attempted to coax him backstage. Kurt then crawled through the rafters, bellowing at the audience, and when he finally made his way down, he told the band he was quitting, then collapsed in tears. The next day on a train to Switzerland, Kurt was robbed. He got so sick, the show had to be canceled. At the final date in England, Nirvana was left with just one guitar, which Kurt threw at Chris, who splintered it with his bass.

On the tour of America that followed, Nirvana had a decent road crew for the first time, and all went fairly smoothly. Members of one of Kurt's favorite bands, Sonic Youth, brought Gary Gersh, their A&R man from Geffen Records, to the gig in New York, but Chris thought the show was so bad, he shaved his head as penance. In Massachusetts Kurt called his girlfriend, Tracy, on her birthday and told her they shouldn't live together anymore. Happy birthday to you.

Bleach was a consistent seller, but due to mismanagement, Sub Pop was floundering and nearly bankrupt. With a guilty heart, Kurt decided to look for a major label. But Kurt's fear of confrontation forced Chris to do the dirty work, so Chris told Bruce Pavitt the band was leaving Sub Pop, taking their seven newly recorded songs with them. Then they fired Chad Channing. Kurt would later say that he and Chad never really got along, but Chad insists it was his decision to leave the band. "I never felt like I was totally in the band. I felt like I was just a drummer. I was thinking, Why don't they get a drum machine—get it over with?" For their final Sub Pop single, "Sliver," Mudhoney's Dan Peters played the drums and did one gig with Nirvana at Seattle's Motor Sports International and Garage. Scream's drummer, Dave Grohl, was in the audience that night and was impressed enough to call the Melvins' Buzz Osborne to get ahold of Chris Novoselic. Chris liked Dave's drumming and invited him to Seattle for an audition, where he was picked up at the airport by Chris and Kurt. When Dave politely offered Kurt an apple, he replied, "No thanks, it'll make my teeth bleed."

Chris said he knew they had found the right drummer two minutes into Dave's audition, and Nirvana was complete. Dave's first gig with the band sold out in one day, and then Nirvana headed for Europe, playing to a thousand screaming people every night, snagging consistent raves. Back in America record labels were champing at the bit to get at the band from Aberdeen,

Washington. Sonic Youth's management company, Gold Mountain, offered assistance, flying Nirvana to L.A. to meet with Danny Goldberg and John Silva, who set up several meetings with record company bigwigs. About one of the encounters Nirvana had with an uptight Capitol exec, Kurt said, "I just wanted to dance on top of his desk with a dress on and piss all over the place." When one label offered a million dollars for the band, Kurt mischievously suggested they take the money and then break up, just like the Sex Pistols' *Great Rock 'n' Roll Swindle*, but after being wined, dined, and serviced beyond their most ludicrous dreams, Nirvana decided on Geffen, even though their offer was considerably lower. Geffen had broken Sonic Youth, after all, and Gary Gersh seemed to actually *understand* Nirvana. Geffen paid off Sub Pop, giving them two points on Nirvana's next two records, which pulled them out of the red and put them back on the map. Kurt excitedly told people that Nirvana were going to have complete creative control over their album. While the band waited for their advance money, Gold Mountain gave them a thousand dollars a month, and they continued to scrape by, pawning their amps and eating corn dogs.

By November 1990 Kurt was spending quite a bit of his meager cash on heroin, and Chris and Dave finally realized the extent of his problem. At first Kurt had indulged once a week, but it was slowly escalating. Heroin seemed to calm his tortured stomach as well as help him sleep. "While I was asleep, my stomach wouldn't hurt," Kurt explained. "Then I'd wake up and curse myself that I was still alive." He often wore pajama tops, just in case a snooze might creep up on him. "I've felt like most of my conversation has been exhausted, there's not much I can look forward to. Everyday simple pleasures that people might have in having conversations or talking about inane things I just find really boring, so I'd rather just be asleep."

The day Nirvana hit Los Angeles to begin recording, they checked into their fancy Oakwood Apartment (which they soon trashed) and went on the Universal Studios tour. Geffen had suggested several hot producers, but Nirvana had already asked their former producer, Butch Vig, to do the honors. Eventually they got their way, and in May 1991 Nirvana started work on *Nevermind* with a budget one thousand times higher than the cost of *Bleach*.

That same fateful month Kurt ran into Courtney Love at a Butthole Surfers gig at the Hollywood Palladium, where they revealed their mutual attraction by slugging each other and wrestling on the floor. "It was a mating ritual for dysfunctional people," Courtney later claimed. Kurt thought Courtney looked like Sid Vicious's girlfriend, Nancy Spungen, and he was smitten. Courtney already had a crush on Kurt, and he still had the trinket-filled heart-shaped box she had given to Dave Grohl for him a few months earlier.

Courtney, a fearless reform-school dropout, had been on the scene for years, appearing in B movies, strip-dancing all over the world, and singing with various bands before forming her own band, Hole. Their first album, *Pretty on the Inside,* had just been completed—a dauntless, driving, self-incriminating, ballsy hunk of music.

Kurt seemed to know that hanging out with Courtney could be a serious matter, and after a few phone calls he decided to concentrate on his record. The basic tracks for *Nevermind* were done in a few days because Kurt refused to do second takes. He fiddled with the melodies and lyrics until the last minute—"Pay to Play" turned into "Stay Away." The anthem "Smells Like Teen Spirit" almost got tossed because the band thought it sounded too much like the Pixies. When he didn't like the way "Lithium" was sounding, Kurt screamed and thrashed while the tape rolled, totaling his left-handed guitar, which ended the session for the day. Butch Vig discovered that Kurt sang so brutally hard that his voice was shredded after only one or two vocals. Kurt hung onto a little bottle of codeine cough syrup, sipping continuously, hoping to preserve his voice along with getting high. Since he didn't know any dealers in L.A., Kurt got stoned on the syrup and a whole lot of Jack Daniel's.

When the album was completed, everybody involved knew it was going to be colossal. Kurt had his usual fun with the bio, claiming that he had been a "sawblade painter specializing in wildlife and landscapes." Nirvana did a short stint with Dinosaur Jr., then opened for Sonic Youth on a tour of European festivals. In England Kurt and Courtney met up and had a few backstage words. During the filming of a documentary, Courtney leaned into the camera and announced, "Kurt Cobain makes my heart stop. But he's a shit." Later Kurt whispered into her ear, "I never would have picked on you in high school," like he knew her inside out. But they still didn't hook up. When the object of her passion left that night with two girls, Courtney yelled, "I hope you get fucked!"

Nirvana began their own headlining tour days before the September 24 release of *Nevermind.* When Courtney heard from a friend that Kurt had been talking about her, she tracked him down on the road and they spent hours on the phone, finally meeting up at a party in Chicago, where the rock-and-roll mating ritual continued. Courtney had brought a bag of sexy lingerie with her, and Kurt tried it all on for her. They were thrown out of the party twice before heading back to the hotel room Kurt shared with Dave. The mating lovebirds were so loud that Dave was forced to spend the night with the soundman.

Nevermind was flying out of the stores, but Kurt was in turmoil. He had always felt it was "us against them" and now a whole bunch of "them" were buying his record. The band took their confusion out on their instruments, thrashing them to bits. Kurt threw fits. "We were feeling so weird because we were being treated like kings, so we had to destroy everything," Kurt said. "I was obnoxious and showing my weenie and acting like a fag and dancing around and wearing dresses and just being drunk. . . . I was out of control."

Said the *Alternative Press:* "In September 1991 Nirvana was just a local cult, the latest alternative morsel to drop down Geffen's gullet. By October they were U2 and Springsteen, Presley and the Pistols, rolled into one snarling bundle." *Nevermind* appeared on hard rock, modern rock, college, AOR, and CHR stations, and *Billboard* called it a "cross-format phenomenon." "It was like I went to bed one evening and everything was fine," Kurt said, "but when I woke up the next morning they said on the news that I was an escaped Nazi child killer."

Courtney showed up at various gigs along the way and Kurt's spirits improved. At the October 29 show in Portland, Nirvana learned they had gone gold. While they were on tour in Europe, they were told that *Nevermind* had reached platinum. In December they knocked Michael Jackson out of the number-one spot. It didn't seem to make much difference to Nirvana. The touring was constant and it was wearing thin. Chris had a severe drinking problem, and despite the fact that Kurt was stressed out and very ill with bronchitis and chronic stomach pain, he and Courtney were dabbling with heroin. Kurt later insisted that *he* had instigated it and did a lot more of the drug than Courtney.

Back in Seattle, Kurt found himself a heroin dealer, determined to get a habit, claiming that it was the only way he could numb his pain. When Hole got back from their European tour, Kurt and Courtney stayed in various L.A. hotels, shooting what Courtney called "bad Mexican L.A. heroin."

During the January 1992 taping of "Saturday Night Live," Chris and Dave realized how bad Kurt's habit had gotten, and Courtney wrongly got some of the blame. *Bam* magazine was the first to point the needle at Kurt, stating that he was "nodding off in mid-sentence. . . . The pinned pupils, sunken cheeks and scabbed, sallow skin suggest something more serious than fatigue." Though Courtney claimed it was a "drug love thing," Kurt insisted he used heroin to kill his pain.

When they got back from New York, Kurt and Courtney moved into an apartment in Hollywood, where they cuddled up and watched TV. Kurt painted and played his guitar. Every morning he would go to the dealer's house and bring home the heroin. Courtney only used a little bit each day, but Kurt had a hundred-dollar-a-day habit. At least his stomach wasn't killing him.

When they discovered she was pregnant, Kurt and Courtney went to a birth-defects specialist who told them that heroin use during the first trimester of pregnancy was virtually harmless, although down the line there could be a minimal risk of learning disabilities. "Having a kid is a big deal," Kurt said. "It's one of the biggest things that can happen to you. It's corny, but all kinds of different people, including punk rockers, do react that way." The couple detoxed together, and Kurt said it wasn't "too bad. . . . I just slept for three days and woke up." Courtney didn't agree. "It was gross. That was a sick scene if ever there was a sick scene."

After the video shoot of the second single, "Come As You Are," Nirvana went to Australia, where Kurt's stomach problems were so intense he called Courtney, sobbing in pain. Everybody assumed he was still shooting heroin. One emergency room doctor believed Kurt was detoxing and wouldn't even treat him. Angry and miserable, Kurt finally located a "rock" doctor who gave him the drug Physeptone, which amazingly took away his pain. Later he found out he had been taking methadone and had become hooked. He was soon back on heroin.

Courtney Love became Mrs. Cobain in Waikiki, Hawaii, on February 24, 1992. The bride was pregnant, the groom was weepy and smacked out. And despite Chris and Shelli's no-show (they assumed Courtney was doing drugs and were making a statement), Courtney said the wedding was "transcendent." In an interview with *Rolling Stone,* conducted under the covers in his pj's, Kurt said his relationship with Courtney was like "Evian water and battery acid," and when you mix the two, "you get love."

Kurt deeply resented his fame, spending almost all his time in the Hollywood apartment with Courtney, doing his drugs in the closet so she wouldn't be tempted. He and Courtney saw a sonogram of the perfectly developing baby girl and Kurt insisted Frances gave him the forefinger/pinkie heavy-metal salute. He refused to tour, because he wanted to be with his pregnant wife, and his relationship with the rest of Nirvana was strained. The band almost shattered when Kurt decided that, since he was the songwriter, he should get 75 percent of the music-writing royalties (they had been splitting it three ways). And the situation got worse when Kurt demanded that the new arrangement be retroactive. Chris and Dave finally agreed to the split, but feelings were bitter.

In April Kurt made another attempt to kick his habit, checking into Exodus Recovery Center, a rock-star rehab in Marina del Rey. He thought the former rocker hippies who ran the place were pretentious. He lasted four days. His habit got worse.

During a short tour in Europe, Kurt convulsed over breakfast in a Belfast hotel because he had forgotten to take his methadone the night before, and was rushed to the hospital. Drug rumors were somehow quashed: The story was Kurt had a bleeding ulcer because of all the junk food he'd been eating. Courtney was six months pregnant, moody and rude. Gold Mountain paid two people to watch over the couple, who were checking into hotels as "Mr. and Mrs. Simon Ritchie" (Sid Vicious's real name). Angry about the monitoring, one night "the Ritchies" made an escape and checked into another hotel. There was pandemonium.

In July Courtney's band, Hole, signed to Geffen for a million dollars. Kurt's heroin habit was now up to four hundred dollars a day. "I ended up doing a hundred-dollar shot in one shot and not even feeling it hardly. I was just filling up the syringe as far as it could go without pulling the end off. At that point, it was like, why do it?" He checked into Cedars-Sinai for a twenty-five-day detox. During that time Courtney's *Vanity Fair* article hit the stands.

Besides describing Courtney as having a "train wreck personality," suggesting that it was she who had turned Kurt on to heroin, the piece by Lynn Hirschberg quoted Courtney as saying that she had knowingly done heroin during her pregnancy. Hirschberg also insisted that "industry insiders" were concerned about the health of the Cobains' unborn baby. And Courtney's wickedly delightful sense of humor was portrayed as just plain wicked. She became so depressed about the piece ("I knew my world was over. I was dead. That was it") that she checked herself into a hospital so she wouldn't resort to getting high. Kurt was too weak and sick to understand what had hit him. While he detoxed, the stomach pain returned with a vengeance, but despite a battery of tests, doctors still didn't have a clue. "He'd been crying for weeks," Courtney said. "It was nothing *but* crying. All we *did* was cry. It was horrible." When Kurt finally rallied, he wanted to kill Lynn Hirschberg. "As soon as I get out of this fucking hospital, I'm going to kill this woman with my bare hands. I'm going to stab her to death. First I'm going to take her dog and slit its guts out in front of her. And then shit all over her and stab her to death."

Frances Bean Cobain was born on the morning of August 18, after Courtney sashayed through the hospital—in labor—to get to Kurt, dragging her IV behind her, demanding that he attend his daughter's birth. He somehow got to the delivery room, threw up, and passed out. During the birth experience, Courtney held Kurt's hand and rubbed his tummy. Named after the Vaselines' Frances McKee ("Bean" came from her kidney-bean shape in the sonogram), Frances weighed just over seven pounds and was perfectly healthy.

Due to the *Vanity Fair* article, Kurt and Courtney were forced by the Los Angeles County Department of Children's Services to hand Frances over to Courtney's sister Jamie when the baby was only two weeks old. It was a devastating, humiliating experience. For the next month Kurt and Courtney couldn't be alone with their baby. The tabloids got in on the action, with headlines like ROCK STAR'S BABY BORN A JUNKIE. Kurt said he and Courtney were "totally suicidal."

But Nirvana played on. They arrived in England with the rock press raging that the band was breaking up due to Kurt's poor health. At the Reading Festival, as a "fuck you," Kurt rolled out onstage in a wheelchair, wearing a white hospital gown—and played the best show of his life.

Kurt wanted to perform his new song "Rape Me" at the MTV Awards, and when the organizers insisted on "Teen Spirit," Nirvana decided they wouldn't play at all. But after considering the repercussions with MTV involving other Geffen/Gold Mountain acts, they grudgingly settled on "Lithium." Kurt freaked everybody out by launching into the first few bars of "Rape Me," "just to give them a little heart palpitation." When he picked up the award for Best New Artist, Kurt smiled and said, "You know, it's really hard to believe everything you read." Backstage, Courtney mouthed off to Axl Rose and he pointed at Kurt, shrieking, "You shut your bitch up or I'm taking you down to the pavement!" Kurt pretended to stand up to Axl, then turned to Courtney and said, "Shut up, bitch!" She laughed her head off. Cutting into the tension, Axl's model girlfriend asked Courtney if *she* was a model. Courtney responded, "No, are you a brain surgeon?"

The Cobains felt like they were under attack again when they learned about an unauthorized Nirvana biography being planned in England. In a total rage about his privacy being poked into one more time, Kurt left several threatening messages on the writers' phone machine: "If anything comes out in this book which hurts my wife, I'll fucking hurt you. . . . I love to be fucked, I love to be blackmailed, I'll give you anything you want, I'm begging you, I'm on my knees and my mouth is wide open. . . . I don't give a flying fuck if I have this recorded that I'm threatening you. I suppose I could throw out a few hundred thousand dollars to have you snuffed out, but maybe I'll try the legal way first. . . ." The book was never published.

Beating out the bootleggers, in December 1992 Nirvana released *Incesticide,* an album of early material, B-sides, and outtakes. Kurt took the opportunity to rant in the liner notes, "Leave us the fuck alone!"

Kurt had his daughter back, but he and Courtney had to undergo regular urine tests and deal with the constant specter of social workers poking into their personal lives. It was all becoming too much. "No matter what we do, or how clean we live our lives," Kurt told Michael Azzerad, "we're not going to survive this because there are too many enemies and we threaten too many people. Everyone wants to see us die."

For someone who wanted to hide, Kurt kept stirring up controversy. The February 1993 issue of the *Advocate* featured Kurt on the cover, and the interview stated that he thought he was gay back in high school: "I'm definitely gay in spirit, and I probably could be bisexual." Later that month Nirvana headed for Minnesota to start work on their new album with producer Steve Albini, booking themselves as the Simon Ritchie Group. In a gutsy move, the band demanded to be left alone. No one from the record company or management would be allowed at the sessions. Albini wanted a live, natural sound, unlike the "controlled, compressed" *Nevermind. In Utero* was completed in two weeks. "They were very well prepared coming into the studio," Albini said, "as prepared as any band I've worked with, and as easy to deal with as any band I've worked with." Kurt's lyrics really impressed him. "They're so simple and to the point and so right. Something that would take me an hour to explain, Kurt would sum up in two words. That's something he has that I've never seen in anyone else." About Kurt's lyrics, Courtney said, "He chews bubble gum in his soul."

Kurt wanted to call the album *I Hate Myself and I Want to Die,* then *Verse Chorus Verse,* before settling on *In Utero* after reading the phrase in one of Courtney's poems. The back cover art, composed by Kurt, is an arrangement of plastic body parts, fetus models, and various flowers. "I always thought orchids, and especially lilies, look like a vagina," he said, "so it's sex and woman and *In Utero* and vaginas and birth and death."

"The grown-ups don't like it," Kurt declared about Geffen and Gold Mountain's first response to *In Utero.* Kurt knew they wanted another *Nevermind,* but said he would "rather die." Steve Albini told the *Chicago Tribune* that he didn't think Geffen would accept *In Utero,* and soon the press was full of stories about Nirvana's unacceptable record. The rumors were tossed around from *Rolling Stone* to *Newsweek,* picking up speed. "We will release whatever record the band delivers," Geffen maintained. Another announcement stated, "Nirvana's Kurt Cobain debunks rumors of Geffen interference with new album." The truth was pretty simple. There were a few things the band wanted to change, and even though the higher-ups agreed with the changes, the press was making Nirvana look like wimps, with Gold Mountain and Geffen as their avaricious tormentors. In the end the album was remastered, two songs were remixed, and acoustic guitar and harmonies were added to "Heart-Shaped Box."

After months of nightmarish legal battles, on March 23 the Department of Children's Services left the Cobains alone with their daughter, deciding that none of the allegations against Kurt and Courtney in Family Court were legally valid. But Kurt was more depressed and reclusive than ever. His friends and family were very worried about him.

Kurt Cobain with wife, Courtney Love, and baby daughter, Frances Bean, caught in the spotlight. (KEVIN MAZUR/LONDON FEATURES INTERNATIONAL)

On May 2 Kurt shot heroin, arriving home trembling, flushed, and glassy-eyed. According to a police report, Courtney had to inject Kurt with buprenorphine, an illegal drug used for heroin ODs, then give him a Valium, three Benadryls, and four Tylenols with codeine to make him throw up. She told the police it had happened before. On June 4 the police were back after Courtney claimed she and Kurt had been arguing over guns in the house. He was booked for domestic assault and spent three hours in jail. On July 23, before a gig in New York, Kurt overdosed again and was brought around by Courtney. He played that night at the Roseland Ballroom. On September 21 *In Utero* was released to glorious reviews.

The fall of '93 was spent on tour. Former Germs guitarist Pat Smear joined the band, and Kurt was able to focus on his vocals. All over the country, people raved about the intensity and passion of Nirvana's live performances. About being onstage, Kurt said, "It's anger, it's death, and absolute total bliss, as happy as I've ever been when I was a carefree child running around throwing rocks at cops. It's just everything. Every song feels different." Offstage was another story. Though he seemed eager to begin a project with R.E.M.'s Michael Stipe, Kurt was silent, withdrawn, and closed, causing deep concern for those close to him. The record company wanted a bodyguard to trail him around, keep tabs on him, but Kurt refused. "Axl Rose has a bodyguard. I'm not Axl Rose."

One of Kurt's joys was bringing his favorite bands to a wider audience, and in October Nirvana performed a Vaselines song and two from the Meat Puppets on *MTV Unplugged*. When the band played London in February, Kurt insisted that the Raincoats open for Nirvana, along with his heroes, the Melvins, who played several of the European shows. But by the end of February Kurt was sick and shows had to be postponed. He was losing his voice and had visited several doctors who told him he shouldn't be singing at all. From Munich, Kurt went to Rome, where he was going to meet Courtney and little Frances at the Excelsior Hotel for a much-needed holiday.

The March 4 announcement from Gold Mountain sounded reasonable enough: "Kurt Cobain slipped into a coma at six A.M. European Standard Time. The coma was induced by a combination of the flu and fatigue, on top of prescription painkillers and champagne. While Cobain has not awoken, he shows significant signs, say his doctors." But Kurt had wanted to die that night. Earlier he had a prescription filled for Rohypnol (a Valium-like tranquilizer) and ordered champagne from room service. Then Kurt unwrapped the fifty tinfoil Rohypnol pill packets and swallowed them all with mouthfuls of champagne. At the crack of dawn Courtney found him unconscious. "I reached for him and he had blood coming out of his nose," she told *Select* magazine. "I have seen him get really fucked up before, but I have never seen him almost eat it." There was reportedly a suicide note left at the scene, but Gold Mountain insisted the note found was not a suicide note. When Kurt awakened from his coma twenty hours later, he scrawled, "Get these fucking tubes out of my nose." A few days later the couple were back in Seattle. "He's not going to get away from me that easily," Courtney said. "I'll follow him through hell."

On March 18 the Seattle police got another hysterical call from Courtney, who told them her husband was holed up in the bathroom with a .38-caliber revolver, threatening to kill himself. According to the report, when the police arrived Kurt came out of the bathroom, saying he had no intention of committing suicide. Four guns and twenty-five rounds of ammunition were confiscated.

Along with a few of Kurt's friends and family members, Courtney started talking to counselors, and on March 25, along with a counselor and ten friends—including Gold Mountain executives, guitarist Pat Smear, and Chris Novoselic—performed an intervention on Kurt. Courtney vowed to leave him if he didn't check into rehab, and Pat and Chris threatened to break up the band. After the difficult, lengthy session, Kurt and Pat Smear went down to the basement to rehearse. When she wasn't able to convince Kurt to check into rehab with her, Courtney flew to L.A. without him, checked into the Peninsula Hotel in Beverly Hills, and started an outpatient detox program. Back in Seattle, Kurt went looking for a gun.

Kurt convinced the best man at his wedding, Dylan Carlson, to go with him to buy a shotgun, reminding him that his own guns had been confiscated and he needed one "for protection." Dylan thought it was strange since Kurt was about to leave for L.A., but accompanied him to Stan Baker's Gun Shop on Lake City Way, where he bought a 61b Remington Model 11 20-gauge shotgun. Concerned, Dylan offered to keep the gun for him until he got back from L.A., but Kurt took the gun home. Then he left for L.A. and checked himself into the Exodus Recovery Center. This time he lasted only two days. On April 1 Kurt called Courtney at the Peninsula, telling her she made a really good record. When she asked Kurt what he meant, he replied, "Just remember, no matter what, I love you." Courtney never spoke to her husband again. That evening, after telling the staff he was going out on the patio to smoke, Kurt jumped the six-foot brick fence and disappeared.

On April 2 Courtney hired a private investigator and canceled Kurt's credit cards. On April 4 Kurt's mom, Wendy, filed a missing persons report. Somebody claims to have seen him in the park near his house a couple of days later, but on April 5 it seems that Kurt climbed the stairs to the greenhouse above his garage and propped a stool against the French doors. Then he removed his hunter's cap, got his drugs from an old cigar box, wrote a letter with a red pen, and opened his wallet to his driver's license, tossing it on the floor as identification. Courtney believes that Kurt then pulled a chair to the window with a view of Puget Sound, took some heroin, pressed the shotgun barrel to his left temple, and pulled the trigger.

Two and a half days later Kurt's body was found by Gary Smith, an electrician who had been hired to install a security system in the house. Unrecognizable, the body was identified by fingerprints several hours later. Heroin and Valium were found in Kurt's bloodstream.

Meanwhile, at 9:30 P.M. on April 7, Courtney was rushed from her room at the Peninsula to Century City Hospital after 911 had been called regarding a "possible overdose victim." She was arrested immediately after being discharged and booked for possession of a controlled substance, drug paraphernalia, and a hypodermic, as well as for "receiving stolen property." All charges were later dropped. (The "controlled substance" turned out to be good-luck holy ashes given to her by her lawyer, Rosemary Carroll.) Courtney hadn't spoken to Kurt for a week and must have been crazy with worry and grief. Released on ten thousand dollars' bail, she went directly to the Exodus Recovery Center, spending one night. The following day her worst fears were confirmed.

Gary Smith had called radio station KXRX-FM with "the scoop of the century," adding, "You're going to owe me a lot of concert tickets for this one." Kurt's mom, Wendy, learned of Kurt's death on the radio. "Now he's gone and joined that stupid club," she said, referring to Jimi Hendrix, Janis Joplin, and Jim Morrison. "I told him not to join that stupid club." Courtney flew to Seattle and stayed with Wendy. She wore Kurt's clothes and carried around a lock of his hair.

While Courtney's taped message played for thousands of sorrowful fans at the candlelight vigil across town, a private memorial was being held at the Unity Church. "A suicide is no different than having our finger in a vise," Reverend Towles told the 150 mourners. "The pain becomes so great that you can't bear it any longer." Chris Novoselic asked that Kurt be remembered for being "caring, generous, and sweet." Courtney read from the Bible and from Kurt's suicide note, including a passage she left out of the tape for the vigil: "I have a daughter who reminds me too much of myself." Gary Gersh read a note from Michael Stipe, and Gold Mountain's Danny Goldberg spoke last: "I believe he would have left this world several years ago if he hadn't met Courtney."

Courtney told the crowd in her taped message that she would read the part of Kurt's suicide note addressed to his fans. The rest, Courtney said, was "none . . . of your fucking business." But before she could begin to read the note, Courtney stopped herself, saying, "He is such an asshole. I want you all to say 'asshole' really loud."

Then Courtney began to read from the suicide note, in which Kurt told of feeling "guilty beyond words." Kurt said that for years he hadn't experienced any thrill at "the manic roar of the crowd." "Well, Kurt, so fucking what?" Courtney said, interrupting her reading. "Then don't be a rock star, you asshole." After Courtney continued to read Kurt's confession that the "worst crime" would be to fake having 100 percent fun as a rock star, she countered, "No, Kurt, the worst crime . . . is for you to just continue to be a rock star when you fucking hate it."

Courtney continued to recite Kurt's self-torturing confession and farewell to his fans. Kurt labeled himself as "one of those narcissists who only appreciate things when they're alone." He wistfully observed that he had it "good, very good," but almost in the same sentence revealed that since the age of seven he had become "hateful towards all humans." Kurt's good-bye concluded with his thanking his fans "from the pit of my burning, nauseous stomach," and his signing off, "Peace, love, empathy . . .'It was better to burn than to fade away . . .' Kurt Cobain."

The crowd then heard Courtney tell them on tape not to put "any stock" in the tough-love tactics that had failed in the end to save Kurt. Courtney said, "I'm really sorry, guys." Her message ended by her asking his fans to "tell him he's a fucker, okay? Just say, 'Fucker, you're a fucker,' and that you love him."

Two months later, on June 16, Hole's bass player, Kristen Pfaff, died in her bathtub of a heroin overdose.

The warm July night I ran into Courtney at Jones restaurant, she seemed beaten up and bruised from the inside out. She was pale and dazed, damp-eyed and disheveled, sitting with a bunch of rock stars in a dark booth. When she saw me she opened up her arms and I held her for a long, sad time. She told me it was hell being a rock widow, and that mourning didn't suit her. "I miss Kurt so much," she said over and over, "but I will survive."

And she has. With rage, passion, and unshakable courage, Courtney has yanked herself out of her anguished fog and fucked with the odds. From her abrasive rants on America Online to the admission that she drowned her sorrows in too many rock guys, Courtney parades through the award shows like a risky princess and curses out Hole's packed crowds while entertaining them to the hilt. She continues to stun and titillate, making headlines like all good rock stars are supposed to do. She recently pleaded guilty to assaulting Bikini Kill's Kathleen Hanna at Lollapalooza, and the judge suspended her sentence on the condition that she "refrain from violence for two years and take anger management courses." But nobody will be able to tame Courtney Love. When we did our interview, I asked her if she felt power by being a rock star. "Fuck yeah, man," she shouted. "I'm a rock star *girl!*" Kurt would be proud.

EDDIE COCHRAN

■

Untamed Youth

■

    hirty-five years ago on a dark, rainy
    Saturday night, a talented, sweet-
natured American kid was thrown through the windshield of a British taxicab
and killed. At twenty-one he was just beginning to cause a stir in the rock
world with his lighthearted, wildfire songs about teenage problems. He
dressed really cool, he shook his shoulders just right, and when he swung his
flashy orange guitar from side to side, a lock of blond hair fell over his fore-
head in a way that made the blossoming girls swoon. He had just started to
raise a fuss and holler—and then he was gone.

The adored baby of a large, seemingly close-knit family, Ray Edward
Cochran loved to play cowboys and Indians and shoot off his capguns, pretending to be Hopalong Cassidy or his hero, Roy Rogers. He led parades
through his picture-perfect Albert Lea neighborhood in Minnesota, banging
pots and pans for drums, and on Saturday afternoons twelve-cent double
matinees at the Rivoli Theater were a big treat. He was a true practical joker,
a mischief maker, always pestering the daylights out of his many nieces and
nephews.

Eddie enjoyed fishing with his cane pole and taking his fancy western-style BB rifle hunting with his dad. He loved scarfing up his mom's soup beans and corn bread, and he played a mean guitar.

When Eddie's older brother, Bill, went into the service, he left the five-year-old in charge of his old Kay acoustic guitar, and soon Eddie was hanging blankets on the clothesline, entertaining the neighborhood kids, who paid a penny each to sit inside the blankets and listen to him play. When his music teacher wanted him to play clarinet in the school band, Eddie insisted that he wouldn't join the band at all if he couldn't play his guitar.

When the Cochran family had to move to California in 1953, childhood friend Shirley Oman says she'll never forget what Eddie said to his mother. "Eddie was standing in his backyard with his silly little cap on, and he said, 'You know, Mom, when we go to California I'm going to make something of myself and you're going to have everything, Mom, you've never had.'"

As I drive down Bernice Circle in Buena Park, I'm struck by the picturesque, unchanged, fifties quality of the suburban stucco bungalows, and the neat, tidy squares of lawn. Except for the glare of ever-present sunshine, I could be Anywhere U.S.A., Anytime U.S.A. Birds chirp, a lawnmower hums. Boys in jeans toss a ball. I'm here to see Eddie Cochran's sister, Gloria, and her son, "Little" Ed—I'm taking them to lunch so we can discuss a beloved family member, lost all those years ago on a rainy night in England.

Little Ed, who was eight when Eddie died, answers the door—a large fellow, now in his mid-forties, with a ready, shiny grin—and leads me into the living room, which is pretty much a shrine to Eddie Cochran. Lots of gold records, posters, portraits, and an oil painting that's such a good likeness, it's scary. Sister Gloria is seventy years old, a sweet little lady with a quiet and gentle demeanor, cloaked in poly-

The all-American Cochran family. "When we go to California," Eddie told his mother, "I'm going to make something of myself." (COURTESY OF GLORIA JULSON)

ester. Everybody has gotten a whole lot older, but Eddie is still twenty-one years old. He always will be. His presence is so overwhelming, I'm curious if Eddie spent any time in this house. "Yes," says Gloria, wistfully. "We moved in here three months before he died." I knew it.

"I thought we'd go to Black Angus," says Little Ed, and although I'm a vegetarian, I charmingly agree and we pile into his mid-eighties Lincoln and cruise through Anywhere U.S.A. to the local steak house.

Unmistakable: It's baby brother Eddie's joyous full-throttle shout coming from the speakers. "I can't listen to him all the time," says Gloria quietly. "It hurts. But this is a special occasion." I listen to Eddie's earliest country-punk efforts with Hank Cochran (no relation), all about a pair of pegged pink slacks, and marvel at his masterful guitar playing and wailing wit.

We settle into the high-backed booth and I order the Black Angus specialty, baked potato soup, while my guests order hamburgers. How did Eddie get so good on that thing so young? I ask his sister. "California was a strange place, and Eddie was alone a lot, so he played that guitar constantly." She smiles. "He didn't think about college. Music was it. He even took his guitar out on dates!" Gloria recalls with a glint in her eye. "He admitted music was his first love." There had to have been girls, right? I know I would have been prowling around. "He had one girl in high school—her name was Johnnie. He went with her for a little, but when he got so interested in his music . . . he took 'em as they come, you know." Gloria seems a tad embarrassed by this revelation, and giggles. "The young girls, when they found out where we lived, would drive by and drop notes in his car."

Eddie got a three-piece band together and played local dates, one of which

Eddie's sister Gloria pulled this picture straight out of the Cochran family photo album. (COURTESY OF GLORIA JULSON)

was the opening of a market, getting his first paying gig a few months later at South Gate Auditorium. He met Hank Cochran at the Bell Gardens music store, and the two teamed up early in 1955, writing songs together and getting a record deal almost instantly with Ekko Records. Eddie was sixteen and decided to drop out of school, against his family's wishes. "Mom didn't like it, but Eddie stuck to his guns," Gloria told me. "He said, 'I want my music, I got this, and this is what I want to do.' He sure was stubborn." The duo took their country-shuffle-with-a-backbeat into barn dances and eventually landed a regular spot on the *California Hayride* TV show. But the three Cochran Brothers singles flopped dismally and, due to Eddie's increasing desire to rock out, the two went separate directions—Hank to Nashville, where he became a successful songwriter, and Eddie back into the studio with Jerry Capehart, who would soon become his manager and writing partner.

Eddie was redefining his style, mixing his country swing with some Ray Charles and Little Richard. He played all the guitars on these early sessions and, listening to his natural ace virtuosity, it's hard to believe Eddie was barely sixteen years old. (He went on to overdub lots of guitars on all his records, a highly unusual practice back then.) Jerry and Eddie signed with a publishing company, American Music, and cut some demos (known then as "dubs"), one of which—a raucous little number written by Capehart, "Skinny Jim"—got Eddie a deal with Crest Records. Though it got decent reviews, the record didn't set the charts on fire, so Capehart took the single and dubs of Eddie singing "Blue Suede Shoes" and "Long Tall Sally" in search of a new deal. Rock and roll was shaking up the *Billboard* charts, and Liberty Records founder Si Waronker dug the dubs enough to sign the teenager, hoping the gifted kid might become a blond Elvis Presley. Coincidentally, while recording some backing music for a low-budget flick, producer Boris Petroff got a load of Eddie in the studio and offered him a cameo in *The Girl Can't Help It,* Jayne Mansfield's trashy, tawdry rock classic. It was a double shot of success that seemed to sit just right with Eddie Cochran.

I spoke to big brother Bill Cochran, and he said Eddie was just brought up right: His family came first and his music second. "He was so down to earth, it was kinda scary. Like I say, he loved his family, and he had music in his heart." Well, Eddie may have had an entire band in his heart, but his familial ties were questionable, says Jerry Capehart. "Eddie's mother, Alice Cochran, was a complete control freak," he insists. "Eddie's dilemma in life was trying to maintain a relationship with his family and having a career. His family wanted to tell him exactly what to do."

It's a brief but potent three minutes in *The Girl Can't Help It* when somebody turns on a TV set to watch Eddie perform "Twenty Flight Rock," a nutty ditty about being "too tired to rock" with his girl after climbing twenty flights of stairs. It almost became Eddie's first single, but someone at Liberty suggested a John D. Loudermilk tune, "Sittin' in the Balcony," for Eddie's big-label debut, giving Jerry and Eddie a day to think it over. When his manager asked the singer what he thought, Eddie said, "Well, Dad, I think it's a hit." He was right. The song was recorded in eight hours with Eddie on guitar and Capehart using a cardboard box for drums, and when it came out in the fall of 1956, it went straight into the Top Twenty. The song was a little schmaltzy and a tad sweet and croony, but Eddie played up the heartthrob angle with a twinkle in his eye, suggesting "There's a whole lot more where this came from."

Back at the house, Gloria and Ed take me into the den and pop in a long-ago black-and-white video clip from Dick Clark's "American Bandstand."

Dick was doing one of his retrospective shows a couple of years back, and Eddie's mother, Alice, and sister Gloria were invited to the festivities, taking with them Eddie's precious Gretsch guitar. We watch the baby-faced blond swinging the same orange guitar, kissing gooey-eyed girls in the balcony, and then, sure enough, there's Gloria and her late mother, Alice, beaming from the audience as Dick sings Eddie's praises, touching the Gretsch like it was God's own instrument. "Dick was talking to Mother, asking if there was anything he could do for her," a misty-eyed Gloria recalls at the end of the mini-Eddie screening, "and she said, 'Yeah, you can give me the tapes you have on Eddie,' and he did. It's so funny," she goes on, "because when this accident happened, Mother tried to buy the tapes and he wouldn't sell 'em." Then Little Ed interjects, "Well, he would have, but the price was so high. . . ."

I call Eddie's other sister, Pat, a soft-spoken lady who runs an office-supply store in Garden Grove. "I consider Eddie the last of the innocents," she begins. "Our teenage kids could use more people like Eddie today. He was a delightful individual for the short time he was with us." She sighs. "Sure, he may have had one too many beers sometimes, but he wasn't into the dope scene or anything like that. I don't want to paint him as not being human—he was terribly human. He loved people, he loved his family, but most of all he loved his music."

"I'm going to tell you some information that very few people have," Jerry Capehart tells me. "Eddie was cast in a feature motion picture called *Rally Round the Flag* with Paul Newman. He had the part, it was all set. I went to pick him up for the first day's shooting, and Alice says, 'We've decided that the part isn't big enough for Eddie.' I argued, but she wasn't going to change her mind. If Eddie had done that part, he would have been as big as James Dean. I used to try and instill in Eddie the positive side of life, but that family of his . . . he felt totally oppressed." What about his father? I query. Did he get involved in the decisions? "Are you kidding? I bet I didn't see Frank a half a dozen times during the years I knew them. He would go to work, come home to his bedroom, and get drunk."

After the success of "Twenty Flight Rock," Eddie put out another single, "Drive-In Show," which didn't quite hit, and made another movie, *Untamed Youth,* starring Mamie Van Doren (in her tell-all tome, she recalls seducing the young rocker). The Warner Bros. film about kids picking cotton in Bakersfield, California, features the charismatic Eddie in the role of "Bong," and one reviewer loved him: "There's a guy who works with Mamie whom I never before heard of—one Eddie Cochran, who writhes through 'Cottonpicker' in a manner that could make Elvis envious. Real frantic, this boy." Eddie may have had some private moments with the blond bombshell, but most of the year was spent touring the country in his white (with wood paneling!) Country Squire station wagon.

I call Gene Ridgio, Eddie's drummer from the very beginning, now working in the gaming industry in Las Vegas, and he's still full of abounding love for the boy snatched from their midst a long time ago. Gene recalls his glory days like they were just yesterday, telling me how he and his band met Eddie at the Rainbow Roller Rink, backed him on a couple of songs, and became his touring band. "Once we did ten weeks of one-nighters," he remembers. "Everyone hated the promoter. We'd go north, then south, then north, west, east, north, south. We would leave a job, pack up, load the trailer, and take off. We didn't sleep in motels; we had to sleep in the car and keep going. Eddie would sleep skewed down in the front seat with his feet up on the dashboard." Gene tells me about the time they were spotted in a gas station after a show with their pay wrapped in rubber bands. Because a local bank had been robbed that day, the station attendant called the cops on the greasy-haired delinquents. "The police pulled us all out of the car," Gene says, "one cop in front, one in back, and one on each side, and they proceed to question us." He laughs heartily. "So they call in to headquarters and say, 'We got the money and it's all in rubber bands.' 'Did you say *rubber* bands? The money was taken from the bank in *paper* bands.'" It seems the jerkwater cops had messed up big-time. "Eddie says, 'Sarge, do you have a daughter?' He says, 'Yeah.' Eddie says, 'She's gonna be very mad at you'—that's how cool he was—and the cop says, 'What's your name, son?' 'Eddie Cochran.' 'The rock-and-roll singer?' 'Yessir.' And the cop says, 'Yep, she's going to be mad, all right.' So Eddie says, 'Tell you what, you want me to give you an autograph so she won't be that mad?'"

Capehart, who was ten years Eddie's senior, tells me that Eddie's family wouldn't sign for his station wagon. "Guess who put his name on the dotted line? Nobody in his family thought enough of their son or their brother to put their name on the dotted line for him to buy a car. So I did."

It's hard for me to imagine sister Gloria being so hard-hearted. Recalling how hard her baby brother had to work, she tells me that when Eddie came home from a road trip, he was beat. "He'd take about three or four days off and go up into the desert with his Buntline," she says. Buntline? What's that? I wonder. "A big gun," Ed fills me in, beaming with pride. "Like Wyatt Earp." Ah. "That poor kid," Gloria goes on, smiling sadly. "He'd go out on these tours, you know, and work his bottom off." Then Ed chimes in, "The band members would get paid, but Ed just didn't get paid!" Little Ed is obviously appalled. His mother continues, "He'd come home broke. I'd feel so sorry for him, putting out all that work and not getting a penny."

Though there wasn't much dough on the road, it was a whole lot of fun, according to Gene Ridgio. "We were doing a show and Eddie, being his beautiful self, was entertaining like you can't believe, and of course the girls loved him, and whether they're with their boyfriends or not, they're gonna show it." Gene is gleeful as he goes on. "Well, this one young man got uptight, a typical guy back in them days—white satin vest, white pants, and white buck sad-dle shoes. After the show we're packing up, this fellow shows up and says, 'Hey Cochran!'—I don't know if you can print this—'I'm gonna kick the livin' shit outta you!' And Eddie says, 'What?' In other words, 'I don't even know you, sir.' But he persists on being the bully and Eddie says, 'You mean to tell me that you and I cannot discuss this thing and resolve it?' And this guy says, 'No way, man, I want a piece of you right now!,' so Eddie says, 'Well, I guess I'm just gonna have to kill you.' With that, Eddie draws his Buntline .45—not pointing at the guy, pointing to the right of him—and fires, and he has a blank in it! The guy stands there in the snow and pees his pants. The snow around his shoes is getting yellow!" Gene is delighted, right there with Eddie again, reliving the moment one more time. "The flame shot out of Eddie's Buntline and just scared the hell outta that guy."

In March 1958 Eddie went to Capehart's pad in Hollywood to go through material for the next day's session. He had a riff running around in his head that he just couldn't shake. He played it for Jerry and, in less than an hour, "Summertime Blues," three minutes of pure, shining, unadulterated rock-and-roll majesty, was finished. The song spoke for all the teenagers who felt they were being bugged, hassled, and bossed around. Eddie Cochran under-stood their plight: how hard it was to hold a job, to get a car, to take your girl on a date. "Sometimes I wonder what I'm gonna do but there ain't no cure . . ." You know the rest.

A lot more touring in the Ford wagon followed, and in January 1959 his second single, the blazing "C'mon Everybody!" hit the charts, inviting all of teen America to come to Eddie's party. As the record climbed the charts, he started filming his third movie, *Go Johnny Go!*, another classic gem of supreme rock-schlock in which he crooned "Teenage Heaven." Ironically, he had to drop out of the Winter Dance Party Tour with Ritchie Valens, the Big Bop-per, and his close pal Buddy Holly due to his film schedule. On February 3 their plane crashed in a field near Mason City, Iowa, and a big chunk of the music died. Deeply affected by the loss of Holly, Eddie recorded a tribute song, "Three Stars," intending to donate the royalties to the three stars' fami-lies, but due to some legalese with Liberty Records, the song wasn't even re-leased until many years after his own death.

Though the success of "C'mon Everybody!" was making Eddie a bona fide teen idol, the panting girls and chartbusters weren't swelling his head. Said his sister Pat, "He loved the success and adulation, but his feet were on the ground. He never lost sight of who he was." I ask her about Eddie's teasing na-ture and she laughs a little. "Oh yes, he used to drive me crazy," she admits. "When I got married, we came out of the church, and he and his friend David really did a job on the car! I jumped in the front seat and landed in a pile of cornflakes. There were cornflakes everywhere! It was crunch, crunch,

crunch!" I can tell the memory is bittersweet for Pat. "Eddie was six years younger than me. He was our baby doll. He was our baby. You know, Pam," she says with a catch in her voice, "it really took a lot out of our little mother when he died. I wish you could have met her."

Jerry Capehart paints a very different picture of Alice Cochran—and a strikingly different picture of the Cochran family baby doll. "Eddie couldn't stand to go home," he says insistently. "When he was home he was there basically just to please his mother. He was still a kid, after all, but Eddie despised going home. He grew up with the refrigerator door always being opened with a cold beer inside. Eddie died an alcoholic." I have never heard that Eddie had an alcohol problem. He liked a little beer, right? I ask Jerry. "No, what Eddie really liked were Black Russians."

In March 1959, when "C'mon Everybody!" hit the charts in England, Eddie wrote a "personal" message to his fans in a teen magazine, letting them know a little bit about his "private" life. As the youngest of five children, Eddie said that made him the "baby" of the family, adding, "It's just something I have to accept although I'm not really the type of guy that likes to be babied." Eddie told his fans about his passion for shooting and gun collecting, stating he was "unlike most youngsters of today" because his favorite car wasn't a "sports model or a convertible" but a station wagon. "No doubt that fits in with the rest of my character, for I like to dress very casually and I'm not too happy in crowds." Eddie ended his message by saying that he hoped to "fix a trip" to England and "say hello" to every one of his fans in person.

The rest of 1959 seemed like one long tour for Eddie. He had become wary of flying, and the nonstop road travel, playing jukebox operators' conventions, sock hops, and roller rinks in the toolies, was starting to make him crazy. He had pretty much decided to concentrate on writing and producing rather than spending so much time with his feet up on the dashboard. And according to Sharon Sheeley, Eddie was ready to settle down.

The Cochran family has tangled-up feelings about Sheeley, a songwriter introduced to Eddie by his friend Phil Everly. "I know Sharon Sheeley says they were engaged," says sister Pat, "but I don't think so. The magazines say he sent for her to come to England, but I find that hard to believe." Bill concurs. "I talked to Ed right before he went to England, we were pretty close, and I'm afraid that isn't true. She says some things that are pretty fantastic, but that goes with the territory, with the entertainment business. I don't feel bad about it. If she wants to think it happened, that's okay." Gloria says that Eddie wouldn't have married Sharon. "Ed liked a home life and he liked to have a woman wait on him hand and foot. He liked to have a woman cook. Mother did it for him, I did it for him. He liked an old-fashioned girl." Gloria then tells me that she believes Eddie was in love with blond starlet Connie Stevens. (Maybe she cooked up a pretty fair dish of beans and corn bread in between takes!)

When I visit Sharon to do the interview, I like her right away. A true eccentric, she laughs wildly, shares willingly, has a zany sense of humor, and a cute little lisp. And I totally identify with her adoration for the long-gone rock boy-god. Black-and-white photos of Eddie adorn her apartment, and once again I'm struck how Eddie Cochran will always be twenty-one while the people who loved him just keep having birthdays. Thirty-eight years ago burgeoning songwriter Sharon Sheeley fell in love for the first time, and she fell hard. After seeing his picture on the poster of *The Girl Can't Help It,* she "set out to get him," spending the next two years "chasing Eddie Cochran." When her songwriting started taking off (Rick Nelson's "Poor Little Fool," Brenda Lee's "Dum Dum," etc.), she signed with Eddie's manager, thus securing herself a constant spot in his presence. Eddie treated her "like a kid sister" for a couple of years, even though she spent all her money on cute outfits and bleached her hair platinum blond so he might pay her some romantic attention. It was when she finally scrubbed off her makeup, put her hair in braids, and arrived at one of his parties in a pair of Levi's that he took notice. She says he professed his love and asked her to marry him on a New Year's Eve night in New York City.

Capehart says he was there and does not believe Sharon's story. "It's so ludicrous I can't even begin to tell you." I ask Jerry if he thinks Eddie was wild on the road. "He sure was! As a matter of fact, he never even had to leave his room. They came to him. But he did care about a little redheaded Irish girl in New York," he says. "Eddie probably fathered two different children. One would be with the Irish girl, and the other was with a girl in Pittsburgh. Hey!" he says as an afterthought. "If there's anybody out there who thinks that Eddie was your father, I'd like for you to come forward! Tell them that Jerry asked you to print that."

"Somethin' Else," Eddie's next single, co-penned with Sharon Sheeley, didn't get too high on the U.S. charts, but over in England it was a smash. British kids were caught in the fervent grip of rock-and-roll fever and were especially mad for American rockers. Even though Eddie had decided not to travel as much, he couldn't very well say no to a five-week British tour with fellow rocker Gene Vincent. After another session at Gold Star in Hollywood, during which he recorded a tender heartbreaker eerily titled "Three Steps to Heaven," he left for England on January 9, 1960.

Eddie Cochran made headlines all over Britain. Girls were fainting. There was chaos everywhere he went and, though he wasn't used to it, Eddie enjoyed the attention. He even went so far as to have "breakaway" suits made because of the frenzied female attacks on his person. But Eddie's humility was in full force when promoters suggested he take over Gene Vincent's headline spot. "The people wanted more to see Ed, but Gene was still the headliner," Little Ed tells me with satisfaction. "But Ed wouldn't take top billing."

A young, unknown guitarist, George Harrison, followed him from Ipswich to Wembley, studying his fingers. "Eddie was an innovator of rock and roll," Gene Ridgio told me with pride. "The way he strung his guitar [was] different than anybody. The two bottom strings were the same so that he could flex them, and they were tuned different." When I asked Gene what made Eddie think he could do that, he said, "Honey, I don't know."

The tour proved so wildly successful, the duo was offered an additional ten-week stint to begin two weeks later. Eddie accepted, then called his mother to tell her the news. "After this," he told her, "I won't have to go on the road anymore."

At the end of March Sharon went to visit Eddie in England: Her twentieth birthday was coming up and she wanted to celebrate with him. She also wanted to see him play for passels of adoring fans. She got there just in time to be with him when he died. Legendary stories have grown up around Eddie Cochran's gravestone like so many tangled weeds. Capehart says that Duane Eddy's manager, who was staying in Eddie's hotel in England, told him Eddie ran out of his room in the middle of the night screaming, "I'm gonna die and there's nothing anybody can do about it." Sharon told me she found him in his room playing Buddy Holly records, which was odd because listening to Buddy had always been too painful for Eddie. Apparently he spoke of how he might be seeing his friend Buddy sometime real soon—he had a lick he wanted to show him. Capehart recalled Eddie telling him that he had a feeling he wasn't going to live very long. And that last song—"Three Steps to Heaven." When he turned up late for the session to face a pissed-off Capehart, Eddie said, "Who's gonna care? It doesn't matter, none of it does."

Sharon and I are looking at a thirty-five-year-old black-and-white photograph of a ruined British taxicab. "I sat right there," she says, obviously hurting. "If he had not pulled me over his lap . . . That's why he died, you know. The autopsy broke my heart. He pulled me over," she says, still amazed at the boy's gallantry. "But of course he would." We come to a shot of Sharon leaving the hospital. "Poor little honey," she says. "Look at me. Dead eyes." Tell me about it, I say gently. "The Virgin Mary came to me and said, 'You will suffer greatly,' and I didn't understand. I knocked on Gene's door and said, 'What are you guys doing in there?' Eddie woke up. . . . You have to understand, all that time in England we didn't sleep together. You didn't know that, did you? We had separate hotel rooms." Perhaps it was the uptight times? I suggest. "It was *him,*" she insists. "I begged Eddie, 'What's wrong with me? Don't you want to make love to me?' I used to dream about it every day of my life. I was a virgin, I was waiting for this big seduction. He told me he loved me. The most beautiful line, which nobody has ever heard but you, Pamela: 'Not tonight. You remind me of a beautiful piece of glass balanced on the edge of a table. If I touch it, it will shatter. . . .' Wouldn't you love to have somebody like that?" Her eyes shine with the memory.

The British tour came to an end at the Hippodrome in Bristol, and instead of taking the train, Gene, Eddie, Sharon, and tour manager Pat Thomkins decided to share a cab to the airport. It was 10:45. The next morning they would fly home to Los Angeles to spend Easter Sunday with their families. On the A4 in Bath, the Ford Consul taxi, driven by nineteen-year-old George Martin, skidded backward into a roadside lamppost and crashed. Wreckage was scattered two hundred yards up the road.

Sharon says that she and Eddie had been discussing their upcoming wedding as they headed for London that night. "He was saying, 'Is so-and-so going to come?' and I'd say, 'Yes.' We had talked to both of our mothers and he was singing, 'California, here I come, right back where I started from! Whoa! I'm gonna kiss the ground when that plane lands!' I asked the driver, 'Don't you think we're going too fast?' and all I remember is feeling like I was on a tilt-a-whirl, everything was spinning. I remember hearing this horrible scream, and thinking, Oh my God, stop that scream, then realizing it was coming out of my own throat. The next thing I remember is waking up in a cow pasture. I couldn't move because my back was broken in four places, my neck in three. The back of my head was split wide open. I just kept thinking it had to be a dream. It was a second after midnight. I couldn't move and I kept screaming, 'Where's Eddie?! Where's Eddie!?' Gene Vincent crawled over to me and said, 'He's fine, he's in the car having a cigarette.' And I knew. I knew Eddie would not be sitting in the car while I'm lying there bleeding to death, and with that I just went out." On impact Eddie's Gretsch flew out of the trunk and rested next to him in the pasture, his hand touching the frets.

Eddie Cochran died at St. Martin's Hospital on Easter Sunday from multiple head injuries. Some reports say that he lived sixteen hours. "He lived for eight hours," says Sharon. "I kept going in and out [of consciousness] asking 'How is he?' 'His condition hasn't changed, it hasn't changed, it hasn't changed.' At four o'clock this stranger walked in my room, took my hand, and said, 'I'm very sorry. He passed away.' It's not like in the movies," she sobs. "You don't scream. The scream is so deep in your guts that it won't come out of your own throat." Sharon starts to cry. "I remember like it was yesterday, and I want to say, 'What do you mean he just passed away, for Christ's sake?' He was the kindest, most wonderful friend—not fiancé, not lover. He was my best friend and he just *passed away*. I wouldn't accept that, but then I felt this chilling breeze go through the room. They pronounced me dead for four minutes, and I remember thinking, Oh God, this feels so good, but then I had to come back into this body that hurt and this heart that hurt."

I ask sister Pat to recall how she heard the dreadful news. "Oh gosh, Pam," she begins, "I remember that like it was yesterday. It was Easter Sunday. I got up and turned on the radio and the first thing I heard was Eddie Cochran was in a horrible accident, but they didn't say he was dead. I called my brother Bill but he hadn't heard anything, so I said, 'I'm heading out to Mom's. We were all getting together that day—Eddie was coming home. By the time I got there, they had heard he was dead. The family never was the same. I always thought my family was invincible until that happened." With thirty-five-year-old tears in her voice, Pat finds it hard to continue. "If I don't expect it and turn on the radio and hear Eddie, it's funny how it still affects me. But it's part of life and you have to learn to live with it. I think if he had lived longer, Elvis would have had to move over a little bit."

Gene Ridgio weeps when recalling that Easter Sunday. "That was it," he admits. "The bottom fell out. I gotta tell you, dear, there's still a void there. When I talk about him, it brings it back." He sniffles. "He was too young. I don't think he deserved to die that way."

"Sometimes you wonder just how God is working," says big brother Bill. "You have to take it and live through it, or you can drive yourself crazy." He says with obvious difficulty, "I wrote a letter to Eddie. Maybe you can get a copy of that." I called the Albert Lea Historical Society and they sent me a copy of Bill's letter:

> Dear Brother . . . You were my buddy and constant companion. . . . I remember I would lay beside you at "nap time" and hum, sing or whistle to the records "Beer Barrel Polka" or "Hot Pretzels." You would hold my thumb and calmly go to sleep. . . . Just before I went into the service in 1942, I bought a guitar. You promised to take care of it while I was gone. I received letters from home saying how you would dust it off every day. Maybe this is when you took your first interest in the guitar. . . . Remember how you would confide in me about your problems, your hopes for your future and many things? Remember our last get-together just before your fatal tour to England? I will always feel honored and will cherish your love for me. . . . May the angels in heaven softly hum the "Beer Barrel Polka" as you rest in peace, baby brother. . . . Bill

When I ask Gloria about Eddie's funeral, it's hard for her to talk about it. "There was quite a few people there, but we didn't publicize it," she says softly, then, "Maybe we could go out and see the plaque." But Ed is concerned about the condition of the gravestone. "The plaque isn't very clean right now," he reminds Gloria. I suggest we clean it off. Ed says he can pick up some cleaning fluid at Forest Lawn, and we head out to the neighboring town of Cypress. As we listen to Eddie wail, Gloria tells me her baby brother was one of the first to be interred. "They had just opened the cemetery up," she says wistfully.

When I ask Jerry Capehart how Eddie's death affected him, he chokes up. "It's still very, very hard to talk about it." After pulling himself back together, he says, "I just want to tell the truth, let the chips fall where they may. I was the one who took him to the airport. None of his family went to see him off. None of 'em. I'm the one who said good-bye to him. When he came home in that pine box, guess what? None of them were there to meet him. Not a one of 'em."

As we walk through clumps of flowers in various stages of dying, Ed wielding a rag and some fluid, it's hard for me to fathom what Capehart has told me. He's got to be mistaken. "He's over there," says Gloria, pointing through some trees, and soon Ed is down on his knees scrubbing the bronze plaque honoring his uncle Eddie. Was it fun having a famous uncle? I ask. "Yeah, but I didn't really think of him that way," he says, scrubbing in earnest, his face getting red. "He was the older brother I never had." I sense this is extremely painful for these simple people, and I'm just about moved to tears myself. "Before I ever thought about having Ed," Gloria says, "Eddie asked me one day, 'If you ever have a boy, will you name him after me? And he was so happy that I did." Ed is holding back a sob. Gloria isn't as successful. When Ed pulls away the weeds and shines up the bronze, I see a lovely plaque of Eddie holding his beloved Gretsch, and a touching tribute poem, written by brother Bob, who died of cirrhosis in 1978.

> *Heavenly music filled the air*
> *That very tragic day*
> *Something seemed to be missing tho'*
> *So I heard the creator say:*
> *"We need a master guitarist and singer*
> *I know of but one alone*
> *His name is Eddie Cochran*
> *I think I'll call him home.*
>
> *"I know the folks on earth won't mind*
> *For they will understand*
> *That the lord loves perfection*
> *Now we'll have a perfect band."*
>
> *So as we go through life: now we know*
> *That perfection is our goal:*
> *And we strive for this.*
> *So when we are called,*
> *We'll feel free to go.*

We head back to Bernice Circle so I can finally see Eddie's legendary Gretsch and his .45 Buntline. I can hardly wait.

As I clumsily handle the cherished .45, trying to pick up the original owner's vibe, I swear I can feel Eddie laughing at me. Does Gloria ever sense the nearness of her baby brother? "I feel him pretty near all the time. I do," she states with conviction. "Mother used to tell me that she would dream about him, that he was in the front room. It may sound silly, but for a long time you could walk in his room and it was just like he was right there with you. It was really something." Ed comes into the room with the aging guitar case, opens it to reveal that vibrant orange Gretsch, and I realize my heart is beating fast. I pick the instrument up and it's light as a feather. I want to hold it like Eddie did, to touch the strings. I put the original hand-tooled "Eddie Cochran" leather strap over my head and pretend I can play. For a brief moment in time I really do feel the presence of Eddie Cochran. I close my eyes, take a deep breath, and look up to see Ed and Gloria smiling at me.

Eddie's gravestone—a tribute from brother Bob. (COURTESY OF GLORIA JULSON)

Eddie Cochran took his Bible with him everywhere he went, says his sister Gloria, and written in Eddie's handwriting on the inside cover, after the phrase "For God so loved the world that he gave his only begotten son . . . ," were the words "And Eddie Cochran."

FREDDIE MERCURY

∎

I've Always

Admired a Man

Who Wears

Tights

∎

Freddie Mercury—Queen's highly eccentric, outlandish diva-dervish front man—was the first major rock star to die of AIDS. After fifteen years of voluptuous, luxurious hedonism, Freddie startled those near and dear by becoming a virtual recluse, rarely leaving his divinely decadent six-million-dollar Kensington mansion, preferring the company of his beloved cats to carousing in London's finest darkened dens of iniquity.

For several years the buzzing rumors invaded Freddie's *very* private mystique, but he didn't announce his dire affliction until twenty-four hours before his death on November 24, 1991. "Following the enormous conjecture in the press," his final statement read, "I wish to confirm that I have AIDS. I felt it correct to keep this information private to date in order to protect the privacy of those around me. However, the time has now come for my friends and fans around the world to know the truth, and I hope that everyone will join me and my doctors and all those worldwide in the fight against this terrible disease."

The son of devout followers of the Zoroastrian religion, young Farokh Bulsara grew up on the exotic, idyllic, friendly islands of Zanzibar and Pemba, which lie in the Indian Ocean off the east coast of Africa. He attended boarding school in Bombay, where he studied piano and was exposed to the classics and opera, which would later become the oddly eclectic inspiration for Queen's ornate, bombastic compositions. But when the family relocated to London in 1959, Farokh (Freddie in English) was teased by the British kids for his dusky skin, protruding front teeth, and clipped colonial accent. The only subject he showed any interest in was art, and at nineteen joined the throng of hip, swinging London teens heading to Ealing Art College, where Who maestro Pete Townshend had recently gotten his Mod band together.

Obsessed with Jimi Hendrix, skinny, velvet-clad Freddie painted copious pictures of his hero, his favorite showing the guitar god as an eighteenth-century fashionable dandy. A classmate recalls that Freddie was prone to the giggles. "When that happened, he would put his hand right over his mouth to cover up those huge teeth of his." A female student remembers Freddie's shyness. "I can't remember him being particularly popular with girls. Freddie only stood out because he was one of only two boys in our class. He was terribly quiet and unassuming."

Shyness aside, moody, mercurial Freddie gave himself the last name "Mercury" after the mythological messenger of the gods, and sang for two different bands before joining Smile with former dentistry student Roger Taylor and physics student Brian May. Although Freddie and Brian May had lived one hundred yards from each other for eleven years, the two didn't meet until the group got together! After going through six bassists, the band finally settled on John Deacon as their fourth member in 1971. Freddie then bravely christened the band "Queen." Years later he told *Rolling Stone,* "It was a very strong name, very universal and very immediate; it had a lot of visual potential and was open to all sorts of interpretations. I was certainly aware of the gay connotations, but that was just one facet of it."

Shopping for outrageous androgynous garb, Freddie met petite blonde Mary Austin at the super-trendy London boutique Biba, and they lived together for the next seven years. Mary encouraged Freddie's dramatic flair by teaching him how to tease his hair and apply makeup. She painted his fingernails black, helping to create his tarty early Queen image. Even after Freddie came to terms with his gayness and their romantic relationship was long over, Mary and Freddie remained amazingly close, and when they stopped living together, Freddie bought her a beautiful flat a few minutes from his new home. Their unusual relationship raised eyebrows through the years, but as Freddie lay dying, Mary kept a constant bedside vigil, and it was she who broke the news of Freddie's death to his distraught parents.

In 1974 Queen's third release on EMI, *Sheer Heart Attack,* included the first of many melodic monster smashes, "Killer Queen," followed by the groundbreaking album *A Night at the Opera.* (The permission notice from Groucho Marx read: "I am very pleased that you have named one of your albums after my film and that you are being successful. I would be very happy for you to call your next one after my latest film, *The Greatest Hits of the Rolling Stones.*" The album's first single, a seven-minute operatic innovation entitled "Bohemian Rhapsody," topped the U.K. charts for nine weeks—the longest run since Paul Anka crooned "Diana" back in 1957. The band spent many weeks in the studio with producer Roy Thomas Baker, during which time the song escalated into a grandiose operetta with more than 180 voices while still retaining a ripping rock feel. Despite the critics' disparaging remarks about pretentious overproduction, "Rhapsody" brought Freddie and Queen to the forefront of the music industry. When the band missed a spot on an important British rock show, "Top of the Pops," they made a film of themselves singing the song instead, starting a powerful new trend in the music industry—promotional videos.

Delighting pop audiences with their ingenious musical hat tricks, Queen followed with another album titled after a Marx Brothers film, *A Day at the Races,* a multilayered, hit-filled extravaganza. Then the band's next album, *News of the World,* went platinum in America due to two bravura tracks, "We Are the Champions" and "We Will Rock You," which became instant anthems in spite of the burgeoning anti-everything punk movement. When Sex Pistol Sid Vicious came across Freddie at Wessex Recording Studios, spewing vitriol and venom ("So you're this Freddie Platinum bloke that's supposed to be bringing ballet to the masses"), Freddie had an unruffled response: "Ah, Mr. Ferocious, we're trying our best, dear."

While the Pistols punished their audiences, Queen gave their fans royal pomp and pageantry and held lavish, bacchanalian bashes. Decked out in satin catsuits slit to the waist to reveal a froth of chest hair, fur coats, ballet pumps, and skimpy short shorts, Freddie Mercury epitomized the unstoppable rock-and-roll showman. With twinkling eyes, he once told a journalist with glee, "I like a nice frock." He was a constant eye-catching vision.

The release party for Queen's fourth album, *Jazz,* was held in New Orleans and featured voluptuous strippers who smoked cigarettes with their vaginas, a dozen black-faced minstrels, dwarfs, snake charmers, and several bosomy blondes who stunned party revelers by peeling off their flimsy costumes to reveal that they were, in fact, well-endowed men. And for the concert launch of *Jazz,* Queen employed fifty naked girls to cruise Wimbledon Stadium on bicycles.

Freddie's campy madcap birthday parties lasted for days and cost hundreds of thousands of dollars, featuring fireworks, flamenco dancers, ladies-of-the-night on the house, pills, powders, and vats of the finest alcohol. He once flew eighty friends first class to a Manhattan penthouse suite, where they consumed fifty thousand dollars' worth of champagne and took copious amounts of drugs, heralding the birth of their most generous rock-star friend. Their host, Freddie Mercury, loved to party and was always on the lookout for Mr. Right (or Mr. Right Now!).

Certainly Freddie's nearest and dearest knew he was gay—a fact he never divulged to the outside world, though speculation was always rampant. A man who didn't like to be alone, Freddie had hundreds of flings and many affairs. On tour he reveled in his stardom, heading directly from headlining stadiums to the town's gay area, which brought innumerable opportunities for wham-bang sexual encounters. He enjoyed straightforward, uncomplicated, and sometimes rough sex—and lots of it—but often complained of loneliness, especially at night. He enjoyed the idea of a true-blue relationship, but was unable to remain committed for very long. "I'll go to bed with anything," he told a friend, "and my bed is so huge it can comfortably sleep six. I prefer my sex without any involvement. There are times when I just lived for sex." He found New York especially titillating. "When I am there I just slut myself," he said. "It is Sin City with a capital S."

Freddie Mercury dressed like a naughty housewife for Queen's "I Want to Break Free" video. (SL/LONDON FEATURES INTERNATIONAL)

And the man loved to shop. "I love to spend, spend, spend," he admitted. "After all, that's what money is there for." Freddie could spend more in mere moments than many people made in a lifetime. Cartier jewelers in London would stay open after hours so the pop star could shop for gems and gold in peace. He collected Lalique glass and works by Victorian masters and by Russian painter Marc Chagall, but his all-time favorites were Japanese woodcuts. On one short trip to Japan he dropped $375,000 on art and antiques. Freddie's exquisite twenty-eight-room mansion took almost five years to complete and was a masterwork of taste and extravagance. His ornate bedroom included a balcony with Romanesque columns surrounding his gargantuan bed. Above the bed, which had to be hoisted up to the top floor by a crane, was an immense domed roof hiding hundreds of colored lights designed to change the bedroom's atmosphere to match Freddie's moods. "I'm fortunate enough to be rich," he confessed. "Sometimes I believe the only bit of happiness I can create is with my money." In the year of his death Freddie created happiness for ten of his friends, spending over a million and a half dollars on homes for them.

In the early eighties, when Freddie exchanged his long locks and androgynous frocks for the macho-man mustachioed leather look, some of Queen's fans turned on him: Razor blades were hurled onto the stage in protest. But Freddie was attracted to the rough, beefcake kind of man he emulated. When he noticed somebody staring at the bulge in his skintight trousers, he would say, "That's all my own work. There's not a Coke bottle stuffed down there or anything." The backlash was inflamed in 1984 when Freddie dressed as a big-breasted woman for the video "I Want to Break Free." Still he disputed press reports that he was homosexual. Some of his friends believe Freddie didn't want to hurt his deeply religious parents; others feel that, as a brilliant businessman, he didn't want to chance losing his fans with the revelation.

Queen's image was further tarnished when they played Sun City in South Africa, breaking the cultural boycott against the racist regime. Though the band stated that they were antiapartheid, the damage had been done in the United States. Still, Queen was massive in other parts of the world, breaking attendance records all over South America and Asia. And in that summer of 1985, when the band took the stage at the Live Aid concert, two billion people were awestruck. "The concert may have come out of a terrible human tragedy," Freddie said that day, "but we wanted to make it a joyous occasion." The newspaper headlines reflected the crowd's reaction: QUEEN ARE KING! The show's organizer, Bob Geldof, concurred: "Queen were absolutely the best band of the day, whatever your personal preference."

But sometime in 1985 Freddie must have found out he had AIDS. He stopped carousing and became more guarded than ever, spending a lot of time at home with close confidants. Queen's final concert was at Knebworth Park in 1986, though Freddie continued to write and record until six weeks before his death. He even collaborated with Spanish opera diva Montserrat Caballe, which resulted in another hit album, *Barcelona,* in 1988.

The AIDS rumors started after Freddie had a blood test at a Harley Street clinic, which he vehemently denied. "Does it look as if I'm dying?" He told reporters that his nights of crazy partying had come to an end because he was forty years old, finally growing up, and "no longer a spring chicken." In spite of his pale and haggard appearance, his Queen colleagues also kept up the facade. The band members weren't even told of Freddie's illness until a few months before his death. After he collected an award with Queen in 1990, standing back meekly as Brian May made the acceptance speech, Freddie Mercury sightings became rare indeed.

Nine months before his death, a pale and ravaged Freddie turned up at Wembley TV studios to work on a video for the band's newest single, "I'm Going Slightly Mad." The crew were told that the singer was having problems with his knee and would have to "take it easy." A bed was installed in his dressing room, guarded by two security men. Freddie disguised his facial sores with thick white stage makeup and donned a black fright wig, plumping up his emaciated body by wearing clothing under his black suit. He wasn't fooling anybody.

During his final months, Freddie was taken care of by his former girlfriend, Mary Austin. Though his doctors tried to comfort him, Freddie suffered from pneumonia, severe body aches, Kaposi's sarcoma, and bouts of blindness. He used painkillers constantly but never complained of the pain. Many of his intimates came and went as the months went by, but it was only Dave Clark, former sixties idol and dear friend, who was by his bedside at the end. "He didn't say anything. He just went to sleep and passed on. It was very peaceful. He was a rare person, as unique as a painting. I know he has gone to a much better place."

Mary Austin said that despite the agony he was going through, Freddie Mercury had no regrets.

A few weeks earlier Freddie had made the decision to rerelease "Bohemian Rhapsody" and donate the proceeds to AIDS charities. Just six days after the song came out, it went to number one, ultimately making more than $1.5 million for AIDS. Mary Austin revealed that Freddie had secretly given away millions to AIDS charities in the months before his death. But that wasn't enough for a lot of people.

Many in the rock world accused Freddie of cowardice by making the decision to keep his affliction a secret. They felt that by not admitting the truth, the flamboyant singer made gayness and AIDS something to be ashamed of. When his will was published in May 1992 and there were no bequests to AIDS charities, the controversy continued. When Mary Austin received the bulk of Freddie's fortune, she vowed to donate part of the money for AIDS research.

"I think the fact that he was so beloved," David Bowie said of Freddie, "straight or gay, will focus some people on the fact that AIDS knows no boundaries." Bowie also said he always admired a man who wears tights.

Six months after their singer succumbed to AIDS, the remaining members of Queen gathered a phalanx of stars to pay tribute to Freddie Mercury and raise money for AIDS research. Guns N' Roses, David Bowie, George Michael, and Freddie's close friend Elton John sang Queen songs to the gigantic teary-eyed crowd who wore red AIDS ribbons to show their support. Despite claims that seven and a half million dollars would be raised for AIDS charities, it was finally revealed that, due to the costs of staging the massive show and providing hotels and limos for the stars and their entourages, the concert made only a modest profit.

There is still no memorial for Freddie Mercury. His ashes haven't been scattered because officials in Freddie's borough of Kensington haven't decided whether he will be allowed a memorial. Said council leader John Hanham, "We do not want a problem like the Paris authorities have with Jim Morrison's grave. And it can't be like Elvis Presley's shrine in America. You have to admit that Memphis is rather different from Kensington High Street."

SAM COOKE

■

A Change

Is Gonna Come

■

The divine Sam Cooke in his prime. (MICHAEL OCHS ARCHIVES/ VENICE, CALIF.)

My favorite living singer is Terence Trent D'Arby. My favorite singer of all time is Sam Cooke. He is also Terence's favorite singer. A lot of people feel that way about Sam. Rod Stewart claims Sam inspired him so deeply that he spent two years listening *only* to his music. "Sam Cooke is somebody other singers have to measure themselves against," said Keith Richards, "and most of them go back to pumping gas." Legendary record producer Jerry Wexler called Sam "the best singer who ever lived. No contest. I mean *nobody* can touch Sam Cooke. . . . Everything about him was perfection. A perfect case."

Sam Cooke was among the first ten inductees to the Rock and Roll Hall of Fame, along with Elvis, Little Richard, and Chuck Berry. Four years before his fatal plane crash, Otis Redding told a reporter that he wanted "to fill the silent void caused by Sam Cooke's death."

Last year ABKCO released the music from Sam's own SAR label—a collection of gospel, pop, and soul that includes Sam's former gospel group the Soul Stirrers, Johnnie Taylor, and the Womack Brothers, along with a few previously unreleased tracks by Sam himself. "Somewhere There's a Girl" is the most inspirational, magnificent, soul-expanding vocal performance I have ever heard in my entire life. The song puts me into a state of prayer and gratitude, reminding me just how transcendent a human voice can be—and how far it can take you. Over thirty years ago Sam Cooke was shot down under very seedy, shadowy circumstances, his glorious voice silenced by a bullet to the heart. How did the well-mannered preacher's son, the Jesus-shouting soul stirrer, wind up in a sleazy three-dollar motel room on the dark side of town, with a shady lady of the night?

In his smooth and graceful way, Sam Cooke broke down musical and racial barriers all during his career. From the age of eighteen he was the premier gospel singer before crossing over to pop. His very first record, "You Send Me," went straight to number one. He was a brilliant songwriter, producer, and arranger, and the first black singer to walk out onstage and refuse to perform unless the concert was integrated.

Son of devout Holiness Baptist minister Reverend Charley Cook, Sam grew up with the church as the central focus in his life. Reverend Cook's service in Bronzeville, Illinois, was the singing, stomping, clapping, shouting kind—praising the Savior with joyous music. Sam's mother, Annie May, sang in the choir, and by the time he could stand up, little Sam was singing for Jesus. As a very young boy, he performed with his four siblings, Hattie, Mary, Charles, and L.C., as the Singing Children, actually making a bit of money to bring home to their folks. Sometimes Sam would even sneak into the local tavern and croon along with Billie Holiday on the jukebox, grabbing a few coins on his own, always offering his take to his mother. Charley Cook took pride in the fact that his wife didn't have to work, and Annie May was a doting mama, instilling in Sam a disarming self-confidence at a tender age. At eleven, in 1942, Sam was dunked in a large tub of water at his father's Christ Temple Church and baptized in the Lord. Soon afterward Reverend Cook became a sort of wandering preacher, traveling to various towns with his message, taking along the Singing Children to praise Jesus in song. At a gathering in Chicago one evening, as the Children waited to sing, they were treated to a rousing performance by the top gospel group, the Soul Stirrers, and watched in silent awe.

Sam's younger brother, L.C., says that Sam knew from a very early age that he was never going to work nine to five. "I said, 'What are you gonna do then, if you ain't gonna work, Sam?' He said, 'I'm gonna sing.' And he had some Popsicle sticks—you know, them wooden sticks? He had about twenty of them and he lined them sticks up, stuck 'em in the ground, and he said, 'This is my audience, see? I'm gonna sing to these sticks.' He said, 'This prepare me for my future.' I say, 'Man, you got to be crazy,' and he sat there and sang to them sticks. You talking about he was nine and I was seven, and he talking about he never gonna work. And he never did."

Sam glided through high school with barely a ripple. Most of his fellow students at Wendell Philips High don't even remember his junior year "First Noel" solo at the Christmas program. His real life was going on outside of school. Sam had formed a gospel group, the Teenage Highway QCs, named after the local Highway Baptist Church (nobody seems to recall what "QC" stood for). With a lot of rehearsal and determination, the a cappella group became part of the quartet circuit, traveling around to perform at different churches. Sam's older brother, Charles, went to see the QCs when he got out of the service and was stunned by the fire in Sam's singing. "He had me in tears, almost."

Sam was about to graduate and was serious about not working nine to five. The QCs hired a "trainer," the Soul Stirrers' R. B. Robinson, to work with them on harmony and tempo, training the ambitious Sam on lead vocals.

A clean-cut Christian image was obviously paramount in his chosen field, but even as Sam charmed his way through the church doors, there were already signs of the ladies' man he was to become. Although he was involved with his childhood sweetheart, Barbara Campbell, Sam got in big trouble with a girl named Georgia when her little sister found some pornography after one of Sam's nighttime visits. Georgia's parents called the police on the preacher's son and he spent ninety days in jail on a morals charge. There must have been some serious shame in the family, but Sam was forgiven his transgression, and now when he sang about the devil's temptation, it rang a little more true. The talk was that this sweet-voiced kid, Sam Cook, was not to be missed, and the next time the QCs played, they got a manager.

Louis Tate saw the group in Detroit and took the clean-cut teenagers on. It was the beginning of a two-year road trip round and round the country. Tate says the boys were very religious—no drinking, no cursing—but that the charismatic Sam couldn't stay away from the women—and they couldn't stay away from him.

It may not have been nine to five, but the QCs were working hard for very little pay, sleeping on a lot of Christian couches along the way. Sam was even more determined and had started writing his own songs, but Tate was going broke and had to get back to his family. It was about this time that the Soul Stirrers lost their lead singer, R. H. Harris, and eighteen-year-old Sam Cook grabbed the much-coveted spot. Now he had to go out and show the Lord he was a Soul Stirrer.

With only one rehearsal, Sam's first performance with his new group took place at his old high school, and he was wringing his hands. After only one line of lyrics, a young girl stood up and shouted, "That's my baby! Sing, baby!" and the house came down for the first of many, many times.

Sam was wearing fancy suits in the gospel big leagues but still had to prove he could take the place of the much-beloved Harris. With his perfect pitch and willingness to learn from the Stirrers' manager, S. R. Crain, in no time at all he did just that. After just a month on the road, the group went to Los Angeles, where Sam would cut his first record. On March 1, 1951, the Stirrers arrived at the studio, where Art Rupe, head of Specialty Records, was surprised to find that Harris had been replaced with a teenager. But as soon as Sam started singing "Jesus Gave Me Water" with that sheer, infectious joy of his, Crain says Sam "awed Art Rupe." One of Sam's own songs, "Until Jesus Calls Me Home," was recorded that day, and the Stirrers were thrilled to have a writer in their midst. "We should sing," Sam cries, "'til Jesus calls."

"Jesus Gave Me Water" was the biggest hit the Stirrers had ever had and made Sam a star in the gospel world. Especially with "Sister Flute." There was one in every congregation—the lady so caught up in the Holy Spirit that she would scream and shout "Amen" until the whole place followed suit, moaning in rapture. The rest of the Stirrers, who were in their forties, were surprised to see girls in their teens, who usually hung back, crowding down front, shouting for Sam Cook. It worried some of the older folks, who believed gospel might get caught up in the blues, but young people heard the sweet hope in Sam's voice and women thought he was absolutely drop-dead gorgeous. Sam Moore (of Sam and Dave) recalls that when the Stirrers came to his hometown of Miami, the Christian girls swooned. "I've seen women just pass out wanting to get him!"

Unbeknownst to "Sister Flute," in 1952 Barbara Campbell had Sam's daughter, Linda, and though Sam stayed in touch and sent money, he wasn't ready to get married. He was having a high old time on the road. In fact, while he was in Cleveland, Sam found out he was going to have another child with a lady named Maxine.

Early in 1953 the Stirrers pitched one of their songs too high for Sam, and when he couldn't reach the note, he cruised under it, bending the note into something magical. The next time he did it again, adding syllables, wo-wo-wo-ing until the girls were on their knees. Sam was able to infuse people with the Holy Spirit. "It's a fire," said Crain about Sam's ability to shake someone's soul. "A fire that burns." One soul reaching out and touching another.

By the third Soul Stirrers album, Sam was bending notes all over the place—and he had fallen in love. It was in Fresno, California, that singer Dolores Mohawk got a load of Sam shaking the spirit out of a whole room full of people, and she wanted a closer look. A much closer look. At the end of the tour, Sam spent two weeks with Dolores, and in October they got married, settling back in Bronzeville with her five-year-old son, Joey. Barbara Campbell was not amused. She had always assumed that someday Sam would be hers. Beautiful Dolores may have landed Sam, but due to his ten months a year on the road, she rarely saw her husband.

Because the Stirrers' label, Specialty Records, was having a lot of success in the burgeoning pop market, Art Rupe hired Robert "Bumps" Blackwell as an

A&R trainee, inviting him to a gospel show at the Shrine Auditorium. After watching the hysterical response to Sam Cook, Bumps immediately thought the soulful singer could cross over into pop music. Sam balked at the idea, fearing he would lose his religious audience, and continued with the Stirrers on tour for another year. He had written three of the group's most recent singles—including the biggest-selling "Touch the Hem of His Garment," while riding in the backseat, after opening to a page in the Bible that told about a sick woman who is healed by touching Jesus's hem. Sam had the storyteller's uncanny ability to pull people into a miracle.

By deciding to enter the pop-music field, Sam was taking a hard-core chance with his career, but that's where the big money could be made. "Making a living was good enough," he said about the musical shift, "but what's wrong with doing better than that?" Still, he recorded his first pop single, "Lovable," in New Orleans under the assumed name "Dale Cook." It wasn't a hit, and the fiction fooled nobody in the gospel world. Sam would have to make a choice.

Dolores Cook was bored and lonely most of the time, and after her desperate suicide attempt, Sam tried to make the marriage work, but his heart wasn't in it. Said Crain, "I think he was just tired of being married. Usually when he was with a woman awhile, he didn't want her no more. Just seems that's the way he acted. Not only her, every woman he had." Sam and Dolores would soon divorce.

Sam recorded one last album with the Soul Stirrers and the song he contributed signaled the change to come. Although "That's Heaven to Me" is still very much a religious song, it states that you can find your God right here on earth.

On June 1, 1957, Sam cut brother L.C.'s song "You Send Me," a sweet tale of young love laced with his breezy wo-wo-wo's, and when the single came out on the new Keen label a few months later, it was an instant Top Ten smash. Sam was soon selling more records in a day than the Soul Stirrers sold in a year. "You Send Me" eventually reached number one and stayed on the charts for six months, eventually spawning eight covers. (Teresa Brewer's squeaky-clean, oh-so-white imitation of Sam's wo-wo's was pretty damn funny.)

All of a sudden everybody wanted Sam Cooke (he added the "e" to his name for his new start). He signed with the prestigious William Morris Agency and got a slot on "The Ed Sullivan Show." But when Sam was cut off in mid-song due to an overlong show, African Americans bombarded the station with complaints and he was rebooked. By that time, December 1958, Sam had a new record, "For Sentimental Reasons," and the national exposure sent him over the top. It was about this time that Sam found out he had fathered another baby, in Washington, D.C. Then, in May 1959, he was arrested on paternity charges in Philadelphia. (He settled out of court for ten thousand dollars.) The man got around!

Sam appeared on "American Bandstand" and "The Steve Allen Show," and with one smash after another, both on the pop and R&B charts, he was selling out shows across the country. In the world of gospel Sam hadn't come up against the race issue, but in his new, wider role, he had to deal with prejudice and the painful problems of segregation every day. Bumps Blackwell tells of an incident at a Howard Johnson's restaurant when he and Sam waited an awfully long time to be served. As they waited for service somebody played "You Send Me" on the jukebox and all the waitresses started swooning over Sam Cooke. "Everybody in the place swooning!" Bumps recalls, but he and Sam never got to eat dinner. Even after receiving warnings from the KKK, Sam chose to go through with an appearance on one of Dick Clark's specials, which happened to be the first integrated audience in Atlanta. A half hour before the show there was a bomb threat, but Sam was the epitome of silky-suave cool and there was no incident. He began to let his hair go natural and take pride in his race. His fans paid attention.

Sam never forgot his first love, Barbara Campbell, and the two became engaged in the fall of 1958. They had known each other since they were kids, and understood each other. Sam said he wanted a home and a family, but he still couldn't seem to settle down.

Almost no singer/songwriter owned his own publishing in 1959, but Sam started heading in that direction. He wanted complete control over his career, which was in full bloom. An avid people-watcher, Sam often said that his astute songwriting gift came from observation. He churned out more hit singles, from "Everybody Likes to Cha Cha" to "Only Sixteen," spending his days in the studio and nights out on the town.

Sam had stayed in close touch with his first wife, Dolores, so her death in March 1959 was a severe blow. Still despondent over her breakup with Sam, Dolores had been drinking and crashed Sam's gift—her new Oldsmobile convertible—into a cedar tree, fracturing her skull. When he attended the funeral in Fresno, Sam was mobbed. Her death hit him hard. He sang "Somewhere There's a Girl" to Dolores.

The white South was torn up with racial tension. Sam was touring with the explosive Jackie Wilson, and when they reached Little Rock, Arkansas, the polite but resolute Sam told the management of the venue that unless the seating was completely integrated, he wasn't going on. Sam went on—in fact, he was the one who walked out onstage to inform the audience that the show would not be segregated that night. In an interview with columnist Dorothy Kilgallen, Sam said, "I have always detested people of any color, religion, or nationality who have lacked courage to stand up and be counted."

Sam finally married Barbara Campbell in Chicago in October 1959, with his father presiding over the ceremony. The press called it "a whirlwind courtship" even though the couple had an eight-year-old daughter. Said his friend Aretha Franklin, "He wore a lot of women down when he got married.

He wore me down. Ooooh, I loved him, I just loved him. That man could mess up a whole roomful of women." He continued to mess up women. Wedding vows didn't seem to slow Sam down.

In January 1960 Sam signed with RCA and recorded "Chain Gang," the first of a long string of hits with the company, but he had bigger ideas. Having already formed his own publishing company, Kags Music, Sam started his own record company, SAR (taken from the initials for his name, Sam, and those of his partners, J. W. Alexander and Roy Crain), becoming the first African American artist to own his own label.

SAR was producing hits, but Sam's first concern was still his own career, and he was bringing houses down all over America. Crain recalled a night at the Town Hill club in Brooklyn. "They throwed them panties," he said. "Sam would catch them and just keep right on singing."

Sam was making it big. Soon after an hour-long national television special, "Sam Cooke Phenomenon," he and Barbara moved to the West Coast and bought a house in the Hollywood Hills with a pool and a marble bar inlaid with silver dollars. They had another daughter, Tracey Samie, and finally Vincent—the son they had been hoping for—was born.

The next few hit singles Sam recorded were about twisting the night away and swinging at parties, but one of the B sides, the passionate ballad "Bring It on Home to Me," in which Sam trades "yeahs" with his friend Lou Rawls, defined what was about to be called "soul music." People rightly started calling Sam "Mr. Soul."

Sam enjoyed spreading his money around, buying jewelry and furs for his wife, new cars for his friends. He was on a major roll, planning his first tour of Europe, when the false rumors started that he was about to die of an incurable disease. Sam made sure to show up at clubs and parties in Los Angeles, proving he was hale and hearty, but the rumors that he was dying—and leaving his eyes to Ray Charles—gave him an eerie feeling. Sam's easygoing manner seemed to undergo a change. He started to drink a lot more and became even more restless than before. Perhaps the thoughts of death prompted Sam to go back to the safe arms of gospel. He performed at a gospel show on New Year's Eve 1962, working his throaty sex appeal into the spirit. Sam's agent, Jerry Brandt, recalls the night with glee. "Sam is taking off. . . . Right next to me, almost, this woman stands up, gives a big shake, and goes out! Lands on the floor, stretcher comes, puts her on it, take her out. I say to my wife, 'I think she just came.' She thinks it's God in her soul, but this chick just had an orgasm that popped!" A few days later Sam recorded a live album at the Harlem Square Club in Miami, and Mr. Soul's sexy, steamy nonchalance had the audience dancing and singing in the aisles. It's without a doubt one of my top ten favorite records. Oooh, I wish I could have been there.

Since Sam had a seemingly insatiable appetite for women, Barbara and he had "an understanding" about his many flings. The *Los Angeles Times* recently reported that Sam often slept with prostitutes to avoid paternity suits. "I didn't accept what he did, but I supported him," Barbara told the *Times*. No matter how unconventional the marriage seemed to be, Sam and Barbara Cooke had been through a lot together. Sam loved his wife and said he would never leave her.

Sam was at his SAR offices, working with Mel Carter on his upcoming LP, when he got the news that his eighteen-month-old son had fallen into the swimming pool. Sam raced to the scene to find that the ambulance had already arrived. He desperately tried to revive Vincent with mouth-to-mouth, but his baby son was already gone. At the funeral Sam broke down at Vincent's casket and had to be helped away. Friends say he was never the same again.

Sam drank through his grief, brooding, blaming himself, blaming Barbara. True to his word, he didn't leave his wife, but their relationship crumbled. He forced himself to work. He got a new manager, the formidable businessman Allen Klein, signed a lucrative new deal with RCA in which he was guaranteed artistic control, and went on the road.

Defying the Southern racial turmoil, instead of staying at the Negro hotel in Shreveport, the Royal, Sam booked his party into the Holiday Inn, only to find upon arrival that his rooms weren't ready. Exhausted and not ready to put up a fight, Sam told off the clerk and left, and had just gotten to the Royal when five cop cars pulled up and arrested the entire party. *The New York Times* ran the news under the headline NEGRO BAND LEADER HELD IN SHREVEPORT, and went on to report that Cooke had been arrested for disturbing the peace after trying to register at a white motel. Press about the incident helped secure Sam's reputation in the civil rights movement. Sam was reading books on African history and spending time with Black Muslim leader Malcolm X and one of his followers, Cassius Clay—soon to become Muhammad Ali. Angered by the discrimination in the music industry, Sam bankrolled a recording studio for emerging black talent, calling it "Soul Station #1," and planned on opening several more around the country.

Bob Dylan's gentle protest song "Blowin' in the Wind" made Sam realize that he could share his activist views with his music, and despite its sorrowful tone, his self-proclaimed "civil rights" song, "A Change Is Gonna Come," was his announcement heralding that change. At its heart, "Change" is a gospel song, a fervent message of hope—even though Sam admits it's been "a long time coming" and he doesn't know what's "beyond the sky." When the song had to be trimmed for a single release, Sam's most poignant lyrics about going downtown and being told not "to hang around" were cut out. He had to live with it.

Sam sang "Blowin' in the Wind" at his June 1964 show at the Copacabana nightclub, blending the coming changes easily into his breezy, sophisticated style. The show, an unqualified success, was recorded for RCA, and *Sam Cooke at the Copa* would remain on the charts for over a year. Sam had done it again—opened the doors for soul music to reach a higher-paying, mainstream (black *and* white) audience.

After a lot of touring early in the year, Sam spent most of the rest of 1964 in Los Angeles, working on "Shake," the last of four singles for RCA that year, and preparing *At the Copa* for release. He screen-tested for Twentieth Century–Fox (for *The Cincinnati Kid*) and the talk was good. But by year's end, his relationship with Barbara was severely strained, and he was having problems with his manager, Allen Klein. Sam told S. R. Crain that he had "found out something" and was planning on getting out of his contract with Klein. He had already made an appointment to meet with Steven Hill, who would later manage Marvin Gaye.

On December 10 Sam had dinner with friends at Martoni's, a showbiz restaurant in Hollywood. He was seemingly in a good mood, talking about a blues album he wanted to start work on, when an acquaintance arrived with an attractive Eurasian girl. Sam excused himself and paid for the drinks, and his friends noticed that, as usual, he had a huge sum of money in his wallet ("several thousand dollars"). Sam didn't return for his main course, and when the couple left Martoni's, they saw him sitting in a booth, talking intimately with the Eurasian woman. Said the friend, "The picture in my mind at the moment was, "'Oh, this is somebody he knows.'" Sam told another friend that he would meet him at PJ's, a nightclub a few miles away, at one o'clock. He never got there. Instead, he took the Eurasian girl, Lisa Boyer, to the Hacienda Motel on Figueroa Street, paid the three-dollar charge, signed his own name to the register, and went into the motel room with Boyer.

Twenty minutes later he was slouched in the motel office's doorway, bleeding profusely, wearing only an overcoat and one shoe. His brand-new red Ferrari was idling in the parking lot, but Sam Cooke was dead.

When the police arrived at 2:35 A.M., the motel's manager, Bertha Franklin, told them that the half-naked man had banged on her door, shouting, "You got my girl in there!" She said he then broke the door down, grabbed her by the wrists, and they tumbled to the floor. "He fell on top of me," she said, " . . . biting, scratching, and everything. . . . I run and grabbed the gun off the TV, and I shot . . . at close range . . . three times." Bertha Franklin said that Sam's last words were, "Lady, you shot me!" Even after the bullet tore into Sam's heart, she said he kept coming at her, "so I got this stick and hit him with that. In the head . . ."

Lisa Boyer had called the police at about the time Sam was shot. They found her in a phone booth a half a block away and took the twenty-two-year-old in for questioning. She said she had met Sam that evening at a dinner party and he had offered her a ride home but instead had kidnapped her and taken her to the Hacienda Motel. "He dragged me into that room. . . . He pulled my sweater off, and he ripped my dress off. . . . I knew that he was going to rape me." When Sam went to the bathroom, Boyer said that she grabbed her clothes and ran out of the room, and that it was just an accident that Sam's clothes had gotten entangled with hers. Later Sam's family testified at the inquest that his wallet was missing, and it was never found.

The body was taken to the County Medical Examiner's, where an autopsy showed that Sam's judgment might have been affected by the 0.14 level of al-

The late Sam Cooke, wearing only an overcoat and one shoe—the ignominious demise of a legend. (UPI/BETTMANN)

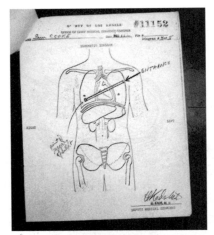

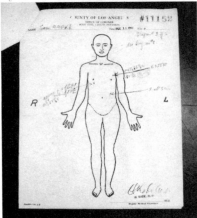

The coroner's report showing Sam Cooke's fatal gunshot wounds. (ADAM W. WOLF)

cohol in his blood. Then he was taken to the morgue and placed in crypt nineteen.

S. R. Crain was indignant. "That's where you put people who ain't got nowhere to go!" he fumed. "You wouldn't put a man like Sam Cooke in the morgue!" But Barbara had been sedated after hearing the dreadful news and was in no shape to handle anything. Sam's body hadn't been claimed. She asked Crain to take care of it, and he called People's Funeral Home in Los Angeles.

Sam Cooke had a double funeral. Thousands of stricken mourners viewed the body in L.A. before it was taken to Chicago so the Reverend Charley Cook and his wife, Annie May, could say goodbye to their son. So many people attended the ceremony that it took police forty minutes to escort the Cook family to their front-row pews. Many of Sam's musical contemporaries turned up to show their respects. Cassius Clay was among the mourners and later voiced his feelings: "I don't like the way he was shot. I don't like the way it was investigated. If Cooke had been Frank Sinatra, the Beatles, or Ricky Nelson, the FBI would be investigating yet, and that woman [Mrs. Franklin] would have been sent to prison." Sam's body was flown back to Los Angeles for the final funeral rites. Outside the Mount Sinai Baptist Church, hawkers sold photographs of Sam in his coffin in Chicago, as throngs of weeping fans crowded into the service, where Lou Rawls and Ray Charles sang heavenly songs for their dear departed friend. As Ray Charles was led down the aisle, he stopped to place his hands on Sam's casket, tears streaming down his face. Sam was buried at Forest Lawn under a small bronze plaque:

SAM COOKE
I LOVE YOU
1930–1964
UNTIL THE DAY BREAK
AND THE SHADOWS FLEE AWAY

A lovely sentiment, but somehow somebody got the year of Sam's birth (1935) wrong. A lot of things were wrong. People who had been to the funeral talked of seeing the young singer Bobby Womack wearing Sam's clothes that day, and less than two months after the death of her husband, Barbara Cooke announced her engagement to the twenty-year-old SAR recording star.

One month after Sam's death Lisa Boyer (a.k.a Crystal Chan Young, Jasmine Jay, and Elsie Nakama), who claimed Sam Cooke had kidnapped and tried to rape her, was charged with

Cassius Clay (soon to become Muhammad Ali) pays his last respects to his friend Sam Cooke. (UPI/BETTMANN)

prostitution. In 1979 she was found guilty of shooting her boyfriend dead and went to prison. Nobody knows where Lisa/Crystal/Jasmine/Elsie is today. According to unconfirmed reports, the motel manager Bertha Franklin, who was awarded thirty thousand dollars from Sam's estate for "battery," died in Michigan a year and a half after shooting him through the heart.

After a brief inquest during which Sam was depicted as a drunken Negro in a rage, the coroner deemed that the shooting of Sam Cooke was "justifiable homicide." It didn't seem to matter that the kidnapper/rapist had signed his own—very famous—name to the register. Or that his ID, credit cards, and money had never been found. And what happened to the ring he had been wearing? Why hadn't anyone staying in the motel heard any gunshots? Nobody was buying the story. But very close confidants feel that Sam had been a victim of his own dangerous habits. Though some wondered why the successful, debonair singer was found in such a seedy neighborhood, pal Johnny Morisette said that he and Sam often frequented the Sands nightclub on Figueroa, also confirming that Sam had a penchant for hookers and knew the Hacienda Motel "very, very well."

Some friends speculate that Lisa Boyer was a prostitute (Bertha Franklin testified that, upon his arrival at the motel, Sam's tie was loose and his shirttails were hanging out of his pants). According to their version, when Sam went into the motel bathroom, Lisa may have stolen his clothes and made a run for it. When he realized what had happened, a bit drunk, his temper hot, Sam went straight to the motel office, broke down the door, and demanded to see the girl who had fled. Then the fifty-five-year-old manager grabbed her gun off the TV set and pulled the trigger three times. According to that version, Lisa Boyer probably invented the kidnap/rape story to avoid questions about what happened in the motel room, wantonly leaving Sam Cooke's reputation supremely and forever tarnished.

Newspaper, TV, and radio reports relayed the cops' version of the events: that Negro singer Sam Cooke, raging drunk and half naked, had kidnapped and tried to rape twenty-two-year-old Lisa Boyer and was killed in self-defense by the motel manager after he wrestled her to the floor.

Allen Klein told the *Los Angeles Times* that he never accepted Lisa Boyer's story. "I was prepared to fight, and asked Barbara if she would like me to keep going on it," he said. "She asked, 'Will it bring him back? Will it get him out of the room with that woman?' I told her no. She said, 'I have two children, and I don't want to put them through this.' So the investigation was stopped." Klein, who later, for a time, managed the Rolling Stones and the Beatles before falling out with both bands, said that he will produce a movie, revealing his theory of how Sam Cooke was killed.

Four months after Bobby Womack married Barbara Cooke, the couple went to Chicago for the wedding of Sam's niece and were confronted by Sam's very angry brother Charles. According to the newspapers, there was a heated argument about Sam's belongings, and somehow Barbara's gun was produced and Charles used it to pistol-whip the newlyweds. To this day Charles says he has no regrets about the incident. Less than six years later the Womacks divorced, and Barbara is now living very comfortably on Sam's royalties.

Sam's old gospel friends feel that Sam was punished for his sinful lifestyle. "When Sam was killed," said Bobby Womack, "there were those who said, 'He thought he got away but God waited on him.' I said, 'Man, God don't do people like that—not this kind of God I know. They do it to themselves.'"

Sam Cooke, the soul-stirring preacher's son, spent his time on earth touching hearts with his voice, creating music that was joyously color-blind. He was a student of black history, a civil rights activist who boldly faced oppression. It's also said that he succumbed to late-night trysts and temptations, gave in to his "earthly desires," and wound up paying for it with his life. But after he died, society's dichotomy between spirituality and sexuality crucified Sam again. A double funeral for a double death.

Despite his tainted reputation, Sam Cooke's music will live forever. I know in my heart that he has found his place "beyond the sky" and that his Lord has forgiven him, body and soul.

MARVIN GAYE

■

Sexual Healing

■

Tragically ahead of his time, and locked in a bitter, bloody battle between his shattered soul and his overpowering sexuality, Marvin Gaye spoke to Jesus Christ as if his Savior were hanging out in the studio while he blatantly sang sexual praises: "Let's Get It On," "You Sure Love to Ball," and "Sanctified Pussy" ("Some girls suck/Some don't dare/Some girls fuck/Some don't care . . ."). It seems Madonna and the Artist Formerly Known as Prince have found a way to integrate sex and the soul, but Marvin was tortured and taunted the Lord with his endless wicked transgressions. Jesus said, "It is done unto you as you believe," and Marvin Gaye believed he was a sinner like no other.

Brought up in a poor area of Washington, D.C., in a very strict, traditional church called the House of God, where his father was a minister, Marvin Pentz Gay, Jr., was singing to Jesus in his high, sweet falsetto at the age of three. Services were often held in the Gay home, where women weren't allowed to show their arms or their hair, much less wear makeup, nylons, or nail polish. There was no television set, no movies, no dancing. From Friday night to Sunday morning, the four Gay children were cut off from the rest of the world, expected only to worship the Lord.

I met with Marvin's younger brother, Frankie, also a beautiful singer—a sensitive, sweet, sad-faced replica of Marvin who has his own recollections. "We knew that being Seventh Day Adventists, we were going to church on the seventh day [Saturday], which to us was the right day, but you have to explain this over and over again to people in order to feel normal. People looked at us as being very abnormal. Marvin and I understood each other, where a lot of people didn't. We were very close." I ask Frankie if he sang in church with Marvin. "As children we all had to do something in church. It was one of my father's rules. Me and Marvin found it better to sing because the rewards were greater. A lot of hugs and 'Oh, you're so beautiful!' We were a dancing, shouting church. Our belief was 'Make a joyful noise unto the Lord.' We used to go to church three or four times a week." Frankie sighs. "I think too much church for any child will have an effect, and because Father was a minister, we were under 'What you do reflects on me.' That always stayed with us. We couldn't do the things that other people do. What we did reflected on his teachings, his discipline. He was very effective in teaching us right from wrong."

The fear of God was instilled early, but young Marvin feared his earthly father far more than he feared the one safely tucked away in heaven. Marvin Sr.—"Father"—beat his sons unmercifully for the slightest bit of imagined defiance, while his long-suffering wife, Alberta, spent a lot of time down on her knees, begging God to stop the continuous torment. All the children had bedwetting problems, and a damp mattress inflamed Father to madness. After insisting that they disrobe, he would whip his naked kids until he could see the welts rise.

Because he was unable to please him, the only attention Marvin could get from his stern, moody Father was negative, so he started to provoke the violence, challenging the older Gay at every turn. But Frankie doesn't feel Marvin was overly defiant. "I don't think he rebelled consciously. He was more of a dreamer. It was an unconscious rebellion." Years later Marvin would insist that Father enjoyed the beatings he doled out and relished the fear he created within his children, saying it was like "living with a very peculiar, changeable, cruel, and all-powerful king." The Jesus that Father believed in demanded sacrifice that he wasn't able to give. Marvin Sr. loathed his own weakness and took it out on his family.

Father's "peculiarity" was that, in private, he enjoyed wearing women's clothing, often stepping into Alberta's panties, shoes, gowns, and nylon hose. Sometimes he wore his hair long and wavy, sometimes he wore wigs. He rarely worked, spending most of his time at home while his wife left at five every morning for her job as a domestic. "Among the many sins I got from Father," said Marvin, "is a love of loafing." The neighborhood kids, sensing something strange about the effeminate Gay Sr., called him a sissy, the ultimate insult. But instead of challenging the attackers, young Marvin ran for his life, mortally ashamed. He would later attach an "e" to Gay, but it wouldn't stop people from adding an "is" in front of his name—"Is Marvin Gaye?" "Man, I can't tell you," said Marvin, "how many guys have asked me that."

In his biography *Divided Soul* by David Ritz, Marvin told the author that his fascination with women's clothing had been handed down to him. "Sexually, men don't interest me. But seeing myself as a woman is something that intrigues me. It's also something I fear. I indulge myself only at the most discreet and intimate moments. Afterward I must bear the guilt and shame for weeks. After all, indulgence of the flesh is wicked, no matter what your kick. The hot stuff is lethal. I've never been able to stay away from the hot stuff."

Motown's golden boy. An early shot of Marvin Gaye. (MICHAEL OCHS ARCHIVES/VENICE, CALIF.)

For someone who would become such a drooled-over object of desire, Marvin Gaye was an extremely shy teenager who felt devastating guilt about his constant masturbation, likening orgasm to "pleasures of the devil." When Marvin entered Cardozo High School in 1953, Father was still giving him whippings, throwing him out of the house, threatening to disown him, calling him a "bum." "I wanted to strike back," said Marvin, "but where I come from, even to raise your hand to your father is an invitation for him to kill you." Instead, Marvin's "unconscious" rebellion increased: He started smoking Viceroy cigarettes and turned to doo-wop music as his deliverance, forming his first group, the D.C. Tones.

Believing school was a waste of time and afraid he would incur the wrath of Father if he failed, Marvin quit after the eleventh grade and joined the Air Force. But he soon found that seeking refuge in the service was a big mistake. Marvin had wanted to learn to fly but instead was stuck peeling potatoes in Kansas. He felt betrayed by his country and thought his superiors were "pompous assholes." Coupled with an almost lethal lack of self-confidence was Marvin's massive ego. He had huge dreams of stardom—of becoming the black Sinatra—and just wasn't capable of taking orders. He faked crazy for a few months and finally got an honorable discharge ("Marvin Gay cannot adjust to regimentation and authority"). When I ask Frankie if Marvin's troubles in the service led to his hatred of Uncle Sam, he balks. "I think 'hate' is very strong. My father taught us not to use that word. You can disagree with the government in certain areas, but I don't think Marvin felt that this wasn't the greatest country in the world, as far as opportunity." Then Frankie admits, "Marvin did say, 'It makes you want to holler, throw up both your hands.'"

Marvin would later say that the only good thing that happened during his stint in the service was that he finally got laid. He had crude sex with a disinterested, obese cathouse hooker, which triggered a lifetime of similar tawdry encounters. In a 1982 interview with the French magazine *Actuel,* he admitted to "needing" prostitutes: "Prostitutes protect me from passion. Passions are dangerous. They cause you to lust after other men's wives."

After his air force discharge, Marvin feared facing Father and crashed on friends' couches, plotting his music career. Along with Reese Palmer, James Nolan, and Chester Simmons, he started the Marquees, a doo-wop group that Marvin claims was named after the Marquis de Sade. "I identified with his wicked ways," he said. "He had a power to raise the blood pressure."

The Marquees played local dances and school assemblies, where Marvin's shy sensuality drove the girls wild. "My singing covered up for the action I wasn't getting," he admitted. "I saw that I was reaching for girls on a mystical level. Almost like I was one of them." The Marquees were eventually brought to the attention of rhythm-and-blues pioneer Bo Diddley, who produced their first record. When "Hey Little Schoolgirl" failed to chart, Marvin got work as a stockboy and then as a dishwasher at People's Drugstore, an establishment that catered to whites only. Every day the black Sinatra had to eat his sack lunch out on a park bench.

Through Bo Diddley, Marvin met a man he would later call his mentor, singer/songwriter Harvey Fuqua, who was quick to spot Marvin's steamy potential. In 1959 nineteen-year-old Marvin headed for Chicago with the latest version of Harvey and the Moonglows, where they were soon recording for legendary Chess Records. None of the songs were hits, but Marvin got his first big dose of the road, hitting the "chitlin circuit" (chitlins—pigs' intestines—being the cheapest meat), with Big Joe Turner and Etta James, being refused accommodations, sleeping in a station wagon or outside on the "cold, hard ground." "Ran into all kinds of racist shit," Marvin said. "I thought about Joseph and Mary being turned away, but that wasn't comfort enough. Jesus turned over the tables in the temple, and I was ready to break down the doors." In the summer of 1960 the Moonglows played to a packed house in D.C. Marvin didn't even know if Father was in the audience.

Harvey Fuqua shared the dream that, with his easygoing, alluring charm, Marvin could become a successful crooner, and after the doo-wop craze died down, they hit Detroit and quickly linked up with Berry Gordy and Motown

Records. "As soon as Berry saw how big my talent was, he made a bid," Marvin declared, "and that was it." When his contract was sold to Motown, he thought he had landed on Easy Street in Motor City, but soon realized he was just another struggling employee in a large stable of talented musicians.

A determined and shrewd businessman, Berry Gordy had started his Motown venture with the royalties earned from Jackie Wilson's "Lonely Teardrops," turning it into the largest black-owned enterprise in the history of American business: "The Sound of Young America." His employees were paid a very low wage, the royalty rates were much lower than elsewhere in the industry, and Gordy kept the copyrights to the songs written by his musicians, but despite everybody jockeying for position, he somehow created a tight, family feel. Marvin, of course, wanted to get closer to his boss, and because of Gordy's longtime friendship with Smokey Robinson, Marvin began his Motown career playing drums for the Miracles, making five dollars a session. In early 1961 Motown had its first million-seller, Smokey Robinson and the Miracles' "Shop Around."

At twenty Marvin began a love affair with Berry Gordy's thirty-seven-year-old sister, Anna, and a lot of people saw it as a calculated attempt to cut in front of the long line at Motown's recording studio. Even if there is some truth to this, Marvin found Anna to be an adoring partner, a wise and worldly teacher who encouraged and inspired him in his pursuit of stardom. The two married in 1961, and Anna called good-looking Marvin her "fine young thing." "We were hot characters," said Marvin, "with hot ambitions." Hoping to slide into the white pop market, with Anna's help, Marvin did get into the studio to record his first album, *The Soulful Mood of Marvin Gaye.* But when the record failed to cause any kind of stir, he was plagued with self-doubt and full of resentment that he needed anybody's help. Outwardly calm, suave, and impeccably cool, Marvin seethed with the pent-up desire to succeed. He watched his boss, Berry Gordy, the international playboy, seemingly on top of the glitzy world, and wanted to run his *own* empire, move people around like so many chess pieces. He called Motown "the gestapo," but added that since Berry was "a loving cat," it was a loving gestapo. Marvin Gaye wanted to fit in, but he couldn't help but stand out.

Marvin recorded six more albums that didn't sell, which kicked his pumped-up delicate ego into a private rage. He slogged around the country as part of a Motown package with Mary Wells, the Supremes, the Marvelettes, and "Little" Stevie Wonder, making sixty dollars a week. He continued to play sessions, but when he started writing, Marvin got his first taste of victory with "Stubborn Kind of Fellow" in 1962 and "Hitch Hike" in 1963, followed by his first crossover hit, "Pride and Joy," written for Anna. But instead of enjoying his hard-earned good fortune, Marvin worried about it being snatched away from him and was in a constant state of angst.

Hit followed hit, and Marvin bought his parents a large, comfortable home in a good neighborhood. He was proud that his mother no longer had to work, but his visits were infrequent. He didn't want to be reminded of his unhappy childhood, and although Marvin ached for his father's approval, he couldn't stand to be around him.

In 1964 "How Sweet It Is (to Be Loved by You)," another declaration of love to Anna, went to number six on the charts, but Marvin wouldn't be satisfied until he got to number one. That same year he headlined the Motortown Revue and recorded *Together* with Mary Wells, the first of many successful duet albums. Clean-cut and boyish, Marvin sang directly to his fans, and they imagined being wrapped up in his arms. More than a few had their wish come true.

Baffled and overwhelmed by his fame, Marvin admitted to being on a "star trip," which was causing serious friction in his marriage. In an attempt to tighten their bond, the Gayes adopted a child in November 1965 and named him Mavin Pentz Gaye III. "I was torn," Marvin said. "I liked the tradition of naming my son after me, but I also didn't want to be reminded of my father. When Marvin arrived, I made the decision: Tradition had to be upheld. That's what we learned from the Old Testament."

Touring gradually became difficult for Marvin, his stage fright reaching paranoid proportions. Sold-out concerts were canceled at the last minute, establishing an erratic lifelong pattern. Falling in line with the Motown program caused Marvin to refer to himself as a "slave" and slowly eroded his fragile self-respect. Because his father was an alcoholic, Marvin stayed away from the evils of liquor but found he could appreciate life through a hazy filter of marijuana and the powerful rush of cocaine. "I'm passionate about good cocaine," Marvin asserted. "No one will ever tell me it's not a good feeling. A clean, fresh high, 'specially early in the morning, will set you free—at least for a minute."

The murder of Malcolm X, followed by the Watts riots, caused Marvin to question the validity of his music. Gordy just wanted to sell records, and Marvin went along with him, but the seed of truth-telling had been planted and started brewing.

The Gayes had a volatile marriage and would often break into loud physical arguments at home and in public places. They took other lovers but still seemed to need each other even though the relationship had started to break down. Once Marvin found Anna at a motel in bed with another man and just went back home. The couple would stay together until 1977, but stagnation had set in. When Gordy moved into his mansion on Boston Boulevard and gave his old house to his sister and brother-in-law, Marvin couldn't help feeling like a poor relation who had lucked out.

Despite the success of his duet records with Kim Weston and Tammi Terrell, Marvin was frustrated by the even bigger success of the Supremes and the Four Tops, who were busy touring the world. He saw much grander things for himself.

Young and spirited, Tammi Terrell was too independent to rouse Marvin's passion, but as a singing partner she was perfection. "While we were singing," Marvin said, "we were in love." During the next two years Marvin and Tammi would record three albums and have nine singles on the charts, beginning with "Ain't No Mountain High Enough," early in 1967. When she collapsed in Marvin's arms during a concert in Virginia, he carried her offstage and his world slowly began to disintegrate. She had six brain surgeries during the next three years, and Marvin spent a lot of time by her hospital bed. When Tammi died in March 1970 at age twenty-four, it was announced that she had a brain tumor, but it was rumored that she had been beaten in the head by a jealous boyfriend. At Tammi's nighttime funeral, Marvin was disoriented, sobbing and speaking aloud to his former singing partner. He saw Tammi as a victim of love. "My heart was broken," Marvin claimed. "My own marriage to Anna had proven to be a lie. In my heart I could no longer pretend to sing love songs for people. I couldn't perform. When Tammi became ill, I refused to sing in public."

Marvin threatened to kill himself for the first of many times. He would hole up with a gun, but could never bring himself to pull the trigger because he believed suicide was a mortal sin. Already in his own private hell, Marvin didn't want to incur the wrath of his Lord.

In November 1968 Marvin finally hit number one with "I Heard It Through the Grapevine," but joy eluded him. In 1969 the deeply personal album *M.P.G.* was released, an exposé about his crumbling marriage and immeasurable loneliness. Though he hungered for huge success, he didn't really feel he deserved it and still refused to tour with his hits. Spending more and more money on drugs, Marvin didn't save any for Uncle Sam. He had learned to despise the government and was bitter about his money paying for the war in Vietnam. He had also come to hate the hustle and hypocrisy of show business. Marvin turned thirty and went into seclusion.

Eager to prove that he could do something outside of the music industry, Marvin went through a strange few months when he decided to become a pro football player. Along with friends from the Lions football team, Mel Farr and Lem Barney, Marvin trained vigorously, running six miles a day, cutting out cigarettes and drugs, intent on becoming a superstar athlete. Motown, of course, killed the idea, but Marvin continued to pursue his passion for sports, later investing in several prizefighters.

He still wasn't performing, but Marvin continued to expand musically and started producing. His first record for the Originals, "Baby, I'm for Real," cowritten with Anna, went to number one on the soul charts. But Motown wanted Marvin to play Vegas and wanted him to grind out another hit record of his own. Restless and edgy, he watched what was going on around him. The murders at Kent State incensed him, and when his brother Frankie returned from Vietnam and recounted the horror stories, Marvin said his "blood started to boil." He demanded an answer to the nagging question "What's going on?"

Frankie recalls telling Marvin about his terrifying experiences in Vietnam: "There was so much pain over there, so much hurt. You hear about things that go on, but there's nothing more terrible than war. Human life becomes cheap. You have to do something to yourself to keep from crying *all* the time, to keep from being afraid *all* the time. Every minute seemed like an eternity. We talked at length about Marvin knowing my feelings. Him being a part of me, it was devastating for him. We cried together. He could feel my pain. 'What's Going On' was his way of fighting. It was his Vietnam."

Using his brother, Frankie, as an inspiration, Marvin came up with his musical centerpiece, an offering of peace and hope, the uplifting and demanding *What's Going On,* the first Motown album to be produced by the artist himself. After the record was initially rejected by the company as "too long and formless," Marvin threatened to never set foot inside a recording studio again unless the album was released. Marvin won this particular war, though his own personal battles continued to rage within. Seen by many as the first concept album, *What's Going On* would be Marvin's most successful record, revolutionizing soul music by revealing the inner workings of the artist's own soul. By gently reminding us that "war is not the answer," and pleading with us to "save the babies!" Marvin was able to tap into his divine nature and sell a whole lot of records in the process. "When would the war stop? That's what I wanted to know . . . the war inside my soul."

Adoration beckoned, and Marvin crawled out of hibernation to receive accolades and awards for what was being hailed as his "masterpiece." On May 1, 1972, he played a triumphant "coming out" concert in Washington, D.C., where he was given the key to the city and called "a hero" by the mayor. He made a little speech at his former high school about drug abuse, despite the fact that he was stoned out of his head. Nobody seemed to notice. His mother rode in a motorcade and waved to the crowds. Marvin later said that he felt like he made his father proud that day.

Due to the massive success of his socially conscious million-seller, Marvin believed his next politically incorrect single, "You're the Man," would also steam up the charts. He was wrong. If he couldn't count on social issues to sell records, he would go to Hollywood and score a movie soundtrack. *Trouble Man* was a cheesy blaxploitation film, enhanced by Marvin's bleak and moody score, which sold well. While he was in Hollywood, Marvin decided he would write screenplays and might even do some acting. His boss, Berry

Gordy, had relocated to Beverly Hills, so Marvin followed suit, moving his entire family to the West Coast in 1973.

Diana Ross was fast becoming a polished actress, and Marvin saw the same for himself. He signed with the William Morris Agency but only got a couple of bit parts in low-budget movies. The screenplays never materialized. He tried to hustle a place in the Hollywood scene but was hustled himself by people who talked him into shady investments. He was soon back in the studio, recording another duet album, this time with Diana Ross, but there was zero chemistry between the two top Motown stars and the pairing failed to live up to expectations.

Ego and soul continued their intense warfare. In an interview with *Crawdaddy* magazine Marvin said, "I don't compare myself to Beethoven. I must make that clear. I just think that I'm capable of all he was capable of." In the same article he announced, "We'll just have to become gods. The world'll be like it started. Maybe God will know Himself. Perhaps He's using us to help Him learn who He is."

During the recording of *Let's Get It On,* the long-planned follow-up to *What's Going On,* Marvin met sixteen-year-old Janis Hunter and fell in crazy, obsessive love. She was seventeen years younger than Marvin. Marvin sang the entire album to Jan, usually coming up with lyrics on the spot, likening the process to the way a flower grows. Jan was placed on the Madonna pedestal that Anna had occupied, being alternately worshiped and scorned, depending on Marvin's quixotic, chemically induced mood swings. He wouldn't divorce Anna until 1977, further complicating his life. Marvin took his new lover to a Topanga Canyon paradise, hiding her from the prying eyes of the public, his mortified wife, and his ever-demanding family.

Meanwhile, the new album's title track, "Let's Get It On," was an instant smash, going straight to number one, and Marvin held out for huge tour dollars. He was worried about Anna getting all of his money and still had a loathsome fear of performing live. After canceling one concert in November, he finally agreed to appear at the Oakland Coliseum on January 4, 1974. As usual, he drove the women wild.

"To know that women love me is gratifying," Marvin told *Rolling Stone.* "Dudes love me too; I can feel it. I sing to everybody. But the first ten rows are always women." Marvin reclaimed his major sex symbol status on his first tour in five years, traveling with four female backup singers, a twenty-piece orchestra, his pregnant girlfriend, his mother, and Frankie—grossing over $1.5 million in August alone. "I was sort of a personal manager," Frankie tells me. "I know what he liked. I knew how to get it right for him, how he liked the stage set up, what should be there for him—the lemon and honey, when to have it there. It had to be the perfect temperature. It couldn't be too hot or too cold. If it's too cold it closes the throat muscles. We had to time it between songs, so that when he'd go to sip it, it wouldn't be too hot, 'cause then he'd burn himself. It was an art." Despite Frankie's brotherly concern, touring made Marvin jumpy, and he tried to snort and smoke his jitters away but could never get enough. It seemed he couldn't get enough of Jan, either. He felt she held him in the palm of her hand. When she gave birth to his daughter, Nona (nicknamed "Pie"), Marvin tried to cancel the rest of the tour but was threatened with lawsuits. He traveled using fake names. Sometimes he wore disguises. When he got back home, he moved his new family into a high-rise in Brentwood, determined to start his life anew. Early in 1975 Anna filed for divorce and Jan became pregnant again.

Marvin saw the divorce action as a personal attack and stopped sending Anna money. He built himself a state-of-the-art recording studio on Sunset Boulevard, complete with a custom-made king-size waterbed and featuring numerous Messiah-like oil paintings of Marvin himself. As a seeming snub to Anna, he bought a five-acre estate for his new family, adding stables, spas, a pool, hot tubs, and a regulation-size basketball court. He already owned fourteen cars, including a vintage Mercedes and a Rolls-Royce. His wife and Uncle Sam be damned.

Even before Marvin proposed to Jan on his next album, *I Want You,* he had already begun the process of tearing the relationship to shreds, turning Jan on to cocaine and insisting that she take lovers. Somewhere inside his double soul, he dreamed of the white picket fence but didn't believe he deserved that kind of happiness. His behavior became more and more erratic as his drug taking increased. He saw himself as an outlaw.

Living outside the law suited Marvin, and his battle with Anna became ferocious. An article in *Variety* stated: "Marvin Gaye faces two consecutive five-day terms in L.A. County jail for contempt of court in an alimony and child support case if authorities catch up with him." But Marvin was back out on the road with Jan and his two babies, seducing and taunting the ladies in the audience with an even sexier stage show. He returned to threats, hearings, and depositions, and the dispute was ultimately solved with music. Anna would receive her $600,000 settlement from Marvin's advance and earnings for his next album, a two-record set succinctly titled *Here, My Dear,* dedicated to his ex-wife. "I had to free myself from Anna," Marvin said, "and I saw this as the way." From start to finish the album recounts the intimate horror of Marvin's failed marriage. When Anna told *People* magazine that she might sue Marvin for invasion of privacy, he responded, "All's fair in love and war."

After four years and two children together, Marvin and Jan got married in October 1977. He was full of remorse for pulling Jan into his private, hellish shame, but he couldn't live without her. Before his first divorce was completely settled, Janis also filed for divorce. "I can't blame Janis for anything," he told *Rolling Stone.* "I fell in love with her, and yet I myself was unable to reform. I continued my wild and reckless ways. I had lost myself, just as I had before Tammi died."

In September 1978 Marvin signed a seven-year deal with Motown for masses of money, and in October filed for bankruptcy with debts of almost $7 million. He toured to half-full houses and collapsed onstage in Tennessee due to "physical exhaustion," spending his usual few days in the hospital. He made attempts but would never quite recover from what he believed to be a blasphemous lifestyle.

Here, My Dear received malicious reviews and didn't sell. Marvin desperately wanted to make a commercial record, but most of the songs on his next album, *Love Man,* were wrenching pleas for Janis to come back to him. There was another threadbare bus tour through the United States with Marvin going through the motions of mopping his sweaty brow and bestowing damp, silky scarves. But if he wasn't in the mood to perform, he would instruct the driver to just keep on driving.

Back in L.A., Marvin turned up at his mother-in-law's house to see Jan and the children and was promptly arrested and beaten up by the police when he refused to leave. His recording studio was shut down and his home in Hidden Hills repossessed. Certain that Jan was in love with Motown's newest cock-rocker, Rick James, Marvin was devastated when another soul singer, Teddy Pendergrass, made off with his woman. When his latest prizefighter, Andy Price, was knocked out by Sugar Ray Leonard in an embarrassing three-minute fiasco, Marvin dropped out, taking his plentiful troubles to Hawaii.

Jan came to visit Marvin in exile when her relationship with Teddy Pendergrass ended, but the Gayes continued their brawling in paradise. "I nearly killed her," he admitted. "I had a knife about an inch from her heart." Marvin claimed to have snorted an ounce of cocaine in one hour, but even though he wanted to die, "God wasn't ready to take me." When Jan left, four-year-old Frankie stayed with Marvin. For a while father and son lived in a bread van. His mother, Alberta, came to Hawaii for a few weeks, paying the rent by pawning her diamonds, but during this harrowing time, Marvin never, ever heard from Father.

Brother Frankie and his wife, Irene, also spent time with Marvin in Hawaii and have some fond memories. "Marvin taught me to make lemonade," Irene says, smiling. "He was very warm and sweet, he really cared about people. He used to tell Frankie that *he* was the rich one because he loved to walk in the garden, spend time with his family." Frankie tries to explain Marvin's erratic behavior: "As an artist you're constantly giving something. It takes a lot from you. But an artist has to give. If not, it's like a bucket of water that's never emptied, the water will stagnate. . . . Or a rose that refuses to give off fragrance. It's gonna die." Does Frankie feel that Marvin's immense fame kept him from having the normal life he seemed to crave? "If you can put it in its place, it doesn't—which is really hard. If someone exalts you, makes you a god, you have to keep your feet on the ground. That's what was so special about Marvin. He would say, 'I'm a human being, I'm with you, I'm no bigger than you. God loves you as much as he loves me.' This is what I admired about my brother more than anything—he never lost touch with the fact that his God wanted him to love his fellow man."

After one of the many times he hit bottom, Marvin realized he still had something vital to say and sent for his musicians to begin rehearsing. The idea of imminent nuclear annihilation began to consume him, and he felt he needed to cut another record to sound a warning. But the message would have to wait for a while. Since Uncle Sam was demanding two million dollars, Marvin took his pain on a tour of Europe. The shows were chaotic and well received, but Marvin was erratic and unpredictable, once climbing out a bathroom window to escape performing. When he kept Princess Margaret waiting for hours, the British press proclaimed SOUL SINGER SNUBS ROYALTY! The drugs were rampant, as were the women. At the end of the tour Marvin couldn't face going back to his many problems in America, and ended up spending months holed up in his London hotel room, freebasing cocaine, before moving across the North Sea to Belgium with a Dutch girlfriend, Eugenie Vis.

While he was away, Motown had released Marvin's unfinished record, *In Our Lifetime,* without his permission, and he vowed never to record for the record label again. "How could they embarrass me like that?" Marvin asked his biographer, David Ritz. "I was humiliated. They also added guitar licks and bass lines. How dare they second-guess my artistic decisions? Can you imagine saying to an artist, say Picasso, 'Okay, Pablo, you've been fooling with this picture long enough. We'll take your unfinished canvas and add a leg here, an arm there. You might be the artist, but you're behind schedule, so we'll finish up this painting for you. If you don't like the results, Pablo baby, that's tough!' I was heartbroken. . . ." The record didn't sell.

A music devotee and longtime fan of Marvin's, Freddy Cousaert, ran a *pension* in the fishing village of Ostend, where Marvin went to stay in the spring of 1981. Cousaert, a successful businessman, was determined to get Marvin back on his feet and back in the studio, where he belonged. Marvin soon became a local celebrity and the subject of a Belgian television special, on which he declared, "I'm disappointed with America, with governments. To govern people is a tremendous responsibility. It should be in the hands of those who are righteous, moral, and sane." He then added, "But I'm disappointed in myself. Because perhaps I'm selfish, perhaps I'm spoiled."

During his stay in Ostend, Marvin started pulling himself together, jogging and riding his racing bike along the beach every day, spending quiet evenings with the Cousaert family. His drug taking was tempered, but it continued while long-distance negotiations went on between Motown and CBS, who finally bought Marvin's contract from Berry Gordy for $1.5 million. Said senior VP Larkin Arnold, "He was one of ten or fifteen tremendously gifted artists. Once I heard he'd become disenchanted, I leapt at the opportunity." Early in 1982 Marvin began recording in Brussels.

Biographer David Ritz gave Marvin the idea for the song "Sexual Healing" during a visit to Ostend. "Gaye's apartment was filled with sadomasochistic magazines and books by Georges Picard, a European cartoonist in whose drawings women were sexually brutalized," Ritz said in *Divided Soul*. "I suggested that Marvin needed sexual healing, a concept which broke his creative block." His old friend and first mentor, Harvey Fuqua, was brought in to produce the album *Midnight Love*.

When the song was released in October 1982, *Billboard* magazine announced that "Sexual Healing" was the fastest-selling soul single in five years. It stayed at the number-one spot for four months, bringing Marvin Gaye back to Los Angeles and back into the much-desired but damning spotlight.

Breaking new musical ground in three different decades just wasn't enough for Marvin. Never deeply satisfied, he fretted over the obscene success of Michael Jackson's *Thriller* and Lionel Richie's middle-of-the-road triumphs. When I ask Frankie if Marvin had a competitive nature, he responds with a knowing grin, "Oh yeah. It's a chess game. It was his craft. I don't think any artist is ever satisfied." Still, when CBS wanted him out on the road, Marvin's paranoia kept him home. When I ask Frankie why, he has a simple answer: "Drugs. Paranoia goes hand in hand with drugs."

While Marvin enjoyed visits with his first wife, Anna, he went on relentlessly pursuing Jan. Despite constant hassles with the IRS, he spent a lot of peaceful time with his children and at the family home in Gramercy with his mother. Then Father returned from six months in Washington and the atmosphere once more became unbearably strained.

Marvin's inner tumult was obvious, but there were some happy times. His divine rendition of "The Star-Spangled Banner" at the 1983 NBA All-Star game brought people to their feet and to tears. In February "Sexual Healing" finally earned Marvin two long-overdue Grammys, but Uncle Sam was always on his case. Realizing that the endless string of bills had to be paid, Marvin reluctantly went back on the road soon after his forty-fourth birthday, in April 1983. He knew that

Toward the end: Marvin finally gets his Grammy. (RON WOLFSON/LONDON FEATURES INTERNATIONAL)

nobody expected him to complete the tour, which was the only reason he vowed to see it through. New York's Radio City Music Hall was sold out eight nights in a row, but on opening night Marvin turned up an hour and a half late, shouting until the curtain rose about how much he hated to perform. He took his preacher and his drug dealer on the road, running madly back and forth from one illusion to the other. "There was more coke on that tour than on any tour in the history of entertainment," said one of the musicians. "Marvin was smoking it, even eating it." Onstage he prowled the stage in a robe and, in a sad sex-symbol parody, stripped down to his underwear during the "Sexual Healing" finale. He was hospitalized again, missing several shows. Marvin didn't trust anyone, even claiming that he was being stalked, that Jan was conspiring to have him murdered. He took to wearing a bulletproof vest, insisting that one of his roadies carry a submachine gun. There were armed guards in the wings and standing watch at his hotel room door. Marvin's paranoia was total but uncannily clear. He believed wholeheartedly that he would soon be gunned down and killed.

When he got back to Los Angeles in August, facing half-filled houses, Marvin was a shattered shell and, despite the presence of Father, crawled back to his mama's house and shut the door forever. He stayed in bed all day, frozen with fear, waiting for the devil. He wanted his mother to sleep by his side every night. Strange people kept coming by, selling him drugs and all kinds of guns. He spent hours sitting against the wall holding a pistol. He rarely ate because he believed somebody was trying to poison him. Marvin took so many drugs, he lost track of who he was. Sometimes girls came to visit, but Marvin Gaye didn't feel he deserved the company of women. His mother, Alberta, told David Ritz that Marvin roughed up a couple of women who came to pay him a visit. "He lost control and hit them. My son, my poor son, turned into a monster." One of his girlfriends, Carole Pinon Cummings, had recently filed a six-figure lawsuit, claiming Marvin had beaten her repeatedly. He couldn't dress himself. He couldn't feed himself. With the shades always drawn, Marvin snorted coke and watched pornography. In the room next door Father drank his vodka. During semilucid moments Marvin ranted at Father to leave the Gramercy house, and Father told the family he would kill Marvin if he came near him.

It was April 1, 1984, the eve of Marvin's forty-fifth birthday, when Father called upstairs for his wife to help him locate an insurance company letter. Alberta was lying beside Marvin in bed, attempting to comfort her tormented son. Marvin hollered back to Father that if he wanted to speak to Mother, he'd better come upstairs. When the elder Gay got there and reprimanded his wife, Marvin became enraged and attacked Father, pushing him into the hallway. Only moments later Father was back. In his hand was the .38 revolver that Marvin had given him a few months earlier. He level the gun at his son and pulled the trigger. Marvin stumbled back against the wall, and as his son lay dying, Father walked closer and shot Marvin one more time at very close range. Alberta was afraid for her own life and begged Father not to kill her, too. But Father had no intention of doing so.

I ask Frankie if Marvin's friends and family attempted to get him some help during those hellish final few months. "He didn't really feel he needed that much help," he asserts. "We were very much into God taking care of us if you asked Him, as far as healing goes, especially as far as the spirit. Man can help you as far as helping you come down from drugs, but to be really strong comes from your

The sins of the father: Marvin Sr. in handcuffs after killing his firstborn. (AP/WIDE WORLD PHOTOS)

faith." Through all of his private turmoil, did Marvin ever question his faith? "You have to ask yourself, 'Did Moses question *his* faith?' It's always the battle between good and evil, and it's how strong you are whether you win that battle or not. You always pray to Jesus for your strength because nothing else matters. If you have Jesus with you, you can win anything with Him, but it's a constant battle. Lucifer has conquered stronger men than me and Marvin and my father."

Four days after Marvin Gaye's death, a line of more than ten thousand passed by his open casket. Stevie Wonder sang to the sobbing mourners, a trembling Smokey Robinson read the Twenty-third Psalm, and then the body was cremated, the ashes scattered into the ocean by his children.

Father gave an interview in jail, saying he wasn't guilty, that he didn't think the gun had real bullets in it, that he had shot in self-defense. "I pulled the trigger," Gay told the *Los Angeles Herald*. "The first one didn't seem to bother him. He put his hand up to his face like he'd been hit with a BB. And then I fired again." Father said he didn't know he had killed his son until hours later when a detective gave him the news. "I thought he was kidding me. I said, 'Oh God of mercy, oh, oh, oh!' It shocked me. I just went to pieces." Later that month a small brain tumor was discovered inside Father's head and removed. In June Alberta Gay filed for divorce after forty-nine years of marriage. In September Father pleaded no contest to the lesser charge of voluntary manslaughter, convincing the judge that he had acted in self-defense. He was sentenced to five years' probation, serving no jail time for the killing of his son.

Marvin Gaye's entire life was made up of the blues. Even when he sang about the sweetness of being loved, the heartache and tears in his high, angelic tenor could easily be heard. He was a reckless, selfish, macho man, but he studied the Koran and was interested in Buddhism. He spoke of writing a book about Jesus returning to modern-day Israel. He wanted to be a pure man for his beloved Lord, and he suffered untold hell because his nature prevented him from standing behind a pulpit, spreading the word of God. But Marvin made the stage his pulpit, the recording studio his church, calling Jesus's name on the final track of his final album. "Marvin was strictly music," says Frankie. "It was his gift. His lyrics are always about love, and they will teach you something."

In the song "Love Party" on *What's Going On,* Marvin announces that the "world is not for long. . . . There's only time for singing, and praying, and having a love party."

"I knew when I heard about [Marvin's death] that it was God's will," said Anna Gordy Gaye. "I thought about the fact, oddly and ironically, the very person who helped bring him into this world . . . God had the same person take him out of this world."

JIMI HENDRIX

■

Bold

as Love

■

I was a little virgin girl the first time I met Jimi Hendrix. When he loped toward me wearing a lopsided grin and that bright, blazing, hand-painted eyeball jacket, his frizzed hair going every which way like electricity on fire, I felt deliciously cornered—and scared to shivers. "What are *you* doing later?" he asked with piercing expectancy, but all I could do was stammer and stutter some lame, polite excuse. I don't believe in harboring regrets, but how about having regrets about something you *didn't* do?

My photographer, Allen Daviau (who is now Stephen Spielberg's cinematographer), called one morning to ask if I would like to dance in a short film with the Jimi Hendrix Experience. My mission was to wriggle around behind the group for their first American release, "Foxy Lady." I had, of course, heard about the Experience: how the Seattle-born guitar god had gone to England, picked up some cute, skinny English boys, then returned to conquer the United States. And I had a serious penchant for skinny English boys. "Gee, Allen," I said, trying to remain calm, "that sounds like fun."

I threw on my favorite blue-velvet rag, hitchhiked over the hill to a crumbling Hollywood mansion-turned-hippie-den, and for many, many hours danced on top of a white column behind Hendrix, Noel Redding, and Mitch Mitchell while "Foxy Lady" blasted down the peeling walls. Jimi kept peering at me from the corner of his eye, but Noel Redding looked like a safer bet to me, and by the end of the day we were holding hands.

My relationship with Noel continued (in various forms) for several years. We are still friends today. I spent a lot of time around Jimi Hendrix and had a whole lot of very naughty fantasies about him (and his guitar!) but never really got to know him. Not many people did. Even though he was deeply private and often said he was from another planet(!), Jimi Hendrix let us all know him in a very profound and personal way through his music. "I sacrifice a part of my soul," he said, "every time I play." Jimi went to another level with his guitar. Pete Townshend agreed: "What the Who were doing was important, but Jimi was an epiphany." According to Bruce Springsteen, Jimi showed us all there was "a deep ecstasy that could be had."

Jimi Hendrix had only a little over three years to make his illustrious mark. His death, which occurred during the early-morning hours of September 18, 1970, when he was twenty-seven, seemed all wrong. Jimi suffocated on his own vomit after ingesting nine potent sleeping pills in the London flat of one of his girlfriends, Monika Danneman, and at 12:45 P.M. was pronounced dead on arrival at St. Mary Abbots Hospital in Kensington.

There were two people I really wanted to sit down and have big chats with: Monika Danneman, of course, and a former girlfriend of Jimi's, Kathy Etchingham, who enlisted Scotland Yard to reopen the investigation two years ago after digging up new "facts" about Jimi's death.

Jimi's childhood was difficult. His mom, the lovely Lucille, was a hard-drinking wild woman, dissatisfied with her lot in life, constantly drowning her sorrows in men and booze. When her husband, Al Hendrix, got out of the army, he found his three-year-old son, Johnny Allen, with a family friend in California and took him back home to Seattle on the train. Suspecting that little Johnny had been named after one of Lucille's lovers, Al changed his son's name to Jimmy Marshall (named after himself and his brother Marshall). Before long Lucille was back (actually back and forth), and after three years of trouble and two more sons, the couple divorced in 1951. It was hand-to-mouth much of the time for Al and his boys. There was a whole lot of moving around and a lot of different schools for Jimmy. Al switched jobs often and he enjoyed gambling. It got so difficult to find work that he eventually fostered out Leon and Joseph, and Jimmy would spend weeks at a time with friends and relatives. Nicknamed "Buster" after Flash Gordon's Buster Crabbe, he escaped into science fiction, painting stars and planets with his watercolors, chasing around whichever neighborhood he found himself in, wearing a handmade cape. He was once suspended from junior high school for wearing bright red pants!

When Jimmy was fifteen, Lucille, the mother he barely knew and rarely saw but adored anyway, died of an alcohol-related illness. His father didn't have a car, and Jimmy didn't make the funeral. Maybe he stayed home out of respect for Al. He had learned, through hardship and through Al's example, to keep his feelings under wraps, but he was destroyed by Lucille's death. He would see her in his dreams for the rest of his life.

I fly to Seattle to meet Jimi's dad, Al Hendrix, now seventy-seven years old and finally the victor after years of litigation over his son's estate. Al and his daughter Janie now control all of Jimi's musical assets. Jimi Hendrix makes as much money now—if not more—as he did when he was alive. His Woodstock guitar recently sold for $750,000.

When Al opens the door of a modest house on the outskirts of Seattle, I am immediately struck by his sweet smile—Jimi's sweet smile. All along the walls are Jimi's gold records, pictures, paintings. When I marvel, Al tells me that the gold records are duplicates, the originals stolen long ago. Who would do something like that? I wonder. He shakes his head. He can't figure it, either. He invites me in and we sit on the couch with Janie (Jimi's stepsister) and one of her toddler sons. When I ask Al how Jimi did in school, he grins. "Oh, he was more or less a visitor." Just like he was in life. "He dropped out of school and went to work with me since I had my own landscaping business. He tried to get jobs otherwise, like a busboy, but that was before all the civil rights. If you were black, well, then you couldn't get that position," he says matter-of-factly. Was Jimi Hendrix a good gardener? I wonder. "First he didn't like to get his hands dirty," Al laughs. Then, after a while there, he found out the easy way to run around doing it, so he enjoyed it." I ask Al if Jimi's musical gift came from him. "Oh, I had it in my mind I wanted to play," he admits, still smiling. "I fooled around with the piano, but then it was the saxophone." Janie tells me that her dad is being overly modest.

Jimmy had wanted a guitar for a long time, pretending to play on a broom, graduating to a cigar box and then to a one-string ukulele. Then Al bought Jimmy a real guitar during a poker game. "I paid five dollars for Jimi's first guitar, an old beat-up acoustic. After I found out he could play the guitar, well, then I went and got him an electric one." It was a white Supro Ozark bought at Myers Music Store on First Avenue. Janie interjects that Al got his saxophone the same time Jimi got his guitar, and the two practiced together, but Al got behind in the payments. "I let the sax go back to the people and kept up payments on the guitar." Wise move.

In the summer of 1959 Jimmy played his first gig with a local group called the Rocking Kings, making thirty-five cents. Pretty soon the teenagers were making sixty-five dollars playing parties, and it was obvious that Jimmy had found his niche. He had huge hands, his thumb almost as long as his fingers, so he could hook it over the neck of his guitar like an extra finger. When he wasn't practicing or spending time with the girls, Jimmy listened intently to

Muddy Waters, B. B. King, Jimmy Reed, John Lee Hooker, imitating the masters. When the Ozark got stolen, which was a traumatic event, Al eventually replaced it with a white Danelectro, which Jimmy tied with feathers and painted red. The quiet kid who kept to himself was already getting a reputation for being eccentric—and extremely talented. When he became a member of the Tomcats, Jimmy quit school. All he wanted to do was play.

After a big fight with his dad and because he couldn't find himself a decent job, Jimmy got it into his head to join the army. He figured he would be drafted anyway, but if he volunteered he would at least be able to choose his post. "What Jimmy wanted," Al recalls, "was one of those 'Screamin' Eagles' patches [as a parachutist for the 101st Airborne] and so the sergeant tells him, 'Well, to do that you have to enlist.' So Jimmy upped and volunteered before he got drafted."

Jimmy left his steady girl, Betty Jean, and headed for basic training at Fort Ord in California, then was stationed at Fort Campbell, Kentucky. He got lonesome right off the bat, writing a lot of letters back home. He didn't like being told what to do, but he seemed to enjoy the thrill of parachuting. Jimi wrote to his dad that he would try as hard as he could "so that the whole family of Hendrix's [sic] will have the right to wear the Screamin' Eagle's patch of the U.S. Army Airborne." A little over eight months later Private First Class James Marshall Hendrix won his much-desired patch, and he wanted out. One of the many rumors that have sprung up about Jimi was squelched by sister Janie. Supposedly after a few tries with the army psychiatrist, Jimmy went so far as to break his ankle on a parachute jump. The truth is, he injured his back and got his discharge in July 1962.

Instead of going back to Seattle, Jimmy and his army buddy Billy Cox decided to take their chances in Nashville, and the two musicians wound up playing the club circuit, backing artists like Carla Thomas and Curtis Mayfield. Jimmy was getting a lot of attention, already experimenting with feedback and nurturing his innate flamboyance. In the spring of 1963 Jimmy went on the road with "Gorgeous" George Odell and wound up spending two years backing various black performers on the "chitlin circuit," driving hundreds of miles without much pay. But Jimmy soaked up the music, playing behind major black acts like Solomon Burke and Jackie Wilson. When a New York promoter caught Jimmy stealing someone's thunder at a club one night, he convinced him to take his guitar to Manhattan.

Luckily one of the first people Jimmy met upon arriving in Harlem was a former girlfriend of Sam Cooke's, a stunning street-smart lady named Fay. She and Jimmy began a tempestuous fling almost instantly. Many years later Fay told *Gallery* magazine, "All our activity took place in bed. . . . He was well-endowed, you see . . . He came to the bed with the same grace as a Mississippi pulpwood driver attacks a plate of collard greens and cornbread after twenty hours in the sun. He was creative in bed too. There would be encore after encore . . . hard driving and steamy like his music. There were times when he almost busted me in two the way he did a guitar onstage." In between steamy bouts, Fay took Jimmy around town, introducing him to all the right people, and late in December of 1963 the twenty-one-year-old was hired for his first sessions with Lonnie Youngblood, a sax player.

Things began picking up: Jimmy won first prize at the Apollo Theater Amateur Night. He met Sam Cooke. He got a gig with the Isley Brothers. Jimmy didn't much like the sideman mohair suit uniform, but he enjoyed the travel, and he loved to play. He toured with the Isleys until he was fed up with the routine and went back to Nashville. In January 1965, going by the name Maurice James, Jimmy landed a gig with Little Richard, but it didn't last long. Jimmy was just too compelling to stay in the background. He played briefly with Sam and Dave and, after a short stint with Ike and Tina Turner, headed back to New York. It wasn't easy but Jimmy was committed. In a letter back home, he told his dad that as long as he still had his guitar and amp, "no fool can keep me from living." Even though Jimmy couldn't even afford to feed himself every day, he vowed he would "keep hustling and scuffling until I get things to happen like their [sic] supposed to for me. . . ." When he heard Bob Dylan's *Highway 61 Revisited,* Jimmy headed in a new direction. He left Harlem for Greenwich Village and started writing his own soul-searching prose. After a few dates with Curtis Knight, Jimmy finally got his own lineup

together, calling the band Jimmy James and the Blue Flames. They made about seven dollars a night playing at the Café Wha?, and though Jimmy was penniless and starving, he was getting a name for himself. He played for a few nights with John Hammond, Jr., at the Café Au Go Go, where British rock royalty—the Stones and the Beatles— got their first shocking

Jimi Hendrix: "Here I come, baby . . ." (ROZ KELLY/ MICHAEL OCHS ARCHIVES/VENICE, CALIF.)

dose of the remarkable guitarist who played his Strat upside down and with his teeth. Without even realizing it, Jimmy was shaking up the music world.

Jimmy lived with different girls during this period, and one of them, Diane Carpenter, claims to have had his child—a daughter, Tamika, who is now in her late twenties. There was a paternity suit, but Tamika has never been formally recognized by the Hendrix family. In 1969 Jimi Hendrix supposedly fathered another child in Sweden, called Little Jimi by his mother, Eva Sundquist. The twenty-five-year old, who looks uncannily like Big Jimi, is now suing the Hendrix estate.

One of Keith Richards' girlfriends, Linda Keith, turned Chas Chandler on to Jimmy, knowing Chas was about to leave his post as bass player for the Animals to go into management with Animals manager Mike Jeffrey. Chandler knew right away that he wanted to work with Jimmy, and after some initial hesitation (he always seemed to lack self-confidence, especially about his singing), Jimmy agreed to go to England when Chas promised to introduce him to Eric Clapton. When he arrived in London on September 24, 1966, Jimmy called his dad in Seattle at four in the morning. "He told me, 'Well, I'm over here in England now and I'm auditioning for a bass player and a drummer. It's just going to be a trio and I'm gonna call it the Jimi Hendrix Experience, and I'm gonna spell my name J-I-M-I.' I said, 'Well, that's a little different!'" Al remembers telling Jimi that the call was going to be expensive and then they both started crying. Al was so excited that he forgot to tell his son that he had remarried.

This is where Kathy Etchingham enters the picture. Jimi got together with the nineteen-year-old the very night he arrived in London. I meet up with Kathy for drinks in a pub near her home in the English countryside. She appears to be a genteel English lady in her mid-forties, dressed in tweeds, who dotes on her teenage kids. She gets fire in her eyes when she talks about Jimi Hendrix. "Jimi said, 'I want to talk to you, I think you're beautiful,' the usual line." She smiles ruefully. "We all went back to the hotel and had drinks. 'Shall we go to my room?' he said, and I stayed the night. The next morning Linda Keith got the maid to open the door, whereupon she grabbed his guitar, held it over his head, and off she went with it!" Kathy is quite gleeful with this recollection. "When I first met him all he had was a guitar in a case, a couple of satin shirts, a jar of Noxema, and a bag of rollers. I used to set his hair in rollers." Jimi eventually got his guitar back from the scorned Linda and spent a large part of the next three years with

Chatting it up with Jimi Hendrix's dad and sister Janie in Seattle. (VICTOR HAYDEN)

Kathy Etchingham. "Jimi had a great sense of humor." She grins. "The English have a dry sense of humor, and he picked it up, slotted in *very* quickly."

Chas was true to his word, and not only did Jimi get to meet Eric Clapton, he had the rare opportunity to jam with Eric's group, Cream, at a concert in London. When Jimmy launched into Howlin' Wolf's "Killin' Floor," Eric just walked to the side of the stage and stood there dumbfounded. It wouldn't be long before the best guitar players in England found themselves trying to keep up with Jimi Hendrix. After hearing Jimi play at the club Blaises, Jeff Beck said, "I think I'll go get a job in the post office."

Jimi held auditions and was soon fronting a trio with bass player Noel Redding and drummer Mitch Mitchell, having already signed management papers with Chandler and Jeffrey. Nobody mentioned Mike Jeffrey's shady past and supposed hushed-up mob connections. Besides, who knew what was going to happen? Bands didn't really think about money in the sixties and were usually kept in the dark about contracts and deal making.

The Experience played some French dates with pop star Johnny Hallyday and headed for the studio, where they cut "Stone Free" and "Hey Joe." Chas worked out a deal with the Who's managers, Chris Stamp and Kit Lambert, to release future Experience records on their new label, Track, if the first single on Polydor was successful. It was, entering at number thirty-eight on the U.K. national singles chart the last week of 1966.

During a gig in Germany, Jimi was yanked offstage by overzealous fans and got pissed off during a gig when he found that his guitar had been damaged. He went nuts and smashed the guitar and the stage to pieces. When the amazed audience ate it up, Jimi decided to put the destruction into his already-flashy act—a tongue-in-cheek version of what the Who were already doing.

The Experience were getting rave-up reviews in the British press and packing houses almost nightly, but Jimi Hendrix remained a soft-spoken, shy, and private man. Meanwhile Chas was trying to establish Jimi as the madman of rock, and accomplished this when *Disc* and *Music Echo* dubbed him "The Wild Man of Borneo." He did look incredible with his electric hair, gold-braided Victorian military jacket, and tight velvet trousers, but despite impending fame and glory, the only thing that ever seemed to matter was the music. And he had unique goals. In January 1967 Jimi told *New Musical Express,* "I want to be the first man to write about the blues scene on Venus."

His music was coming from a place to which few had dared venture. A British journalist let the tape run after an interview, while Jimi was talking to Eric Clapton: "Music, man, it means so many things. It doesn't necessarily mean physical notes that you hear by ear. It could mean notes that you hear by feeling or thought or by imagination, or even by emotion. . . ."

The second single, "Purple Haze," was obviously written about Jimi's frequent forays into the land of LSD, but he wisely told the press the song had come from a dream about walking around under the ocean. Jimi had, in fact, been experimenting with various illegal substances for quite some time. "Purple Haze" went to number three on the charts, followed by a third smash, "The Wind Cries Mary," written after a horrendous argument with Kathy (her middle name is Mary).

The first time Jimi burned his guitar, journalist Keith Altham says the band was backstage trying to figure out how to stir up the Finsbury Park audience, when Altham pulled a lighter out of his pocket and jokingly suggested Jimi light up his guitar. Lighter fuel was produced, and the rest is legend.

The first album, *Are You Experienced?*, reached new dimensions and is still impossible to categorize. It soars. In "Foxy Lady" Jimi announced, "Here I come, baby, I'm comin' to *getcha!*" and a million girls opened up their arms.

His concerts were becoming more free-form, and like one of his inspirations, jazz great Ornette Coleman, Jimi never played the same solo twice. He played behind his back, on the floor, with his teeth, shoving, pushing, humping the speakers while roadies struggled to keep them upright. The night he boggled minds and split open hearts at London's Savile Theatre by starting the show with the just-released Beatles song "Sgt. Pepper's Lonely Hearts Club Band," an astonished Paul McCartney was in the audience, along with Pete Townshend and Eric Clapton. At the end of the set Jimi threw his guitar into the audience, and on the back of the white Fender Jimi had written a love poem:

> May this be
> Love or just
> Confusion born out of
> frustration wracked
> feelings—of not
> being able to
> make true physical
> love to the
> Universal gypsy Queen
> True, free expressed music
> Darling guitar please
> rest. Amen.

After altering the course of music in Britain, Jimi headed back to America to play the Monterey Pop Festival, a three-day love fest for the free-love generation, which was being filmed by director D. A. Pennebaker. Jimi's only request was that he bring along good friend Brian Jones to introduce the Experience. He wandered through the trippy-hippie crowd with Buddy Miles, Eric Burdon, and a very high Jones, ingested an intense new drug, STP, and painted his new Strat, looking forward to kissing the California sky. "I'm so high, living on my nerves," he told Burdon. "The spaceship's really gonna take off tonight." The Experience was scheduled for one of the final slots on Sunday night, and the Who were so petrified at the thought of following Jimi that Papa John Phillips flipped a coin to find out Who would follow whom!

As legend has it, when Jimi lost the toss, he stood up on a chair and played mind-altering guitar while everybody stood by and gaped.

Brian Jones introduced Jimi as "the most exciting performer I've ever heard" and the Experience attacked the stage with a frenzied combination of rock/blues/jazz/Dylan that completely totaled the agog audience. Jimi rode his guitar, had sex with it, prayed to it, and then "sacrificed" the newly hand-painted Strat by squirting it with lighter fluid, killing it with fire, and then raising it from the dead. Pity the poor Mamas and Papas, who had to step onto that charred stage to close the festival. The *Los Angeles Times* said that after the Monterey spectacle, Jimi had "graduated from rumor to legend." As the Experience went on to stun American audiences, they found that nobody wanted to follow them or open for them. After one show at the Fillmore in San Francisco, the headliners, Jefferson Airplane, just hid out until the Experience left town.

The band ripped up the Whiskey-a-Go-Go in Los Angeles. I was there—the entire building was full of raging, unearthly sound. But as the Experience changed the frequency in L.A., Mike Jeffrey was booking them on a tour with the Monkees. What could he have been thinking? The screaming teenybops just didn't get it, and Jimi played most of the gigs with his back to the audience. Jimi did get friendly with Peter Tork, but the Experience lasted only a few days with the TV pop stars. Jimi's sense of humor surfaced when he told *NME* that he thought the Monkees were replacing him on the tour with Mickey Mouse.

When asked by *Open City* magazine about "sexual and violent" live shows, Jimi responded, "A lot of people think what I do with my guitar is vulgar. I don't think it's vulgar sex. . . . It's a spontaneous act on my part, and a fluid thing. It's not an act, but a state of being at the time I'm doing it. My music, my instrument, my sound, my body are all one action with my mind. . . . " Jimi was still tripping on psychedelics, his mind wide open to astrology, numerology, the *I Ching*. During sessions for the second Experience album, *Axis: Bold as Love,* he was even experimenting with the ancient meanings, dynamics, and energy patterns of colors, weaving reds, blues, and greens into his rainbow of pounding sound.

The band played 255 shows in 1967. There was almost too much road travel. After a short Christmas break they were back at it again, and Jimi got into some trouble in Sweden. He had had a few drinks and proceeded to destroy Mitch Mitchell's room and everything in it, putting his hand through the window before Mitch finally had to sit down on Jimi to stop the devastation. The police were called and Jimi was charged with criminal damage and hustled off to the hospital. For such a gentle, spiritual soul, Jimi seemed to have had quite a temper, sometimes taking it out on the women in his life.

Axis went straight into the American Top Twenty, and another successful tour of the United States followed. When I'm asked what my favorite live show is, I always say the Jimi Hendrix Experience at the Shrine Auditorium on February 10, 1968. I felt like part of a levitating congregation in an electric church, awash in colored holy lights, drowning in screaming guitar chords.

When the Experience hit Seattle, Jimi was met at the airport by his father, Al, his new stepmother, Ayako, and her daughter, Janie. Jimi must have been nervous about playing his hometown, because reviews for the show were mixed. But Al seemed to have had fun at the concert: "We were all going in the back door, and of course the security were all around, and a lot of fans around there saw Jimi." Al laughs, wiping away tears. "And we were going in and the guy got this big, large door open, and some of the fans just surged forward and Jimi says, 'You just go on in!' and the security guy said, 'Hey! No!' He was having a hard time holding them back, and ol' Jimi, he's going to let them go on in!" After an uncomfortable appearance at his old high school, the band headed for Texas.

Nonstop life on the road was (and still can be) dangerous and confusing, with kiss-ass strangers offering musicians double doses of all kinds of drugs, which were usually gobbled up for escape, sleep, and to beat off boredom. I remember Mitch taking a handful of downers and then asking someone else for more, having completely forgotten that he had just ingested enough to knock him out cold. And there were internal squabbles. Sometimes Jimi was moody and irritable, taking it out on his constant companions, Mitch and Noel, though Noel seemed to get the brunt of Jimi's outbursts. And there were too many women. Devon Wilson was always around, a wild, wiseass black beauty, always on the hustle, but Jimi had a hot spot for her. He had a problem saying no and regularly had several girls on his arms, in his lap, and under the covers. And they were constantly at each other's throats. There were riots at every gig. Every night was full of chaos, and everybody wanted a piece of it.

At the gig in Montreal a drunken Jim Morrison tried to get up onstage and help Jimi out, but Jimi wasn't interested. "Hey, do you know who I am? I'm Jim Morrison of the Doors." Jimi responded, "Yeah, I know who you are, and I'm Jimi Hendrix." A friend of mine saw Jimi jamming at the Scene club and recalls Jim Morrison "slithering" across the dance floor to the stage, crawling up Jimi's body, and attempting to unzip his pants. She says it was obvious Morrison wanted to give Jimi head, but that Jimi was into his playing and "brushed him off like an unwanted pest."

Oddly enough, the Experience was booked into the black district of Newark the night Martin Luther King, Jr., was shot, and instead of the usual set, Jimi walked out onstage and said, "This is for a friend of mine," and for a change the audience was silent and tearful. Not long before Jimi died, he was approached by the Black Panthers, who wanted him as a spokesperson, but according to Noel Redding in his book, *Are You Experienced?*, "Jimi was never heavy about being black, he was into being *Jimi*—human being, pop superstar. When his blackness became an issue, he dealt with it, but he never put it out front."

Jimi Hendrix was dissatisfied. He wanted to stretch further than he thought the Experience could go. He was weary of the constant touring, bored with his "wild man" image. And there were problems with Chas Chandler. Jimi felt he was being held down creatively. The sessions at the Record Plant became big parties full of hangers-on looking for a buzz. Chas thought Jimi's LSD taking had gotten out of hand, claiming that Mike Jeffrey and Jimi were spending too much time in the acid zone together. Mike, whose prime concern was making money, soon became Jimi's solo manager. A whole lot of money was being made, but where was it going?

I spoke to a friend of Jimi's, Alan Douglas, who now runs the nonprofit Jimi Hendrix Foundation, and he told me a story about Jimi's first hundred-thousand-dollar offer. "It was all booked. He called me up one night and said, 'I gotta talk to ya.' I said, 'Come on over,' and he's sitting there all night long telling me he's getting a hundred thousand dollars in Cleveland and what are the kids gonna think? I said, 'Just go play. It shows respect for your talent.' After hours of conversation, he slept on the couch in the back room. Gerry Stickells [the road manager] calls at six and says, 'I'm coming over with the limo at seven-thirty for an eight-thirty plane.' I woke Jimi up, gave him a cup of coffee, and we're walking downstairs and he was in front of me. There's the limo driver, uniform on, standing there with the door open. Jimi takes three steps up the stairs, hesitates, turns right, and runs down the street, and nobody saw him for two days! He ran, he ran his ass off. I looked down the street and he was gone. Mike had the police out."

More touring of Europe and the States, one tour running into the next, a stoned-out crazy blur. At JFK Airport Jimi was thrilled to see Jerry Lee Lewis and offered his hand to the Southern rock legend. Jerry Lee snubbed Jimi. It wasn't the first time Jimi had had to face racial prejudice. Many hotels and restaurants had refused him entrance. In Mitch Mitchell's book, *Inside the Experience,* he says, "Noel and I never really understood the pressures an American black person went through. . . . Hendrix wouldn't go in certain restaurants or stores with us. We'd say, 'Hey, why not?' and he'd go, 'No, I just do not want to go in there. . . .' The potential racial problems were also magnified by people disliking not just Jimi for being black, per se, but because he was playing with two white boys." Jimi seemed to have no color at all, said Kathy Etchingham: "Even though he helped break down the barriers, he didn't see color and neither did anybody else."

By the time the third album, *Electric Ladyland,* was finished in November 1968, Jimi, Mitch, and Noel had decided to take a sabbatical from one another. Jimi spent some time in Los Angeles before returning to London and moving into Handel's former home with Kathy Etchingham. Jimi was thrilled to be residing where Handel had composed his masterpieces and vowed to compose some of his own. To a reporter Jimi said, "This is where Handel used to live. He's got a blue plaque outside the door. I swear I'll never need a plaque to remember me by."

The Experience reunited for another tour of Europe, and in Copenhagen a young ice-skating teacher, Monika Danneman, was about to take her place in rock-and-roll history.

It has taken me quite a while to find Ms. Danneman—who was with Jimi the night he died and claims to have been his fiancée—and even longer to convince her to give me an interview. It seems she's been raked through the rock-and-roll coals recently and is hesitant to say another word about the day Jimi Hendrix died.

My trip to East Sussex is a pain in the butt. The trains have been rerouted due to pounding rains, and I find myself bouncing through the storm in a crowded bus. Monika is a slim, angular, soft-spoken platinum blonde, sort of ageless but I suppose in her late forties. As I enter her cottage, "Little Thatch," I'm surrounded by many, many images of Jimi—beautiful, frighteningly realistic paintings done by Monika. I am taken by one in which Jimi is lying in a pool of water reaching out for a slim blonde who stands above him. Monika offers me a grilled cheese sandwich and a cup of tea, and as her cat purrs at my feet, I ask how she and Jimi met. It's a story of two different worlds colliding— the sheltered ice-skater and the scary rock god meeting at a hotel bar and seeing mutual stars. Monika went to a couple of Jimi's gigs with him and, after spending time with Jimi, realized he was "a very gentle, kind, considerate person." She went to London a few months later, and though Jimi was still living with Kathy, Monika says he was spending a lot of time with her also. Kathy begs to differ. "She knew him for only four days," she insists. "It's well documented, and nobody will argue that he was on Brook Street with me. There was no sign of this woman. In fact, I had never met her. She met him in January '69 in Dusseldorf, and she didn't meet him again until September 15, 1970, and he was dead by the morning of the eighteenth."

In her clipped accent, Monika tells me Jimi was "deeply spiritual": "The spiritual path came through in his music." Jimi had started calling his music "electric church music," and in April of 1969 he told the *International Times,* "Jesus shouldn't have died so early and then he could have got twice as much across. They killed him and then twisted up so many of the best things he said. Human hands started messing it all up and now so much of religion is hogwash." On the bedside table, according to the interviewer, Jimi had a massive array of drugs and alcohol that he kept dipping into during the course of the interview. He told another journalist, "I've wanted to go into the hills sometimes, but I stayed. Some people are meant to stay and carry messages." Jimi didn't have much time left.

In May 1969 Jimi was busted for possession of heroin and hash resin at the airport in Toronto, where he was charged and then released on ten thousand dollars' bail. Jimi, who had no interest in heroin, swore that the drugs had been planted, and with the trial scheduled for December 8, a seven-year sentence loomed over Jimi's head like an invisible curse.

At the end of a blistering Experience set at Mile High Stadium in Denver, Jimi told the awed audience, "This is the last gig we'll ever be playing together." It was news to Noel, and even though he had been working with his own band, Fat Mattress, he was deeply hurt by Jimi's public announcement and flew straight back to London. Mitch would continue to play drums with Jimi off and on until Jimi's death.

Jimi was weary of being a rock star, very much needing to recuperate from the constant stresses. He needed time to expand and explore, telling one journalist he was tired of "being a clown." Mike Jeffrey rented Jimi a rambling ranch house in Woodstock (Mitch called the place an "obscene mansion") and it was soon full of an ever-expanding assortment of musicians bearing cocaine and psychedelics. Jimi started painting, he cruised around in his new silver Corvette, he even attempted some horseback riding. Calling his new group "A Band of Gypsys," Jimi delivered a loose, freewheeling set at the Woodstock festival, concluding with a searing version of "The Star-Spangled Banner" at six A.M. Monday morning while the muddy groovers packed up to go home.

There were too many people at the Woodstock house, and Jimi was under pressure to deliver another record while everybody was living well and getting high on his largesse. All the drug taking was creating a tense paranoia, and despite making fortunes around the world, Jimi never seemed to have enough money. Mike Jeffrey was about to buy a Manhattan recording studio in Jimi's name—Electric Lady—and Jimi began to suspect Mike of ripping him off and talked often about leaving him. As a favor for some of Mike's mob pals, Jimi opened a club called Salvation, only to be kidnapped by supposed mobsters and taken to a hideout for a couple of days. It was all a big screwup and Mike Jeffrey rushed in to save the day, but the damage had been done to Jimi. Who could he trust? Monika says Jimi was living in fear. "After he was rescued he wondered how Mike knew where he was. Then it clicked with Jimi that it was a setup by Mike to scare him. Jimi was constantly trying to get away. There were various threatening things happening." Monika says it was too dangerous for Jimi to bring her to New York. "Jimi thought Mike was capable of anything and might use me for blackmail," she told me, adding that Jimi just couldn't up and leave Jeffrey. "Besides the contract there was loads of unreleased material, and for Jimi, losing control of his music was the biggest crime—that's why he was fighting, trying to find a way out, at the same time realizing there was nothing in his bank account. He wanted to investigate and was getting threats because of that. He even felt the drug planting in Toronto could have been Mike trying to teach him a lesson."

Alan Douglas, who was working with Miles Davis at this time and hooked

Jimi up with jazz musicians like John McLaughlin, says that Mike was having a change of heart. "Somewhere along the way he took some acid or something, and he was changing his sense of values. Jimi was very intelligent, he knew when he was being conned in a second. The agents wouldn't set up the tours in [geographical] sequence, everybody was taking it off the top, and Jimi wasn't making any money. Mike wasn't paying enough attention to that. And Mike didn't give Jimi time to rest; he had no time to write, to record. Before he could finish overdubbing, he'd be pulled out of the studio, on the road. No time for contemplating. All these ideas kept popping in his head. He only had time to begin but never to finish. I think at the end Mike began to realize that it wasn't right."

The Jimi Hendrix Experience with a couple of friends. (MICHAEL OCHS ARCHIVES/ VENICE, CALIF.)

Jimi may have told Judge Joseph Kelly at his December trial in Toronto that he had outgrown drugs, but as soon as the not guilty verdict came down, a very relieved Jimi went out and got bombed. He continued to hassle with Mike Jeffrey, who wanted him to re-form the Experience; he rehearsed the Band of Gypsys; he flew to England in May to try to talk Kathy Etchingham out of getting married. Monika says this was when Jimi called and proposed to her. "Naturally it made me happy because it meant he wanted not just a boy-girlfriend relationship, but even a step deeper than that."

The Band of Gypsys toured the United States, and when Jimi hit Seattle, he spent time with his family before heading off to Hawaii, where Mike had arranged for him to play and appear in a youth-oriented film called *Rainbow Bridge*. The film's director, Chuck Wein, is an old friend of mine, and he recalled the night Jimi filmed the rambling, spontaneous monologue about seducing Cleopatra and making love to her in front of the Great Pyramid.

"The whole point of *Rainbow Bridge* was to get Jimi's inner process to reveal itself a bit," Chuck enthuses. "He was so much more profound than anybody ever understood. Look at the lyrics—they're initiatory. He challenged people. Instant in your face, and either you go for it and live to be a friend or you're out. There was so much intensity. On the night we were going to do his scene, he was real solemn. He said, 'Nobody gives a fuck what we do here anyway. Nobody has a clue about spirit, it's worthless trying to do anything as part of "the message," so why don't we just kill ourselves?' He proposed a triple suicide, which I was not about to start taking seriously." I had always assumed Jimi had been high on acid for that scene, but Chuck assures me otherwise. "All he had was a bottle of rosé wine."

With Jimi's million-dollar studio, Electric Lady, finally completed, he started recording "The First Rays of the New Rising Sun" and by August had completed several new tracks. The haunting ballad "Angel" was written about his mother, Lucille, after one of his many dreams about her. "Dolly Dagger" was for Devon Wilson. In fact, she was in the studio, and you can hear Jimi say, "Watch out, Devon, give me a little bit of that hell, eh?"

Right in the middle of the sessions, Mike booked Jimi a tour of Europe following an appearance at the Isle of Wight festival in England. Jimi was exhausted and staggered through Sweden, Denmark, and Germany, and when his bass player, Billy Cox, suffered a paranoid breakdown and went back home to his parents, Jimi decided to spend some time in England. Although he checked into the Cumberland Hotel, Monika says that Jimi asked her to rent a private flat so they could "have some peace." She also insists that Jimi wanted to hold a "really big" press conference to announce their engagement, but because her father had just suffered a heart attack, she didn't want to, as the shocking news might have killed him. "So I said, 'I just can't do it—on maybe the death of my father,' and he understood that completely, but he was very upset, I was very upset. At the end Jimi talked to my mom, asking how long until he could do the press conference, and my mom said, 'Wait till tomorrow, tomorrow might be better.' And it went on for a few days—he never made it because he died."

On September 14 Jimi went to see her at the private flat in Notting Hill, and the following night the couple went to Ronnie Scott's club, where Kathy Etchingham says that Devon Wilson kicked Monika right out of her chair. (I believe it. Devon crashed my twenty-first birthday party and stole all my presents!) On Wednesday, the sixteenth, Jimi spent the day with Monika, and she claims he was with her the entire night, but according to Chas Chandler, he and Jimi had a business meeting, and Alan Douglas maintains that Jimi then spent the night with him and some friends and drove Alan to the airport the following morning.

On September 17 Monika took some photos of Jimi in the backyard, holding a basket of flowers. "He was full of plans," she says. "He was working aggressively, attacking the old view of himself. The photographs of him in the garden show him very naturally [as] the gardener. He just wanted to show his natural side and not this image that had been following him for years." I ask Monika if Jimi seemed content the last day of his life. "He was very happy, making plans in regard to us getting married, having children. He had already chosen the name for our first son—translated, it was Thunder. I was at that time still very conservative, so to name a child this way was very unusual. I was so much in love with him, I said all right. If he wanted that name, that name it would be." Then the couple went shopping, where, oddly enough, they bumped into Kathy Etchingham and then Devon Wilson, who invited Jimi to a party that night. He accepted. Monika says he was going to the party to tell Devon to leave them alone. Kathy Etchingham says that is "utter claptrap."

At one A.M. Monika drove Jimi to Kit Lambert's party and he asked her to pick him up in half an hour. People already at the party, however, said that Jimi got there much earlier than one A.M., and when Monika called on the intercom, he didn't want to leave but finally went downstairs after several buzzes. Chuck Wein says he has it on eyewitness authority that Jimi went to the party that night to see Devon, so that he could tell her he loved her and say goodbye to her.

Mitch Mitchell says he called Jimi at the Cumberland, inviting him to jam with Sly Stone at the Speakeasy about midnight, and Jimi had enthusiastically agreed. When Jimi didn't show, Mitch says he had an odd feeling that was "hard to define."

Monika says she and Jimi stayed up talking until past dawn. "He had a huge amount of faith in God and the higher power. I just loved listening to him because the things he told me were so amazing! He couldn't find very many people who were interested in that, and for him it was very, very important. He was in both worlds, he was on a higher plane." She says she fell asleep in Jimi's arms and woke up a little after ten A.M., to find him sleeping soundly. Knowing he had smoked his last cigarette, she went "quickly to a shop not far away," and when she came back with the cigarettes, Jimi was still asleep, but she noticed "some sort of something dripping out of his mouth." When she attempted to wake him up and wasn't successful, Monika says she realized Jimi was in trouble. She called Eric Burdon's hotel to speak with a friend of Jimi's, Alvinia Bridges, "who was very much with musicians," trying to locate Jimi's doctor, but Alvinia didn't know who Jimi's doctor was. "I told her Jimi was sick and I couldn't wake him up, and I had found in the meantime that there were some sleeping tablets missing—nine altogether—and she said, 'Get the ambulance.'" According to Eric Burdon's autobiography, Monika called him "at the crack of dawn," and in an interview with the fanzine *Straight Ahead,* Eric said that when he told Monika to get an ambulance, "she argued about it, saying that there [were] incriminating things in the flat, which I guess she took care of."

Monika says that when the ambulance man got there (at 11:27 A.M.) he checked Jimi's eyes and assured her that everything would be all right, that "most likely in the afternoon we could both walk out of the hospital and would be laughing about the whole affair." It didn't quite happen that way. "They didn't seem worried, so I wasn't worried," she insists.

Reg Jones and John Sua, the ambulance crew, told a different story to journalist Tony Brown: They remembered finding the door ajar, and nobody home except Jimi, who was lying on the bed. "It was horrific," said Jones. "He was covered in vomit. There was tons of it all over the pillow—black and brown it was. . . . We felt his pulse between his shoulders, pinched his earlobe and nose, shone a light in his eyes. But there was no response at all. I knew he was dead as soon as I walked into the room." Monika says she rode in the ambulance with Jimi. "He was still alive and they recorded the death almost an hour later when he got into the hospital. Some people say I was not in the ambulance. How could I have known which hospital to go to? They didn't go to the hospital which was the nearest because at that time in the morning they were full up and we were directed by radio to the other hospital." John Sua says that Monika was not in the ambulance; the only people present were "me and the casualty, and Reg the driver. Nobody else." In 1992, the London Ambulance Service conducted their own investigation of Monika's allegation, and concluded: ". . . it is apparent that the ambulance men acted in a proper and professional manner. There was no one else, except the deceased at the flat . . . when they arrived. Nor did anyone else accompany them in the ambulance to St. Mary Abbots Hospital."

According to Monika, she waited around the hospital for some news. "Some time later a sister came to me and said that Jimi's heart had stopped but that everything was all right now and not to worry, but I could tell the doctor was not taking anything serious. That's when I said I wanted everything to be first class. They didn't know who Jimi was because I didn't tell them, but I did tell the doctor at that moment, 'Listen, this man is a very famous composer and musician, you have to do everything you can do.' Much later I did find out that there was no first-class treatment at all in this hospital. It didn't exist. While they were treating him I went twice into the room. One time I saw them working on Jimi and they chucked me out, the next time they chucked me out immediately. In one statement the doctor said he came unconscious to the hospital. A little bit later he said Jimi must have died in either the flat or the ambulance. Later he made a statement I couldn't believe—he said that Jimi must have died hours before! They wouldn't have tried all kinds of treatment on him if he had been dead for many hours! I said to myself after reading that statement, 'What kind of doctor is he? Under what kind of care was Jimi at that time?'

"I had promised Jimi a lot of things—one of the things was that, if he died, I would help to look after him for three days because he didn't want to be buried alive. I can't go into it, it's too deep. Because I was not married to him, the next best thing I could think to ask was to see Jimi. They allowed me to see Jimi and my tears were just streaming, but the minute I saw Jimi in this little room, I just had to stop because he had a smile on his face and he looked so alive. There was no agony, it was just like he was asleep and had a beautiful dream." But according to Doctor Seifert, who spoke with writer Tony Brown, this lovely scene never took place. "No one would have been allowed to look at him, or stand over him," the doctor insisted. "That would never have been allowed." And when Brown asked Monika who identified Hendrix's body, she contradicted herself. "As far as I know, Gerry Stickells [Jimi's road manager]. I didn't want to see him. They asked me, but I just couldn't." Hmmmm.

Still, I commiserate with Monika. No matter what kind of relationship she had with Jimi, she was obviously in love with him and must have been completely devastated. "I went from seventh heaven into hell," she says sadly. "He was the love of my life."

Eric Burdon recalls calling Monika back the morning of September 18: "'Monika, it's Eric. Listen, just do what I say and don't ask any questions. Phone an ambulance, now, quickly!' She came back at me with 'I can't have people round here now, there's all kinds of stuff in the house.' 'I don't care, get the illegal stuff and throw it down the toilet, do anything you can, but get an ambulance now, we're on our way over.'" When I ask Monika about Eric's recollections, she says, "Eric Burdon is so identified with Jimi that he lost a bit—the reality."

Kathy Etchingham says she believed Monika's story at first, but after reading a manuscript supposedly written by Monika years later, she "smelled a rat." "I realized she didn't know Jimi at all! Describing how he rolled joints! I knew and everybody else knew that Jimi couldn't roll a joint! I was the joint roller!" So Kathy went straight to her lawyers, and eventually to Scotland Yard, who began a new inquiry into Jimi's death—twenty-three years later. I ask why she thinks Jimi left Kit Lambert's party that night and went back to Monika's flat. "She must have come back and demanded that he go with her. She had his favorite guitar in the car and he would have gone if his guitar was any way at risk. Monika's been seeing Al Hendrix twice a year for twenty-four years. She's convinced the old man that they were great lovers, about to be married, and he gave her a letter that this is true," Kathy states with horror. "She uses this now to prove she was the great love of his life." I ask Kathy if she thinks there was some kind of foul play. "I don't believe there was a conspiracy to kill him, but Monika could have done more to save him. I think it was simply a catalog of falling errors. Gerry Stickells says he was called between eight-thirty and nine A.M., and when you consider that the ambulance wasn't called until eighteen minutes past eleven—what's going on? She wasn't even on the ambulance." Kathy shows me a stack of legal documents signed by doctors and ambulance men. "The ambulance men say she wasn't there when they arrived, the door was open and just the body on the bed, covered in vomit, and he was dead on arrival at the hospital. They confirmed he was definitely dead."

The Accident and Emergency Admissions officer at the hospital says he never even made out a patient's admission card for Jimi because he was never officially admitted, having been pronounced dead on arrival. Dr. Seifert said that even though Jimi was taken into casualty as a matter of routine, he remembers that the monitor was "flat."

Monika tells me she welcomed the new inquiry. "Scotland Yard said that if they had been able to prove Jimi had died earlier, they would have reopened the case, but when they found out what had been said at the inquest twenty-four years ago was the truth, they decided not to. They looked into whether Jimi died a few hours earlier, which is a shame, really, instead of 'Why did he die?'"

Though the cause of death was officially declared as "inhalation of vomit due to barbiturate intoxication," blaring headlines around the world announced that the wild man of rock had overdosed on downers. And why had Jimi Hendrix taken so many sleeping pills—nine times the prescribed dosage? Recalling my own encounter with Mitch Mitchell (among others!), I figure Jimi took a few tablets, then took a few more without remembering the first handful. A friend of mine recalls giving Jimi a couple of Mandrax tablets a few nights earlier, and an hour later he asked her, "Where are those Mandies?"

One of the numerous surrealistic paintings of Jimi that Monika painted after his death.
(COURTESY OF THE MONIKA DANNEMANN ESTATE; © MONIKA DANNEMANN)

Since Jimi had no will stating otherwise, his body was flown to Seattle for the funeral, which was held on October 1 at the Dunlap Baptist Church. Hymns were sung, brother Leon read a poem, a family friend read the eerily prophetic lyrics to "Angel," the last song Jimi recorded, describing what his angel told him: "Today is the day for you to rise . . . You're gonna rise." Then Jimi's fellow musicians, friends, and admirers tearfully filed by the open casket (Noel and Mitch held hands as they viewed Jimi's body) before it was taken to Greenwood Cemetery, where Jimi was laid to rest near his own "angel"—his mother, Lucille.

Jimi had written a song the night he died, "The Story of Life (Slow)." These are the final two verses:

> *I wish not to be alone*
> *so I must respect my other heart*
> *Oh, the story*
> *of Jesus is the story*
> *of you and me*
> *No use in feeling lonely*
> *I am you searching to be free*
>
> *The story*
> *of life is quicker*
> *than the wink of an eye*
> *The story of love*
> *is hello and goodbye*
> *Until we meet again*

When interviewed at Jimi's funeral, Mike Jeffrey said, "Last week I was looking at a film script Jimi was working on, and in the margin he had written, 'Don't raise me up; I am but a messenger.' . . . He realized the power of the soul, as one of his own songs said. . . . To my mind his music was the music of the new religion." On March 5, 1973, Mike Jeffrey was flying to London to find out if he would be inheriting Jimi's U.K. royalties when the DC-9 crashed, killing all forty-seven passengers. Soon after Jimi's death, Devon Wilson, who had become addicted to heroin, fell through a plate-glass window and died. When Monika Danneman's book, *The Inner World of Jimi Hendrix,* came out in 1995, Kathy Etchingham took her to court again, claiming that Monika had repeated allegations that Kathy was "an inveterate liar." (Kathy had previously sued Monika for libel for those allegations and won. Monika had to pay a thousand pounds in damages and costs.) Two days after she was found in "contempt of court," Monika was found dead in her fume-filled Mercedes, near her lovely little cottage in Seaford. Sad, sad, sad. Said Kathy, "I'm sad that it should all end like this."

Alan Douglas recalls the time he took Miles Davis to see Hendrix play. "Miles was freaked. He said, 'What the fuck's he doing?' He couldn't figure him out. I'll never forget the day I played Jimi for Dizzy Gillespie, and he just didn't say anything, just got up and walked out of the room. I didn't see him for a few days and when I did he said, 'I don't want to talk about it. I can't talk about it.' Jimi amazed them so much, they didn't know where he was coming from, or how to get there. Jimi used to go so far out that you'd think he'd never make it back, but the sucker always found a way back in. He flew without a net."

Jimi Hendrix often spoke about being a messenger. His hope was that his music might somehow pierce our hearts and heal our souls. He finally did go so far out that he couldn't find his way back in, but he did us all a huge favor— he left his music with us.

RICK JAMES

■

Slow

Draggin'

with the

Devil

■

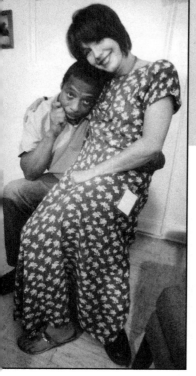

took a chance and sat on Rick's lap in
il. "Where else," he asked, "can you
arn to make bombs out of
othpaste?" (ADAM W. WOLF)

One hundred degrees and climbing. Another blinding California heat blast. On the long sweaty drive out to the California Rehabilitation Center, I wonder about air-conditioning facilities in jail. Am I wearing the proper attire? What do you wear to prison, anyway? I've never visited a locked-up human being before, and I'm one nervous chick. This particular locked-up human being gives me the willies. The heat is making me feel light-headed and wary as I watch anxiously for the freeway exit that will lead me to CRC. It has taken weeks of back-and-forth phone calls to set up this interview with the "Super Freak" king of funky stuff, Rick James, incarcerated in September 1993 following his trial for the assault and false imprisonment of two Los Angeles women.

In his slay-day Rick James was a brilliant, innovative monster music maker—singer/songwriter/producer—a swaggering, strutting, pompous picture of decadence and dastardly obsessions in spangled skintight jumpsuits and Jheri curls.

When his debut album, *Come Get It,* went double platinum, Rick moved into a mansion once owned by William Randolph Hearst. "I was livin' large," he said, "inside a *Citizen Kane* fantasy." Many smash hits followed, and "Super Freak," the song most closely associated with James ("She's a very kinky girl/the kind you don't bring home to mother"), brought all shapes and sizes of adoring, kinky girls into his life. He once told *People* magazine he spent a million dollars in one year "on cars, wine, women, and booze." And cocaine. Lots of it. His partying-down days are a large part of legendary rock lore. Nobody parties like Rick James.

After winding my way into the hills of Nowheresville, I find family clumps of every race, creed, and color congregating in front of formidable high-assed gates, waiting for passes to visit loved ones. I go round and round through the barbed-wire parking lot in search of a space for my T-Bird as steam rises in waves from the baking pavement. I have a one o'clock appointment. It's 12:58.

After spending over eight months in the CRC drug

Rick James—slam-bam punk-funk sensation. (MICHAEL OCHS ARCHIVES/VENICE, CALIF.)

rehab program while officials decided whether he should be formally admitted, James has just been ruled ineligible to complete the program due to his assault conviction, and may have to do a five-year prison stint instead of being freed in a few months. I bet he's seriously pissed off. The kind of sex 'n' drugs 'n' rock 'n' roll superfreak freedom Rick James had must have been oh-so-hard to give up. I read in the *L.A. Times* that his attorney, Mark Werksman, was baffled by the court's decision. "They just looked at the whole package and said, 'We don't like this guy.'" As I finally slide into a parking space, I wonder if I will.

There were two separate cases against Rick James and his girlfriend, Tania Anne Hijazi. In the first, in July 1991, twenty-six-year-old Frances Alley alleged that James burned her leg and knee area with a crack pipe, applied alcohol, slapped her across the face with a gun, and burned her groin and torso area with a hot knife. In her testimony about the night in question, Alley—a friend of a friend of James who had left a rehab program in Georgia and was working in a massage parlor in Beverly Hills—alleged that James was "going to teach her a lesson" because he "couldn't find his eight ball." "He made me take my clothes off and sit in the chair," Alley testified. "He ordered Tania to go to the kitchen and heat up the knife until it was red hot." James then supposedly tied her to the chair with neckties. "Rick poured alcohol all over my knees. He started smoking crack. Every time he took a hit, he held part of the crack pipe to my knees."

According to her testimony, James slapped her across the face with a handgun, saying, "No one fucks with Rick James in his house." She then testified that he burned her with a Bic lighter and kept reheating the knife with the lighter or a candle, burning her inner groin area, and from "the abdomen to the pubic line." "He burned Hijazi twice on the back for smoking outside. I then went into the bathroom and put cold towels on my burns. We then went into Rick's room and smoked crack." Besides the torture and mayhem accusations, Frances Alley testified that James had forced her to perform oral sex on his girlfriend. "He told me to lay back and Tania was going to take care of me," she said. "Then Tania went down on me. He made me do the same to her. I was laying on my back, she got on top of me and kind of straddled me and starts peeing on me, on my burns and stuff. It hurt real bad.

Q. Were you still afraid?

A. Of course I was afraid. I was grossed out. It was nasty.

Q. Then what happened?

A. Then he told me to put my fingers in her.

Q. Did you do that?

A. No. Every chance she and I got, we faked it. We faked giving each other head.

Rick's publicist has already told me that he won't discuss the case and claims Rick is innocent of the charges. I had wanted to ask him about remorse and repentance. Oh well.

I show a weary security guard all of my identification and then wait on a sticky brown Naugahyde couch for Lt. Annette Hissami, the warden, to walk me down to her office, where we will meet Inmate N63609. It's way past one o'clock now and the sweat is running down my sides.

When she finally appears, I'm surprised to see that Hissami is a young, attractive lady in a pretty cool-looking suit. She leads me to her office through the penitentiary grounds, explaining why CRC, with its red-tiled roof and pink walls, looks more like a luxury hotel than a jailhouse. Back in the thirties it had been the Lake Norconian Club, visited by Hollywood celebrities and political bigwigs. "The inmates do the gardening," she says proudly as we pass through perfectly manicured rosebushes. "This is a *medium*-security prison," she emphasizes, and we settle into her office and wait for the inmate to be brought down from his cell. Lieutenant Hissami graciously offers Adam (my photographer) and me a Pepsi. We accept. It's now two o'clock. She tells me I was lucky to get this interview, that James is going back to court next week.

During the "*ménage à trois*–type thing," Frances Alley alleges, James told her, "I needed to learn how they live in California. He said it was nothing. Everybody in California does that, and I was sexually ignorant and inexperienced."

According to Alley's testimony, when James realized the extent of her burns, he sent her to a pharmacy. "The lady looked at my leg and said, 'Honey, honey, we can't do anything for that.' Then I went to the L.A. Free Clinic. They said, 'We can't do anything. This is way too severe. You need a burn unit.' Then we went to Cedars [Cedars-Sinai, a hospital in Beverly Hills]." After doctors examined Alley, the police were called. But she didn't want to press charges at that time. Apparently James wanted to apologize to Alley and she went back to his house. "It must have been the crack," he said and allegedly gave her a check for $320 made to cash. "Here, take this," he told her. "Go buy yourself something nice. I will take care of you. I will buy you a ring as big as your head." She stayed a few more days, getting high, and James didn't bother her anymore. "When everyone was asleep, I left without making a noise," she testified. "I came back the same night. Rick started calling me a slut, a whore, and a cheap nasty bitch for telling everybody that he did this to me, and I better backtrack, go back and tell all these people that I had supposedly told, that a pimp did it to me. Not Rick James. A pimp. He said he would rip out my tongue. He then said he'd pay five thousand dollars to have me killed. He also said he'd have acid thrown on my face on the street if I didn't clear his name. It was his girlfriend that opened her mouth, not me. All right. It was his girlfriend. It pissed me off so bad. The next day I went and pressed charges."

There's a power outage in Lieutenant Hissami's office while we wait for inmate N63609. No air conditioning for a while. She gets on the phone and twenty minutes later it's blessedly cool again. She keeps looking at her watch, wondering when the prisoner will be brought down for his interview. After making a few calls she finds that the prisoner has been taken to the wrong place. Oh boy. The prisoner is going to be in a great mood for this interview. It's pushing three o'clock.

The second incident supposedly took place in November 1992 at the swankpot St. James Club and Hotel on the Sunset Strip. Mary Sauger, an old friend from the music business, testified at James's trial that she met him and Tania Hijazi to discuss James's new record label, and after they all got high on cocaine, Rick and Tania began to argue. Sauger tried to leave and was supposedly slapped by Hijazi and James repeatedly until she lost consciousness. They allegedly brought her back by throwing water on her, but continued to strike her. Then James choked her. She was able to leave after being held for twenty hours.

Rick James and Tania Hijazi in court. His prayers didn't work—Rick was convicted of assault, imprisonment, and furnishing cocaine. (TOM RODRIGUEZ/GLOBE PHOTOS)

She testified that she received a phone message offering money to "shut up," but she, too, went to Cedars-Sinai and the police were called. James was arrested two weeks later.

Of all the charges brought against him—assault with a deadly weapon, aggravated mayhem, torture, false imprisonment by force, forced oral copulation, assault with a deadly weapon, sale or transportation of a controlled substance, terrorist threats—he was convicted of only three: assault and false imprisonment of Mary Sauger and furnishing cocaine to Frances Alley. The jury deadlocked eleven to one on the other charges, and in September 1993 he was sentenced to five years in prison. Prosecutors declined to retry James on the other charges, and he pleaded no contest to a simple assault charge against Alley. Tania Hijazi pleaded guilty to assault charges against Sauger and was sentenced to four years. (Her sentence was later reduced due to improper contact between an investigator in the district attorney's office and Frances Alley [a.k.a. Michelle Allen] while Alley was in jail before Hijazi's trial.)

The phone rings in Lieutenant Hissami's office. "He'll be right down." She smiles. She seems relieved. Adam turns on his lights and fiddles with his cameras, looking slightly embarrassed in his orange pantaloons. I take several deep breaths. As Rick James finally strides through the door, I can see that he's not amused and grin way too brightly at him. We shake hands. He's put on some weight, and of course the long, braided dreads have gone the way of the studded knee-high boots and foot-long spliffs.

He's wearing jailhouse blues but looks healthy and, as I expected, is heartily pissed off. He sits down across from me, and I decide to use the irritation and ask about the court date next week. "I've been excluded from this program," he says matter-of-factly, his eyes spitting fire. Why? I query. "Because of who I am. That's the real reason. They say, quote, if you're convicted of any violence, you're not allowed here. I have one charge of assault, and of giving cocaine. On my arrest sheet, of course, there were a lot of allegations and alleged reports of torture and mayhem, kidnapping, and all that kind of shit. They say you're not allowed here with excessive violence. Me and my attorneys, we're going to debate that. Number one: I was never convicted of this excessive violence, and on the second hand, I'm going to show that there is biasness [*sic*] within the realms of this institution." My eyebrows raise in indignation, and he continues. "There are people here with murder, mayhem, arsons. I know a guy that has been retained with an arson and a double murder. And he was *convicted* of these charges. The judge and the D.A. are aware of what went on in my trial . . . all the lies and false allegations that went on in my case. There are some set laws here that an institution has to follow. If they're going to retain some people and exclude others on the basis of their name, race, or . . ." Celebrityhood, I offer. "Right," he agrees, warming to me a bit. "Follow the law or don't follow the law. I've done everything that's required of me to be here. I'm a drug addict. My case revolved around drugs. I had maybe three or four months left to do here, so you can imagine how devastating it was to find out I was going to be excluded from the program. Justice is justice. Just because you're a drug addict, it doesn't make you not human. Just because you're incarcerated, it doesn't make you a true prisoner. You know what I'm sayin'? Yes, incarcerate but rehabilitate. We subpoenaed the warden and a lot of the records. I'm not gonna take this lying down, I've never laid down, I'm not gonna lay down, and I never will lay down."

Rick James learned a lot of life's hard lessons as James Johnson. His mother worked the numbers racket, and his dad, James Johnson, Sr., deserted his family of seven, leaving them in the all-white projects of Buffalo, New York. Rick lied about his age and joined the U.S. Naval Reserves, thinking it would keep him out of Vietnam. But when he got placed in active duty in 1966 and was assigned to a ship headed for the war zone, he fled to Toronto, where, as Ricky Matthews, he joined up with Neil Young and found peace and love with his first band, the Mynah Birds.

Eventually the band went on to Detroit and amazingly landed a deal with

Motown, but Ricky's soul swoon was short-lived. Motown didn't want an AWOL act on the label. In 1971 James did eight months in a navy brig in Brooklyn and then bummed around Europe for a while, fronting a blues band, the Main Line, in London. After becoming Rick James, he jammed with California dreamers like Jim Morrison—eating up acts like Sly Stone whole—then put his own soulful jazz, R&B shock-rock band together and went back to Motown. In 1978 he cowrote "You and I," his first big-time single, and the rest of *Come Get It*. He was an overnight slam-bam, punk-funk sensation—an outspoken sensation. In 1981 James told the *L.A. Times* that what he really wanted to do was play rock and roll, but as a black man he couldn't. By then he had three smash albums under his studded belt but was unable to make the move, afraid of losing his black audience and unwilling to take the time to win over a white following. When hosting a Grammy show, James spoke out against MTV's reluctance to show videos by black artists, but by the time MTV began to wise up, Rick's career was stalling. He fell out with Motown in 1985 and his first album for Reprise barely made the charts. By the time M.C. Hammer sampled the "Super Freak" riff in "U Can't Touch This," Rick James and his pipe were trapped in his gloomy room.

I tell Rick that he will soon be back in the news, and he's very enthusiastic. "Yeah. It's gonna be top, *top* news. If I can get past O.J. Simpson," he adds with sarcasm. "There have been a lot of people here with criminal records worse than Rick James. Especially because I was not convicted of a lot of these things."

They deadlocked, right? I inquire. "Yeah, somebody could testify 'he made love to a pig, he brutally beat this pig, he brutally beat the woman who owned the pig, and he had sex with a horse'—in other words, a person could say outrageous things, then when you get to court, the judge finds you not guilty of all these things, but when you get to prison, they say, 'We can't keep you here because it says you made love with the pig and beat the pig and beat the pig's owner.' If you're going to build your laws around allegations and fabrications, then what the hell's really goin' on?"

All this talk about barnyard animals and sex is sort of freaking me out, considering what he's in here for. I look for a way to change the subject, but he's not finished. "It looks like I came here and was a fuck-up. I find myself trying to defend myself. I've done everything a man can possibly do. I haven't gotten any write-ups, I haven't been in trouble, I graduated top of the CCP drug class [Civil Commitment Education Program]." I admit that it doesn't make much sense. "No, it doesn't make sense, and we're going to fight it."

There's something about this guy that I like. He's full of heated charisma and bad-assed attitude that nine months in prison hasn't even slightly dented. "Don't get me wrong," he continues. "I'm very bitter about how I've been treated. There are some things I want to bring into the light, but I'm glad I came here. This is the longest time I've been straight and sober. But if I wanted to get high tomorrow—my drug of choice—I could do it in this penitentiary. It comes with the territory. But I fight the feeling."

I ask if he's treated like a celebrity by the other inmates. "When I first got here it was pretty hectic," he sighs, "signing a lot of autographs for people. After they got used to me, it became second nature that I was here. I became just another inmate." Rick James, king of superfunk, just another inmate. Has it given him humility? "Oh, I was humbled when I was at L.A. County, sleeping in a six-by-six cell with rats and roaches. Humbility [*sic*] became quite easy." He's relaxing, calling me by name. "When I lost my mother in 1991 of cancer, Pamela, that was a very traumatic experience for me. When one loses his best friend, that's a humbling, humiliating experience. You start to question your spirituality, your religion, you question God. Even with my addiction, there was this layer of humility [*sic*]. When I was acting out the Rick James persona, one of the things about him, he was not a humble cat! That was

The Superfreak behind bars. (ADAM W. WOLF)

a facade, Pamela, you have to understand."

Why did he need a facade? I ask. "I chose to create that persona. I read about the Masai warriors in Africa and put braids in my hair. They used to weave horse and lion hair into their braids. They believed if you wore the hair of powerful animals, you would gain their power and spirit. After I saw Kiss onstage, I wanted my show to look like the Fourth of July. The persona of Rick James was wild and crazy—sex, drugs, and rock and roll. . . ."

I remark that I think it's odd how he refers to himself in the third person. "I relinquished Rick James," he announces with relish. "I set him free and buried him. He nearly killed me! I've always third-person'd him. It was always strange to hear my mother say 'Rick.' My name is James Johnson. Rick never sat with me right. It was always uncomfortable." I ask if he considers himself a violent person and he shakes his head. "If anything I consider myself nonviolent. I'm from the hippie era—peace, love, groovy. You know where I'm coming from. I found the violence coming out of me later, after my mother passed away. Not so much violent, but angry." Were there things left unsaid? "There were a lot of things left unsaid and undone," he says sadly, leaning closer to me. "My cocaine addiction was running so rampant, I didn't know how to stop it. I didn't understand the sickness." Perhaps he was too high? "That's one reason," he concedes. "And if I was sick, everybody around me was. Everybody did it. You can't have rock and roll without drugs, you can't have rock and roll without sex. It's a vicious circle and I became angry. I was angry when I was young. I was mad about living in a white tenement slum, run off from school by Polish people. I was mad about my mother being in the numbers rackets, working for the Mafia. I was angry about the fact that my father would beat my mother on a daily basis, and that my mother would take it in turn and beat on me. I was an abused child. I was mad about all those things, very bitter and very angry."

I ask if he's still in touch with Tania. "Yes. She's incarcerated, and God knows she's having her share of problems. There's a lot of jealousy with those women up there. They're like really tripped out, you know, that we have a relationship. Tania's my best friend. We've been able to elevate past the bullshit. Plus, we've got this son. He's being taken care of by a nanny. His name is Tasmin, like a Tasmanian devil." He smiles. "We call him the Tas Man." I get down to it and ask if he feels justice was served in his case. "As far as my being here? Absolutely not. I'm not saying this because of my ego or profession, but if anybody needs help with drug addiction, it's me. . . . Here I am trying to do the best I can to deal with it and they won't let me." Rick James also told me as an aside that he had done drugs on occasion with many other people, including O. J. Simpson.

When did the drug bug bite him? "I started smoking Mary Jane when I was fifteen. And I was snorting an ounce a day when I was recording albums in the seventies and eighties. I sat with a bottle of Black Jack, a bottle of Quaaludes, and an ounce a day." It sounds a bit excessive to me. Did that seem like the normal thing to do? "It seemed like the way to make a record!" He laughs ruefully. "Everybody did it. Some of them took that extra hit, that extra pill, and died. Jimi, Janis, a few others. A lot of us died inside. When I was smoking five or six thousand dollars of dope a week, I think subconsciously I was looking to die. I was too chickenshit to take a gun to my head or jump off a building." I empathize. It must have been a horrific way to live. "'Sucking on the devil's dick,' that's the way I looked at it. I'd look at the fire and the insanity, and the fact that I hadn't left my room in three or four weeks. I'd look at the deviants around me, how low I had sunk. The room was my gloom."

Did the deviants around him take advantage of his superstardom? "Sure," he admits sourly. "I supported everybody who came around me. I had millions of dollars in the bank, Rolls-Royces up the ying-yang, houses all over the place. I bought cars for everybody, clothes and Learjets. I was very sick. That was my way of showing love. If I did these things, maybe everybody would forget about Rick James and see who was really me. Maybe they would put this fake, false image aside, forget the braids, forget what color I was, the way I looked, forget what I wrote about, and see some other person. Maybe they'd like him better. It was all an illusion. It was all bullshit, but it sounded good at the time." When did he see that it was bullshit? "Somewhere in the eighties," he says after a moment of pondering. "Me and Steve Tyler were in rehab together. We've been in rehab twice together, and I'm so pissed! He's staying sober and I've relapsed left and right. Finally I got some therapy. Finally I let a person look inside of me." Does he accept responsibility for all the fuckups? "I accept responsibility for everything that has happened to me. But I know, and most people who know me know, that without the drugs, most of these things wouldn't have happened. I was dancin' with the devil, Pamela, we were doin' the cha-cha-cha. We were doin' the slow drag." What an image. But it's over now, right? I say hopefully, "Now you live one day at a time?" He laughs heartily. "I live one millimeter of a second at a time!"

The guard comes to collect the prisoner and take him back to his cell, but while Lieutenant Hissami is on the phone, looking the other way, I jump up on his lap and Adam snaps a photo. I don't know what's possessed me.

We shake hands again, and I ask one more question: Does he feel he has people to make amends to? And Rick James bellows, "Hell, no!" Then James Johnson continues, "Yeah, there are people. That's so far off. I've got to get myself together first, Pamela. I gotta wake up to the sunshine, throw my son up and down, live my life like none of this happened. I just needed a period of time to get this stuff out of my system. It took this incarceration to do that, and I'm thankful. I'm back in touch with God, *my* God, my Lord. I thank him for bringing me here." Then Rick James is back. "Where else can you learn how to make bombs out of toothpaste and machine guns out of toothbrushes?"

It's a few days later and Rick James has gotten some superbad news. Judge Michael Hoff told the Grammy Award winner that he was lucky he wasn't headed to prison for a dozen years, perhaps even for life, calling the shorter sentence (five years and four months) "a gift" (because of the discovery of the investigator's improper contacts with Frances Alley). James's lawyer, Mark Werksman, was mighty angry. "For fifteen years he has been known as the Super Freak. They rejected the Super Freak. They never bothered to learn about the real Rick James." Or the real James Johnson, I suppose.

Today he's serving out his very hard time in Folsom Prison. The experts who evaluated Rick James agreed that he would have benefited from the state's drug program and probably would not have hurt the women if he hadn't been sucking on the devil's dick.

BRIAN JONES

■

Standing

in the

Shadows

■

The flaxen-haired founder of the Rolling Stones, Brian Jones, the foppish dandy—bastard son of Oscar Wilde and Muddy Waters—was the first of the rock-and-roll giants to die under debauched, drug-related circumstances. It was a brutal wake-up call for the love generation.

I met him only once. Just a kid in the Rolling Stones candy store, I was hanging around the Ambassador Hotel, circling the hallowed Hollywood bungalows, waiting for a glimpse of the gods, when Brian sauntered by wearing thick red cords and a black turtleneck sweater. It was a gloomy day and his blond mane shone like a halo. When he said hi to me, I was struck dumb by the dazzling incandescence. He had an amused expression on his face, haughty and expectant—too much awareness. Later I peered into his bungalow window and saw Brian wearing skimpy underwear and a long red scarf around his neck, being very naughty with two Spanish ladies wearing black garters. My teenage heart was pounding at the illicit sight. There was banging at his front door, interrupting his pleasure fest. As I watched, agog, Brian threw open the door, grabbed hold of a broom with one hand and his privates with another, and said, "If you girls don't get the hell out of here, I'll drag you in here and fuck you." The teenybops scampered back into the sunshine, squealing with a mixture of fear and delight. Wow. Brian Jones said the "F" word with such aplomb, and it was only 1965.

Brian Lewis Jones was a huge fan of R&B and already appearing in clubs and coffeehouses when he got his first important gig, playing a mean slide guitar with British bluesman Alexis Korner in April 1962. In the audience that night were two very impressed Dartford lads—Mick Jagger, a bored student at the London School of Economics, and delinquent art pupil Keith Richards. Fascinated with his rooted musical vision and haughty bravado, the two friends successfully auditioned for Brian's new band, which he named after Muddy Waters's "Rollin' Stone Blues." Apparently Mick and Keith despised the name but had to accept it because, after all, it was Brian's band.

Brian's band went on to ignite the music world—to scare, shock, and dismay parents of panting teenage girls and stir tepid authority figures to unparalleled rage, and the press to taunting headlines: WOULD YOU LET YOUR DAUGHTER MARRY A ROLLING STONE? The Beatles had long hair but they also had little matching suits and smiled for the cameras. The Stones were a dangerous-looking lot—scruffy and snarling, mismatched and menacing. As their records dominated the charts, the Stones' reputation as a real threat to proper society grew.

It was a deserved reputation. By 1965 Brian had already fathered three illegitimate baby boys with three different adoring girls (all in all, Brian would have six sons). In fact, two paternity suits were filed at the same time. Pat Andrews alleged breach of marriage, enticement, and association for toddler Mark Julian, and Linda Lawrence sought a lump-sum settlement for baby Julian Mark. Pat Andrews said, "I would never have gone public about Mark until I read it in the papers about Linda, and their call-

Brian Jones, the Prince of the Monterey Pop Festival. (HENRY DILTZ)

ing the baby Julian Mark." What was Brian thinking? Already a hard-core drinker, Brian plunged headfirst into drugs, flamboyantly leading the way like a psychedelic, bejeweled Pied Piper.

Brian was undoubtedly the leader of the band in the early days, golden-haired and gorgeous, by far the most popular Stone. He could pick up any instrument, from a saxophone to a sitar, and master it in thirty minutes. There were even times when Brian threatened to "get rid of Mick" because his voice was too weak to sing night after night, and the two of them constantly vied for the spotlight, each attempting to upstage the other. But when Mick and Keith began to write songs together, it affected Brian's confidence in a big way. He felt left out, pushed aside, unimportant, and pissed off about it.

Still, Brian invented and then epitomized the British pop star, reveling in the opulent, hedonistic Rolling Stone lifestyle. A friend of mine, fourteen years old when she and Brian had their fling, had this to say: "Brian was totally self-obsessed—in the mirror with the silks and satins, brooches, pins, floppy hats, frock coats, feathers, and velvets, capes to the floor. He couldn't get out of the bloody mirror, he was so in love with his image. But he was brooding and uncommunicative, and talked to you like he was holding court, very grandiose. And he would take anything—Tuinals, Mandrax, acid, always mixing methedrine and whiskey." I asked what sex with him was like, and my friend smiled. "Oh, he was wild in bed. A wild man. Highly sexed. One night he wanted me to pee on him, and I wouldn't do it. He was insistent on it, for hours he harped on it. He was so disappointed. He wanted a three-way with Anita, but I wasn't into it. She saw us at a party together and broke a bottle of champagne over his head. Brian and I went back to the hotel and had sex anyway."

Into the libertine stew waltzed Anita Pallenberg, a mischievous, wanton, clever minx who would eventually tear out Brian's heart. For a while, however, Anita and Brian were the zenith of rock royalty. After being introduced to him backstage at a gig in Munich, Anita says she "decided to kidnap Brian. . . . He seemed to be the most sexually flexible. I knew I could just talk to Brian. As a matter of fact, when I met him I was his groupie, really. I got backstage with a photographer. . . . I had some amyl nitrate and a piece of hash. I asked Brian if he wanted a joint and he said yes, so he asked me back to his hotel and cried all night. He was so upset about Mick and Keith still, saying they had teamed up on him. I felt so sorry for him. Brian was fantastic, he had everything going for him, but he was just too complicated."

The reigning couple began to walk, talk, dress, and think alike, taking up astrology and magic, consorting with young dukes, lords, and ladies, turning their high-born admirers on to the potent joys of LSD. Brian felt he had one up on Mick and Keith, knowing they secretly coveted his majestic, lean-and-mean mistress, but deep down he had a wicked fear of losing her. Passionate and volatile, the couple argued about everything, with Anita usually coming out the victor. Ultimately, Brian challenged her with his fists one too many times, and she found solace and compassion in the arms of Keith Richards.

The Stones were being relentlessly pursued by British police after a series of sordid exposés in the *News of the World* about their shameless, debauched lifestyles. After a tip, supposedly from this illustrious newspaper, Keith Richards's stately pad in West Wittering was raided. Traces of cannabis were found, as well as four pep pills in Mick Jagger's jacket. This was only the beginning of a dauntless quest to destroy these "menaces to the establishment."

Keith made plans to escape the media tirade and hired Tom Keylock, Brian's burly minder/chauffeur, to drive him to France, and Brian suggested he and Anita join them and extend the trip through Spain and Morocco. Some have said Brian overdosed in the backseat halfway through the drive and had to be taken to the nearest hospital, but it's likely that the thin air affected his asthma, which made him ill enough for the hospital visit. Either way, Anita went on with Keith, leaving Brian to torment himself on his twenty-fifth birthday, sleepless in the South of France. His fears were warranted: Keith and Anita slept together that night in Tangier. Even though Anita met Brian back at the hospital so they could fly to Marrakesh and meet the others, Brian immediately suspected what had happened and dealt Anita the first of many pummelings on the trip. The next day, after observing Keith and Anita eyeing each other by the pool, Brian disappeared, returning with two tattooed Berber whores, and invited Anita to join them. When she declined the offer, he viciously beat her again as the naked prostitutes watched.

Then a plan was hatched that confirmed all of Brian's twisted, paranoid nightmares: Brion Gysin, a friend along on the trip, was told by Mick, Keith, and Tom Keylock that a posse of British reporters was headed for Marrakesh, and to take Brian out for the day to keep him from talking to the press. Brian, excited by the prospect of taping his beloved Joujouka musicians, went happily to the huge town square, getting bombed with two self-proclaimed holy men, the "Hash Head Brothers," taping his precious music, feeling more lighthearted than he had in quite a long time.

Upon returning to the hotel with tapes and pipe in hand, Brian realized he had been abandoned and became frantic, running around the hotel, demanding over and over that the desk clerk make sure no note had been left for him. When he broke down, sobbing uncontrollably, Brion Gysin feared his friend might be suicidal and called a doctor, and Brian was sedated.

This treacherous act on the part of his girlfriend and band mates had a devastating effect on Brian, and a feeling of desertion and loneliness set in from which he never fully recovered. To his friend Dave Thompson, Brian said,

"First they took my music, then they took my band, and now they've taken my love." He checked into Priory Clinic in Roehampton, suffering from depression, but two weeks later had to be out on the road with the Stones. Not surprisingly, Brian quadrupled his drug and alcohol intake, seeking escape from the dire humiliation of standing onstage with Anita's new amour, Keith Richards. Then he was the next Stone to be busted. After being held overnight and charged with "unlawful possession of dangerous drugs," Brian sent his parents a telegram: "Please don't worry, don't jump to nasty conclusions and don't judge me too harshly."

Two of Brian's psychiatrists concluded that he was suffering from paranoia, but what they didn't realize, even though it was often drug induced, was that it was paranoia based on reality. Said *News of the World*'s Trevor Kempson, "Of course, Brian was being set up, all through 1967 and later in 1968. First the police would be tipped off that Brian was holding drugs and a few minutes later the tip-off would come to me. I think that what happened was that someone in the Stones' organization also wanted him out of the way."

After another bust, Brian narrowly escaped several months in Wormwood Scrubs Prison when his psychiatrist testified on his behalf: "It would completely destroy his mental health, he would go into psychotic depression, he might even attempt to injure himself." When he was almost caught with drugs in his Rolls-Royce, Brian leapt from the car, threatening to jump into the Thames. Rescued by his driver, Brian once again checked into the Priory Clinic. He tried to slip away quietly, but as ever, headlines blared BRIAN JONES IN NURSING HOME.

Needless to say, relations with the Stones were strained for Brian, but he had been uncannily accurate in his brutal assessment of the *Sgt. Pepper* copycat album, *Their Satanic Majesties Request,* and was given more musical leeway on *Beggar's Banquet,* which the critics would hail as "Brian's singular triumph." It was to be his last album with the Stones.

On the morning of May 20, 1968, Brian was awakened by pounding on the front door, then a loud crash as three policemen started digging around in his flat. They came up with a piece of cannabis, hidden in an unlikely ball of yarn. Hustled off to Chelsea Police Station, Brian was deathly white, clumsily dressed in mismatched clothes thrown on during his arrest, claiming he was innocent of the charges: The wool wasn't his. Understandably, when the trial got to court, Brian expected the worst.

Brian's defense lawyer was Lord Michael Havers.

JONES: I was asleep when I heard this loud banging at the door. I did not immediately become aware of what it was. A minute might have passed before I knew it was somebody very intent on entering the flat. I put on a caftan-kimono sort of thing, went to the door and looked through the spy-hole.

HAVERS: What did you see?

JONES: I remember seeing . . . three large gentlemen . . . of a sort I don't usually *see* . . . through the spy-hole of my door.

HAVERS: Who did you think they were?

JONES: Police perhaps, or agents . . . I was afraid.

HAVERS: Of the police?

JONES: Yes, since last year I seem to have had an inborn fear of the police.

FRISBY (PROSECUTOR): If it please the court, *inborn* means you've had it all your life.

JONES: Ah, an acquired fear. I went back to the bedroom on tiptoe. I couldn't make up my mind whether to call my secretary or my solicitor. I was very worried.

HAVERS: The police have said that ten minutes passed before they came into the flat. Do you agree with this estimate?

JONES: I can't agree or disagree. Some time passed. Certainly long enough to have disposed of anything I shouldn't have had.

HAVERS: How did you feel when they showed you the resin?

JONES: I couldn't believe it. I was absolutely shattered.

HAVERS: When Constable asked if the wool were yours, did you say, "It might be."

JONES: I never had a ball of wool in my life. I don't darn socks. I don't have a girlfriend who darns socks.

HAVERS: Later when you were at the police station, you said that you never take cannabis because it makes you so paranoid. What did you mean?

JONES: That refers back to the events of last year. The effect of the drug for me was a heightening of experience that I found most unpleasant. That made me very frightened of it.

HAVERS: Would you be advised what would be the consequences of breaking probation by using drugs?

JONES: Yes sir. I have taken no chances.

HAVERS: Had you the slightest knowledge that the resin was in that wool?

JONES: No, absolutely not.

The jury retired for forty-five minutes, bringing back the verdict of guilty, and Brian slumped in his seat. "No, no, no, it can't be true," he moaned. But Chairman Seaton, who had seemed so callous at Brian's previous hearing, rapped his gavel and said, "Mr. Jones, you have been found guilty. I am going to treat you as I would any other young man before this court. I am going to fine you . . . according to your means. Fifty pounds with a hundred and five pounds' costs. . . . You really must watch your step and stay clear of this stuff."

Immensely relieved, Brian grabbed hold of the latest blonde in his life and posed for photographs in front of the courthouse. "It's wonderful to be free," he said. "Someone planted that drug in my flat but I don't know who. I will state to my death that I did not commit this offense."

On a visit to Ceylon, just before the year's end, Brian had his astrological chart done and supposedly received a curious warning: "Be careful swimming in the coming year. Don't go into water without a friend."

Weary of being harassed in London, as well as of being the only Stone who hadn't acquired his own stately manor, Brain bought A. A. Milne's Cotchford Farm, his very own house at Pooh Corner, filling the cozy fifteenth-century farmhouse with priceless antiques, rugs, screens, and tapestries, amassed from his frequent sojourns to Morocco. He would drag friends through the copious gardens, showing off the life-size statue of Christopher Robin, proudly announcing that Milne had buried the original Pooh manuscript under the sundial. Brian slowed down his drug intake, built a music studio, swam laps in his beautiful swimming pool, got friendly with the locals—his life finally on an upswing. And despite his angst over Anita Pallenberg, Brian never lacked for female company, once claiming to have bedded sixty-four women in one month. One blonde had moved into Cotchford with him and, soon after, another had taken her place—Anna Wohlin, a Swedish student with a striking resemblance to Anita. Even though things seemed to be going well for Brian, his precarious position in the band kept his mind troubled. He started putting on weight, the bags under his eyes getting heavier and darker.

Some alterations needed to be done on the house, so Brian took Keith's recommendation that Frank Thorogood, an old school chum of Tom Keylock's, do the job for him. Frank moved into the garage flat, hired several workmen, and renovations began. From the beginning, however, Brian complained about Thorogood, telling his friend Tony Sanchez, "Those builders aren't doing what they're meant to be doing! They act as if they own the place, as

The pool at Pooh Corner where Brian Jones drowned. *(PA NEWS)*

if I wasn't there! People just arrive saying they have come to fix this or that and they stick around for days." The builders soon became party guests, and the renovations took second place to revelry. Cotchford was constantly in chaos. Brian, never one for confrontation, actually let Thorogood move into the main house, bitterly resenting the intrusion, distrustful but saying nothing.

When Charlie Watts, Mick Jagger, and Keith Richards paid a visit to the farm one warm June night, Brian knew he was out of the Stones. Some reports have him begging and weeping, others that he felt relief and excitement about starting up his own band with the likes of John Lennon, Mitch

Mitchell, Steve Marriott, and Steve Winwood. To Tony Sanchez, Brian said excitedly, "We're going to be bigger than anyone would believe," announcing that he wanted to "go back to real rock and roll, and cut out all the commercial crap the Stones are putting out." Brian was offered a hundred thousand pounds on top of his share of Stones royalties, and it was reported that he left the band to work on his own solo projects. Then Brian Jones was replaced by John Mayall's guitarist, twenty-year-old Mick Taylor. An announcement was made soon after that the Stones would play a free concert in Hyde Park. To Anna Brian said bitterly, "I'd probably be the only one they would charge to get in."

On Tuesday, July 2, Frank Thorogood went to the Stones' offices to pick up wages for himself and his workmen and found out a bit of bad news: Brian had requested that all payments to Frank and his builders cease immediately. True to form, Brian had someone else do his dirty work for him. When Frank confronted his boss at Cotchford, Brian made good on his decision to sack the builders, telling Frank that he and his girlfriend, Janet Lawson, were to start packing. Frank demanded that more money was owed him, and an uneasy truce was reached: He and his builders would be paid in full on the condition that they leave the next day.

That night, just before midnight, Brian Lewis Jones, age twenty-seven, drowned in his swimming pool at Pooh Corner.

Despite the fact that Brian was deemed to have drowned while swimming under the influence of alcohol and drugs—"death by misadventure"—the conflicting reports given by the three people with him have caused speculation for over twenty-five years. According to Anna, at about 10:15 Brian was keen to swim and went over to Frank and Janet's to ask them to join him. At about eleven P.M. Brian changed into his trunks and, followed by Anna, got into the pool to swim. Frank swore in his police statement that "Brian was staggering, but I was not concerned because I had seen him in worse condition and he was able to swim safely." Janet Lawson disagreed: "I saw that Brian had great difficulty in holding his balance on the springboard." As to what happened next, none of the three statements confirms the exact sequence, except that the women left the pool area and went into the house before Thorogood, leaving him alone with Brian in the pool for more than a half hour. Then Anna claims that the phone rang and, as she answered it, "Frank came in and picked up the phone in the kitchen, then I heard Janet shout, 'Something has happened to Brian!' I rushed out about the same time as Frank. Janet was there and I saw Brian lying on the bottom of the pool." Janet says that when Frank came into the house, he asked her for a towel. "Then I went to the pool and on the bottom I saw Brian. He was facedown in the deep end. He was motionless and I sensed the worst right away." Thorogood told police, "After we had been in the pool about twenty minutes I got out and went into the house for a cigarette, leaving Brian in the pool. I honestly don't remember asking Janet for a towel. I know I got a cigarette and lit it, and when I went back to the pool, Anna appeared from the house about the same time. She said to me, 'He is laying at the bottom,' or something like that. I saw Brian facedown in the deep end of the pool." Each of the witnesses had a different version of how Brian was pulled from the pool. "I felt Brian's hand grip mine," claimed Anna.

The Stones found out while in the studio that Brian was dead, and though it's been said that Charlie Watts couldn't stop crying, they continued to record and went ahead and taped a spot for "Top of the Pops" that same evening. A few days later the Rolling Stones, featuring Mick Taylor, played the free gig at Hyde Park in front of a gigantic blowup of Brian's face. Clad in a billowing white dress, Mike Jagger appealed for quiet: "Cool it and listen," he said. "I want to say something for Brian." He then read two verses from Shelley's "Adonais," after which thousands of white butterflies were released from cardboard boxes. "Peace, Peace! he is not dead, he doth not sleep! / He hath awakened from the dream of life. . . ."

On November 7, 1993, Tom Keylock went to the North Middlesex Hospital to visit his old friend Frank Thorogood. "When I saw Frank, I feared the worst," Keylock said. "He looked really rough. We started talking and he told me he wanted to put his house in order. 'There's something I have to tell you. It will probably shock you, but we've been friends for so many years that I feel I can tell you.'" Thorogood asked Tom not to speak about what he was about to tell him while he was still alive. "'It was me that did Brian,' he said. 'I just finally snapped, it just happened, that's all there is to it.'" Tom wanted to ask a lot more questions, but Thorogood couldn't continue. He died that night.

Someone else says that Thorogood didn't act alone. One member of the rock group the Walker Brothers said that Brian invited him to a party the night he drowned, and that some of the men at the party were hostile toward Brian, poking fun at him and taunting him. He saw one man holding Brian down in the pool, and another standing on Brian's head to keep him from getting out of the water. It was dark, he said, and he couldn't tell whether or not they were just trying to scare Brian. He left the party to avoid involvement. A. E. Hotchner, the author of *Blown Away,* dug up one of Thorogood's builders, referred to by the pseudonym "Marty." "There was two guys in particular really had it in for Brian," Marty said. "Been on his back for weeks, I mean always making remarks, the rich fag, all that kinda stuff. . . . Anyway, this night Brian was swimming a lot. He could swim good, bounce off the diving board, lots better than any of us lads, and the girls was watching him, also because he was a celebrity they sort of gave him attention. These two guys got pissed about that—they was drinkin' pretty good by then—it was kind of like when it started, kind of like teasing. Sort of grabbing Brian by the leg and pulling him down, meanwhile saying bitchy things. . . . Then it started to get rough and these lads really got worked up at Brian the more he resisted, I mean really bad-mouthing him now and ducking him and then sort of holding him underwater and keeping him under and then letting him up for a coupla seconds and he was gasping and then down again. . . . They seemed to get more steamed about Brian the more they pushed him down, and I could tell it was turning ugly as hell. Finally one lad wanted to let Brian out, but the other wouldn't let him and they was kind of tugging on him. It got real crazy and the next thing I heard somebody say was 'He's drowned.' That's the first we knew what these guys had done and someone said, 'Let's get the hell out of here,' and we ran for it."

And so the life of Brian Jones was snuffed out. How could it have happened? Even though foul play was suspected by some, on August 7, 1969, Detective Chief Inspector Lawrence Finley said that the police had no further interest in the death of Brian Jones, and the case was officially closed.

Spacey-eyed Brian staring out to . . . who knows what. (LONDON FEATURES INTERNATIONAL)

Brian was buried on July 10, 1969, at the Priory Road Cemetery in Cheltenham, a few yards from the church where he sang as a choirboy. Canon Hopkins, who conducted the service, read aloud to the mourners Brian's own epitaph: "Please don't judge me too harshly." Only two members of Brian's band turned up—Bill Wyman and Charlie Watts.

A few days after Brian's funeral, a beaming Anita Pallenberg announced that she and Keith Richards would soon be parents.

JANIS JOPLIN

■

Buried

Alive

in the

Blues

■

When Janis Joplin overdosed on heroin in a tacky Hollywood motel on October 4, 1970, her death was perceived as yet another nail in the free-loving, hedonistic, swinging-sixties coffin. Jimi Hendrix had died a raunchy death two weeks earlier, but somehow Janis's death was more shocking and unseemly, so much more sordid and ignoble, simply because she was a woman. Her high-priestess hippie crown was quickly replaced with a shameful tiara of thorns.

Janis Joplin made no apologies. With her passion for the frenetic moment and disdain for outmoded, fictitious values, she took a stab at the shaky status quo every step of the way. Proud and uncompromising, Janis was also a severe addict and lived her short life in a state of heightened, frightened hysteria. Her voice was shredded rapture, a howling plea for release. She shared her pain with us like it was a swig from her blessed bottle of Southern Comfort.

A year before her death Janis told a journalist about her early days in San Francisco: "I just wasn't serious about anything," she said. "I was just a young chick. I just wanted to get it on. I wanted to smoke dope, take dope, lick dope, suck dope, fuck dope, anything I could lay my hands on, I wanted to do it, man."

Music kept Janis on the planet for twenty-seven years. She was a doomed diva chock-full of soul. "There's no patent on soul," Janis said. "You know how that whole myth of black soul came up? Because white people don't allow themselves to feel things. Housewives in Nebraska have pain and joy; they've got soul if they give into it. It's hard. And it isn't all a ball when you do."

As a young girl Janis Joplin tried to fit all that soul into her stifling middle-class neighborhood in the fading oil-refinery town of Port Arthur, Texas, but

Janis onstage—the only place she felt safe: "The one thing that felt honest and right." (HENRY DILTZ)

instead she felt like an un-attractive sore thumb. Her mother dolled Janis up in ruffles and organdy, gave her piano lessons, took her to the First Christian Church every Sunday to instill values. She and her younger siblings, Laura and Michael, went on fre-quent trips to the library with their father, who en-couraged them to read the classics and do something meaningful with their lives. When precocious Ja-nis showed an interest in art, she got lessons with the best art teacher in town, even though it was hard on the Joplin bank account. She was raised right, but in school she asked too many questions, wouldn't pay attention to the teachers, didn't show "good sportsmanship." Highly intelligent and un-derchallenged, Janis Lyn Joplin was bored.

In 1957 Janis volunteered at the library, painting posters and bulletin boards, eventually appearing in the *Port Arthur News* with the headline LIBRARY JOB

BRINGS OUT TEENAGER'S VERSATILITY. Even though she joined the Junior Reading Circle for Culture, was a member of the glee club, and sang a solo in the Christmas pageant, during her first year of junior high Janis was already questioning authority. She ridiculed Top Forty radio, preferring black soul music, and when she announced her adamant belief in integration, students accused her of being a "nigger lover." By the tenth grade it was obvious that she would never be a feminine Southern belle—she wasn't graceful and she wasn't pretty—so Janis started hanging with the local bad boys, getting an undeserved "reputation." When she and some male friends took her dad's car to a New Orleans honky-tonk, crossing invisible color lines to hear the right music, they were stopped by the cops. The incident started hushed whispers about illicit liaisons and barroom brawls and Janis became even more of an outcast. She was loud and crude and spoke her mind. She laughed in a screechy cackle, dressed like a slob to hide her weight, and bit her nails down to the quick. Her complexion had started erupting and was giving her horrible grief. Next to the bouffanted, polished Maybelline debs, Janis felt ugly, cursing her "little pig" eyes and horrible pimples. But she had a large ego and was defiant and uncompromising. Seemingly the slings and arrows from her peers did little to alter her hell-bent course, but deep down Janis was confused and hurt.

Somehow Janis got good grades, even though she didn't make it to school all the time, and she graduated in May 1960. She worked part-time as a waitress and sold tickets in a local theater. Her Modigliani-inspired oil paintings were on the walls of a beatnik coffeehouse, and she even managed to sell a few. Discovering the alternative, edgy Beat poets Kerouac and Ginsberg helped Janis feel that she might not be alone in the world after all. She started speaking in hipster slang, she found the blues, and when she started to sing, her own voice astounded her.

Janis also learned about the numbing glory of booze by reading the Beats. In fact, most of her literary icons seemed to have been alcoholics. She somehow equated creativity with liquor and began her lifelong passion for the bottle. It became her constant companion and most trusted ally. She would never put it down.

Hoping to please her increasingly distraught parents, Janis tried a semester of college in Beaumont, Texas, but she did a lot more partying than studying. When she got back to Port Arthur, the parties were getting crazier and they didn't stop. There was even a brief stint with a psychiatrist. Frightened for their wild-eyed, skittish daughter, the Joplins shipped her off to Los Angeles to stay with Aunt Mimi and Uncle Harry. After a few weeks with her relatives and a fleeting job as a keypunch operator, Janis met a guy at the bus stop headed for Venice, and she went with him. Excited by Venice's post-Beat energy and array of hip, racially mixed coffeehouses, Janis rented a funky little apartment near the beach and started singing. She probably dabbled with methedrine and maybe even heroin during this period, but her fascination with the fading glory of Venice didn't last long. Janis hitchhiked to the hallowed Beat ground of City Lights Bookstore in San Francisco, then headed back to Texas.

She tried going back to college, took a job in a local bowling alley, even went intermittently to church, but having gone from beer to Thunderbird to bourbon, Janis needed more and more excitement to keep herself buzzing. She spent a lot of time across the river at Louisiana blues bars, getting into trouble, pissing off the locals, rubbing her newfound hipster consciousness in their holier-than-thou faces. Once again she took her father's car on a weekend excursion, this time to Austin, and found that she liked it there. When she told her concerned parents she wanted to study at the University of Texas, they hoped for the best and Janis enrolled at UT in Austin during the summer of '62.

School was just a sidebar to Janis's burgeoning social life. One of the few to make it onto the dean's list of designated "troublemakers," she fell in with a cynical, reckless, intellectual crowd, who lived in a funky complex called "The Ghetto." Like Janis they had come to be proud of their outsider status, prodding and poking sacred Texas traditions, reveling in the havoc it created. She had only short-lived romantic relationships, and even though Janis seemed to have a voracious sexual appetite (which included several flings with women), she was seen by her clique as just "one of the guys." Despite her loud-mouthed bravado, she felt helplessly plain, unfeminine, and insecure. Janis dressed in black, grew her hair long and wild, didn't wear makeup, and littered conversations with her favorite word, "fuck." She also sang and played autoharp at a converted gas station called Threadgills, and despite her growing rep for eccentricity, people were starting to pay attention. "Her voice was magnificent," recalls Clementine Hall, friend and founding member of the Thirteenth Floor Elevators, "rich and clear, with a deep burr in it."

The campus newspaper, *The Summer Texan,* ran a story on Janis titled SHE DARES TO BE DIFFERENT! The favorable article revealed that Janis went around barefoot and wore Levi's to school "because they're more comfortable," and that she took her autoharp everywhere she went "in case she gets the urge to break into song. . . ." The journalist said that the "squares" would most likely call Janis a "beatnik," but that she preferred the world "jivey" to describe herself. "She leads a life that is enviously unrestrained. She doesn't bother to have her hair set every week, or to wear the latest feminine fashion fads, and when she feels like singing, she sings in a vibrant alto voice. . . ."

The crowds loved Janis—she was really getting a feeling for the blues—but there were painful brush-offs when she auditioned at certain bars, because she wasn't slim and doe-eyed like Joan Baez. And despite the *Summer Texan* article, Janis's fellow students were angered by her freewheeling disdain for the values they held on to so dearly. When one of the frat houses jokingly entered her in a school contest for "The Ugliest Man on Campus," Janis was mortally wounded when she found that fellow students were actually voting for her. She felt hemmed in, ugly as sin, and deeply misunderstood.

When a former UT student and fellow liberal, Chet Helms, heard Janis sing at Threadgills, he swore she could be a sensation in San Francisco, where he thought the folky music scene could benefit from her rich, raucous wail. In early January 1963 the two hitched across the country, and just two days later Janis was singing in North Beach at Coffee and Confusion, earning fourteen dollars her first night.

Janis became a regular on the coffeehouse circuit and she and Chet crashed all over town until a couple of fans let her live in their basement. She worked regular jobs sporadically (including a brief stint at the American Can Company), and along with her ever-increasing booze consumption, Janis became a consistent drug user—mainly methedrine. Speed made her feel as if she could accomplish anything. She had flings with men and women, but Janis still felt unsettled and lonesome. In the summer of 1964 she just had to check out the Greenwich Village scene and took off for New York, moving into a hotel full of creative stoners—and quickly becoming one of them. She did a lot of speed, sang in Village clubs, and had a short, lusty affair with a black girl, but by August she was restless and drove her yellow Morris Minor convertible back to San Francisco, stopping just long enough in Port Arthur to worry her mom and dad sick.

According to Bob Dylan, times were a-changing, and Janis felt she was an integral part of the movement, determined to live every second *right now.* She moved into a little dump on Geary Street with a friend, Linda Gottfried, and ravenously pursued her "art." "Janis called herself the first black-white person," Linda said, "a candle burning on both ends," announcing she knew she would die young, often wondering, "When am I going to burn out?"

She listened to Bessie Smith, studied Hesse, Kant, and Nietzsche, hunting the truth while she shot meth, which she felt made her more creative. She even dealt the drug for a while before trying to commit herself to San Francisco General Hospital for being "crazy." They told her she was sane and to go away. Then early in 1965 she fell in love with another speed freak, a well-dressed, intelligent charmer with impeccable manners and a mysterious past. He had big dreams and so did Janis and they connected, but together they shot so much methedrine that their dreams turned into hallucinations. Janis got down to eighty-eight pounds, and her boyfriend actually did wind up in a mental hospital. She visited him daily and the recovering couple decided to get married when he was well enough.

Realizing she had hit bottom, a reformed Janis went back to Port Arthur to ready herself for the upcoming wedding. It seems that deep down she must have desired that idealized notion of normalcy. Back at home, she heartily attempted to redeem her wicked past by enrolling at Lama State, becoming an ardent college student. With her unruly hair tucked into a prim bun, she wore ordinary dresses—with long sleeves to cover the tracks on her arms.

Janis's love arrived a few weeks later and asked Mr. Joplin for his daughter's hand. He seemed to be a sincere, devoted fiancé, spending quality time with the Joplin family before leaving to take care of his own "family business." It wasn't long before Janis found out that her "fiancé" was already married and his wife was expecting a baby! He convinced Janis he was going to get a divorce, and she carried on making her Texas Star quilt, shopping for linens and china while her mother stitched her wedding dress.

Janis saw a counselor about her former drug use, got B's in her boring classes, and waited for Mr. Right, who told her he was bringing her an engagement ring for Christmas. When he didn't show, Janis took the rejection hard. Her last-ditch trip to Normalville hadn't worked and she started spending more time in Austin clubs, belting out her brokenhearted blues, which earned her a great review in the *Austin American-Statesman:* "But the most exciting portion of the program [was] JANIS JOPLIN—the only female performer on the bill—who literally electrified her audience with her powerful, soul-searching blues presentation."

For almost a year Janis had stayed away from drugs, so when she got an offer from old friend Chet Helms to audition for Big Brother and the Holding Company in San Francisco, she thought long and hard before accepting the offer. It's true that drugs were rampant in San Francisco, but Janis had finally realized music was the only thing that made her feel good—"the one thing that felt honest and right," said her sister Laura. Still, Janis made Chet promise to buy her a Greyhound ticket home if she didn't make the grade with Big Brother.

When Janis hit Haight-Ashbury in June 1966, it had been taken over by thousands of rebellious tuned-in, turned-on, dropped-out young peaceniks, swaddled in velvets and thrift-store castoffs, flying high on LSD and creating their own culture. Bands like the Grateful Dead, Jefferson Airplane, and Quicksilver Messenger Service were sharing their kaleidoscopic secrets at the Avalon Ballroom and Bill Graham's Fillmore. Janis's first mentor, Chet Helms, managed the Avalon and ran a rock-and-roll corporation called the Family Dog, and Big Brother already had an avid, tripped-out cult following. All they needed was a chick singer to make it happen. But when Janis walked in, plain and pudgy with a scarred and pitted complexion, the band didn't know what to think.

I recently met with Big Brother guitarist Sam Andrew in the bar of a fancy-schmantzy hotel in San Francisco. He's slim, dressed in leather, his shiny blond-gray hair hiding his much wiser eyes. "She was very feminine," he tells me, recalling the day Janis auditioned. "Texas is a really strange place, particularly the time she grew up. Anything emotional or passionate was real suspect. 'Don't do that. That's not the way to be. You should be a lady.' Getting that all her life—and being so much the other way—must have been confusing." Sam smiles. "When she came to sing with us she was wearing short-shorts, tied at the side. A little cotton cut-off blouse—basic Texas tacky. Nobody knew how to dress then anyway—we were making it up as we went along." The band had misgivings about the terrified, plain-Jane girl from Texas until she opened her throat and cut loose. Janis was hired instantly and six days later played her first gig with Big Brother at the Avalon Ballroom.

In a letter back home Janis said, "I'm not at all sold on the idea of becoming the poor man's Cher," adding that she was really trying to "keep a level head and not go overboard w/ enthusiasm." Janis was concerned that her parents believed that her "self-destructive streak" had gotten the best of her again, and apologized for being a "disappointment" to them. She admitted she understood their fears and even shared some of them. "I really do think there's an awfully good chance I won't blow it this time . . . and please believe you can't possibly want for me to be a winner more than I do. . . ."

The first thing Janis did was to fall in love with Big Brother guitarist James Gurley and, though he was married, the two lived together for a short and blissful time. When the fling was over, Janis became close with James's wife, Nancy, who taught her the art of bead-making, as well as getting her back into the hyperactive rush of speed. As Sam Andrew told me, "It was just the times. There were no boundaries. Everybody was high on something."

Big Brother became the house band at Avalon Ballroom and, along with wives, lovers, dogs, cats, and babies, moved into a rambling pad in the canyons of Lagunitas, where they lived, ate, drank, and shot music. At last Janis felt accepted, even loved, for who she was. In August she wrote her family, "I/we got an ovation," the biggest of the night, which led Janis to exclaim, "Wow, I can't help it—I love it! I'm somebody important. SIGH!! . . ."

With her newfound confidence, Janis started dressing with more aplomb—tight bell-bottoms, boots, spangly blouses, and antique dresses along with ropes and ropes of handmade beads. She was radiant. Instead of getting in trouble for who she was, Janis was being adored, and she bloomed.

When Big Brother played the Mother Blues club in Chicago, Bob Shad offered the band a deal on his small record label, Mainstream, and in September Janis and her boys were in the studio. In late 1966 a couple of singles were released, but even with some good local notices, nobody paid much attention. But Janis wasn't discouraged. She had gigantic hopes.

At a gig in Los Angeles Janis picked up a busboy, a young Peter Tork, at the Golden Bear club, and it took a bit of convincing, but Tork, who later became one of the Monkees, told me about their off-and-on relationship. "Janis made no particular point of displaying her intelligence," he said, "but this came up and she couldn't help setting me straight. She had her bottle of Southern Comfort right there, and I told her she would get 'sclerosis' of the liver. She corrected me on my usage of the word, 'No, it's *cirrhosis* of the liver.'" Peter laughed. "In those days acts were booked for a week, and there we were! For a while every time I saw Janis, she was happy to see me, hugged me, gave me that great big old laugh, and the next thing I knew we were rolling in the hay together. Then one day I caught up with her at a Who concert and she wasn't friendly to me at all, and I said, 'Okay, I get it, she's after one of these *other* guys!' That was that."

Surrounded by colorful, high people, Janis found she was still lonely. She got herself a little puppy and called him George. She worked at staying off speed but still managed to drink a pint of liquor a day. Trying to be productive, she bought an old sewing machine and made herself some velvet clothes. She decorated her pad and wrote probing songs about her new life. She saw a dermatologist about her miserable complexion and started taking antibiotics. She had endless parties. But nothing seemed to take away the loneliness.

Janis had been so deeply hurt by the aborted marriage that men became sex objects to her. She picked up "pretty boys" in the Haight and practiced free love for all she was worth. She had her share of girls, too. One of these girls was Peggy Caserta, who later wrote an X-rated tell-all called *Going Down with Janis.* The opening two sentences: "I was stark naked, stoned out of my mind on heroin, and the girl lying between my legs giving me head was Janis Joplin. She was stoned blind on smack, too, but the junk flowing through her veins and saturating her brain hadn't diminished the skill with which she used her mouth on me." The book is full of hot sex, pledges of love, hard drugs, and jealous rages, but many people close to Janis say that Peggy greatly embellished and exaggerated their relationship.

She may have been brazenly "doing her own thing," but for Christmas Janis asked her mother for "a good, all-round cookbook, *Betty Crocker* or *Better Homes.*" When her aunt Barbara came to visit, Janis put on a bra and played golf, proudly sending her scorecard back home. She seemed to be a complete dichotomy.

Early in 1967, Big Brother had had enough of too-cozy family living and Janis rented an apartment with a friend of Sam Andrew's, Linda Gravenites, and the girls became very close. Linda was a costume designer and saw Janis as a dazzling and exciting performer, dressing her in low-cut satins and antique lace. Janis wore flowers in her hair and even started using makeup. She posed for a "High Priestess of the Haight" poster with one of her nipples showing, and began a fun and flashy love affair with Country Joe McDonald. In her scrapbook Janis wrote, "For a while it was Country Brother and the Holding

Fish." The first hippie pin-up doll and the leader of Country Joe and the Fish would traipse hand-in-hand through the Haight like the king and queen of cool. But their careers got in the way of Cupid. The affair lasted six months.

Discontented and hypersensitive, Janis *needed* continuous attention to keep her even slightly satisfied. She craved it like a drug. Although she may have seemed in sync with the mellow, laid-backward flower children, her desire for success was paramount. Said her roommate Linda, "Janis wanted to succeed in capital letters. On her own terms. To be famous and show everybody." Janis's deepest wish was about to come true.

Big Brother helped to bring in the Summer of Love at the Monterey Pop Festival and, along with Hendrix and the Who, garnered raves that shook up the industry. The reviews in *Newsweek* (which featured a photo of Janis) and *Time* magazine were glowing, reflecting the feelings of the forty thousand who were electrified by Janis's razor-scalding rendition of Willie Mae ("Big Mama") Thornton's classic, "Ball and Chain." She tore out her heart and hurled it into the audience. They couldn't get enough.

She rehearsed with the band every day and played gigs on weekends. Big Brother kept on getting raves, with Janis being singled out as the Second

Big Brother and the Holding Company bring in the Summer of Love with the "High Priestess of the Haight." (MICHAEL OCHS ARCHIVES/VENICE, CALIF.)

Coming of the blues. As a direct result of their combustible Monterey performance, in November 1967 the group signed with Dylan's brilliant, arrogant manager, Albert Grossman, who had a reputation for adoring the dollar and recognizing major talent. His only request was that the band stay away from heroin, which was proliferating in the Haight, and they all agreed. He immediately got Big Brother a high-figure deal at Columbia Records. Janis called him "Uncle Albert" and believed she would finally be taken care of and understood. Grossman did watch over Janis's career but stayed out of her personal life, which was always chaotic. Surrounded by acid- and potheads, Janis still preferred the sweet whiskey Southern Comfort and, as a Texan, held her liquor proudly. Walking in the park with her dog, George, she met an elusive young junkie, and when they got romantically entangled, Janis started dallying with heroin, even after having made that promise to Uncle Albert that she wouldn't.

In December 1967 I dropped a fat blue tab of mescaline and wandered down the brilliant, melting maze of the Sunset Strip into the Whiskey-a-Go-Go to see Big Brother. I oozed down front where Janis was on the floor begging us to take another little piece of her heart. "Take it, take it, TAKE IT!" she pleaded, aflame with furious abandon, nothing held back, nothing left for herself. She left the stage weak and wet. I was full of her passion for days. I was so grateful I got to see her perform.

Christmas was spent with her family. Janis was making money, and along with copies of Big Brother's new single, "Down on Me," she brought generous gifts all around. She caused a commotion in the local 7-Eleven, did interviews with the local press, and suggested that her little brother grow his hair longer. Then she went to Mexico and had a botched abortion. It took her weeks to recover.

But she didn't stop working. Todd Schifman was Big Brother's booking agent at the time. "They were playing the Kaleidoscope in L.A. . . . I get a call from the road manager about six o'clock and he says, 'Todd, you'd better get down here, there's big problems.' The mob had come in, walking around with guns, threatening to cut the wires on the P.A. system, and there was a line three blocks long outside. I go into the dressing room and Janis is lying on the floor, sick. I had to carry her to the phone, and she called the hospital. She had just had an abortion and something was wrong. She was in terrible pain. After the call she laid out on the floor and I told her she couldn't go on. We had a perfect out! I told the road manager to postpone it for a night, but they opened up the doors and all these kids swarmed in. I said to Janis, 'Just so there's no problem, maybe you could go up onstage and tell these people to come back tomorrow.' So I help her up onstage, and I couldn't believe it, she calls the band up there and she says, 'There's some shit goin' on here tonight, guys backstage runnin' around with guns. Well, fuck 'em, we're gonna play for you!' And she did an hour-and-a-half show. You never would have known she was in pain. She could have killed herself, but that's the type of person she was. She told it like she felt it."

Big Brother signed their contract with Columbia in New York after playing a scorching set at the Anderson Theater. Reaction from the press was unexpectedly swift and glorious. The review in *The New York Times* the following day proclaimed, "There are few voices of such power, flexibility and virtuosity in pop music anywhere." Janis veered from frenzied ecstasy to abject insecurity, and she needed constant assurances from her friends and band mates about her appeal. Sure, audiences were eating her up, important journalists were vying for twenty minutes of her time, but was she fat? She was already getting wrinkles, wasn't she? To her folks she wrote: "Wow, I'm so lucky—I just fumbled around being a mixed-up kid (& young adult) & then fell into this. And finally it looks like something is going to work for me. Incredible." In a letter to her roommate, Linda, she said, "Tomorrow (please let me brag—it's just about the only satisfaction I'm getting) I'm being interviewed for a thing in *Life,* and *Look* is going to do us when we get back to S.F. . . ." Success was finally hers, but it didn't make Janis happy. With all her inner tumult, Janis didn't seem to realize that she was shoving the door wide open for women. The *Village Voice* said: "The girl gap is an easy term for a hard problem that's been facing the music industry. The plumage and the punch in the last few years' rock has remained the province of men. . . . Now, with Janis all that is over."

In between recording sessions, Big Brother toured. Janis was getting so much solo attention that the guys felt like her backing group. When Grossman changed the billing to "Big Brother and the Holding Company, featuring Janis Joplin," there was a whole lot of grumbling in the band. And Janis didn't think they were cutting it in the studio, once storming out of a session shouting, "I ain't gonna sing with them motherfuckers!"

At the time of the *Cheap Thrills* (originally *Sex, Dope, and Cheap Thrills*) sessions, Janis had an infamous encounter with Jim Morrison, a bang-up battle that she asked her publicist, Myra Friedman, to play up in the press. Janis told Myra that Jim had been slobbering drunk and had pulled out a "whole bunch" of her hair, and she cracked a bottle of scotch over his head. According to Chet Helms, who says he was there, "He unzipped his pants and put his penis in her face, and she hauled off and whacked him good!"

True to the hippie credo, Janis tried to live smack dab in the moment, telling *The New York Times,* "Maybe I won't last as long as other singers, but I think you can destroy your now by worrying about tomorrow." She prided herself on being totally uninhibited and unconventional, yet was always surprised by the consequences of her actions.

Cheap Thrills went gold in three days, with *Cash Box* calling Janis "a mixture of Leadbelly, a steam-engine, Calamity Jane, Bessie Smith, an oil derrick, and rot-gut bourbon funneled into the twentieth century somewhere between El Paso and San Francisco." Fans started trying to get at Janis onstage. They wanted to *touch* her. When fame engulfed her, she needed even more testimonials to her greatness. She gave so much onstage, she got so much back, that Janis needed to feel that profound audience adoration twenty-four hours a day. When asked *how* she could sing like *that,* Janis always answered, "I close my eyes and feel things."

Big Brother must have felt it coming, but getting the boot from the chubby Port Arthur girl who auditioned in tacky short-shorts must have stung. Only Sam Andrew was asked to be a part of her new group. Janis played her last gig with Big Brother on December 1, 1968, at a benefit for the Family Dog. She premiered her new band three weeks later.

The *Detroit Free Press* called her 100-PROOF JANIS JOPLIN, and Southern

Comfort became Janis's trademark. She carried the bottle onstage with her and held on to it during interviews, claiming that it tasted like "orange petals in tea." In appreciation, the liquor company bought Janis a lynx coat, which she flaunted in grand style. But the Southern Comfort bottle was conveniently hiding her escalating heroin problem. Not that she thought it was a problem. In her most notorious quote, Janis told *The New York Times Magazine,* "Man, I'd rather have ten years of superhypermost than live to be seventy by sitting in some goddamn chair watching TV. Right now is where you are, how can you wait?"

Janis often shot dope with "Sam-O," Sam Andrew, who OD'd after a triumphant gig at Albert Hall in London. That night she and Linda saved Sam's life by getting him into a tub of ice-cold water, then walking him around and around the room. Janis herself was revived at least half a dozen times after overdosing on heroin. She was shooting two hundred dollars' worth of dope a day. When Linda asked why she did so much heroin, Janis said, "I just want a little fucking peace, man." Her favorite combination of booze and junk would prove to be lethal.

Janis's career was at its zenith: She did "The Ed Sullivan Show" and traded wits with Dick Cavett, all dolled up in her trademark beads, bangles, and rings on every finger. The girl nominated for "Ugliest Man on Campus" was now setting swinging fashion trends in *Vogue* and *Glamour.*

Janis relished her time onstage, but the road just seemed to remind her that she was alone. Said her lawyer, Sam Gordon, "Sure, Albert was there a phone call away and the band was there for tunes and the wine store was down the block and there were freaks in the lobby for her entertainment. But after that, it was just a situation with four walls, a chick lying in a fucking hotel room with nobody and nothing."

The week she was supposed to be on the cover of *Newsweek,* General Eisenhower had the audacity to die, and an irate Janis told the British paper *Melody Maker,* "Fourteen heart attacks and he had to die in my week! In *my* week!" Seven days later she did grace the cover of *Newsweek,* but Janis was devastated by the mean-spirited *Rolling Stone* cover story, which called her "The Judy Garland of Rock and Roll." The *Kozmic Blues* sessions had started and they were full of turmoil. Band members were leaving and being replaced on a regular basis. Sam Andrew finally split for good. And then her beloved pooch, George, disappeared. Janis believed he had been stolen by a fan and pleaded for his return on the radio, but the dog was gone. The only time Janis seemed to feel good was onstage, but her performance at the Woodstock festival suffered due to her escalating use of heroin and alcohol. In *Going Down with Janis,* Peggy Caserta describes a horrid scene in which Janis shoots smack in one of the grotesquely foul mobile toilets before being literally carried to the Woodstock stage to sing. Her usual vitality and enthusiasm had turned into peevish demands and tortured tantrums. She played the role of diva–dervish, living up to her JANIS JOPLIN persona, which was so huge and overwhelming she didn't know how to handle it. When the cops in Houston requested her help in controlling the crowd by asking the frenetic groovers to "move back and cool off," not only did Janis refuse, she told the cops where to go. When the same thing happened in Florida, Janis cursed out the cops for the entire audience to hear, and was instantly yanked offstage and arrested for "vulgar and indecent language." Janis had had a brief fling with Joe Namath, and onstage at Madison Square Garden she called plaintively for the football star: "Joe, Joe, where are you, Joe?"

Peggy Caserta claims that Janis had a better time with Dick Cavett than she did with Joe Namath. "'Guess what? I balled Cavett after appearing on the show,' she said. Can you *imagine?* She started laughing then, and I wondered as she went on if she was making it all up. 'You'd never guess it,' she said, 'but Cavett has a much bigger cock and is a better lay than Namath. Poor old Broadway Joe,' she said, almost crying she was laughing so hard. 'He was a disaster. He could hardly even get it to stand.'"

According to her psychiatrist at the time, Dr. Ed Rothchild, Janis sincerely wanted to stop using heroin, attempting several methadone cures. He described her as "just intellectually bordering on brilliant. . . . One of her problems was that intellectually she was so advanced, and her emotions were childlike and uncontrollable. . . . She was unbelievably 'on' all the time." Janis also seemed to have an alarming appetite for sex—always blabbering about who she just "balled"—and she couldn't get enough junk food and sweets. She ate gooey pies and cakes for breakfast and washed it all down with Coke floats. Her weight fluctuated wildly from 115 to 155 pounds. She was a mess.

The painfully soulful *I Got Dem Ol' Kozmic Blues Again Mama!* was released in November 1969 to mediocre reviews. Distraught and ready for a life change, Janis made another sincere effort to settle down, buying her own home in Larkspur, a little community north of San Francisco in Marin County. With redwood decks and lots of glass, the back of the house opened onto a lush woodland paradise. Janis bought loads of antique furniture, Oriental rugs, and bric-a-brac. She started piano lessons, and to replace George, Janis rescued several mutts from the pound.

Determined to kick junk again, Janis went with Linda Gravenites to the Rio carnival in Brazil, where she met David Niehaus, a down-to-earth fellow who didn't even know who she was. After spending two romantic days with her, David announced, "You know, you look like that rock star Janis Joplin." She felt he cared about her for who she really was, and with David's help, Janis did manage to kick heroin. When Uncle Albert telegraphed Janis to come home and get back to work, she wired back, "No. And don't lay that guilt trip on me." She was having one of the only carefree times of her life. On March

20, during a press conference at her hotel, Janis declared, "I'm going into the jungle with a big bear of a man named David Niehaus. I finally remembered I don't have to be onstage twelve months a year. I've decided to go and dig some other jungles for a couple of weeks."

At the end of the idyllic three-month vacation, David planned to return home with Janis but had some trouble with his visa. To make it just a little worse, Janis hollered at the official in charge, "You're a cunt and this is a cunt country!" And by the time David arrived in Larkspur two days later, Janis was back in persona mode and back on heroin. What had happened to the vivacious, colorful woman he danced with on the beach? David gave the relationship a royal try but couldn't stand to see what Janis was doing to herself. When he found her in bed with Peggy Caserta, he sadly left to continue his world travels. Her roommate Linda couldn't handle Janis's addiction, either, and moved out of the Larkspur house. This shook Janis up enough to take another cure, and according to her next roommate, Lyndall Erb, Janis managed to kick dope entirely. But never booze—she was up to a quart of tequila a day.

In April 1970 Janis put together a new band, the Full Tilt Boogie Band, and began rehearsals in her garage. Looking for the "real" Janis, she gave herself the nickname "Pearl," which was supposed to embody her stage personality, but she seemed to have trouble telling the two apart. She even had a fake voice for Pearl, a nasally whine with the vowels left out. Was it Pearl who picked up the pretty young boys, calling them "talent"? Was it Janis who threw them out of her bed in the wee morning hours?

In the middle of rehearsals, friend Bobby Neuwirth dropped in with Kris Kristofferson, and an afternoon of knocking back tequila turned into a three-week binge that Janis later called "The Tequila Boogie." Daily the trio covered the local bars and boozed through the nights, with Janis hanging on to Kris as if he were her saving grace. She was wild for Kristofferson and had a large fantasy about him, but he remained noncommittal during their brief affair. She did get a killer song out of the deal, "Me and Bobby McGee," but once again Janis was left alone with her dastardly habits. The Full Tilt tour was kicked off at a party for the Hell's Angels, which turned into a free-for-all that had a very drunk Janis slugging it out with a biker's girlfriend after she lunged for Janis's precious bottle. People who were there recall naked dancers and a couple having sex onstage. The only way the Full Tilt tour could go was up.

There were a couple of disastrous concerts and Janis realized she couldn't get drunk and perform. She cut back on her pre-show booze consumption and her performances reflected the discipline. The tour went fairly well, but Janis was unbearably lonely, often calling home to Port Arthur, complaining of exhaustion. But she needed the love that poured all over her from the audience, she *had* to have it. It was the only thing that could fill the gaping hole in her heart. The mood swings were unbearable. When she was happy, she was maniacally ecstatic; when she was sad, she was morbid. In her despair she ranted wildly, making up tawdry sexual escapades if she was lacking for horny anecdotes. She freaked out about getting old, insisting she was "ugly," and why couldn't she look like a movie star? She attacked and insulted her friends, she was tortured and missed the deadening relief of heroin. Myra Friedman observed Janis in a dressing room one night, reading a book on philosophy. A few moments later she overheard her saying. "Well, I have to go and change into Janis Joplin. She's upstairs in a box."

After announcing her intentions on "The Dick Cavett Show," Janis dragged three of her male friends to her ten-year high-school reunion in Port Arthur. What was she expecting? She had been misunderstood in high school, even taunted and abused. The slights must have grown to elaborate proportions and Janis probably wanted to "show them" that the outcast had attained megastar status. Decked to the nines wearing purple satin and gold-embroidered velvet, bracelets, baubles, beads, and the usual pink and blue feathers in her hair, Janis agreed to a press conference. Facing reporters at a long table, she grinned. "Looks like the Last Supper, doesn't it?" When asked if she entertained in school, she joked, "Only when I walked down the aisles." Somebody wondered if she went to her high-school prom. "No, I don't think they wanted to take me," she said, "and I've been suffering ever since. It's enough to make you want to sing the blues." I'm sure she was only partly kidding.

Janis had wanted her royal ass kissed, and it hadn't happened. After the reunion she took her younger sister, Laura, to a Jerry Lee Lewis show and introduced her to the legendary "Killer." "You wouldn't be half-bad-looking—if you weren't trying to look like your sister," Jerry Lee snapped. Janis slugged the obnoxious superstar in the face, and before hauling off and belting her back, he said, "If you're gonna act like a man, I'll treat you like one!" Janis was mortified and proceeded to get blind drunk. Instead of filling the hole in her heart, the trip back home had stirred up painful, shameful memories that wouldn't be put to rest.

The Doors' producer, Paul Rothchild, had always wanted to work with Janis but had been concerned about her addiction. When he found that she had been clean for a few months, he went to some Full Tilt gigs and agreed to produce the record. "She was singing and I was enraptured," he enthused, "because I was listening to one of the most brilliant vocalists I had ever heard in classical, pop, or jazz music. What a voice! I went, 'Oh my God!' All of the woman was revealed."

During the first week of September Janis and the band checked into the notorious rock-and-roll Landmark Hotel in Hollywood for the *Pearl* sessions at Sunset Sound Studios. An ugly stucco building on Franklin Avenue, the Landmark catered to a questionable clientele. Several of my all-girl freak band, the GTOs (Girls Together Outrageously), lived there for a while. So did Alice

Cooper. Painted sunburst orange and bear brown, the lobby featured psychedelic swirls on the walls and a very tolerant attitude. The hotel's manager, Jack Hagy, said, "It was Janis's kind of place."

A few weeks earlier Janis had met twenty-one-year-old Seth Morgan and was falling hard for the dark, cocky, intelligent Berkeley student. His brash self-confidence enabled Seth to deal with Janis/Pearl's superstar status, and since he came from an affluent family, for once Janis didn't feel she was being used. She encouraged him to stay in school, thinking it would be a kick to share her life with a college graduate. Other than a few temper flare-ups, they had been living a fairly quiet life in Larkspur, reading the morning papers over coffee, strolling through the woods. She announced that she would limit her touring, maybe even get pregnant. Janis had even cut back on her drinking, and the couple were talking about a wedding at sea when she left for the sessions in L.A. The plan was for Seth to join her at the Landmark on the weekends.

When Seth turned up in L.A., Janis was wrapped up with Paul Rothchild, listening to tapes and choosing songs for the album. Seth felt like an outsider and didn't spend as much time with Janis as she would have liked. She wanted total adoration from Seth, but nobody had ever been able to give Janis the attention she demanded. When she discovered that Peggy Caserta was also staying at the Landmark—*and* still addicted to heroin—Janis was irate, insisting that Peggy find another hotel. But it wasn't long before Janis was doing dope with Peggy. She had been clean for five months this time, and when she got back on the needle, Janis explained it away by saying she couldn't drink and get to the studio on time. She said she needed to mellow out after a session and would stop shooting dope when the album was finished, no problem. She told a friend she shot junk again just to see if she wanted to do it anymore.

Janis started out buying only fifty dollars' worth at a time but was swiftly heading back into the trap. She had been back on heroin for a week when Jimi Hendrix died. To Peggy she said, "It just decreases my chances. Two rock stars can't die in the same year." To her publicist, Myra, Janis reflected, "I wonder what they'll say about *me* after I die."

Janis had been getting herself a tan at the Landmark pool and had blond streaks woven into her hair. She visited her lawyer, who was drawing up a prenuptial agreement for her marriage to Seth, and signed her revised will: Half of her estate would go to her parents, the other half to her siblings. She allocated twenty-five hundred dollars so that her friends could have a party when she died, and before she left, Janis made her lawyer promise there would be a big party.

The recording was going well, there were high hopes for *Pearl,* but Seth wasn't around enough and Janis was desperately lonely. He was supposed to arrive in L.A. on Saturday, October 3, but there had been a heated argument on the phone and he said he would be there on Sunday. Saturday night Janis listened to the instrumental track for "Buried Alive in the Blues," looking forward to singing the vocal the next day. Then she stopped at Barney's Beanery for a couple of screwdrivers and at twelve-thirty was back at the Landmark, alone in her room.

Earlier that day Janis had bought a supply of heroin from her regular dealer. She only bought from this particular guy because he was always careful to have his dope checked out by a chemist. Unbeknownst to Janis, the chemist had been out of town that day and the heroin she bought was four to ten times stronger than what she was used to taking.

Janis under arrest.

Skin-popping the drug, instead of finding a vein, delays the high for up to ninety minutes, which is what Janis chose to do that night. She then discovered she was out of cigarettes and went to the lobby and got change from Jack Hagy at the desk. He was the last person to see Janis alive.

When Janis didn't show up for her Sunday-evening session, her road manager, John Cooke, got a key from the desk at the Landmark and went to her room. Finding her facedown on the floor, John touched her cool skin, hoping it wasn't too late, but Janis Lyn Joplin had been dead for seventeen hours. Her body was wedged between the table and the bed, her lip was bloody, her nose appeared to be broken, and a red ball of fresh needle marks punctured her arm. Janis was wearing only a blouse and panties and in her closed fist were four dollar bills and two quarters—change from the cigarettes.

The police found Janis's hype kit neatly put away in a drawer. They called her death an "accidental overdose," though there was talk about suicide. "Some people say it was murder, some say suicide," Sam Andrew tells me, shaking his head, "but that stuff is way out. One of the things about heroin being illegal is there's no controlling the dosage. It's amazing it doesn't happen more often. You let it sift through the strainer and it gets real strong," he says. "There's such a fine line." Janis's supplier lost several more customers that week with his lethally pure batch of heroin. I knew one of them. I ask Sam what he did when he found out Janis had died. "I went out and scored some smack," he admits. "We all gathered over at the drummer's house, had some kind of wake. They scattered her ashes in Marin County off the coast. I didn't go."

Peter Tork blames Janis's death on low self-esteem. "She died with a needle in her arm," he says. "It may be genetic or environmental or both, it's hard to know. If you don't have a sense of community or a higher power, then you blame yourself, think bad of yourself, so you struggle and try to divert. One form of diversion is entertaining. If you can make those thousands love you, you'll be all right. In fact, it makes no fucking difference. It's a kick when you're onstage, but an hour and a half later it starts all over."

Sam Andrew and I finish our coffee and get ready to leave the posh hotel lounge when he takes hold of my arm. "Janis had more fun than people thought," he says intently, "but then there was that other side—the insecurity was there all the time, too. She'd say, 'Was I good? Do you love me? Did I go flat on that ending? Was it okay?' She knew it was okay, but she needed to hear it. At the same time she had more fun than anyone." Sam looks around the stuffy, elegant room. "Janis Joplin had more fun than anyone in this room will ever have."

KEITH MOON
"THE LOON"

■

Hope

I Die

Before I

Get Old

■

"I think I must be a victim of circumstance, really. Most of it's my own doing. I'm a victim of my own practical jokes. I suppose that reflects a rather selfish attitude. I like to be the recipient of my own doings. Nine times out of ten, I am. I set traps and fall into them."

I had much firsthand experience with the Who's deranged, severely damaged, and very dear-hearted drummer, Keith Moon. I met him in 1971, on the set of Frank Zappa's breakthrough video film, *200 Motels,* the avant-madcap story of "life on the road" with the Mothers of Invention. I was playing a ga-ga groupie-girl news hen and Mr. Moon was hired to conjure up a maniac nun, which he pulled off quite nicely. His excessive amounts of savage energy and scathing wit frightened me at first, but after observing from a safe distance, I soon realized that his court-jester desire to be loved kept impish-faced Mr. Moon pretty much harmless (to everyone but himself and hotel rooms!). Keith was always on the lookout for mischief, and his huge, wide-open, cocoa-brown eyes never missed an opportunity to shred an otherwise sane or boring moment. "It was another 'oliday Inn. When I get bored, I rebel," he told *Rolling Stone*. "I said, 'Fuck it!! Fuck the lot of ya!' And I took out me 'atchet and chopped the 'otel room to bits. The television, the chairs, the dresser. The cupboard doors. The bed. It happens all the time."

Notes written on Keith Moon's report card in 1959 suggest that his tendency toward lunacy started early: "Retarded artistically," wrote his art teacher, adding, "Idiotic in other respects." His physical education teacher had this to say: "Keen at times, but goonery seems to come before anything." How right he was. The music instructor's comments were more telling: "Great ability, but must guard against tendency to 'show off.'" No such luck. It seemed that Keith was born with an unfinished nature that made him impossible to embarrass, and this quirk left him free to do and say things that most thinking people wouldn't dare.

Keith started playing drums in 1960 at the age of fourteen, left his Wembley school a year later, and joined a series of bands with names like the Mighty Avengers and the Adequates, playing weddings and parties on weekends. By 1964 Keith had lost twenty-three jobs and was fond of telling friends the many, many fascinating ways he had found to get fired. Because he was wildly into California surf music, his next band, the Beachcombers, were

Keith Moon and me—all dolled up with a whole lot of places to go. (RICHARD CREAMER)

heavily influenced by Jan and Dean and the Beach Boys—breezy sun-and-fun, sand-and-surf music far removed from the London chill. One warm California night, many years later, I introduced Keith to Dean Torrence of Jan and Dean, and in the back of a limo the two of them sang, "Goin' to Surf City, gonna have some fun/Goin' to Surf City, where it's two to one. . . ." It was glorious.

Keith had been following a local Mod band called the Detours, headed by a stalk-slim guitarist with an imposing hooter, Pete Townshend. Keith harbored a secret desire to audition for the band and one night, in April 1964, a pie-eyed pal approached the stage, announcing that his friend with the dyed bright orange hair, Keith Moon, could play better than the guy they had on drums. With his mum watching, not only did Keith pass the test, he played with such reckless ferocity that he busted up the session drummer's bass pedal and high-hat—a sure sign of things to come. Singer Roger Daltrey asked Keith what he was doing the following Monday. "We'll pick you up in the van," he said, and Keith was an instant member of the Detours.

The Detours were already locked in constant combat, Peter and Roger vying for power, and, with the addition of seventeen-year-old Keith Moon, they became an even more volatile entity. Instead of disagreements being bottled up and shoved aside, they were heatedly tackled and thrown into the music. Bass player John Entwistle had difficulty with Moon's lunatic soloist tendencies. He was all over the place full force, hammering every drum at once with no real backbeat, playing more like a guitarist than a drummer—taking his own leads, thrashing and bashing, twirling his sticks, standing up behind the kit, cocky and insistent, demanding attention. Pete and John already had massive amplification, so in order to keep up, Keith added a second bass drum and loads of cymbals and tom-toms. Soon other rock drummers followed suit until oversize kits became commonplace.

The Detours became the High Numbers and got their chance in the studio, recording two R&B covers for Fontana Records. Despite a mini-rave in *Disc* magazine—"They're up to date with a difference—they're even ahead of themselves"—the single wasn't a hit. Due to the glut of cool records out, including the Beatles' "A Hard Day's Night" and the Stones' "It's All Over Now," the High Numbers' single just wasn't good enough. Still, the band was gathering more and more fans at gigs.

On the outlook for a local group on which to base a pop film, Kit Lambert turned up to see the High Numbers at the Railway Tavern on a tip from a friend. Impressed, the following week he brought his partner, Chris Stamp (brother of actor Terence Stamp), who said, "All we could hear was a great dirty noise. Still, we sensed this amazing excitement all around us, and we knew that it had to be wild." The pop film was out the window. "Instead, the pair became the band's managers, converting their name back to an earlier idea of Townshend's—the Who.

Stamp and Lambert took the boys to Max Factor on Bond Street for theatrical makeup lessons and to Carnaby Street for stage clothes, which they wore on a daily basis to maintain their Mod image. Despite their recording flop, the Who could fill venues and started modifying the stage to accommodate their ever-growing theatrical pranks. Pete had crazed episodes of arm windmilling, mowing down the audience with his machine-gun guitar; Roger leered, whipping his mike cord round and round in a vast circle; and Keith Moon loomed behind his gargantuan kit, sweating maniacally, tossing his sticks in the air, while John gazed menacingly. By this time John, Keith, and Pete were heavily into "leapers," potent amphetamines that brought out a lot of innate aggression. Personally, they couldn't stand each other, and it all came out onstage. But the legendary Who instrument-bashing came about by accident. Trying to control feedback at a club with a very low ceiling, Pete got pissed off, accidentally smashing the neck of the guitar against the ceiling, which created a quirky sound. He repeated the action, and the audience wanted more. During the second set, after a challenge from some art-school friends, Pete banged his axe so hard that the neck broke. "I had no recourse but to completely look as though I meant to do it," Pete recalled, "so I smashed the guitar and jumped all over the bits. It gave me a fantastic buzz." The following night the joint was jammed. The destruction may have thrilled the punters, but the band couldn't afford to replace ravaged instruments. After a disappointed crowd left the club, Keith got so frustrated he kicked his drum kit to smithereens and word soon got around. The next gig was packed, and both Pete and Keith destroyed their instruments to such a huge response that, despite the cost, destruction became a semiregular event. The demolition symbolized the fury of rock and roll and the audience demanded it.

When Lambert booked the Who into London's R&B Marquee Club, he came up with the slogan "Maximum R&B," which is exactly what the Who played—spiked, hard-core, rocked-out versions of Chuck Berry, B. B. King, and Bo Diddley. "The Who should be billed as not only 'Maximum R&B,' but as 'far-out R&B,'" announced London's hip rock paper *Melody Maker*, adding that the Who were one of the trend-setting groups of 1965. The review was timely. A week later the Who released their first single, "I Can't Explain," one of Pete's earliest attempts at songwriting, inspired by the Kinks' "You Really Got Me."

An amazing slab of pop history, the song is highlighted by the suspenseful, fearless slam-bam flair of Keith's cut-loose drumming. He had the uncanny ability to climb inside a song, fill it to the bursting brim, and bang his way out with his drumsticks. In the process Keith Moon elevated and reinvented rock drumming, setting a formidable standard that few have been able to follow. And he was rock's first superstar drummer.

As the record climbed the charts, the Who became regular faces on "Top of the Pops" and "Ready, Steady, Go!" "It wasn't until Townshend started smashing up guitars and I started smashing up the drums that producers of the shows began to realize that there was more than the singer in a band," Keith said. "They'd actually line up a camera for the drums, which was a first. People started to actually notice the drummer." It's not surprising. Mr. Moon made it his life's work to be noticed.

"I Can't Explain" hit the British Top Ten, but all the money went to replace smashed-up instruments. Despite impending success, animosity within the band raged. "Roger is not a very good singer at all," Pete told *Disc* magazine. "The pretty one," Keith Moon, did an article for the teen magazine *Fabulous*, entering the room with an axe, which he slammed down on the table. "What's that for?" inquired the stunned interviewer. "That's for Roger," said Keith with manic glee. "You 'aven't seem 'im, 'ave you?"

As Modism faded with the fashion craze, Pete turned more to pop art for his inspiration. "We stand for pop art clothes, pop art music, pop art behavior," said Pete. "We live pop art." For Keith it was "just a way of dressing up the music and putting it across."

The sales of the second single, "Anyway, Anyhow, Anywhere," were fueled by controversy. Pete had started telling the press that he advocated drugs and was a drug user himself. In a *New Musical Express* survey, Keith listed his favorite food as "French Blues," certain happy pills that he enjoyed enormously. Though the Rolling Stones actually got arrested for pissing against the wall of a gas station in the English countryside, at the end of a show in Paris the Who peed in an alley and it was filmed live for French and British cameras!

The drug taking got so ferocious that singer Roger Daltrey (who was already cleaning up his act) threatened to quit the band during a tour of Sweden. At a show in Denmark Roger emptied Keith's profound pill supply down the toilet, and when Keith got pissed off, Roger knocked him out. Weary of the constant aggro, the band then threatened to fire Roger. After a humiliating meeting, Roger agreed to keep his temper in check. The massive drug and alcohol consumption continued to escalate.

The band's first album, *The Who Sings My Generation,* put them over the top. Every kid in the universe hoped they would die before they got old. Keith Moon's drumming continued to lambaste any preexisting limits and challenge any and all ground rules. His personality and his musicianship were completely intertwined. Keith was so bombed at the "Substitute" session that he had no recall of playing on the track, insisting that it had been someone else, expressing fear and outrage that he was being replaced. He relished his pop stardom, the rampant, doped-up endless nights, so proud of being *the* very baddest bad boy in rock. He married his longtime sweetheart, Kim Kerrigan, in March 1966, but the wedding vows did nothing to tame his unfinished nature.

War within the band never ceased. When Keith turned up late at a gig, Pete beat him over the head with his guitar, and for a few days Keith tried to persuade John Entwistle to leave the Who with him and form a new band. Keith also wanted to sing, despite his lack of vocal talent, and spiteful rows always ensued.

Keith soon became was the father of a new baby girl, Mandy, but this sobering fact did nothing to sober him up. The parties at his home in Chelsea went on for days with gargantuan amounts of drugs and alcohol consumed, gallantly provided by everyone's ever-ready host. Kim and the baby would disappear upstairs into an entirely different (and much saner) world.

When the Who finally got to New York City in March 1967, manager

Stamp arranged for regular shots of amphetamines, adding doses of penicillin just in case. Free-spirited females were around in abundance, and the Who took full advantage. Though the gigs proved to be stunningly received, the band was tossed out of the first two hotels due to Keith's nearly perfect destruction of his room. He eventually made hotel-room trashing into a fine art and, like his drumming, the annihilation was often imitated but rarely duplicated.

In May the Who were invited to play the Monterey Pop Festival, where ruthless, respectful competition with the Jimi Hendrix Experience elevated both bands into the stratosphere. This high-profile exposure got the Who booked on a ten-week American jaunt with Herman's Hermits, one of Britain's squeakiest-clean exports, and the Who got their first taste of the long and winding endless road. Keith coped in his inimitable way by securing five hundred cherry-bomb explosives and gleefully blowing up dozens of hotel-room toilets—until word got around and a five-thousand-dollar security deposit was demanded before the Who could check in to any hotel in America. Keith's twentieth-birthday party was held at the end of a ragged gig in Flint, Michigan (Keith announced vociferously he was turning twenty-one because in most states that was the legal drinking age), and when the Holiday Inn manager had the unforeseen gall to tell the partygoers to turn down the music, the birthday boy took hearty offense. The first to go was the five-tiered cake from Decca Records (by some accounts, right into the manager's face). Legend has it that Keith raced through the hotel hallway, grabbed a fire extinguisher, and sprayed every car in the lot, ruining many paint jobs, before wrecking his hotel room, stripping naked, and jumping into the pool—which was empty! In an interview with *Rolling Stone* a month before his death, Keith said he drove a new Lincoln Continental into a *full* swimming pool that night. "Today I can think of less outrageous ways of going than drowning in a Lincoln Continental in a 'oliday Inn swimming pool, but at that time I 'ad no thoughts of death whatsoever," he told Jerry Hopkins. "There was none of that all-me-life-passing-before-me-eyes-in-a-flash. I was busy planning. I knew if I panicked I'd 'ave 'ad it." Keith made a Houdini escape from the Lincoln, arrived back at the room dripping wet in his underwear, tripped through the doorway, slipped on some marzipan, and knocked out his front tooth. He was rushed to the dentist and then spent the day in jail. Happy birthday, Mr. Moon, happy birthday to you.

The Who's appearance on the Smothers Brothers' TV show was rebel rock at its finest: Between rehearsal and tape time, Keith hurtled around, giving stagehands a bit of cash and a swig out of his brandy flask, charming them into putting ten times the usual dose of gunpowder into his drum kit. As Pete went into the final windmill whip at the end of "My Generation," Keith set off his drums and the blast sent him flying off the riser, a razor chunk of cymbal slicing into his arm. Pete's hair caught on fire and his left ear took the brunt of the blast, which probably contributed immensely to his future hearing problems. When Tommy Smothers walked onstage wearing an acoustic guitar around his neck, despite being half-dazed Pete seized the moment, yanked away Tommy's guitar, smashed it to the ground, and put his foot through it. Backstage, Bette Davis fainted into Mickey Rooney's arms.

Rolling Stone named the Who as rock-and-roll group of 1967. "I Can See for Miles" was a Top Ten hit in England and the United States, but Pete Townshend was restless. After reading books on Indian avatar Meher Baba, Pete became an outspoken, devoted disciple. He stopped taking drugs and began to write for the Indian master the music that became his masterwork, the rock opera *Tommy*.

The road always beckoned and Keith got bored easily, but blessed with an ingenious, devilish imagination, he battled to keep the boredom at bay. And of course he had his image to uphold! Sleep never came easy for Mr. Moon: Once he spent hours nailing hotel-room furniture to the ceiling exactly as it had been on the floor. He would take the screws out of cabinets and put them back together so they seemed untouched; drag furniture outside, piece by piece, leaving his room all but empty; dump catsup in the tub along with plastic arms and legs to shock the maids; toss priceless antiques into the fireplace with a lit cigarette; hurl endless TV sets out of plate-glass windows; literally swing on sparkling chandeliers until they crashed down all around him. What else was a poor boy to do with all that pumping adrenaline? After being cheered by thousands? After ruling the world for two hours? After popping half a dozen multicolored pills and downing a full bottle of Courvoisier? The after-gig anticlimax must have hurt like dull arrows, and Keith dealt with it the best way he knew how. "Things get broken," he said. "If you're sitting around after a show and there's something you don't like, you just switch it off by throwing a bottle through the screen."

Thrashing and bashing—altering rock drumming forever. (MICHAEL OCHS ARCHIVES/VENICE, CALIF.)

The *Tommy* album came out in May 1969 and everything changed for the Who. They went from being a solid kick-ass rock band to a theatrical pop event that was not to be missed. Touring with *Tommy* all through 1969 and 1970 (including a blistering set at Woodstock), the Who brought the deaf, dumb, and blind boy to a huge international audience, turning the world on to bright possibilities. By the end of 1970 the Who were finally millionaires.

Except for Mr. Moon. He spent his money quicker than it came in. Along with a new pyramid-shaped home, Keith bought himself his very own pub, as well as many, many cars that he was fond of totaling. He lived his life as if he was always on the road, becoming British tabloid fodder as "Moon the Loon," stalling his hovercraft on the train tracks, which delayed British Rail for a day, dressing up in full Nazi regalia, or stepping out stark, raving nude. He was proud of how many chemicals and vats of liquor he could get down, and more than once he was rushed to the hospital for a stomach pumping. He would bring strange women home with him, so of course his marriage was always in deep trouble. Despite his obvious love for Kim and Mandy, he was out of control and couldn't seem to help himself. His wit was matchless, and though he could make everyone around him double up with laughing fits, he was a sad, sad fellow.

On January 4, 1970, things got worse for Mr. Moon. An incident took place that resulted in the death of his driver/minder, Neil Boland, coloring the rest of Keith's life very dark indeed. My dear old friend "Legs" Larry Smith, of the Bonzo Dog Doo-Dah Band, was with Keith that night. "Keith and I had gone to quite a large pub and discotheque in North London, in the suburbs, really," Larry recalled. "Not particularly wonderful, but Keith always accepted invitations. It was about half past ten and this place was going to close about eleven, and things started to get a bit crazy. Keith was looping about with the boys, but I had an odd sense of the evening. I felt we should get the hell out and beat the closing time, but Keith said, 'No, no, no, dear boy, I'm going to have another dance,' and waltzed out into the crowd again." Larry got the keys and waited for Keith in the backseat.

"Ten minutes later Keith and eight thousand people came tumbling out of the pub," Larry continued, "the driver Neil behind him, and suddenly all the rabble realized that they were going to have to wait in a bus queue for twenty minutes and we were going to go gliding in the comfort of a pink Rolls-Royce! They snapped, started emptying their pockets, and we were being rained upon by small change! Because Neil was so proud of the Rolls, he got out and started to run at them, which was even crazier. Neil had put the car in drive, and it was crawling forward. Suddenly we found ourselves rolling toward the main road with no one driving the damn thing! Keith slid over to the driver's seat, not being able to drive, of course—Keith couldn't do things like that. At this point people had surrounded the car and were raining down fists, kicking, smashing the windows. Neil was out having a bash with them. I leaned up over the backseat, put my arms over Keith, and started to steer. People were screaming, getting hysterical. When we turned onto the main street, Neil was running alongside the car, still fending off these attackers, and he must have tripped and fallen under the car, so we actually must have rolled over Neil. The car rolled on and on, and Keith finally stopped it somehow. We didn't feel anything, we were carrying right on, we didn't know that Neil's body must have been in the middle of the road. The police came, the reporters came, we were holed up in Keith's house for two weeks not answering the phone."

Larry tells me that Neil was more than Keith's driver. "We were mortified because Neil was family. He was a soft, lovable Irishman who picked up the pieces of our excesses very well. It's an art form in itself." It seems Keith, Larry, and Neil pulled a few pranks together. Once Larry walked into a large department store asking for a pair of "strong work trousers," which the salesman supplied. "I took the trousers and started pulling the legs apart. 'How can I be sure these are strong work trousers?' I ask the salesman, who's starting to flinch. At that point Keith Moon comes into the store and says, 'Good morning! I'm happy to test those trousers!'" The two madmen proceeded to pull the trousers in half while the shocked salespeople looked on. "We hadn't paid for these trousers," Larry laughed. "The assistant got the union representative. We were just about to be arrested and dear Neil walks in and says, 'I'll pay for those trousers!' All eyes were suddenly turned on Neil—a total stranger offering to pay for a pair of ripped trousers! I said, 'Can, I have two bags please? One for each leg?' We did the same thing in a Mothercare shop. We ripped a baby's little fluffy jumper in half and the sales assistant just wept." Larry had one more little story to tell me: "Keith had a microphone and two speakers built into the front of his car, and we drove around this little seaside town making terrifying announcements: 'This is the Plymouth Police Department, this is an official message. There is a large tidal wave approaching Plymouth Beach. Would you please evacuate the beach, but stay in your shoes. Repeat, stay in your shoes.' We were in the back of the Rolls with a fucking microphone. How we were not arrested that day, I do not know."

Though he was cleared of all charges, after the death of Neil Boland, Keith had even more trouble sleeping. In Los Angeles with me one long, tortuous night, he woke up a dozen times, screaming that he was a murderer and didn't deserve to live. Each time he would douse his grief with copious capsules and gnash his way back to temporary oblivion. Only his drums and his sense of humor kept him going. We were staying at the Century Plaza Hotel because the notorious Mr. Moon had been expelled from almost *all* of the L.A. hotels, and he had come up with yet another way to keep himself amused (he always felt an obligation to keep *everybody* entertained). As I stood watching from the balcony, Keith appeared down below, pouring a giant box of powdered soap into the hotel fountain. He soon joined me on the balcony and together we watched the chaotic froth wreak bubbling havoc as great clumps of suds foamed down the street.

He was a man of innumerable accents and personalities that he would switch at will whenever evil boredom struck. Even during sexcapades he would turn from a fumbling virgin boy to a dastardly rapist within the space of a few moments. He dressed in the finest costumes and disguises money could purchase, drank deeply from hundred-year-old bottles of cognac, and was never satisfied. Meanwhile the great Who beast rolled along—*Live at Leeds, Who's Next, Meaty Beaty Big and Bouncy*—tour after tour after tour.

Keith continued to demolish his marriage, wreck cars, strip naked in pubs and bars in various countries, and drown himself in cognac, seemingly imperishable. He did a couple of blazing star turns in the David Essex movies *That'll Be the Day* and *Stardust,* but nothing seemed to quell the fact that he was lonely and mad. When *Quadrophenia* was released in October 1973, Kim took Mandy and moved out for good. "We led separate lives under the same roof," she told a journalist. "He'll get up in the morning and decide to be Hitler for a day, and he *is* Hitler." Keith took the loss like a swift kick to the heart. Even his playing suffered. He never got over it.

During a tragic U.S. tour in late 1973, in which the band often came to blows, Keith collapsed onstage and, as he was carried off, Pete announced to the audience, "We're going to try to revive our drummer by punching him in the stomach and giving him a custard enema." It wouldn't have helped. Keith had ingested too much PCP (an animal tranquilizer) and was taken to the hospital. When the tour got to Montreal, the band and their crew ruined a Bonaventure hotel room so thoroughly (actually ripping out the floor) that sixteen people, including the Who, wound up spending the night in jail.

Keith was so pissed off that his Uncle Ernie role in *Tommy* had been trimmed that he refused to play on the movie soundtrack, instead taking off for Malibu to drown his sorrows in the sunshine. In March 1975 he released *Two Sides of the Moon,* a typical sun 'n' surf tribute—the album's single, a schmaltzy "Don't Worry Baby," didn't set the charts on fire.

Though he was getting a good suntan, Keith was a very sick man, addicted to his precious cognac and Hollywood's drug of choice, cocaine. He teetered around town with Harry Nilsson and Ringo Starr, pretending to be having a ball. When the Who toured again, Keith once more spent time in jail for kicking a British Airlines ticket terminal to pieces, and he collapsed onstage in Boston. He had a very close call at the Navarro Hotel in Manhattan—he kicked in an offensive painting and cut his foot so badly that if the Who's manager Bill Curbishly hadn't found him, Keith would have bled to death.

Back in Malibu on a break from touring, Keith had a bit of a problem with his neighbor, Steve McQueen. A very private and quiet movie star, McQueen was distraught about the noise and chaos that the Who's drummer brought to Malibu Colony. He had zero appreciation for one of Britain's finest rock eccentrics, and the police were called on several occasions. Keith harassed and bugged McQueen until the actor was forced to build a fence between the properties.

The rest of the band thought about getting rid of the ever-troubled drummer but ultimately decided against it. As John Entwistle said, "What would Keith Moon do without the Who?" As the tour dragged on to Miami, Keith's boredom after two days off culminated in another arrest. He walked through the hotel halls with the Who's music shrieking from a tape recorder, and when told by an assistant manager to "stop making so much noise," Keith turned down the volume, dragged the manager back to his room, loudly trashed it, invited the manager to observe the mess, saying, "*That* was noise," then, turning the music back up, "*This* is THE WHO!!!" Curbishly bailed Keith out of jail and promptly checked him into the hospital for "psychiatric evaluation." He was out in three days.

In Los Angeles Keith was seeing a lovely blonde, Annette Walter-Lax, but still hadn't gotten over the loss of his family. He was paranoid about losing his position in the Who, and his drinking and drugging were finally starting to show. He had a potbelly, his once wiry body was soft and puffy, his big eyes were constantly bloodshot. Pete Townshend was writing new Who material but the band was afraid to take Keith on another tour.

In 1978 Keith returned to London with Annette, taking up residence in Harry Nilsson's flat in Mayfair (strangely, Cass Elliot of the Mamas and the Papas died there in 1974). In between recording sessions, Keith actually went to a health farm and seemed temporarily together, but his lifeblood drumming just wasn't the same and it knocked him off the wagon (drum stool) forever. Keith couldn't keep time and couldn't follow arrangements. Once again the band talked of replacing him, but Pete couldn't bring himself to do it.

On a holiday with Annette, Keith tired of the long plane trip and, losing all control, dashed into the cockpit and drummed on the flight engineer's table, then attacked a stewardess and some crew members. He was thrown

Keith, the night of his death. "It was like a sacrifice," said Roger Daltrey. (MICHAEL OCHS ARCHIVES/VENICE, CALIF.)

off the plane, taken to a local hospital, and pronounced "unfit to travel." These continuing incidents dashed hopes that Keith might get better. Despite Pete's loyalty, the band was ready to relieve Keith of his drummerly duties—but he did it for them.

On September 6, 1978, Keith and Annette attended Paul McCartney's midnight screening of *The Buddy Holly Story.* Paul owned Buddy Holly's catalog and celebrated Buddy's birthday every year with a spectacular bash. Keith was in his element that night, sitting at the head of the star table with Paul and his wife Linda, gregarious, charming, and flamboyant as ever. The couple got home at four-thirty, whereupon Keith took a handful of sleeping tablets and a sedative called Heminevrin (a relaxant that curbs alcoholism and mania—he definitely suffered from both!) and fell asleep to *The Abominable Dr. Phibes,* a Vincent Price horror film. His eyes flew open at seven-thirty and, after unsuccessfully trying to get Annette to cook for him, he went to the kitchen, made himself a steak, drank some champagne, swallowed a few more Heminevrin pills, and died before he got old.

Keith's ashes were interred at Golder's Green crematorium during a small funeral ceremony for the band, his family, and a few friends. Roger Daltrey's floral tribute was a TV set with a champagne bottle smashed through the screen.

"In a way it was like a sacrifice," Roger said. "We can do anything we want to now. I have very odd feelings. I feel incredibly strong and at the same time incredibly fragile."

"Keith has always appeared so close to blowing himself up in the past that we've become used to living with the feeling," Pete Townshend said at the funeral. "But this time Keith hasn't survived, he hasn't come round, he hasn't thrown himself off the balcony and landed in one piece. Everybody laughed at Keith and his antics, but they never saw the other shoulder was wet with tears."

JIM MORRISON

■

The

Lizard of

Aaaaahs

■

I was one of the few hundred people who watched the rise and demise of the Lizard King. In the early, early days, right in front of my greedy eyes, he would slink around the Sunset Strip, black leather unzipped, devilish grin, cocky and unremorseful. "Aaaahh," we all whispered. "What goes on behind that flawless face? Where does he go when the lights go all the way down?" Tousled, tormented, and highly in demand, he led the parade with dangerous indifference. Even the naked facts do nothing to alter those early images: dark, messy ringlets, love beads, angry, penetrating scowl. Come hither, but be careful.

The first time I witnessed Jim Morrison slither onto a stage, I was bombed out of my mind on a very early version of PCP called Trimar. My friend Jerry Penrod, the bass player for Iron Butterfly, smuggled it out of the hospital where he worked during the day. He got it in quart jars and handed them right to me. Wasn't I just the lucky one? An itsy-bitsy vial sold for ten dollars on the street, so I was very popular that balmy night in Hollywood. The underground cavern club Bido Lido's was packed. I held on to sopping lace hankies full of this incredibly dangerous drug—inhaling, giggling, waiting.

The news was out all over town that this new band, the Doors, had a gorgeous, hot singer who actually *sucked* the microphone, and all of us wild, loony girls couldn't wait to get a load of him. The anticipation was high and so were we. The band played pretty cool, with lots of moody organ, and then Jim Morrison was onstage. Somehow he just *appeared,* holding the microphone like it was trying to get away, clutching it hard like it might just be alive, moaning, eyes closed, feeling enough pent-up pain for everyone in the room. And *God,* what did he look like? I had to get a closer eyeful. I struggled and squeezed my way down front and gazed up at a future rock legend in delirious wonder. HE'S HOT, HE'S SEXY, HE'S DEAD. Remember that *Rolling Stone* cover? I had never seen such blatant sexuality onstage. He writhed in horny anguish, demanding that everybody in the stormy, sweltering room light his fire. "We want the world, and we want it *now.*" He hooked us all together. We wanted the entire fucking world, and we wanted it right this *minute!* I had seen the Stones a couple of times and Mick Jagger inspired some steam dreams, but he had his frenzy under control. Jim Morrison was so out of control that it scared people. It scared me close to imaginary death and I loved it. While Mick suggested that danger lurked in his trousers, Jim grabbed hold of it and shook it in our faces. He defied the system with his dick, like a rock-and-roll Lenny Bruce. While the flower dolls urged us to live in peace, Jim bellowed about insanity, incest, and murder. His defiance was catching and we all wanted a piece of it. When he took a dive into the audience without premeditation, we all held him up, snatching some of his scary stuff oh-so-briefly.

Instead of telling journalists that his father had been a captain in the navy and he had been a navy brat, traveling around the country, changing schools on a regular basis, Jim Morrison told the press that his parents were dead. It was easier. Although witty and charming, Steve Morrison had been a strict disciplinarian who barked orders at his sons and daughter, demanding that Jim follow rules that he seemed determined to break. Mother Clara upheld her husband's position, and there was a constant battle to tame Jim's innate rebellious nature.

When Jim was barely five, the Morrisons were taking another trip across the country when they were waylaid by a deadly accident involving a family of Indians. "Jimmy was very much affected," Grandmother Caroline said. "He wanted to do something." The highway police and an ambulance were called, but Jim was so upset that his father said to him it hadn't really happened, that he had just been having a bad dream. It was a dream that never died, and Jim would later claim that the souls of the dying Indians jumped into his head that afternoon.

While his siblings were content to walk the line, Jim was constantly prodding the facade of fifties morality. With an IQ of 149, he mercilessly tore into his teachers, demanding answers they were unable to give, and, in fact, he would always have a smoldering disdain for authority figures. To pass the time he read *Mad* magazine and drew stacks of twisted, sexually explicit drawings.

Jim's George Washington High School experience in Alexandria, Virginia, was just something to get through. He didn't participate in any school activities, but because good grades came so easily to him, he was bored and always looking for a way to shake things up and get noticed. When he was late for school, he claimed to have been kidnapped by gypsies. Once he left class early, saying he was having brain surgery that very afternoon. He called to friends in the hallway—"Hey, motherfucker!"—many, many years before it was even slightly acceptable. He painted copies of de Kooning nudes, and he was wild for words, foraging through poetry books, glomming on to Blake, Rimbaud, Balzac, Camus, and Beat writers Lawrence Ferlinghetti and Jack Kerouac, who gave Jim permission to ". . . burn, burn burn like fabulous Roman candles exploding like spiders across the stars. . . ."

His high-school girlfriend, Tandy Martin, while captivated by Jim's sensitivity (one of Jim's poems for her stated, "But one / The most beautiful of all / Dances in a ring of fire / And throws off the challenge with a shrug"), still had to put up with his wicked sense of humor, which often

The Lizard King crossing the imaginary line to the dark side of the moon. (HENRY DILTZ)

brought her to tears. She was devastated when Jim was asked to join the all-important AVO fraternity and he had no interest whatsoever. When the couple broke up, Jim threatened to cut her face up so nobody would look at her but him, but Tandy never believed he would do it. Jim seemed to have quite a few friends but somehow remained a loner, spending more and more time at a club on Route 1, listening to the blues. He graduated in June 1961 but, much to the dismay of his folks, didn't attend the graduation ceremony. Jim Morrison's diploma was sent to him in the mail.

The constant battle with his parents about the clothes he wore (the same dirty shirt for a week), the length of his hair, and his smart mouth began to escalate when, at sixteen, Jim discovered Friedrich Nietzsche, who confirmed Jim's suspicions that, like the philosopher, he, too, was a free spirit and "a philosopher of the dangerous." He began writing poetry and keeping a journal, inspired by Franz Kafka. He blew minds by asking friends to read a passage out of any one of his collection of books, then proudly telling them the title and author.

Hoping to steer their errant son in the right direction, Steve and Clara enrolled Jim at St. Petersburg College in Florida and shipped him off to Steve's parents' house to live. He took psychology courses and tortured his very sober grandparents by leaving empty wine bottles in his room and blaring Elvis. After school he hung out with a guy known to be gay, who told Jim that when he cruised for guys, he always left his underwear in the drawer. "Always show your meat," he instructed Jim, advice he would later follow.

In 1962 Jim switched to Florida State University and moved in with five other college students but was soon asked to leave, relocating to a tiny trailer behind a girls' boardinghouse, where he boned up on protest philosophies. He peed in the public fountain. He exposed himself to trick-or-treaters. He encouraged a few of his friends to start a riot during a campus seminar, to show that a crowd could be controlled. "We can make love to it," he enthused. "We can make it riot!" He had no takers.

The Morrisons had moved to California, and Jim hitchhiked across the country to tell his parents of his decision to study film at UCLA. They adamantly rebuffed his request, adding that he had better cut off his unruly hair, and he angrily went back to FSU, moving into a seedy motel. Though he continued to get top grades, amazing teachers and fellow students with his grandiose ideas, Jim was unhappy and couldn't stay out of trouble, once getting arrested and handcuffed for "disturbing the peace, resisting arrest, and public drunkenness."

Against his family's wishes, in February 1964 Jim hitched back to California and enrolled at the UCLA Theater Arts Department, where he attended classes with Francis Ford Coppola and a like-minded, well-read eccentric, Dennis Jakob. The two discussed forming a band, "The Doors—Open and

Closed," based around the statement by William Blake: "If the doors of perception were cleansed, everything would appear to man as it truly is, infinite." Jim also spent a great deal of time with a moody, wired, arrogant freak, thirty-four-year-old Felix Venable, who inspired Jim to pursue his poetic decadence and to experiment with all sorts of mind-expanding drugs. Jim's drinking accelerated. He teetered naked on the edges of tall buildings. He set his bed on fire, threw darts at *Playboy* centerfolds, filled the men's-room walls with rancorous graffiti. The chaotic, controversial, subversive film he managed to come up with—a half-naked girl stripping on top of a television set featuring Nazi storm troopers—earned him a "complimentary D," and Jim Morrison dropped out of film school to wander Venice Beach and smoke pot. He took fistfuls of LSD. When the array of drugs in his system failed to disqualify him for army duty, Jim convinced the army doctors he was a homosexual. Soon afterward he played harmonica on his first gig with fellow student Ray Manzarek's band, Rick and the Ravens, and said it was the easiest money he'd ever made.

Jim's own mind fascinated him beyond anything else, and he began staying on the rooftop of an abandoned office building at Venice Beach, dropping acid, pondering his options, writing poetry, meditating, opening himself up to the great unknown, ready for absolutely anything. And the words started to pour out of him in a torrent. Years later he recalled this time: "It was a beautiful, hot summer and I just started hearing songs. This kind of mythic concert that I heard . . . with a band and singing and an audience—a large audience. Those first five or six songs I wrote, I was just taking notes at a fantastic rock concert that was going on in my head. And once I had written the songs, I had to sing them." With a diet of drugs and very little food at his disposal, when Jim Morrison came down from the rooftop, his appearance had altered dramatically. No longer pudgy, he was lean and suntanned, his dark hair curling around his angular face, deep-set eyes hypnotically intense. Ray almost didn't recognize him.

One of rock and roll's legendary cosmic moments took place that summer of '65 when Ray Manzarek ran into Jim on the Venice Boardwalk and asked what he had been up to. "I've been living on some rooftop writing songs," he said, and Ray wanted to hear Jim sing them. About the fortuitous meeting, Ray later said, "Somebody must have planned it."

Knocked out entirely by what he heard, Ray insisted they start a rock-and-roll band and "make a million dollars." Jim said that was what he had in mind all along, suggested they call themselves "the Doors," and moved into Ray's house that afternoon, where they worked on the songs and Jim's tentative singing for two weeks straight. Ray met drummer John Densmore at the Maharishi Mahesh Yogi's Meditation Center and asked if he might be interested in playing in a new rock band. John's first rehearsal was in Ray's parents' garage: "Ray said, 'This is Jim, the singer.' He had never sung. But they showed me some of the lyrics and I was attracted to them. Songs like 'Moonlight Drive' and 'Soul Kitchen' were real out there, yet I could see the fluidity and rhythm to them and right away thought, God, put this to rock music? Yeah! . . . Jim was real shy and sung facing the corner of the garage, but he was different and great looking. He didn't know anything about chords or any of that, but he was a genius for melody—he heard them in his head. . . ."

Along with Ray's brother on guitar, the burgeoning group recorded a demo and, surprisingly, were signed right away by Columbia's Billy James, then left to sit and wait. While they waited, Robby Krieger replaced Ray's brother on guitar, and the music really started to happen. They were serious, rehearsing five days a week, but when the Doors auditioned for a few local clubs, they were turned down because they had no bass player. Believing their sound was exciting and different, the Doors refused to compromise.

Jim wrote to his father to tell him of the exciting new developments in his life, but the elder Morrison wrote back to Jim, objecting angrily, stating that what Jim was doing was "a crock." Jim never wrote to his father again.

Still hell-bent, getting arrested, tearing up friends' apartments, breaking girls' hearts, getting high as a helium balloon, Jim somehow managed to make the all-important rehearsals. Just as they were about to relent and get a bass player, the Doors were offered a running gig at London Fog, a tiny dump on the Sunset Strip. At first Jim was shy, singing with his back to the small audience, but still managed to attract a slim, freckle-faced redhead, nineteen-year-old Pamela Courson, who quickly became his beloved counterpart. Although he would certainly veer off wildly in other directions—including my own—in his heart Jim Morrison was very much a one-woman man. Seemingly reserved and acquiescent, Pam could not only match wits with Jim but give as good (or as bad) as she got. She was the only one who would dare tell Jim that he needed to see a psychiatrist (he went twice) or that he'd been wearing his leather pants so long that he smelled. She nagged him about his excessive drinking. When he fucked around, she fucked around. Jim could be brutal, sometimes tying her up, insisting on anal sex. When he stayed away for days at a time, she wrote "Faggot" on his favorite vest and cut his clothes into tiny pieces. Although she called herself "Jim's creation," Pam was hot-tempered, demanding, and fearless, and somehow managed to hang on to her wild-child man for the rest of his life.

Realizing he had too much musical competition, Jim developed his stage show so that it became increasingly fraught with danger—he would take acid, pop amyl nitrate before going onstage, collapse in a heap, start fistfights. After four months the Doors were shown the London Fog door—just in time to get hired at the Whiskey-a-Go-Go, the showplace for rock's biggest acts, where Jim's antics started causing quite a buzz. People (like myself) turned up just to hear Jim alter lyrics to songs like Them's "Gloria": "She come on my bed, she come in my mouth, little girl suck my . . ." It was almost too much.

Dropped by Columbia, the Doors were free to seek another record deal, and word was out that the singer was a true madman. Encouraged by Arthur Lee of Love, Jac Holzman checked out the Doors and offered them a deal at his small label, Elektra. This was incredible news for the Doors, but already the band members were plagued by the consistently destructive behavior of their singer. One night when Jim didn't show up for a Whiskey gig, John and Ray found him at the eight-dollar motel he was so fond of, flying on twenty doses of acid. "He really wanted to get out of himself," marveled John, "totally go to the ends, as far as you can go, every time. Find out!" The Doors had been fired and rehired at the Whiskey over and over again, but this would be their final Whiskey gig. During "The End" Jim shouted to the expectant revelers that he wanted to fuck his mother.

Recording on the Doors album began in September 1966, produced by Paul Rothchild on a four-track recorder at Sunset Sound Studios, and totally capturing the sensual feel of a live Doors show. According to Rothchild, Jim had no fear about revealing himself. "He was exposing his soul and that was bravery in the extreme in those days when everybody was posturing." The first time the Doors attempted "The End," Jim was high on booze and acid, repeating the words "Fuck the mother, kill the father" until they became a twisted mantra and the session was over. But the following day Rothchild described as "the most awe-inspiring thing I'd ever witnessed in a studio . . . one of the most important moments in recorded rock and roll." They got it on the second take, and Ray described the experience as Jim taking everyone on a "shamanistic voyage." Jim later said that "The End" was about three things: "sex, death, and travel . . . liberation from the cycle of birth-orgasm-death." When the music was over, everybody went home, but Jim came back alone and destroyed the studio, pulling a fire extinguisher from the wall and spraying chemical foam all over the control board. Ray said there had been too much heat and that Jim was just "calming the whole thing down." The bill was sent to Elektra.

After a controversial stint at New York's Ondine Club, Jim moved in with Pam Courson in Laurel Canyon at 1812 Rothdell Trail, a little green wooden house above the Country Canyon Store—right next door to a friend of mine!

This little story illustrates how wide open Jim Morrison was to whatever came his way, and what Pam had to deal with on a daily basis. I didn't know my friend lived next door to the Doors' lead singer, and one afternoon when I was alone in the house, inhaling some of that strange PCP liquid, I heard some very familiar music. Aaaahhhh. I had heard the songs often enough to know that somebody must have had a prerelease copy of the Doors album, and they were playing it very loud. I went out into the blasting sunlight and down a hundred rock stairs until I was surrounded by that glorious music, which was pouring out of the house next door! I could see the naked back of a guy digging around in his fridge, humming along with "The End." He grabbed a beer and when he turned around and started to knock it back, I let out a minor shriek. Lord have mercy on my teenage soul, it was Jim Morrison himself, with those black leather pants unzipped to the danger zone. Armed with fictitious chemical confidence, I proceeded through the green door and went into a perfect backbend (purple velvet dress over my head) in the middle of the tatty Persian rug. Despite my whacked-out condition, I soon realized I wasn't alone with the Lizard King. I opened my eyes and stared into the face of a very pissed-off redhead. Jim was backed into a corner, curled up, hissing "Get it on!" Then the redhead very unpolitely asked me to leave. So un-neighborly! As I careened back up the stairs, I was too high to have been embarrassed, even though I should have been.

A few minutes later I heard a racket downstairs and then Jim was tapping at the door. He wanted to know what I was on, and could he have some? I assumed the sparkling liquid was on the planet for my pleasure. Much later I found out it was used to knock out gorillas, elephants, and whales. I still mourn the brain cells that bit the dust in those days. But that sunny California afternoon I gave Jim Morrison the quart jar, and soon we were rolling around on the floor like old friends. The following night, as I left for a Doors show at the Hullabaloo Club, I had to step over a whole bunch of shattered Doors demos that Pam had hurled at Jim when he attempted to come back home. I waited for Jim at the backstage door, and he took me by the hand to the hallowed backstage area. I offered him a spot of Trimar and we poked around and found a ladder leading to a small musty stage area. Jim laid out my muskrat jacket like it was a set of silk sheets. Up, up, and away. We landed in horny nirvana, throbbing and pulsating, making out like maniacs, until we heard the first few chords of "Light My Fire" from somewhere over the rainbow. His gorgeous face loomed before me, and I could see him trying to figure out where he was, what he was doing, and what he was supposed to be doing. Then realization hit and he was down the ladder and gone. I lay there, looking at the glowing spot where his face had been, trying to gather up my limbs and make them function. Then I followed him. Very dumb move. I walked right onstage with the Doors and stood there gaping like a goon. Jim was already squirming at the microphone, and a large roadie came to lead me gallantly from the stage. I guess I should have been embarrassed one more time, but I wasn't.

When the gig was over, Jim climbed behind the wheel of my 1962 Olds and we cruised the hot Hollywood night. After some date-nut bread and O.J. at the now-defunct Tiny Naylor's, Jim headed for the hills, grabbed the jar of Trimar, and hurled it into some overgrown ivy. "That stuff could hurt our heads," he drawled. "Now we won't be tempted." Had it been anyone other than Jim Morrison, I might have been seriously pissed off, but I took it like a big girl. He actually gave me a small lecture on the evils of drugs, and told me that his disorderly stage persona was just an elaborate act to go along with his music. I felt like a privileged insider, but I didn't believe it for a minute. I had my head on his shoulder and he was calling me "darling." It was a sweet summer dream come true. Predawn I dropped him off at the cheesy Sunset motel where he stayed when Pam threw him out. He told me to come and see him the next day, but when I flounced in with high hopes, I found that he had already checked out. He was back on Rothdell Trail. I listened to Jim and never, ever took another whiff of Trimar. Too bad he didn't follow his own astute advice on the evils of drugs.

That long-ago night Jim also told me that he really considered himself to be "a poet." So did Pam, and it became one of the consistent battles in their relationship. She wanted him to leave the rowdy rock life and spend his time writing poetry.

The Doors' press kit contained some Jim gems. He was awesomely quotable:

> We are from the West. The sunset. The night. The sea. This is the end. The world we would suggest would be of a new, wild West. A sensuous and evil world. Strange and haunting, the path of the sun. . . . I like ideas about the breaking away or overthrowing of the established order—I am interested in anything about revolt, disorder, chaos, especially activity that seems to have no meaning.

He also insisted that his parents were dead.

"Break on Through," the first single, didn't even crack the Top 100, but the Doors were rampaging across America, grabbing devotees, and by the summer of 1967, "Light My Fire" was climbing to the top spot, followed by the album, which hit number one and stayed on the charts for two years.

While the Beatles and Stones led the Summer of Love kids on a merry chase, the Doors represented the shady side of rock and roll. Jim Morrison was a bona fide damp dream, the unruly Pied Piper who led us willingly into chaos. He slept anywhere, fell down in the Sunset Strip gutters and was carried away by strangers. He drove cars into trees and left them behind. He was the real thing. Said John Densmore, "Morrison was devastating in those days. He wore his leather pants twenty-four hours a day and looked like some kind of swamp lizard out on the border."

The second album, *Strange Days,* which included the astute "People Are Strange," was recorded in three months and the Doors went back on the road. According to *Crawdaddy* magazine, "The Doors, in person, have become the best the West has to offer . . . the best performers in the country, and if the albums are poetry as well as music, then the stage show is most of all drama, brilliant theater in any sense of the word." And though they were starting to make a fortune, it didn't seem to matter to Jim, who never carried any cash. True to his credo, Jim continued to overthrow the established order. At a drunken show in Long Island, Jim tried to remove all of his clothes. Right after a gig at Yale University, Jim climbed to the bell tower, stripped naked, and swung out on the bell-tower shutter, hundreds of feet above the scattering crowd. He was promptly arrested.

Jim's mother, Clara, refused to stay "dead," finally reaching her missing son through Elektra, inviting him home for Thanksgiving, adding that he had better cut his hair. After the conversation Jim told one of his roadies not to accept her calls. Backstage at a Doors show in Washington, D.C., she was unable to see her son. During "The End" that night, Jim stared at Clara at the side of the stage. "Mother? I want to . . . FUCK YOU!" Jim never saw or spoke to his mother again.

In August 1966 the Doors played the Cheetah Club in L.A. I was front and center, swooning when Jim seemed to topple into the audience. It wouldn't be the last time he took that precarious dive. We started to expect his sweaty madness in our upraised arms.

In September the Doors performed on Ed Sullivan's very important TV show, making rock history when they were told to excise the word "higher" from "Light My Fire." The promise was made, but Jim didn't keep it. They never played "The Ed Sullivan Show" again, and Jim didn't care.

Validated by *Time, Newsweek,* and *Vogue,* who called him "shaken-loose and mind shaking . . . as if Edgar Allan Poe had blown back as a hippie. . . ." Jim kept taking chances onstage. "Sometimes I just stop the song and let out a long silence," Jim said, "let out all the latent hostilities and uneasiness and tensions before we get everyone together." The music stopped for minutes at a time, the audience stopped breathing. "I like to see how long they can stand it, and just when they're about to crack, I let 'em go." In a highly quoted interview, Jim told *Time* magazine that the Doors were "erotic politicians" who were looking for "an electric wedding," adding that he was more interested in "the dark side of the moon."

Jim's close friend and photographer, Paul Ferrara, told me that Jim was well aware of the pandemonium his icon status created. "One time we were watching *The Misfits,* and he said, 'The thing about Marilyn Monroe is that she lets it all hang out. She's everything to all people.' Jim had the same vulnerability that Marilyn had. The fact that he brought it up makes me think that he was totally aware of the 'thing' he was experiencing."

The day after Jim's twenty-fourth birthday, December 9, 1967, he crossed the imaginary line to the dark side of the moon. Backstage at a gig in New Haven, Connecticut, he was making out with a young girl in a shower stall when a cop stormed in, insisting that no one was allowed backstage. When Jim grabbed his crotch and told the cop to "eat it," his face was sprayed with Mace. The cop realized he had made a big mistake and, along with the Doors' manager, Bill Siddons, bathed Jim's face with water, but Jim wasn't amused. He was mad at the pigs. During the instrumental break in "Back Door Man," Jim put on a thick Southern accent and insulted the entire New Haven police force. After the tirade, he shouted, "The whole fucking world hates me!" and a police lieutenant climbed up onstage to tell Jim he was under arrest. "Okay, pig," he taunted, "come on, say your thing, man!" Then there was chaos. Jim was dragged offstage and down a flight of stairs, beaten, and kicked before being thrown into a cop car and taken to the station house—arrested for "indecent and immoral exhibition." Not to mention "breach of the peace and resisting arrest." The charges were eventually dropped. A couple of months later a very loaded Jim was in trouble again after being whacked over the head by an incensed guard at an X-rated Las Vegas movie theater. The police arrived and Jim called them "redneck stupid bastards" and "chickenshit pigs." He was arrested for "public drunkenness" and taken to jail. It was becoming a very common occurrence.

Paul Ferrara told me a tale that describes Jim's everyday behavior pretty well. "There were three of us in Jim's Ford Shelby. We turned onto Sunset Boulevard after a night of partying. Jim floored it in front of the Whiskey and ran through about four red lights—foot on the floor, about one hundred miles an hour, cars zooming across in front of us! All I remember saying was, 'I want the fuck out of this car!!' It freaked me out! I felt he was playing Russian roulette with all of our lives—the same as pulling a trigger on a gun you're not sure about. I was angry, but not as angry as when he killed himself. He was trying all the time. It was like he was saying, 'I can walk across the tightrope and you can't.'" When I asked Paul if he

Jim Morrison's mug shot in New Haven, Connecticut, after his arrest for "indecent and immoral exhibition." What else was new? (POLICE SHOT)

thought Jim lived in the moment, he said, "It was a very pagan moment. He was just in a different consciousness—he had switched over, broke on through."

During the recording of the third album, John Densmore quit the Doors because Jim was so drunk he was unable to sing, lying on the floor in his own urine. It didn't last twenty-four hours. The Doors hired the first of Jim's "caretakers," people who followed him around attempting to keep him out of trouble. Needless to say, it didn't work. The rest of the Doors had to tiptoe around their leader's increasingly erratic lunacy. Almost every song on *Waiting for the Sun* took twenty takes. Jim tried to recite a rambling poem, "The Celebration of the Lizard King," but was too wasted. "I am the lizard king!" he shrieked. "I can do anything!" His drinking pissed everybody off, so he drank more. He arrived at the studio with a motley assortment of scary hangers-on. He was late. He was very late. Sometimes he didn't show up at all.

Up until now, Jim had enjoyed the heady power he had created, but was getting edgy about the pressures of fame. He was the antithesis of his glamorous image and preferred the bleak anonymity of a cheap motel. He didn't own anything (like a home), didn't *want* to own anything, and constantly gave away any belongings he happened to accumulate. When he did buy clothes, he would leave his old ones behind as if he were shedding a skin. He carried one credit card and a torn-up driver's license. Bored with the skintight Adonis image, he trimmed his long ringlets, gained weight, became bloated and pale. He felt that due to his fame, people had stopped being honest with him, and he was alone. In June of 1968 he actually tried to quit the band, saying, "It's not what I want to do," but was convinced to stay. The Doors caused riots out on the road. Jim crawled around on the floor, curled himself into a fetal position, and howled. Critics called him "mesmerizing," "spell-binding," "demonic." There was a disastrous meeting with Janis Joplin at a pool party, and Jim was so brutally obnoxious, she wound up clobbering him over the head with her bottle of Southern Comfort. Paul Ferrara was there. "Janis and Jim were sitting on the couch, waiting their turns at pool, and they started arguing really loud, beating on each other, so we separated them. Then they were both gone and we heard a honking out in the driveway. We all ran out and Janis was beating Jim with a bottle in the front seat of the car." Jim was disappointed when she didn't want to see him again.

A good friend of mine was there the night Jim crawled across the floor at New York's Scene Club to the stage where Jimi Hendrix was playing. He wrapped himself around the guitarist and shouted, "I want to suck your cock!," actually attempting to remove Jimi's velvet trousers. "I was the guy who broke the thing up," Paul Ferrara told me. "Poor Hendrix was trying to do his set, and his fans started beating Jim up. He was flailing and I gave him this massive bear hug, took him in my arms, and dragged him away."

"Hello, I Love You" was the Doors' first smash in Europe, and the tour went well until they reached Amsterdam and Jim took every drug that was handed to him by enthusiastic fans. He gyrated wildly onstage for a minute or two, then collapsed into a heap and was taken to the hospital.

Waiting for the Sun went gold the day it came out, and it looked as if the Doors were about to become "acceptable," which irked and confused Jim. When critics barked that the Doors were going "commercial," Jim needed to prove that he was more than a rock-and-roll commodity while he headlined the Forum. Assisted by his booze buddy, poet Michael McClure, Jim met with a literary agent, hoping to get his poetry published. The agent was very encouraging, which gave Jim the impetus to eventually publish it himself. Meanwhile the Doors worked on their documentary, and by the end of October Jim was devoting all of his time to editing *Feast of Friends*.

Todd Schifman was Jim's booking agent and ally. "We had a line of communication that was pretty unique. I got to know his character pretty well. Because I wore a suit and tie, I think he was kind of surprised by my liberal ideas." When I asked Todd about Jim's relationship with Pam, he said he thought it was "abusive and unhealthy," adding, "He was the sadist and she was the masochist. . . . Here's an area where I hesitate . . . In private, at parties, I certainly got the impression that [Jim and another male celebrity] were involved in a full-blown relationship. I've been at social gatherings where they were a couple. Jim was not the dominant one." I told Todd that perhaps bisexuality was just one more way for Jim to push the limits. "I think Jim was gay," he said categorically. What about Pamela and Patricia? I asked. "That doesn't mean he wasn't gay. Those were not successful storybook relationships. And Pam always seemed like a little boy to me. I know for a fact that Jim was into being gay."

Jim's constant drinking was messing with his performances, the once-spontaneous collapses and falls becoming rote and predictable. Sometimes he could barely stand up, hanging on to the microphone, finally finishing the show from the floor. After a riot in Phoenix, the *Gazette* reported: "Blame it on the Doors, possibly the most controversial group in the world. Lead singer Jim Morrison appeared in shabby clothes and behaved belligerently. The crowd ate up Morrison's antics, which included hurling objects . . . cussing and making rude gestures." When Jim realized his words and music were taking second place to his terrifying persona, he tried to rein it in during a pivotal show at the Hollwood Bowl. He just sang his ass off. But the audience had expected a Doors freak show. There was no encore that night, and Jim bitterly accepted his fate. At a concert with the Who in Queens, New York, Jim went ballistic and was downright disgusting, chanting on about "a Mexican whore sucking my prick." When he grabbed his dick and let out a scream of obscenities to a girl down front, her boyfriend responded by going for Jim with a chair and all hell broke loose. By the time it was over, all the Doors' equipment was destroyed and twenty people were hospitalized. But Queens was just the foreplay for Miami.

While Jim struggled with his massive success, Pam dug it. Jim bought her a new XKE and spent $250,000 so she could run her own trendy boutique on Sunset Boulevard. She started taking cocaine and dabbling with heroin, which pissed Jim off. They had severe arguments but were too caught up in each other's drama to make a move. Jim continued his downward drinking spiral. At a show at Madison Square Garden, Jim pointed to one side of the hall and said, "You are life," then to the other side, "You are death," then announced, "I straddle the fence—and my balls hurt."

Along with friend Paul Ferrara, in February 1969 Jim attended several performances of the highly avant-garde Living Theatre, which really stirred him up. The performers interacted with the audience, agitating, confronting, and frightening them, finally ending the play by stripping down to loincloths and forming a pyramid that spelled out "ANARCHISM." Jim was inspired and planned to add these confrontational tactics to his very next show—in Miami. "I think he was liberating himself, just the way he saw the Living Theatre do. We were totally blown away by the freedom," Paul Ferrara told me. "He was about experimenting to the max. He was looking to open all the different doors. Scientific expedition—'I'll take six of these and see where I get.' And he had this humongous secret life. I knew him as a devil and an angel at the same time. He couldn't separate them. He was the most generous

Jim on the floor—a typical place to find him. (MICHAEL MONTFORT/MICHAEL OCHS ARCHIVES/ VENICE, CALIF.)

person I knew, but sometimes he did the angel thing, sometimes the devil thing."

Somebody should have seen it coming. The capacity crowd was over-charged by the time the Lizard King finally made it to the stage with a mad gleam in his eye and so far gone that he probably couldn't see. The Doors played some music, but their singer couldn't hear it. "I'm not talking about a revolution!" he howled. "I'm talking about havin' a *gooooooood* time! Hey, lis-ten! I'm lonely, I need some love, you all. Come on, I need some good times. I need some love-ah love-ah. Ain't anybody gonna love my ass?" While the Doors gamely played behind him, Jim waited for a response to his plea. "No-body gonna come up here and love me, huh? All right for you, baby, that's too bad. I'll get somebody else!" After a few words of "Five to One," Jim began his confrontation. "You're all a bunch of fucking idiots! Lettin' people tell you what you're gonna do! Lettin' people push you around! . . . Maybe you love gettin' your face stuck in the shit. . . . You're all a bunch of fuckin' slaves!" He hoarsely tried to sing, then shouted, "THERE ARE NO RULES!" He put down the state of Florida, and when a freak from L.A. handed Jim a lamb, he said, "I'd fuck her, you know, but she's too young." A few words of "Touch Me," then the tirade continued. "Hey, wait a minute! Wait a *minute*! You blew it, you blew it! I'm not gonna take this shit! I'm coming out! I'm coming out!! FUCK YOU!" He grabbed a cop's hat and sailed it into the audience, cham-pioning the Living Theatre. "I wanna get on the trip, I wanna change the world!" Over and over he repeated, "I wanna see some action out there!" Then "Let's see a little skin. Let's get naked! Grab your fuckin' friend and love him! I'm talkin' about some love! Love love love love love love love." People started taking off their clothes, and then it happened: "Do you want to see my cock? You didn't come here only for *music,* did you? You came for something else, didn't you? WHAT IS IT? You want to see my cock, don't you? That's what you came for, isn't it?! YEAAAAHHHH!" He then ripped off his shirt and started fiddling with his belt buckle. Nobody knew it, but Jim was wear-ing boxer shorts, planning to pull a "Living Theatre," but when he started un-buckling his pants, a roadie came to the rescue and tried to stop it.

Nobody seems to know what happened next. "See it? Did you see it?" Jim asked the flabbergasted audience. "There are no rules, there are no limits!" he insisted. "C'mon, this is your show, anything you want, let's do it!" and fans started to swarm the stage. He prowled through the frenzied crowd, pretend-ing to masturbate; he got on his knees in front of Robby and, when he was knocked offstage, led a whip dance through the concert hall while several fights broke out. The Doors played a seething version of "Light My Fire" un-til the electricity had to be turned off. "Uh-oh," Jim later said to manager Bill Siddons, "I think I might have exposed myself out there."

Jim and the Doors missed the heated response to the show, flying out the next day to the Caribbean, where Jim had a perfectly miserable time on his little holiday (without Pam—they were in another battle). When asked about the concert, Jim admitted he had been too drunk to remember what happened. Meanwhile warrants for Jim's arrest were being drawn up in Miami. One felony—lewd and lascivious behavior (stating that Jim did "lewdly and lasciviously expose his penis and shake it . . . simulate acts of masturbation upon himself and oral copulation on another)—and three misdemeanors—"indecent exposure, open profanity, and drunkenness." Headlines across America shouted GROSSED OUT BY THE DOORS and GET RICH QUICK—BE OBSCENE, proclaiming Jim "King of Orgasmic Rock." The Doors were banned in concert halls all over the country, gigs were canceled, and they were dropped from radio playlists. Jim's life had changed irrevocably, and he dragged the rest of the Doors along with him. Everything seemed to hinge on the trial. The band was never the same again.

Jim turned himself in to the FBI on April 3, 1969, then buried what remained of his sex symbol status by growing a full beard, rarely bathing, wearing the same clothes endlessly. He began recording his poetry, worked on his own movie, *HWY,* about an aimless young hitchhiker, and waited for the trial. He and Pam moved to Beachwood Canyon. Life wasn't much fun. Pam's heroin use had escalated and she was trying to hide it. And Jim was drinking so much, he rarely satisfied her. "Some sex symbol," she scrawled on the mirror in lipstick. "Can't even get it up!" In a telling interview with Jerry Hopkins, Jim said that getting drunk was "a choice. . . . I guess it's the difference between suicide and slow capitulation."

The fourth album, *The Soft Parade,* took eight difficult months to record, and by the time it was completed in June, the Doors were starting to get a few bookings despite the "Miami incident." Jim grumbled about the five-thousand-dollar bond that had to be posted for every show, calling it a "fuck clause," but the shows were well received and without incident.

On July 3, 1969, Brian Jones was found dead in his swimming pool and Jim wrote a touching poem for him, "Ode to L.A. While Thinking of Brian Jones—Deceased." Strangely, two years later to the day, Jim himself would be found dead in water.

In November Jim returned to Miami and entered a not-guilty plea. Bail was set for five thousand dollars, with the trial scheduled to begin the following April. And he was about to get in trouble again. After a rowdy plane ride to a Rolling Stones show in Phoenix, a very inebriated Jim and his friend Tom Baker were arrested upon landing, charged with "drunk and disorderly conduct" and "interfering with the flight of an aircraft," a very serious offense. Both of them had a heated argument with the captain, and Tom, in particular, had made suggestive remarks to the flight attendant and grabbed at her thigh. He and Jim were held in the Phoenix jail for eighteen hours. Back in

L.A., Jim had a car accident that destroyed five trees on La Cienega Boulevard, where he left the car behind, claiming it had been stolen. At a party for his twenty-sixth birthday, a half-comatose Jim whipped out his member and proceeded to pee on an expensive rug. Guests caught it in goblets so the rug wouldn't be destroyed. A day later he told Bill Siddons that he thought he was having a nervous breakdown.

One night around this time, I was at my den of iniquity away from home, the Whiskey. I must have been pretty hard up because the 1910 Fruitgum Company were playing, but I was determined to rock out. I was sitting with Miss Lucy from my group, the GTOs, when Jim Morrison slid into our booth and hollered, "Get it on! Suck my mama!" Jim definitely had a thing about his mom, no doubt about it. Anyway, we were nice to him (I still harbored a secret adoration), but he was in one of those infamous moods again, and very drunk, too. He reached across the table, yelled, "Get it on!," grabbed Lucy's beer, and hurled it into her face. She got pretty upset and told him it wasn't very nice. He said, "I know," with a sad, sorrowful voice, as if he couldn't help it. Right before he crawled across the dirty Whiskey floor to climb onstage with the startled Fruitgum Company, he slapped me real hard across the face for no reason. It was as if he was trying real hard to feel something. With my cheek throbbing and mascara running down my face, I watched him grab the microphone away from the singer, moan, and shove it right down his pants. The owner of the Whiskey finally had to turn off the lights and sound to get Jim out of the way. The lights are turned out, I couldn't help thinking, so I guess the music's over.

Not quite. The relative failure of *The Soft Parade* got the Doors back into the studio within six months, where Jim pulled out his final bag of tricks. Critics raved about *Morrison Hotel Hard Rock Cafe. Rock* magazine said, "Morrison isn't sexy anymore, you say; he's getting old and fat. Well, you can't see a potbelly on record, but you can hear balls. . . ." Jim claimed much of the album, including "Roadhouse Blues," was written for Pam. He loved her but was also involved with a writer from New York, Patricia Kennealy, a white witch. When the Doors played a four-night stint at the Felt Forum, Jim spent his afternoons with Pam and his evenings with Patricia.

Worries about the Phoenix "skyjacking" allegations were put to rest when, on April 6, the flight attendant changed her testimony, and Jim's appearance was rescheduled. On the twenty-seventh Jim was acquitted of the charges. "They were just trying to hang me because I was the one that had the well-known face," Jim said. "The trouble with these busts is that people that don't like me like to believe it because I'm the reincarnation of everything they consider evil. I get hung both ways."

After the *Morrison Hotel* tour, Jim took the master tapes for the new live Doors album back to New York and stayed with Patricia Kennealy. Although his relationship with Patricia was as haphazard and unpredictable as all the rest, on June 24 the couple were married in an ancient Celtic pagan ritual at Patricia's apartment. A high priest and priestess performed the Wicca wedding, in which Jim and Patricia took vows and a few drops of their commingled blood were mixed with consecrated wine. Jim fainted after the ceremony, said Patricia, because of the huge amount of energy created inside the magical circle, and not because of the ritual bloodletting.

"What Pam and Jim had was a total love affair," Paul Ferrara told me. "But there were those days when he disappeared. I've heard homosexual stories, I've heard everything. There were so many weirdos throwing themselves at him. Who knows? If they had the right drug at the right time—'Hey Jim, let's step in the alley and get off.' I married one of Jim's girlfriends. I slept with Pam. We were fairly liberal with our girlfriends. The night she took me home, she said, 'Well, he's with somebody else!' Jim found out about it, but it wasn't talked about. Maybe he cared, but he didn't show it. He was with somebody else!"

After a three-week jaunt to Paris, Jim waited several edgy days in Dade County, Florida, for Judge Goodman to finally begin the trial. The state's first witness was a tiny teenage girl, Colleen, her hair in a ponytail. "He pulled down his pants," she said, appalled, "and . . . stroked it. . . . It was disgusting." She clutched her hanky and whined that she had been "shocked." Colleen's boyfriend confirmed her testimony, then Mom hit the stand and agreed that her daughter had been "visibly upset" when she arrived home from the concert. The shocking audio evidence was played for a solemn jury. Two different people testified that Jim had exposed himself for "five to eight seconds." Then somebody refuted their testimony, saying he had seen no oral copulation or exposure. On and on it went, like a *Mad* magazine nightmare, with Jim Morrison in the role of spoof scapegoat. Initially Jim took an interest in the workings of the law, copiously filling notebooks as the trial progressed. By the last few days he was amusing himself by giving the jurors nicknames.

While the trial dragged on, Patricia Kennealy called Jim in Florida with the news that she was pregnant. He asked her to join him, but after their first evening together avoided her for the next two days. When she showed up in the courtroom, Jim was forced to deal with the situation, telling Patricia that a child would ruin their relationship, ultimately convincing her to have an abortion. Patricia says that she and Jim both cried, and he promised to be with her when the time came. But he didn't even call.

Due to Doors gigs, the trial plodded on for a month. The 150 photographs displayed as evidence showed no exposure of any kind. When Jim finally took the stand, for four hours he was calm, eloquent, and gracious, all the while insisting that he didn't expose himself or simulate oral copulation on Robby. After deliberating for two and a half hours, the jurors handed down a mixed verdict: innocent of lewd behavior and drunkenness, guilty of indecent exposure and profanity. (Jim had exposed himself, but it wasn't lewd!?) Released on a fifty-thousand-dollar bond, Jim told the press that the verdict would do nothing to alter his lifestyle because he had done nothing wrong. The Doors had lost over a million dollars in bookings, and Jim now had to await sentencing.

During the trial Jimi Hendrix died, two weeks later Janis Joplin OD'd, and Jim's imbibing increased. Ominously he told his friends, "You're drinking with number three." He and Pam fought so ferociously that she went to Paris, where Jim later heard that she had taken up with a French count. He became more and more morose and disillusioned.

On October 30, Jim faced Judge Goodman, who handed down the stiffest sentence he could—sixty days of hard labor at Dade County jail for each count, followed by two years and four months' probation as well as a five-hundred-dollar fine. Jim's lawyer filed an appeal. Jim drove back to L.A. after the sentencing, stopping in New Orleans, where he dashed off a postcard—"The Sacrifice of the Divine Lamb"—to the Doors' office: "Don't worry; the end is near, Ha Ha."

Elektra released *13,* a Doors greatest-hits package, and Jim and the Doors went to work, writing new songs for a new album, *L.A. Woman,* which included the anagram for his own name, "Mr. Mojo Risin'," and the eerie "Riders on the Storm." But Jim was very unhappy. There was a bright spot when he recorded more of his poetry, but at a gig in New Orleans Ray Manzarek claims that he could see Jim's spirit leave him. "He lost all his energy midway through the set. He hung on the microphone and it just slipped away. You could actually see it leave him. He was drained." In defiance, Jim pounded the microphone stand into the stage, over and over until the wood splintered, then sat down on the drum riser. The rest of the tour was canceled. The last song Jim Morrison sang onstage was "Light My Fire." The Doors never performed in public again.

Todd Schifman had gotten Jim together with MGM head Jim Aubrey, who Todd says was a "stone believer" in Jim. "We negotiated a contract with Jim that was unbelievable," Todd said. "It gave Morrison the right to three pictures at MGM, to direct, produce, write, star, write the music—unbelievable artistic control. He set up offices and started writing, but his self-destructiveness wouldn't allow him to really make what he should have out of the deal. After the first year nothing was accomplished, so Aubrey wouldn't pick up the option."

Demoralized and at his lowest ebb, Jim started snorting piles of cocaine, on the prowl for a woman who would stretch the limits with him. While he was staying at the Chateau Marmont, he spent a few wild nights with a buxom neighbor, instigating three-ways and once waking up in a tangle of bloody sheets after they shared champagne glasses of each other's blood. As if on cue, Pam returned from Paris. Patricia Kennealy arrived soon afterward, and the two women took their turns with Jim, actually encountering each other one mad, stoned night. After a couple of months, however, Jim was spending most of his time with Pam, and Patricia went back to New York.

When asked to do an antidrug "Speed Kills" radio spot for the Do It Now Foundation, Jim surprisingly agreed, screwing up every take until the representative fled in abject frustration. Jim couldn't seem to help himself. "I never did a song on speed. Drunk, yeaaahh . . . Shooting speed ain't cool, so snort it. . . . Don't shoot speed, you guys. Christ, smoke pot! . . . Please don't shoot speed, try downers. . . ."

Jim worked hard on the *L.A. Woman* album, and according to many of his friends, he then quit the Doors and quietly made the decision to leave for Paris, where he would pursue his life as a poet. Some of Jim's friends say he was enthused and excited about the move; others, like Patricia Kennealy, disagree. She spent a week with him in L.A. while Pamela searched for an apartment in Paris. "I took one look at him and knew he wasn't going to be around very much longer," she said. "It seemed not to be *him* anymore; the dark side was taking over." He walked the streets, sleeping with a different girl every night, smoked three packs of Marlboros a day, coughed blood, and mixed tequila, vodka, whiskey, and gin until he was violently ill. Another one of his girlfriends had an abortion. At barely twenty-seven, Jim told Michael McClure that he felt forty-seven. In a note to *Creem*'s Dave Marsh, Jim closed with "I am not mad. I am interested in freedom. Good luck, Jim Morrison."

L.A. Woman was garnering raves and the single "Love Her Madly" was the Doors' first Top Ten hit in two years, but instead of the usual chaotic touring, Jim was cramming his poetry notebooks with reflective, scathing insights, trying to put some order back into his disorderly life. For a very brief time, at 17 rue Beautrellis on the Right Bank in Paris, it seemed as if Jim might be able to make some sense of it all. He lost weight, shaved his unruly beard, didn't drink as much, and wrote daily, telling people he'd finished one book and was beginning another about the Miami trial. He and Pam seemed to be living inside a gentle truce, but wicked habits die hard—or not at all. Creativity soon fled, and Jim sat for hours in front of an empty page. There was a new set of drinking buddies, sleazy, unexplored nightclubs to fall down in at four A.M. But on July 1, 1971, Jim once again resolved to overcome the battle with his old demon, alcohol. On July 3 he was dead.

The statement that Pam gave police the day Jim died says that she and Jim returned from a Robert Mitchum movie about one A.M. Jim watched some home movies while she washed dishes, then they listened to some records and fell asleep about two-thirty. Jim's noisy breathing awakened her about an hour later, and after pacing the room a few times, Jim told her he didn't feel well and wanted to take a warm bath. While he was in the tub, Jim felt nauseated and Pam brought him a pot from the kitchen and he threw up. When he threw up a second time, Pam noticed some blood, but Jim said, "It's over," he was feeling better, and not to call a doctor. Pam woke up a while later and found that Jim was still in the tub. She said his head was tilted to one side, his eyes were closed, and he was smiling. She thought he was joking with her and she told him to stop it, until she noticed blood dripping from his nose and started shaking him. After trying to get Jim out of the tub, she called some friends, Alain Ronay and Agnes Varda, saying, "I can't wake him up, I think he's dying."

When the police arrived and confirmed that Jim was dead, Pam told them his name was "Douglas James Morrison" and that he was "a poet." The official cause of death was listed as "natural causes." The doctor decided that Jim must have had "coronary problems" that were exacerbated by heavy drinking, complicated by a lung infection, which caused "myocardial infarction"—a heart attack.

It wasn't until July 5 that the rest of the Doors found out that Jim was gone. Bill Siddons was the first to get the call about rumors that Jim had died, and finally reached Pam, who confirmed the horrible truth. When Bill arrived in Paris the following morning, Jim's body was in a casket, still in the apartment with Pam. He was buried on July 8 at the Père-Lachaise cemetery, exactly where he had told Pam that he wanted to be—close to Balzac, Chopin, and Oscar Wilde, near the grave of Molière. Only a few people attended, and there was no service.

But did Jim Morrison really die that way? Was he dead at all? Back in 1967 Jim proposed faking his death as a publicity stunt. He had once spoken to *Rolling Stone* about someday turning up with a whole new identity. Nobody wanted to believe Jim was dead, and the rumors flew.

According to a dealer in Paris, Jim scored some heroin that was too pure, snorted it in the men's room of the Circus club, and was carried to his flat, where he later died. Friends insist that Jim preferred cocaine to heroin. A cocaine overdose? What if Jim had found Pam's stash of heroin and she told him it was cocaine? Or maybe he had been

"This is the end, beautiful friend." (LOUISE DECARLO)

killed as part of an elaborate conspiracy aimed at the dangerous hippie counterculture? Jim had worked on a screenplay about someone disappearing into a jungle. Had he perpetrated an elaborate hoax, just so he could finally disappear and get a little peace?

In a story told to *Paris Match* magazine by Alain Ronay and Agnes Varda in 1991, something close to the truth finally emerged. Ronay says that while the doctors examined Jim's body, Pam pulled him aside and told him that she and Jim had been snorting heroin for two days, heroin that *she* had supplied. Racked with guilt, she went on to tell Ronay that Jim had been listening to the first Doors album when he took one more hit, and they both nodded out. She did awaken to Jim's heavy breathing and, concerned, got him into the bathtub, then went back to bed and fell asleep. She woke up later and panicked when she realized Jim wasn't in bed with her. She found him in the tub, his nose bleeding, and he threw up three times into the pot, telling her he felt better and to go back to bed. Then he died. "Jim looked so calm," Pam told Ronay. "He was smiling."

In 1969 Jim had named Pam his sole heir, but the will was tied up in court for the next two years. Pam believed she was Jim's common-law widow, demanding an advance on the estate, and when Jim's lawyer authorized a loan, she promptly bought a mink coat and a VW Bug. It has been reported that she worked as a prostitute, partly because Jim predicted it would be so. Pam never stopped grieving and continued her heroin use. She sometimes sat by the phone, waiting for Jim to call. Just when the final accounting of Jim's estate was being made, Pam died of an overdose. She would have gotten half a million dollars immediately, and a quarter of everything the Doors would make in the future, which would have added up to many millions. In a grotesque twist, in 1975 Jim's share of the Doors' earnings was split equally between Jim's parents and Pamela's parents. The antiauthority rebel now supports a retired admiral and a retired high-school teacher.

"A hero is someone who rebels or seems to rebel against the facts of existence and seems to conquer them," Jim told *Circus* magazine. "Obviously that can only work at moments. It can't be a lasting thing. That's not saying that people shouldn't keep trying to rebel against the facts of existence. Someday, who knows, we might conquer death, disease, and war. I think of myself as an intelligent, sensitive human being with the soul of a clown."

RICK NELSON

■

Some People

Call Me

a Teenage

Idol

■

Ricky Nelson brought the devil's music into the homes of millions of Americans every week in crisp, clean black and white. He was neat and tidy. He had good manners. He was drop-dead handsome yet winsomely non-threatening. And his proud parents, Ozzie and Harriet, were always in the audience, grinning their approval as he rocked. Teen idol Ricky Nelson made rock and roll palatable and wholesome, something the average nuclear family could enjoy together every Tuesday night in their very own living room.

As part of radio and then television's "America's Favorite Family," the "irrepressible Ricky" spent three cloudless, blissful decades parading through ideal domestic events that never took place in his real life. Sometimes Ozzie and Harriet were his real parents, sometimes his fictional "Mom and Pop," and the rest of the time his ever-watchful employers.

By the time Ozzie and Harriet Nelson became parents of their second son, Eric Hilliard Nelson, in 1940, they were an established big-band couple, settling in Hollywood when offered a slot on Red Skelton's "Raleigh Cigarette Program." Their good-natured humor helped make the show a runaway success, and two years later "The Adventures of Ozzie and Harriet" hit the airwaves to much acclaim.

Every Saturday stolid David and his mischievous younger brother, Ricky, would dress up in their cowboy outfits and take the Hollywood Boulevard streetcar to the movies, where they fired their cap guns at the bad guys on the screen. The boys walked to Gardner Street School, two and a half blocks from home, coming back each day to their delighted English setter, Nicky. It seemed like the flawless family suburban dream, but every growing pain, every argument behind the closed doors on Camino Palmero, became fodder for the radio show. And in 1948, when David and Ricky were twelve and eight, producer Ozzie added his sons to the cast. "We knew David could handle it," said a writer for the series, "but we weren't sure if Ricky was old enough." From the first day, irrepressible Ricky stole the show with his high-pitched voice and knowing smirk. David played a passive character, setting up his younger brother for the laughs, but if resentment was brewing, the older boy kept it inside.

Young Ricky Nelson—wholesome, tortured teenage TV idol. (AP/WIDE WORLD PHOTOS)

With twenty years of show biz under his belt, Ozzie demanded and received more control over family projects, cowriting *Here Come the Nelsons,* a lightweight, lighthearted film romp that did surprisingly well at the box office. Skinny eleven-year-old Ricky, with his brush cut and braces, had a ball in front of the cameras, excitedly viewing each day's footage with the grown-ups. The following adventures of Ozzie and Harriet would take place on the small screen—for 435 charming, sanitized episodes.

The TV Nelsons lived in a timeless, nameless neighborhood. *The Honeymooners'* Ralph Kramden drove a bus; Lucy's hubby, Ricky Ricardo, played bongos and sang "Babalu," but the viewing audience never found out what placid Ozzie Nelson did for a living, even though he would sail into the house with his lunch pail and announce, "Harriet, I'm home!" Nothing from the frightening headlines ever found its way into the pristine, sparkling pad on Rodgers Road, Anywhere, U.S.A.

Within his domain, Ozzie was the big boss, expecting perfection from everyone, especially his kids. David was rarely unprepared, but Ricky was having too much fun to take it all too seriously, often arriving without his lines memorized. He started planting his dialogue around the set, peeking into the cookie jar and opening drawers during scenes. The boys addressed their parents at home the same way they did on the show: "Yes sir," "No sir," "Yes ma'am," "No ma'am." "Ozzie ruled with an iron hand," said one of Rick's first girlfriends. "He was an extremely domineering, intimidating person and expected an awful lot from Ricky and David. They didn't want to let him down."

Though Ozzie certainly wouldn't have given his approval, at fourteen Ricky lost his virginity to a plump blond hooker in an alleyway on a trip to London, which led to further excursions with many ladies of the night. Teenage Ricky loved to speed around in fast cars and spend a lot of time steaming up the windows, but his main interest was rapidly becoming rock and roll. He wanted to sing like his rockabilly idol, Carl Perkins, but would keep his secret for two more years.

By the time Ricky was sixteen, he was a huge star with half a million dollars in the bank, but still received only a fifty-dollar weekly allowance from his parents. He never wanted for anything. It was all taken care of for him. He rarely dealt with his money, and it remained an abstract concept, which would become a ferocious problem for him later in life.

Ricky finally made up his mind to rock because of a girl. When his new crush, Arlene, cooed dreamily about Elvis Presley, Ricky found himself telling her that he was about to make a record himself and not long afterward did a campy Elvis portrayal on "Adventures." When the response to the show was positive, Ricky told Ozzie that he wanted to cut his own rock-and-roll record. Having been a musician, Ozzie treated his son's request with respect, but proceeded with caution, booking Ricky and his guitar into Knotts Berry Farm's Birdcage Theater with no fanfare. When the reaction was good, Ozzie took a tape of Ricky singing a squeaky-clean version of the Fats Domino hit "I'm Walkin'" to several record companies, who turned him down flat. Only Norman Granz at independent Verve Records was willing to take a chance on the sixteen-year-old TV star. Two weeks after he sang the song on an episode of "Adventures" called "Ricky the Drummer," in which he snapped his fingers and shook his legs while the girls sighed, Verve released "I'm Walkin'." By Ricky's seventeenth birthday, the song had reached number four on the *Billboard* charts and sold over a million copies. Former crush Arlene called Ricky to gush, but he didn't see her again until backstage at one of his concerts fifteen years later.

In his first year of recording, Ricky turned out half a dozen rockabilly hits, all performed on "Adventures" as girls got closer to the stage and swooned in black and white. While the show was on hiatus, Ricky toured with his new band to uproarious screams, fainting females, and damp panties hurled on-stage. With a touch of mascara on his long lashes and his hair in a slight pom-padour, just a hint of Ricky's smile sent his ga-ga fans straight to sweetheart heaven. Though plenty of teenage jailbait could have been his for the pluck-ing, he preferred prostitutes, sometimes three or four at a time, which were procured for him by road managers. Wow.

As a young girl, I was a devoted viewer of the "The Adventures of Ozzie and Harriet." If I had known that Mr. Angel Face Teen Idol was bonking a bunch of hookers, I would have fainted dead away. People just didn't do that kind of thing then, did they? Ha-ha. But Ricky Nelson was a walking di-chotomy, living two, maybe three lives at once.

Off the road, depression set in. Ricky would go through the same old mo-tions on the show, but feeling that his family could never understand the strain of rock stardom, he began to spend his spare time with like-minded musi-cians—Johnny and Dorsey Burnette, Gene Vincent, the Everly Brothers, Ed-die Cochran—playing music and gunning motorcycles on Mulholland Drive way past midnight. He even got close to Elvis Presley, playing football with the King and his cronies at Bel Air Park. It seems Elvis never missed an episode of "Adventures."

Despite his harlot-filled road dates, Ricky was sheltered and tethered by his fame. Playing himself within the confines of an average American family, liv-ing his real life as anything but an average American teenager, must have done some serious damage. At eighteen he carried his family's TV show—an unbe-lievable pressure. He was a millionaire with no checkbook of his own, uncertain if people liked him for any real reasons, increasingly remote and withdrawn yet at the same time naively trusting. His parents held the reins, allowing America's Boy Next Door to rock only so far, and it hurt him deeply when critics questioned his "authenticity" and dedication to rock and roll.

In fact, Ricky almost quit his big feature film *Rio Bravo* because he had to sing a couple of corny Western ballads. Johnny Cash had given him a cool tune called "Restless Kid" for the movie, but Ozzie and musical director Dmitri Tiompkin ultimately prevailed and a forlorn Rick was forced to croon "My Rifle, My Pony and Me." The Johnny Cash song eventually wound up on the album *Ricky Sings Again*. After another good role in *The Wackiest Ship in the Army*, Ricky was offered a meaty part in Lillian Hellman's *Toys in the At-tic*, but was forced to decline due to ABC's threats to cancel "Adventures" if he temporarily left the series. How could he put his entire family out of work? He did showcase his records on the weekly show, but Ozzie also forced his son to sing schmaltzy clinkers and soggy-stringed ballads. Ricky Nelson was being stifled by playing Ricky Nelson when what he really wanted to do was cut loose, rock out, and sweat. In subconscious rebellion, Ricky took control with dangerous hobbies. He almost burned up in a racing car, he actually took up bullfighting, and he earned a black belt in karate. Following the fiery racing accident, Rick said he'd entered the demolition derby to show the crowd he wasn't afraid. Afraid of what? Ozzie's shadow?

At twenty-one Ricky became Rick and had the biggest double-sided hit of his career, "Travelin' Man" backed by "Hello Mary Lou," which reached number one in twenty-two countries and sold six million copies. The album *Rick Is 21* spent nearly a year on the charts. Though his mom still shopped for his food, Rick was finally in his own bachelor digs, dating actresses culled from the *Players Guide* casting directory. The girls Rick dated all describe a romantic, respectful young man who brought flowers and gifts and kissed them for hours. A former Miss California fondly recalls Rick's hair tonic all over her dress. He may have been innocently necking with beauty queens, but Rick was also involved in a hidden relationship with a wild young bohemian blonde addicted to heroin. She disappeared to New York after a horrifying illegal abortion, telling friends she was so in love with Rick that she didn't want to destroy his life. He was devastated, and for years afterward tried to locate his "only true love." He never found her.

Kris Harmon had dreamed of marrying Rick Nelson from the time she was eleven. She kept a photograph of the two of them taken at a celebrity basketball game on her wall with the inscription "Nothing Is Impossible." The power of the mind is an amazing thing. The Harmons and the Nelsons had been friends for many years, so when Rick started dating Kris after encouragement from Harriet, the two sets of parents almost pushed the couple down the aisle.

Kris's father, football great Tom Harmon, and her mother, Elyse, an artist and former actress, raised Kris to be an obedient Catholic girl, but she defiantly admits to being the family's black sheep. Strong-willed and bold, she took over Rick's life where Ozzie hadn't even left off yet. On April 20, 1963, the glamorous young couple were married in a Catholic ceremony, after Rick, a nonpracticing Protestant, brushed up on Catholicism. A daughter, Tracy Christine, was born six months later and the press releases stated that she'd been delivered prematurely. *Very* prematurely. Apparently Rick told a friend, "If Rick Nelson got a girl pregnant, Rick Nelson got married." Recently Tracy Nelson, now a successful actress, told me that she had not really been premature, but was hidden away "because Grandpa didn't want people thinking that Mom and Dad had had sex before they were married."

David had married a year earlier and, as always, Ozzie incorporated his sons' lives/wives into the show. It must have been so weird. Six family members playing themselves—but not really. Even Ozzie's grandchildren appeared in an episode. By 1965 the Nelson family seemed antiquated. The world outside was in color, and it had moved on. At twenty-five, Rick and his pals were still hanging out at the malt shop. Even though Ozzie attempted tragic hipness with shows like "Ozzie a Go Go," "Adventures" was not renewed for the 1966 season. Having worked nonstop for eighteen of his twenty-six years, Rick must have felt nothing but relief.

Rick had stopped touring but continued to record, having signed a twenty-year contract with Decca Records, which enabled him to experiment and branch out musically. But British Invaders—the Beatles, the Stones, the Who—and profound prophet Bob Dylan were stomping all over the twenty-six-year-old former teen idol. It must have hurt so bad. Still he persevered, writing naked autobiographical songs like "You Just Can't Quit": "Don't feel sorry for me / 'Cause can't you see / I'm still me / And I just can't quit." But nobody was listening, nobody was buying. Nobody cared if he quit or not.

But Rick didn't quit. In 1969, heartily inspired by Dylan's country-flavored "Nashville Skyline," he rounded up a batch of excellent musicians, formed the Stone Canyon Band, and started playing live again. Despite vigorous protests, his fellow players convinced Rick to add a few of his oldies to the set, along with the new material, which included three Dylan tunes. Released in 1970, *Rick Nelson in Concert* met with respectful raves and the single, Dylan's "She Belongs to Me," reached number thirty-three on the charts, Rick's highest-ranking single in over five years.

Rick looked different: He had let his hair grow long, he wore boots and bell-bottoms. Some of the audiences he faced wanted the Ricky Nelson black-and-white version. They wanted him to take them back to their tight, bright, unlined bobby-sox days. But he wanted to move on. Rick's next album, *Rick Sings Nelson,* was languishing at the bottom of the charts, so he grudgingly agreed to take part in an "oldies" package show at Madison Square Garden. After going through the "Mary Lou" oldie motions, he launched into a raucous version of the Stones' "Honky Tonk Women." The crowd's enthusiasm turned hostile and the audience of twenty thousand started booing. At least it seemed that way to Rick. Accounts vary—some say only a few people booed—but Rick got the point and it must have stung him like a hive of angry bees.

Rick went home and channeled his account of that hellish evening in one sitting on a single piece of paper, and the insightful result was "Garden Party," in which he realizes "You can't please everyone / So you got to please yourself." After he penned the final killer lyric, "If memories are all I sang / I'd rather drive a truck," Rick called his cousin / manager, Willy Nelson: "Willy, I wrote one! I think I just wrote a hit!"

Fifteen years after "I'm Walkin'" hit the *Billboard* Top Ten, Rick Nelson struck gold again with "Garden Party," giving his waning career another jump start. He went on to write deeply heartfelt songs about his burgeoning belief in reincarnation and the sorrows of lost love, and took them on the road.

After life on "Adventures," Kris found that she didn't have a career and deeply resented Rick for spending so much time touring. They were close to separating when Kris found she was pregnant with twin boys—Matthew and Gunnar. Though they stayed together, the couple grew steadily apart and any real communication ceased, despite the birth of their fourth child, Sam, in 1974. Kris was so jealous of Rick's music that she didn't even allow his guitar in the house.

When Ozzie died in June 1975, Rick slowly fell apart. The spark created by "Garden Party" flickered and went out, the songwriting fizzled. He turned up late to sessions and rehearsals, keeping band members waiting around for hours. He rarely got dressed, preferring to stay in his robe all day long. The thirty-five-year-old star had never written a check, never used a credit card. He had entrusted all the financial decisions to Ozzie and then to Kris, and her outlandish spending had just about broken him. To escape his deeply troubled marriage and to pay for the endless heaps of bills, Rick went back on the road and stayed there for the rest of his life.

Rick believed that entertaining was his life's calling. He felt comfortable on the road—the great escape from reality. He had to be at a certain place at a certain time and someone woke him up and took him there. When he was hungry, he called room service. When he wanted sex, there was always a pretty lady close by who knew all the words to "Travelin' Man" by heart. He always stopped to sign autographs and had a ready smile for his fans. Sometimes the venues were less than desirable. Said a member of the Stone Canyon Band, "Rick played as hard for sixty people as he did for twelve thousand."

Rick was in Monroe, Louisiana, where director Taylor Hackford was filming a TV documentary on the singer, when Kris made her perfectly timed call to announce that she had filed for divorce. He was devastated. When she picked him up at the airport, she drove him to his new house. "You live here now," she informed him. Rick hadn't been at his new pad for a month when Kris arrived to find her estranged husband cavorting in the Jacuzzi with two Rams cheerleaders. Kris promptly smacked the naked girls, screaming at them to leave while Rick hid in a closet. Rick has told friends that he bedded thousands of women. I'm sure it's true. Against the advice of his business manager, in 1978 Rick bought salacious actor Errol Flynn's former estate, complete with several unusual naughty features, one of which was a two-way mirror in the master bedroom.

Rick and Kris briefly reunited, but due to her flagrant buying sprees and their constant arguing, Rick was on the road 250 days a year, which Kris found intolerable. Kris started drinking heavily, insisting that Rick quit music and go back to acting, which he, of course, refused to do. They broke up for good in 1980, and although the relief must have been blessed, Rick couldn't help but compare his embittered, messy marriage to his parents' seemingly perfect forty-year union. As he mourned, Kris went on a hell-bent rampage to remove from Rick every cent he ever made. And then some.

To add to his grief, in 1981 Rick was slapped with a paternity suit. A blood test proved that a one-night stand in New Jersey had favored Rick with another son, Eric Crewe. Kris was wearing him down with depositions and money demands, and since Rick refused to be a fossil on the "oldies" circuit, he turned into a recluse, hanging around the house in his robe, playing the piano along with Carl Perkins' forty-fives.

I talked with a petite brunette named Linda who visited Rick several times during this period, and got a pretty miserable story: "The first time I went up there, these fellows were sitting around, but he wasn't there. He was watching us from a telescope in his closet. He was in the closet getting high on freebase and he finally asked me to come in. I think he had just gotten into it. I could tell by the way he handled it, he was really still enjoying it. It gets to the point where you hate it, but you do it. It's instantly addicting. It took me to my knees. It's like a cancer in this world that we've never seen the likes of. He was a total gentleman, sweet, kind, just precious. He had his new wardrobe all lined up in there and was looking at some new pictures through a loupe. He said, 'Help me pick out the best of my head shots,' but it seemed like something that would never get done. He was torn because he knew he had to work, but when you have that pipe in your hand, there's nothing more important."

Linda went to visit Rick again and found him in the closet watching pornographic movies. "He took me on a tour of the house," she recalled. "He was real proud of the house but very angry because Kris had gone to Sears and bought all of these cheap aluminum fixtures and replaced all the original brass fixtures in the bathrooms. He was so embarrassed. 'She spent eighty to a hundred thousand dollars on junk, she has no taste,' he said. He was very resentful. He took me into his room and he had just gotten his father's chair delivered from his mother. He said, 'Sit in this chair. It's the only thing left I have of that man.' He started telling me about his father—he was a real overbearing, real tough guy. He said all he ever wanted to do was play professional tennis, he was extremely shy and never wanted to act, that he was forced to work, that his father was a tyrant. But he was so happy to have his father's chair in the bedroom. He admired David because he went out and became a lawyer. He talked about how proud he was of his sons that they played tennis. Once I was up there and he apologized that he couldn't cook me anything. He had these two guys up there taking care of him. He picked the lid up off a frying pan and said, 'This is all I get anymore, this chicken-fried steak. I'm sick of eating like this.' He was lost. A lost soul. Rick was crippled."

Rick signed his divorce papers in December 1982, but the legal warfare with his former wife was far from over. Plagued with debts, Rick finally made the decision to join his peers and hit the road with his classics. Friends laughingly nicknamed him "Ledge," short for "legend," and Rick Nelson finally seemed to accept that he really wouldn't rather drive a truck. Just like another rock maestro, Pete Townshend, who really didn't want to die before he got old.

When a fellow musician had one girl too many in his room at the Riviera Hotel in Las Vegas, he offered pretty, blond Helen Blair to Rick, and he accepted. Rick was very lonely and twenty-one-year-old Helen soon became his constant companion, happily bending to his topsy-turvy lifestyle, eventually moving into the Errol Flynn house with her two long-haired cats and Afghan hound. Rick seemed content, but his friends were concerned about Helen's heavy drug abuse, in particular her addition to cocaine. She also had a penchant for shoplifting. When Harriet discovered that Rick and Helen were engaged, she threatened to write him out of her will, but Rick always explained away his fiancée's troubles by saying she had had a horrible childhood.

Rick finally met his idol, Carl Perkins, after thirty years of emulating his style, and Perkins was taken by Rick's sincerity: "One of the last things Ricky said to me was, 'I would really like to open some shows for you next year, Carl.' I said you've got the cart before the horse—*I'll* open for *you*, but Ricky said, 'No way.' That was very special, and when I heard about the accident, it really tore me up."

The day Rick's twin sons, musicians Matthew and Gunnar, turned eighteen, they moved in with their father. Daughter Tracy remembered her father saying, "I feel like I have a home again."

Rick was feeling pretty good. Having done a couple of pilots, he was hopeful about renewing his television career; his all-age crowds were more enthusiastic than ever, and he had just completed a soulful new country-tinged album for Curb Records that featured a tender, moving version of Buddy Holly's "True Love Ways." He had even spent a comfortable Christmas Eve with all four of his children and Harriet, David, and Helen.

Because Kris had her attorney send Rick a letter saying he was behind in his payments and owed her money, Rick and his band booked a short tour that started the day after Christmas 1988. As usual, Helen joined Rick on the trip. It was a grumpy group that boarded Rick's 1944 Douglas DC-3 that night. More than a plane, the "traveling house" DC-3 had recently been plagued with problems. In

Rick with Al Kooper. His T-shirt speaks for him. (GARY NICHAMIN)

September Rick and the band had missed the first Farm Aid concert due to a malfunctioning spark plug. Drummer Ricky Intveld's brother James told me that the band was afraid to fly on the DC-3. "Rick liked it because he thought it was a cool old plane. My brother used to call from the road and say, 'The plane's cheesing out. I don't want to get on it. What do I do?'"

On Monday, December 30, Rick closed his show in Guntersville, Alabama, with Buddy Holly's "Rave On," shouting joyously to the crowd, "Rave on for me!" before patiently signing autographs for a long line of fans. Tuesday morning upon arriving at the airport, the sleepy travelers learned that there would be a delay due to a clogged primer line that prevented the left engine from starting. Finally, at a little after one o'clock, the DC-3 took to the gray skies. At 5:08, 120 miles from their destination, copilot Ken Ferguson radioed the Fort Worth Air Route Traffic Control Center: "I think I'd like to turn around, uh, head for Texarkana here. I've got a little problem." At 5:11 another radio transmission: "Smoke in the cockpit. Have smoke in the cockpit . . ."

At 5:14 Rick Nelson's DC-3 disappeared from the Fort Worth air-traffic controller's radar screen.

The plane severed two power lines as it went down, snapped a utility pole, crashed into a tree that tore off its left wing, and plowed into a heavily wooded area. From two hundred yards away, eyewitnesses could feel the heat from roaring flames seventy-five feet high. Both pilots struggled from the wreckage and watched the inferno in horror. Firefighters wouldn't let anyone near the blaze, and the flaming sepulchre, holding seven bodies, was left to smolder all night long.

Harriet Nelson learned about her younger son's death on a TV newscast. Rick's son Matthew was enjoying "Garden Party" on the radio when the deejay announced sadly, "A tribute to Rick Nelson, killed in a plane crash earlier today."

When he heard the tragic news, an old friend of Rick's, newscaster Charley Britt, remembered Rick telling him the two ways he didn't want to die: in a plane crash or a fire.

Even before the funeral, Kris threatened to sue for part of Rick's life-insurance money, and to avoid a court battle, David let her have the money from one of Rick's two policies. Kris also attempted to get control of the estate from David, who was the appointed administrator of Rick's last will and testament. Two weeks later a judge rejected her request.

The funeral, held on a bright blue Monday, was full of tension and hostility directed toward an ashen and defiant Kris. David told a touching childhood story, all of Rick's children delivered moving eulogies, and Matthew and Gunnar brought tears to the mourners' eyes as they sang their father's song "Easy to Be Free." Nobody mentioned Rick's fiancée, Helen Blair.

As the funeral ended, Kris and daughter Tracy got into a fight about Kris's plan to sue for the life-insurance money. Kris knocked her daughter to the ground and hit her with her purse. A few days later Kris arrived late for the private burial.

Rick Nelson was laid to rest near his father and maternal grandmother on a green hill overlooking the San Fernando Valley. Following the short prayer and interment, stolid David finally spoke his mind to his brother's ex-wife. Turning on Kris, he roared, "Murderess!"

On January 15, 1986, the *Washington Post* headline trumpeted DRUG-RELATED FIRE SUSPECTED IN RICK NELSON PLANE CRASH. Because of the discovery of eighteen aerosol cans (sometimes used as freebase solvents), the media speculated that one or more of the passengers had been freebasing cocaine, perhaps starting the fire on the aircraft. Although no evidence of paraphernalia was found in the wreckage and everything pointed to a malfunctioning or faultily repaired Janitrol gasoline heater, the rumors still persist today that Rick Nelson, in a drug-induced daze, heedlessly set fire to his own plane, killing all the passengers. In fact, when the smoke-filled plane went down, the teen idol, "irrepressible Ricky," gallantly covered his fiancée's body with his own.

I was working on a magazine project a little while back and had Rick's daughter, actress Tracy Nelson, interview her twin brothers, Matthew and Gunnar, of the band Nelson.

GUNNAR: All of us have grown up in a really weird way and we've had a *lot* of serious pain in our lives—you can go either way with that pain.

TRACY: It's a lot like Pop with "Garden Party."

MATTHEW: Can you imagine anything more awful than that? To be out there in front of all those people who used to love you, and it's not like you're unproven, you've been proven. You've had to be taken off the Atlantic City Boardwalk in a helicopter 'cause you couldn't get through with a car, and then you've got all these people booing you onstage—the same people.

GUNNAR: That was around the time he showed up to play that rock-and-roll revival show and was going through a huge personal renaissance—the first time he was writing his own material.

TRACY: And he was out from under the shadow of Grandpa.

GUNNAR: For the first time he was really getting into himself and what made him tick. It was a really gutsy thing to do—to come from all that success and just decide, "Hey, I'm going to be real now, I'm going to do it on my own." When I saw him happiest was after the "Garden Party" date, when he turned that incredibly horrid situation around, getting booed off the stage and turning it into a hit song. He was so happy. Even when he wasn't as commercially acceptable or successful, he loved writing, he loved playing his own stuff.

TRACY: I've told you guys this before—one of my most important memories is his music room being right below my bedroom. I would get out of bed and take my blanket and lie on the floor and listen to him play the piano—

that's how I'd fall asleep, with my ear to the floor, listening to that piano. I think we grew up with a certain amount of pressure. Our family is the only family that has an exhibition at the Smithsonian. It was like an institutionalized morality that everybody felt compelled to protect. I don't deal with it as well as you guys do. I have a certain amount of resentment. . . .

GUNNAR: Like a stigma?

TRACY: I told you the story about how I thought I was premature? And it turned out that I was actually put in an incubator when I didn't need to be because Grandpa didn't want people thinking that Mom and Pop had had sex before they were married.

MATTHEW: Right. But then again, it was a different time.

TRACY: I know, but what's so amazing to me is people would watch television and they'd think, "This is the way we want to be." And Grandpa was actually writing about his childhood in the thirties. In a way, Pop did all the work for us, because he broke free of that.

GUNNAR: I had somebody come up to me in New York and say, "If it wasn't for your family show, I wouldn't have been a good person. I think I would have really fucked up. I didn't feel a part of my family, but once a week I sat down in front of the TV, and got to feel a part of yours."

TRACY: When I think about Pop and all the shit that was said about him when he died, the thing that infuriates me is here's a man who was basically a public servant from the time he was a child. . . .

MATTHEW: It's strange. A guy who interviewed us said, "How your dad died, I was really disappointed—the cocaine and all that stuff. I had been led to believe that he was flawless." And I said, "Well, first of all, that's not true. The shit's not true." We unfortunately still have people thinking it was freebasing that caused the crash. The truth is, as you know, the heater blew off the plane. It was an accident. We feel that we can be real, and part of being real is having feelings. That shit hurts, you know, some kids lost their father.

TRACY: I can remember being with Pop in an airport and him racing for a plane and he never turned anybody down when they wanted to shake his hand or talk for a minute.

MATTHEW: Not once, ever. It didn't matter what kind of hurry he was in.

TRACY: Yeah. And I think part of the problem he had in life was that he let people take a little too much and didn't stand his ground enough because he didn't have the security of knowing he could do it on his own.

MATTHEW: Then you get to the issue of being nice as opposed to being real.

TRACY: Exactly. In a funny way this family has got a certain amount of light about it. It always has, from the beginning. What's really wild is that we are a lot more real than they were. The fifties stuff with Ozzie and Harriet, there was a lot of trauma and a lot of pain, but it was never expressed. For us to be able to do that . . .

MATTHEW: . . . brings a sense of reality in this family that has never been there.

TRACY: You know that line in your song . . . "Listen from my heart / He's never lied to me. . . ." It's so true. You always do the right thing if you listen from there . . . that little voice you're always talking about. Do you feel like maybe that's Pop?

GUNNAR: I do. 'Cause I didn't have it before he died. Call it coincidence or whatever, call it growing up. But I do. I feel like I've got someone watching over me.

GRAM PARSONS

■

Fallen

Angel

■

One of the finest moments of my entire life happened at the Whiskey-a-Go-Go in the summer of '69. It might have been my finest musical moment of all time. Gram Parsons was singing, wrapped up in the splitting sorrow of "She Once Lived Here," an aching George Jones sob song about this poor guy who couldn't bear to stay in town because his ex-girl used to reside there. Seemingly all alone in the half-crowded rock den, Gram was a lost man, hurting through his voice better than anybody I have ever heard. He hurt so damn good, so *hard,* he made a pitiful broken heart feel beautiful and profound. His voice cracked, it caught, and sometimes it was ragged, but Gram Parsons was a visionary soulman extraordinaire. He bled for his audience, whether they noticed it or not.

As usual, I was front and center for the Flying Burrito Brothers' weekly foray into the rock world. They would play the Palomino on Monday nights and the Whiskey on Tuesdays, attempting to unite the two seemingly different universes of country and rock to sparse and skeptical audiences. The heady mantle of "country-rock pioneer"—a term he came to despise—was settling itself on Gram's head like an ill-fitting cowboy hat. He preferred to call his music "white soul" and "white gospel"—"cosmic American music."

I was swaying on the dance floor, in sync with Gram's exquisite pain, and when he launched into the bridge "I see her faa-aace in, the cooo-ool of the evenin'/I hear her voice in each bree-eeeze loud and clear," tears started sliding down his face as he gazed into the lights, his heart so stuffed with emotion, I could feel my own swelling love-pump pressing against my rib cage. It literally took my breath away. I forgot to breathe.

When I came out of the spinny-fit and found myself back on the Whiskey dance floor, I looked around to see what Gram's sopping display of angst had done to the rest of the audience, but they seemed absurdly unchanged. But Gram had validated all the pent-up heartache I had ever felt in my life by shamelessly exposing his own shattered heart.

Gram Parsons's short, tangled life was like one of George Jones's weepy songs—full of Southern madness, backstabbing, cheating, suicide, liquor, lawsuits, more drugs than should be allowed, too much family money, and too little love.

By November 1965 Gram had escaped to Harvard. In a letter to his little sister, Avis, who was desperate to get away from the family, Gram wrote that he hoped they could learn from their difficult past, make some changes, and be "real people," not "sick or haunted" by what life had put them through. Gram believed that he and Avis actually had an advantage because of the poor family examples set for them. They could see that some people "permit life to tangle them so badly that there is no escape." He told Avis he felt they still had time. "[L]ife can be real and beautiful if you build it that way honestly so there will be no lies or shadows to be afraid of later."

Unfortunately, the way Gram saw fit to exorcise his shadows in the little time he had left on the planet was to drop, pop, shoot, inhale, and imbibe every available life-threatening substance known to man. As his musical career progressed, so did his intake of lethal misfortune. The fact that he was never without a lot of cash, due to his trusty trust fund, made it all too easy.

Gram Parsons got real high with Keith Richards, and Mick Jagger gave him the song "Wild Horses." Nudie, the renowned "Rodeo Tailor," put naked ladies, cubes of acid, Tuinals, and marijuana leaves climbing up Gram's cowboy suit, and in the end, Gram's dead body was stolen, driven out to the desert in an old hearse, and set on fire. Pretty legendary stuff. His old friend Keith had this to say about Gram's influence: "He kind of redefined the possibilities of country music for me, personally. If he had lived, he probably would have redefined it for everybody."

But in a letter to an old friend in late 1972, Gram admitted that his music was "still country" but felt that there were no boundaries between "types" of music. "I keep my love for variations, even tho I've some sort of 'rep' for starting what (I think) has turned out t' be pretty much of a 'country-rock' (ugh!) plastic dry-fuck."

Before he died a mysterious, drug-addled death in the desert at his beloved Joshua Tree, Gram recorded his second album with Emmylou Harris—sweet, bleeding songs that dreams and nightmares are made of. In that late September of 1973, the trailblazing, sad-eyed Southern boy had just filed for divorce from his wife, Gretchen, and was about to go back out on the road with Emmylou. Some of the life tangles finally seemed to be clearing up. Gram didn't mean to die, he just couldn't help it.

When people asked Gram where he was from, he'd answer, "The Swamps." Smack dab on top of the Okefenokee Swamp, Waycross, Georgia, is a town of twenty thousand with well over a hundred churches and only eight bars, where regular Ku Klux Klan meetings are still held. Raised by his strict, moneyed, alcoholic citrus-heiress mother, the former Avis Snively, and the charming, hard-living Ingram Cecil "Coon Dog" Connor, Gram was a privileged child—friendly, well mannered, and popular with peers as well as teachers. Catered to by black servants, Gram had weekly parties in the sunroom and spent his weekends on the yacht. Coon Dog led Gram's Boy Scout troop, took him camping and hunting. Piano lessons began at age eight, and in the fourth grade, Gram had already written his first song, "Gram Boogie." At nine precocious Gram took two teenage girls to see his hero,

Gram filming flying saucer flick *Saturation 7* in the Joshua Tree desert, where he died. (ANDEE COHEN)

Elvis Presley, at City Auditorium, sneaking them backstage after the show to get an autograph. Then Gram got a guitar, pomped his hair, and started entertaining the neighborhood, lip-synching to Elvis records while the little girls swooned.

After reading about the Bolles School in *Harper's Bazaar,* Avis shipped her son off to the military academy for the sixth grade, where despite all the rules twelve-year-old Gram seemed to thrive. But his well-heeled, idyllic world was about to be turned upside down. On December 21, 1958, Coon Dog dropped his family off at the train station, signed some checks at the office, then blew his brains out with a .38 pistol. He left no suicide note but a few weeks earlier had told his brother Tom that he had finally figured out a way to break free from his job in the Snively citrus business. And there had been whispers that Avis was having an affair. The night before Coon Dog's funeral, Avis had a huge party, and friends and family were appalled by her seeming lack of grief. She waited until the day after Christmas to tell Gram and little Avis that their father was gone. Gram was desolate. Everything fell apart. Citing him as a "bad influence," in June 1959 the Bolles School sent Gram back home. After a summer of traveling across the country by train, Avis took her children to the Snively home in Winter Haven, Florida, to start over again.

Just as Gram was pulling his life back together, Avis married a shrewd, good-looking salesman whom family members believed to be "in it for the money." Robert Ellis Parsons lost no time, immediately adopting Avis and Gram and arranging for new birth certificates, which stated that Robert was their father. Gram Connor was now Gram Parsons.

At their new house on Piedmont Drive, Gram had a piano in his room and his own private entrance, which soon became the neighborhood hangout where Gram and his friends listened to records by Ray Charles, Roy Orbison, and favorites Jake and the Gospel Soul Stirrers. For Gram at fourteen, music had become his solace and reason for living, and he formed his first band, the Pacers, playing and singing Top Forty hits at all the local teen spots, actually making decent money. He was getting comfortable with his voice and good on the guitar, winding his absurdly long, beautiful fingers around the Fender neck almost a time and a half. A year later Gram left the Pacers to join another cover band, the Legends, with Jim Stafford, who was called "the fastest guitar in town." The band became regulars on a local radio show, but there wasn't enough work to keep Gram happy. He also played with the Rumours, headed by Kent Lavoie, who would later become Lobo. Then, bolstered by the success of folk groups like Peter, Paul and Mary, Gram and his girlfriend Patti Johnson formed the Vanguards.

He kept himself busy with music, but Gram's family life was a shambles. His mother, Avis, was pregnant and drinking heavily. Bob was cheating on her and the entire town knew about it. Gram started rummaging through Avis's copious prescription-drug stash, looking for some relief. He failed his junior year at Winter Haven High and Avis got Gram reinstated at Bolles, where he would have to repeat eleventh grade.

Gram and Patti were thwarted in a slapdash attempt to elope by Patti's outraged parents, who stopped the couple as they perused their getaway map. They were kept apart until Gram went back to Bolles. People remember Gram carrying his guitar into every class, entertaining schoolmates at the fountain, enjoying all the female attention. He asked an artist friend to make him up some business cards that said "It's okay, I'm a musician." Gram competed in the Debate Club, became a member of the Centurions fraternity, and on the weekends played with his newest group, the folky Shilos. The band made enough money to get themselves new instruments, traveling as far as South Carolina and Chicago for gigs, getting paid a few hundred dollars a night. The Shilos almost got a booking at the Bitter End in Manhattan, but didn't get the job when it was discovered they were all underage and still in high school. But having experienced the hipness of Greenwich Village—playing with people like Richie Furay, who would later form the band Poco—Gram would never be the same.

In late March the Shilos booked time in a local recording studio, cutting nine songs in one hour. To friend Paul Surratt, Gram wrote, "I'm sure my music is going to be as big as dylans [*sic*], and after my album we will have the advantage of owning my music." But nothing happened with the tape and the Shilos broke up.

Trouble in Parsons's paradise caused Gram to decide to leave for Harvard after graduation. "I wanted to find out what Tim Leary and Richard Alpert were up to," he later said, but the truth was closer to home. Bob's continuing infidelity led to a horrible, gossipy mess that caused Avis to turn more and more to the companionship of booze—against her doctor's warnings.

As he was rehearsing for Bolles graduation ceremonies, Gram was told by his English teacher that his mother had died, but he decided to participate in the ceremonies anyway, keeping his feelings safely stuffed and under wraps.

For Gram, Harvard turned out to be a place to hone his varied and eclectic musical influences and form another band, the Like, with Ian Dunlop, John Nuese, Tom Snow, and drummer Mickey Gauvin. The Like merged R&B with Gram's country influences and were often joined by actor Brandon de Wilde (*Shane, Hud*), who sang beautiful harmony duets with Gram. A lot of experimenting with drugs occurred. After a long weekend on LSD, Gram confided to a friend that he was desperately concerned about his little sister Avis, who was now trapped with Bob Parsons and his new wife, Bonnie, and forced to watch them tossing around her dead mother's money. Gram wrote letters of encouragement but felt powerless to help.

Gram had a good excuse to leave Harvard when Brandon de Wilde asked the Like to play on some demos he was cutting in New York. The band rented a huge furnished house in the Bronx and started rehearsing, determined to get a record deal. Trading in "the Like" for the "International Submarine Band" (taken from a "Little Rascals" episode), they struggled to find their musical direction. Inspired by Ray Charles's *Country and Western Meets Rhythm and Blues,* the ISB had the unusual opportunity of being able to rehearse constantly without the hassle of bill paying, blessed by Gram's ever-flowing Snively nest egg. They took their odd mixture of country, rock, and soul to the clubs, where reactions were always mixed. Gram's first shot at fame was shot down. The ISB cut a promo single for the movie *The Russians Are Coming, The Russians Are Coming,* but the diverse Southern stew, as Gram later said in an interview, was misunderstood. Next came a single deal with Columbia Records, which never panned out, and Gram was getting restless. Visiting Brandon, who was making a movie in California, Gram fell madly in love for the first time, insisting that the band relocate to Los Angeles. They were game.

I drove up the coast to Santa Barbara, where Nancy Parsons lives in a lovely old white wooden house, so we could reminisce about her "old boy," Gram. Nancy was happily living with David Crosby when Gram came into her life. "I was secure and happy and fulfilled with David," she says warmly. "When I saw this guy who looked like a coon dog/drowned water puppy come up the driveway, it was not in my mind to be unfaithful." But bells and destiny chimes sounded in Nancy's head when Gram said, "I've been looking for you for a long time and I'm going to take you with me." They were both nineteen. "It was written, it had to happen," she insists. "I was making up the big bed, fluffing a sheet into the air, and David said, 'Nancy, where are you? You're a million miles away.' I looked at him: 'Don't you understand? I've met Gram Parsons and I have to leave with him.'" Nancy says that for an entire year her life with Gram was "a vision of love and harmony and heaven on earth."

Moving in with his lady love, Gram rented a Laurel Canyon house for the rest of the band and plotted his grand future in the City of Angels. Through Brandon's connections, the International Submarine Band performed at a party scene in a Roger Corman movie, *The Trip;* then the movie's star, Peter Fonda, recorded one of Gram's songs, "November Nights," for the small Chisa label. Gram was rubbing elbows with the near-greats but had to enter the Palomino club's weekly talent contest to get up on a stage. It took him two years to win, after losing out to corny comedy acts and whistling cowboys. A few years later, in a tragic attempt to get good enough to sing with the Burrito Brothers myself, I entered the Pal contest and lost to a piano-playing duck.

Nancy was pregnant and Gram panicked. "I was actively fighting for this little soul in my belly because Gram's manager wanted me to have an abortion on my very own bed. Gram didn't know what to do. He was so young, so scared, and so confused. A baby wasn't part of his vision for us." But Nancy refused the idea of an abortion. "We couldn't make a go of it. He couldn't give up his kismet, his contract to come to earth and do his mission with his music. He had to choose and that's where the pain started. That tore him up, it tore me up. For me it was Gram and his happiness or Polly and her life. His choice was to get the music here. He said, 'Now I know what I have to do,' and I said, 'Don't leave me here.' I knew he was going to split apart from me and what we represented, and make his music happen and leave in a blaze."

Just after the ISB broke up, Gram was offered an album deal with Lee Hazlewood's new label, LHI. John Nuese stayed with Gram while the others played the circuit, calling themselves the Flying Burrito Brothers. Gram corraled his friends Bob Buchanan and John Corneal, and the International Submarine Band album, *Safe at Home,* featuring four G.P. originals, was recorded in two sessions. Released in the spring of 1968, the album—and Gram specifically—received an excellent review in the *L.A. Times:* "His voice and pen seem meant for the medium, neither sounding artificial in the homey feel of good country music." Gram went to Nudie, the Rodeo Tailor, and decked himself out in country flash, but the initial buzz on the International Submarine Band was soon over, and Gram was ready for a move.

After meeting Byrds bassist Chris Hillman in a bank, Gram was brought in to audition for the group, and Roger McGuinn asked him to join that very day. Roger later recalled the meeting for *Fusion* magazine: "We hired a piano player and he turned out to be Parsons, a monster in sheep's clothing. And he exploded out of this sheep's clothing. God! It's George Jones! In a sequin suit!" The Byrds had dabbled in country and, along with Chris Hillman, Gram devotedly pushed the group in that direction, which culminated in *Sweetheart of the Rodeo,* considered the breakthrough album that led to what would come to be called "country-rock"—long-haired weirdo rockers daring to tamper with the C&W mainstream. Having decided to record in Nashville for authenticity, the Byrds were booked to play the hallowed halls of the Grand Ole Opry. At twenty-one years old, Gram Parsons had reached Mecca and decided to run with it. After a decent reception from the wary audience for the Merle Haggard song "Sing Me Back Home," Tompall Glaser announced another Haggard song by the Byrds, but Gram had his own agenda. "We're not going to do that one tonight," he said cheekily. "We're going to do a song for my grandmother, who used to listen to the Grand Ole Opry with me when I was little. It's a song I wrote called 'Hickory Wind.'" This was a surprise to the Byrds, who were flying high on the pot they had smoked backstage, but they followed Gram's lead and managed to piss off the entire Opry hierarchy.

At the end of their European tour, the Byrds played London's Middle Earth, spending that rainy night at Stonehenge with Mick Jagger and Keith Richards. Roger spoke about the Byrds' upcoming trip to South Africa, and Keith made sure to tell Gram his feelings about apartheid, the policy of blacks being separated from whites. He told Gram it was like growing up down South and being "the wrong color," and that the Stones wouldn't even think of playing there. So when it came time for the Byrds to leave for South Africa, Gram refused to go. Though Chris Hillman went into a rage, he later admitted Gram had been right. "I was ready to murder him, but then we did make up and become friends again. The South Africa tour was a stupid farce and he was right. We shouldn't have gone, but he shouldn't have let us down by copping out at the end. . . ."

Gram had been a Byrd for a little over four months. The landmark *Sweetheart of the Rodeo* was the lowest-selling Byrds album to date, only reaching number seventy-seven on the *Billboard* charts. However, not too long ago *Rolling Stone* named *Sweetheart* one of the top two hundred albums of the last twenty-five years.

While the Byrds suffered in South Africa, Gram and Keith Richards found some kind of common ground and started hanging out. To England's *Melody Maker*, Gram announced he had already started another group, "a Southern soul group playing country and gospel-oriented music with a steel guitar."

Back in L.A., Gram found that Chris Hillman had quit the Byrds and, after apologies, convinced him they should start a band. Along with "Sneaky" Pete Kleinow on pedal steel, Chris Ethridge on bass, and eventually ex-Byrd Mike Clarke on drums, Chris and Gram stole the name "Flying Burrito Brothers" and took off, the former Byrds easily getting a record deal with A&M Records, a label that was trying to branch out and get hip. With the advance, Gram took the Burritos directly to Nudie's and outfitted them in

Gram and best pal, Keith Richards (left), jamming and flying high at the Stones' villa in Nellcote, France. (COURTESY OF JOHN DEL GATTO/PHOTO BY DOMINIQUE TARLE)

festive country-trash garb. Instead of the usual roses on his short white jacket, Gram insisted on naked ladies, cubes of acid, Tuinal capsules, marijuana leaves, and a blazing red cross shooting rhinestones across the back.

It was about this time that we became friends. A fiendish Byrds fan, I saw one of Gram's only L.A. Byrds performances at the trippy-hippie Kaleidoscope on Sunset Boulevard. Chris Hillman, my first love, introduced me to the slinky bedroom-eyed stranger, and his Southern manners just slayed me. I was around for the early Burrito days, spending time with Chris, getting to know Gram, baby-sitting his baby daughter, Polly, drinking up the magic at Burrito Manor. Gram and Nancy had never really broken up, and she often brought Polly to town from their sweet little pad in Santa Barbara to visit Daddy.

Miss Mercy, my partner-in-crime in the GTOs, wrote a piece on Gram for

L.A. Weekly, describing her first glimpse of G.P. at the *Yellow Submarine* premiere: "[T]he lights dimmed and a tall, lean cat in a sparkling Nudie drifted by. He was true glitter, true glamour rock. The rhinestone suit sparkled like diamonds, it had submarines all over it and the color was scarlet red. It sparkled so bright it made Gram sparkle through the movie show. . . . His Nudie belt hung on his hips like a gunslinger, and that was his ammunition, his exaggerated entrance into my life. . . ."

Chris, in the middle of a hellish divorce, and Gram, who was going through grief with Nancy, both moved into a cowboy ranch pad in the San Fernando Valley and started work on *The Gilded Palace of Sin.* Chris says it was one of the most productive times of his life. "It's being familiar with your partner, knowing and anticipating what Gram was thinking about, because we were sharing a common thing then," he remembers. "We were sitting in the middle of L.A. . . . Our old ladies had left us. That's what caused the creative working condition."

Mercy and I visited Chris and Gram during this fertile period, and they greeted us with a grocery bag full of pot and played us a bunch of country forty-fives on a portable record player. "This is George Jones," Gram said in his weepy drawl, "the King of Broken Hearts," then broke into plaintive sobs while George crooned. "Imagine," said Mercy later, "crying over a hillbilly with a crewcut." I felt like I was being let in on a very important secret—Chris and Gram turned me on to country that night, and I've never gotten over it. The Burritos invited Mercy and me to sing in the chorus of "Little Hippie Boy," and in turn we invited them to the GTOs sessions with Frank Zappa. In between ditties, Gram took my roommate, Miss Andee, and me into a little room where he played us a bleeding ballad for Nancy called "Hot Burrito #1." As he looked at his exquisite hands on the piano keys, Gram said, "Sometimes I wonder where these hands came from. I keep expecting to see stitches around my wrists."

Gram must have been thrilled when he read Robert Hilburn's *L.A. Times* review for *The Gilded Palace of Sin,* praising his vocals as "straight from the sentimental George Jones heart of country music." He kept his feelings bottled up inside, but Gram's blues came out in his music.

One afternoon Nancy gaily announced that Gram had proposed to her, but the gaiety was short-lived. Unbeknownst to Nancy, Gram had devised a publicity scheme, reminiscent of Hank Williams marrying one of his wives onstage in between concerts. Gram would invite all his showbiz pals, play a set, and maybe even be able to get the wedding on television! He told Nancy that the invitations were being made up and to create her wedding dress with good ol' Nudie, and leave the rest of the plans up to him. She did as she was told, had a dress made from the same fabric as Gram's naughty Nudie suit, and waited. And waited. "Gram played a lot of games. I went to Nudie's and found that Gram hadn't been forthcoming with the money. [The thousand-dollar wedding dress was never paid for.] 'I never saw an invitation. It got real crazy after I saw Nudie and found out that Gram was using me as another stage prop." Nancy felt humiliated and retaliated in the only way she could. She spent the night with his old friend Mickey Gauvin. Some friend. "There's no honor among men," Nancy insists. "I didn't have to sink to that level, but remember the sacred sexuality, the ancient temples? I wasn't getting back at Gram, I was fulfilling myself with a temple boy!" Nancy must have known she was ending her relationship with Gram once and for all. "I knew already that it was a big, awful, horrible joke. The fact that he would set up this elaborate ruse—this is the man I loved with my immortal soul—one hand beckoned me forward, the other pushed me away." It's such a sad story. "It was in Gram's cellular memory to be sad," Nancy sighs. "The Southern way breeds sadness. I wish I would have known to say to him, 'Even if your father knocked himself off, just because your mother knocked herself off, doesn't mean that you have to follow the script too.' But he thought he did, and that's very Southern, Tennessee Williams, dark and willow-hung." It's expected, isn't it? I ask. "There, you've hit it on the head," Nancy agrees. "Who was he to go against that? When he saw that his vision wasn't gonna happen, then he went back to the only thing he knew and fulfilled it. He thought I was the Madonna? Yeah? Well, I'll show you!"

In their spare time, the Burritos played serious poker. I remember one night cooking my first fried chicken for "the boys" while they threw money around and cursed one another out. They may have been stoned-out hippie freaks, but their women were not allowed to play cards. I was dancing at the Whiskey one night when Mike Clarke walked in wearing the hand-beaded cowboy shirt I had made for Chris. When I asked how he got it, Mike sheepishly confessed he had just won it in a poker game. The all-important coked-out poker games continued on the road.

Gram had a drastic fear of flying. So in February 1969 Brandon de Wilde and I were at the train station to send the Burritos off on their cross-country tour, so high we were almost blind. Gram had been tottering through the well-wishers, shoving globs of cocaine into already stuffed noses, reeling, almost delirious. Even though I had indulged myself, I was concerned about Gram, who seemed to have no idea how to stop. The drug-addled tour was part poker, part fun, but mostly a fiasco. Sometimes Gram sang like an outlaw angel, other times he fell apart. One late night Gram called me from somewhere in Middle America, telling me that he made the band wear jeweled turbans onstage, then he sang to me on the phone. It was some kind of grievous heaven.

Back in L.A. the rowdiness escalated. Gram moved into the infamous Chateau Marmont, for a time sharing a bungalow with director Tony Foutz, who was making a movie about UFOs called *Saturation 7*. Gram was soon spending his days in the Joshua Tree desert looking for flying saucers while the cameras rolled. The project collapsed when the money man pulled out because he thought the film was going to be "too political."

When the Rolling Stones came to town, they all crammed into the tiny Corral club in Topanga Canyon to see the Burritos. Upon noticing that Mick Jagger was taking an interest in me, from the stage Gram said, "Watch out for Miss Pamela, she's a beauty but she's tenderhearted." He knew my weepy heart well.

As a loving observer, it appeared to me that Gram and Keith Richards were turning into each other. They huddled in corners together, getting high, dressed in each other's clothes. One night the Burritos played the Troubadour and Gram was wearing Keith's scarves and belts, makeup scrawled on his face and drunk as a skunk. Chris Hillman was so pissed off he turned his back just in time to miss Gram thrash his own acoustic guitar, then kick it off the stage. When the Stones were in town, Gram missed rehearsals and turned up late for gigs. The Burritos felt that Gram wanted to be a Rolling Stone, and that the Stones were ripping off Gram's countrified soul, giving him no credit. To *Rolling Stone* Gram admitted, "I think they've done a few country-sounding things since I got to know them." Burrito roadie Jim Seiter complained that Gram was "getting faggier by the day." When Chris Ethridge had had enough and left the band, Chris Hillman took over on bass, adding Bernie Leadon on guitar.

Sixteen-year-old actress Gretchen Burrell was invited to a Stones rehearsal where they were celebrating Gram's twenty-third birthday, and sparks flew through the air. She soon took up residence with Gram at the Chateau Marmont, sliding comfortably into his chaotic, stoned-out life.

Gram was still making occasional contact with Nancy, checking up on Polly. "One night he called me in Santa Barbara at four in the morning," Nancy recalls, "and he was crying and hysterical like I'd never heard him before, and he said, 'She's shooting up in the bathroom, she's shooting stuff in her arm with a needle, Nancy!' I said to him, 'You don't have to be a lunchbox and think you have to experience it to make it okay.' I shouldn't have said that. He would take things like that and process them in a very odd way. He saw things from the back of the mirror, you know what I mean?"

The first Burrito album hadn't made a dent in the charts, selling only forty thousand copies, but they were gearing up for a second. Chris said he and Gram were "walking on different roads" and that sessions for *Burrito Deluxe* were strained and difficult. They couldn't seem to get any songs together, and lucked out when Keith Richards sent Gram a tape of the Stones' "Wild Horses" to see if Sneaky Pete might add some pedal steel. Gram asked Keith if the Burritos could record the song and he gave his permission. Mercy and I were at the "Wild Horses" session and Gram was as proud and happy as a little kid. He sang it like a fallen angel.

Through his tight friendship with Keith, Gram landed the Burrito Brothers an important gig with the Rolling Stones at Altamont Raceway outside San Francisco on December 6, 1969. The Stones even picked up the Burritos' travel tab. The free "thank-you" concert at Altamont was supposed to rival Woodstock, but the vibe was so shockingly bad that I left right after the Burritos' set, hooking up with them later at the Stones' hotel—where the vibe was even worse. The Hell's Angels were providing "protection," and a fellow in the audience had been stabbed to death as the Stones played. Mick was guilt-ridden, talking about quitting rock and roll forever. Gram and Keith were in each other's pockets. Gram was wearing black leather and eye makeup, Keith had on cowboy gear. They were nodding out on the floor. It was harrowing.

Burrito touring was always difficult, made worse due to Gram's increasing paranoia about being up in the air. High as a kite, yes. Up in the air, no thank you. During the *Burrito Deluxe* tour, Gram swallowed so many downers that he usually had to be taken to the plane in a wheelchair, drooling and sobbing. In Seattle he wasn't allowed on the plane at all. "They'd see some guy slobbering in a chair," Chris explained, "wearing these outlandish clothes and a top hat. . . ." Avis had been institutionalized by Bob Parsons in New Orleans and needed her big brother's help, but Gram was unable to provide any. After the troubled tour, back in L.A. Gram had a horrible accident on his Harley. He had been riding with friend John Phillips. In the aftermath of the accident, Phillips thought Gram was dead until Gram whispered, "John, take me for a long white ride."

I brought Gram flowers in the hospital and didn't recognize him. His face was a puffy purple balloon. I worried hard that Gram was trying to keep up with his friend Keith and didn't have the constitution. When I left I said, "Take care of yourself, Gram Richards." He tried to laugh.

After a disastrous Burrito gig at the Brass Ring, Chris Hillman finally boiled over, firing Gram and snapping his favorite guitar in two pieces. Though he felt bad about it, Chris said, "It was better than hitting him in the head."

In producer Terry Melcher, Gram found an appreciative audience and another drug buddy. Convinced that Gram was "the white, country Jimi Hendrix," Terry got him a solo deal on A&M, but he and Gram were so wasted that the sessions amounted to nothing. Gram fell off the stool while he was singing. Terry fell asleep at the soundboard. Years later Terry said that Gram saw himself as a victim. "He thought he was too much of an artist to be understood by the industry. He was such a romantic character. He was one of these people who thought it was great to die young."

In March 1971 Gram took Gretchen to England, hoping for some inspiration. Instead he got hooked on heroin. An occasional user for years, Gram, along with Keith, got so strung out that they went through a couple of cures together. Aware that he is the target for Gram's ultimate demise, Keith said he didn't teach Gram very much about drugs. "Gram was just as knowledgeable as I was about chemical substances when I met him. And he had very good taste." According to writer Stanley Booth, Keith once declared that "Gram gets better coke than the Mafia."

Gram started telling the press that he was going to record his upcoming solo album for Rolling Stone Records. Meanwhile he languished in the Stones' villa in Nellcote, France, jamming with Keith and flying high. At first Mick Jagger accepted Gram, but he was now becoming wary of his constant presence. "Mick is very jealous of anybody that I get close to," Keith said. "He's an old woman like that with me. . . . But I have to understand from Mick's point of view that Gram was pretty out of it and outrageous at the time. . . ." So outrageous that he was finally asked to leave. Gram took Gretchen to old friend Ian Dunlop's farm in Cornwall, where he proposed marriage. In a very odd move, Gram asked his stepfather, Bob Parsons, to hold the wedding at his home in New Orleans. None of Gram's friends came to call.

When the married man arrived in L.A. he got together with Chris Hillman, who told him about an amazing singer he'd discovered in a little club in Washington, D.C.—Emmylou Harris. Since Chris was busy with Stephen Stills's *Manassas,* he encouraged Gram to look her up—which he did. Knocked out by her lilting voice, Gram met up with Emmylou after her show and they sang together for hours. Gram vowed to work with the sweet-voiced songbird as soon as possible. It turned out to be almost a year.

Gram had become an alcoholic. He was fifty pounds overweight and miserable. His fancy duds were tattered and didn't fit him anymore. Back in L.A. without a plan, Gram roamed around, getting wasted, until hooking up with former Byrds manager Eddie Tickner, impressing him with news that Keith Richards wanted to produce his solo record. Even after discovering that Keith wasn't available, Eddie convinced Warner Bros. to sign Gram, suggesting that country great Merle Haggard produce the record. Gram spent an idyllic few days in Bakersfield with Merle, calling him a "nice, sweet cat," but Merle's wife left him and the plans fell apart. Chris heard that Gram had been drinking too much and that Merle thought he was wild. Years later *Bam* magazine queried Merle about G.P. "He was a pussy," Merle claimed. "Hell, he was just a long-haired kid. I thought he was a good writer. He was not wild, though."

Another recuperation in his beloved Joshua Tree desert, and Gram had decided to produce his own album. The first thing he did was to hire Elvis's band, then he sent Emmylou a plane ticket. Opening day of the *GP* sessions found Gram on the floor, totally incapacitated. He was so chagrined that he abstained from booze for the rest of the recording process, even though his constant shakes confirmed the severity of his problem. Emmylou seemed to calm Gram, and his passionate, tear-stained vocals brought people to tears. *Rolling Stone* applauded Gram's singing: "That amazing voice, with its warring qualities of sweetness and dissipation, makes for a stunning emotional experience." But nobody was buying. Nobody was ready to pay for that much pain. Bernie Leadon had joined the Eagles, and their light country-rock songs were climbing the charts. Gram called the Eagles "bubble gum": "It's got too much sugar in it. Life is tougher than they make it out to be." Gram found solace in heroin and became so tragic that Chris Hillman had to throw him out of his birthday party. I saw Gram one last time at the Troubadour, haggling with his dealer on the phone. He was bloated and confused, his divine hands hanging at his sides like forgotten flowers, but his smile could still give me the shivers. I loved him.

The haphazard rehearsals for the Fallen Angels tour took place in road manager, "executive nanny" Phil Kaufman's ramshackle place in the Valley. On the very first night of the tour, Gram's bus was slammed by a truck, destroying his name painted on the back. It didn't get better from there. Gram and Emmylou had some magical moments, but Poco's Richie Furay witnessed opening night: "It was one of the most pitiful things I ever saw." Gretchen couldn't stand Phil Kaufman and wasn't happy with the stage sparks between Gram and Emmylou. She constantly picked fights with Gram, and the Fallen Angel entourage thought Gretchen was schizophrenic—"a downer, a whiner." A blazing argument in Arkansas got Gram Maced and beaten up by local police and sent off for a night in jail. Phil Kaufman describes the scene in his book *Road Mangler Deluxe:* "We heard screaming and yelling coming from the room next to ours. Gram and Gretchen were beating each other up once again. They couldn't find the stash. . . . I was in the Blytheville police station and I could hear Gram mouthing off. Every time he'd mouth off, I heard the thud of a nightstick hitting bone. Gram just wouldn't shut up." As the music got better, Gretchen got worse and was finally forced to go back home. The blistering fights continued when Gram got back to L.A. Even when Emmylou's boyfriend arrived, Gretchen continued to fly into jealous rages.

There was an inevitable last ditch to save the ruined marriage. In the spring of 1973 Bob Parsons and his wife, Bonnie, invited Gram and Gretchen on a cruise to the West Indies. But instead of rest and relaxation, Gram was forced to listen to his drunken stepfather unload his guilt, revealing that he had made martinis for Avis in the hospital, hastening her death. Gretchen said that Gram was traumatized by the disclosure and started having seizures. Following a stay in the hospital, Gram was back in rehearsals with Emmylou. He wrote one of his finest songs, "In My Hour of Darkness," after he lost three friends: Dear Brandon de Wilde was killed in a car accident, guitarist Clarence White was killed in a hit-and-run, and Gram's dealer, Sid Kaiser, died of a heart attack. "Death is a warm cloak," Gram told *Crawdaddy* magazine. "An old friend. I regard death as something that comes up on a roulette wheel once in a while. It's sad to lose a close friend. I've lost a lot of people close to me. It makes you a little bit stronger each time. They wouldn't want me to grieve. They would want me to go out and get drunk and have one on them." At Clarence's funeral Gram broke down, telling Phil Kaufman not to let anybody bury him.

"You can take me to the desert and burn me. I want to go out in a cloud of smoke." Gram's house burned down a week later. All he saved was a handful of lyrics. He stayed briefly with Gretchen at her father's house but soon moved in with Phil Kaufman. His marriage was over; he would soon file for divorce.

Gram and Emmylou rehearsed hard for the second album, *Grievous Angel,* and it paid off well. Emmylou was thrilled. "I finally learned what I was supposed to do," she said. "I felt like Gram was on his way to getting himself under control." Gram was delighted with *Grievous Angel,* telling friends he had finally made the record he had always wanted to make. With a tour of Europe scheduled, Gram was looking forward to a few relaxing days in the desert.

Taking along his roadie Michael Martin, Martin's girlfriend, Dale McElroy, and an old flame, Margaret Fisher, Gram left for Joshua Tree on September 17, renting two rooms at his favorite haunt, the Joshua Tree Inn. So much pot was smoked that Michael had to go back to L.A. for more, leaving Gram with the two women. He drank and shot his meals the next day, and that evening he had a close call. According to Dale, Margaret ran into her motel room, asking for some ice cubes because Gram had OD'd. "I did what she asked and arrived at this other room to find Gram on the floor unconscious," Dale recalled. "Margaret quickly took down his pants and pushed two or three ice cubes up his ass. To my astonishment, in a matter of seconds, he had regained consciousness, had made some joke about what we were doing with his pants down, had gotten up and was walking around the room." A little later Margaret returned to Dale's room, asking Dale to sit with Gram while she went to get some coffee. Gram slept while Dale read, but when his breathing "turned into a guttural rasping sound," she gave him mouth-to-mouth for twenty minutes. Afraid that there was no one else in the hotel, Dale kept trying to revive Gram, but soon realized that she was losing him. "I found out later that there had indeed been other people in the motel at the time. Had I yelled out, somebody else might have been able to get an ambulance for him and Gram might still be alive today. . . . I made a mistake and the guy died."

When Margaret came back, she called an ambulance and Gram was taken to the Hi-Desert Memorial Hospital, where he was pronounced dead at 12:15 A.M.

Dale said she was the last to see Gram alive. Margaret insisted *she* had been alone with Gram and given him mouth-to-mouth but it was too late. She told the San Bernardino County coroner that she left Gram at about eight P.M. to get something to eat, stating that he "did not look well." When she called "some friends" to check on Gram at eleven o'clock and couldn't reach anybody, she hurried back to the Joshua Tree Inn and found that Gram wasn't breathing. To add to the mystery, the son of the motel owners, Alan Barbary, had his own version of what happened. He and Gram drank tequila all day long, smoked some pot, and when Alan left for a swap meet, he believes Gram scored some morphine. When Alan returned at ten P.M., he says he found

Gram in bed with one of the girls on her knees masturbating him, calling his name, pleading for him to wake up.

Phil Kaufman was called and he arrived in Joshua Tree an hour and a half later, scooping up the women and taking them back to L.A. They were never questioned by the police.

The official cause of death: "drug toxicity, days, due to multiple drug use, weeks." Weeks, months, and years, actually. Years and years. The autopsy report described puncture wounds on the back of Gram's left hand, along with other scars in the left elbow. Cocaine, amphetamines, and morphine were found in his system.

Acting fast, Bob Parsons arrived in L.A. to claim Gram's body. By burying him in New Orleans, Bob hoped to establish that Gram was a resident, and glom on to his estate. Without discussing it with Gretchen or anyone else, Bob planned the funeral, telling Gram's friends it would be a family affair.

Phil Kaufman, remembering his promise to Gram at Clarence White's funeral, decided to try and help out his old buddy. After finding out which airline was shipping Gram's body to New Orleans, Phil and roadie Michael Martin borrowed Dale's funky old hearse, claiming they were to collect "the Parsons remains" because the family had decided to use a private plane. They loaded Gram's coffin into the hearse and took off for Joshua Tree. When the two bombed-out thieves reached Cap Rock, they somehow got the coffin out of the hearse and lifted the lid. "It squeaked open and there was Gram lying there naked," Phil reported. "As a matter of fact, later on the police tried charging us with stealing jewelry and clothing off the body. I told them he was naked. All he had was surgical tape on his chest where they had done the autopsy. . . ." Phil poured gasoline all over Gram and set him on fire. "We watched the body burn. It was bubbling . . . you could see it melting. . . . His ashes were actually going up into the air, into the desert night. The moon was shining, the stars were shining, and Gram's wish was coming true. . . ."

Gram got more press for being scorched in the desert than for his heart-boggling musical legacy. When I told people I had just lost a dear friend, Gram Parsons, they would say, "Oh, wasn't he that guy who was burned up in the desert in some sort of weird ritual?"

Phil and Michael were arrested for grand theft of a coffin, since there were no laws against stealing a body (Phil later called it "Gram Theft Parsons"). The day before the arrest, what was left of Gram was buried in a simple New Orleans cemetery, the Garden of Memories, under a gravestone that reads "God's Own Singer," the title of a Byrds song that Gram had nothing to do with. Bob Parsons never got any of Gram's coveted inheritance and died a year later from alcohol abuse.

On November 5, Phil and Michael pleaded guilty to misdemeanor theft and were each given a thirty-day suspended jail sentence and fined three hundred dollars. It would have been Gram's twenty-seventh birthday. To help pay legal costs Phil had a truly tacky event called "The Gram Parsons Funeral Party," charging five dollars to watch Bobby "Boris" Pickett mince between papier-mâché tombstones, singing "Monster Mash." Phil sold G.P. T-shirts and bottles of beer labeled "Gram Pilsner—A Good Stiff Drink for What Ales You." Tasteless and crass items, but I still have both of them.

A couple of weeks after Gram died I went to the Joshua Tree Inn and spent the night in room number eight, sending him love and praying for light on his long white ride.

"Gram was special," said Keith Richards. "If he was in a room, everyone else became sweet. Anything that Gram was involved in had a touch of magic to it."

"He cut straight through the middle with no compromises," Emmylou Harris said. "He was never afraid to write from the heart, and perhaps that's why he was never really accepted. It's like the light was too strong and bright, and people just had to turn away . . . because it was all too painful. It could rip you up. Not many people can take music that real."

Nancy, his ex-wife, says, "There has never been anyone I've ever known who had such archangelic charisma." "When Gram was fully present and in his full power, you would have walked off a cliff for him. Early in our rela-tionship, he told me, 'Do you understand what a fallen angel is? It's an angel from the divine realms who comes to earth, loves a mortal woman, is wronged by her, and sullies his grace—thereby falling from grace.'" It sounds like what happened in real life, doesn't it? I ask gently. "Mickey was just a pawn in the game," she insists. It's a shame about the depth of Gram's pain, I say. "You've heard Gram say this: 'How can you write a country

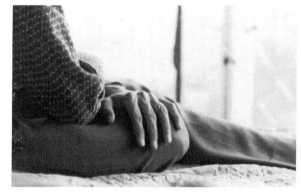

G.P.'s amazingly long fingers—"Sometimes I wonder," Gram told me, "where these hands came from." (ANDEE COHEN)

song unless you go through pain?' You say Gram was in such horrible pain, but that's all part of it. He was loyal and true in his younger years, would come to the aid of his friends, had the most pristine, clear vision—he knew there could be heaven on earth, that we could all be in harmony and love one another— and when he saw his visions, one by one, crumbling, he wasn't strong enough. The great, heavy Southern sorrow was part of the act and then it became a re-ality. When you play Jesus Christ, you walk across swimming pools. You act the part! For Gram it became the real thing. It caught him." When I tell Nancy that I'm calling Gram's chapter "Fallen Angel," she says, "Good. He called it. He became it. He lived it. He did his mission and he left."

JOHNNY THUNDERS

∎

Too

Much

Junkie

Business

∎

"**O**kay. You got it. I'm gonna die tonight," Johnny Thunders would announce from the stage. "I'm gonna die up here." But Johnny's fans wouldn't get that twisted privilege. On April 23, 1991, the New York Doll/Heartbreaker guitarist died alone in a New Orleans hotel room under bizarre circumstances that are still being investigated.

Johnny's older sister, Marion, tells me there is a lot of mystery surrounding her brother's death. "I spoke to him that evening and he sounded fantastic," she recalls. "I believe there was foul play. I've been to New Orleans and nobody wants to talk to me. I went to the police department and the coroner's office and when I mentioned Johnny's name, everybody shut up. Nothing corresponds—the time on the death certificate, the time we were called." With obvious frustration she said that by the time she went to New Orleans, there was a different coroner. I ask Marion if she got a look at the police report. "Conveniently enough, there's only half the police report; the other half they can't seem to find."

Born in Queens, New York, in July 1952, John Anthony Genzale was raised by his mother, who was a supermarket cashier, and older sister, Marion, to be an altar boy, but at eight years old Johnny was following his earliest dream—to become a baseball player like his hero, Mickey Mantle. An average student, Johnny excelled in his favorite sport until his high-school teacher demanded he cut his thick mop of hair to get on the team. Johnny impolitely refused.

His second salvation was music. Seven years older than Johnny, Marion was into the sixties girl groups, turning young Johnny on to the Shangri-Las and the Crystals, which inspired his own musical discoveries—Howlin' Wolf, Gene Vincent, Eddie Cochran, the Stones, MC5. "He started when he was three," Marion tells me. "He was already imitating Elvis Presley!" At sixteen he formed his own band, Johnny and the Jaywalkers. At seventeen he spent months prowling the streets of London, seeing a different band every night for inspiration.

Back in New York, Johnny quickly fell into the tumultuous 1969 rock

junkie in the bathtub—Johnny's big dreams were always on hold. (MARCIA RESNICK)

scene, hanging in bars like Max's Kansas City and Nobody's, where he met the cocky David Johansen, an expelled Catholic school student from Staten Island who was busy forming a band called "Actress" with Arthur Kane, Sylvain Sylvain, and drummer Billy Murcia. Johnny joined the foursome, briefly becoming Johnny Volume before settling on Johnny Thunders. Actress soon became the fabulous New York Dolls.

They rehearsed in Rusty Beanie's Cycle Shop, playing seedy joints before landing a regular Tuesday-night gig at the Mercer Oscar Wilde Room and finally becoming the semipermanent house band at Max's Kansas City. Velvet Underground's Lou Reed proclaimed the Dolls "cute," and Max's was soon chockablock with fawning rock stars and decked-out Dolls devotees, who imitated the band's fishnet-stocking androgyny, wearing plastic pop beads, teetering on eight-inch platforms, their mascara thick and lip gloss gooey. "Before going onstage," claimed *Rolling Stone* magazine, "the Dolls pass around a Max Factor lipstick the way some bands pass around a joint." Jerry Nolan, who joined the Dolls a bit later, told the *Village Voice* that you could spot Johnny Thunders and his girlfriend Janis "from ten miles away." "Janis got Johnny into his look. He was wearing high heels, and you remember that teased hair look? That Rod Stewart look? Johnny's was like that, but even more dimensionalized and exaggerated, teased all the way up like in a crown. It was so long. He would have a platinum blond streak down the back . . . a girl's blouse on, and on top of that, a sparkling girl's vest. And then maybe a cowboy scarf. Mixing in cowboy stuff with glamorous forties girl stuff was something the Dolls liked to do. And he wore makeup, which really set him off."

Former promotions man Marty Thau pulled in Steve Lieber and David Krebs as financial managers and took on the formidable task of trying to get the Dolls a record deal. He set up some gigs in London and demo recording time at Escape Studios in Kent, but after only a couple of sessions and before the Dolls' first scheduled date at Manchester's Hardrock club, Billy Murcia became a tragic rock statistic. The drummer had gone to a party in Chelsea, soon found himself in the usual state of alcoholic obliteration, and passed out cold. It seems that Billy's new companions feared for his life and tossed him into a full bathtub, hoping to bring him around. The verdict: misadventure—death by drowning. Johnny and the rest of the band were shook up, but Dolls momentum was building, and Billy Murcia was quickly replaced with a well-respected New York drummer, Jerry Nolan. Jerry believes that "real abuse" caused Billy's death. "He went to a party with a lot of highbrow, stuck-up, rich teenage kids. They had these pills called Mandys. They were a heavy barbiturate down. All day long kids kept giving him these pills. . . . When Billy fell asleep everybody fucking panics. . . . They throw him in the goddamn fuckin' bathtub to try to shake him out of it. They fucking drowned him!

They drowned the kid! These fucking rich kids freaked out and ran away. They all split on the guy. What a fucking waste."

Jerry slotted right into the Dolls lineup and almost no time was lost. Record companies came in droves to gigs but were too afraid to sign the "obscene" band until rock critic Paul Nelson convinced Mercury to give them a deal. But there was internal conflict right away in the choice of producer. Despite fevered protests from Johnny and Jerry, David Johansen chose Todd Rundgren to helm the first record, and he didn't really do the band justice. Said Johnny, "He fucked up the mix

The New York Dolls, in the band's trashy transvestite drag, "passing around a Max Factor lipstick the way some bands pass around a joint." (MICHAEL OCHS ARCHIVES/VENICE, CALIF.)

really bad. Every time we go on the radio to do interviews, we always dedicate 'Your Mama Don't Dance and Your Daddy Don't Rock and Roll'—know that song?—to Todd." Although some of the Dolls' trashy magic was muffled in the mix, their 1973 debut album still managed to sell 110,000 copies. Mercury's clever catchphrase—"The New York Dolls: a band you're gonna like whether you like it or not!"—helped propel the first single, "Trash," onto the *Cash Box* charts and secure a tour with Iggy Pop. The tour was a raging success, ending with all the Dolls being arrested in Memphis for "profane language." Johnny was handcuffed right onstage. Said Jerry Nolan, "We once got off a plane in Paris or someplace, and we were walking through the lobby, and there was some press there, cameras and reporters. Johnny had been really sick on the plane, just not feeling well, and when he got off he really barfed out, right in front of the press." It got to where people expected the Dolls to do something disruptive and/or disgusting. And Johnny was more than willing to accommodate. That night at the Paris gig, he didn't appreciate being spit on and bashed his guitar over the offending fan's head.

Notorious British journalist Nick Kent, writing for *New Musical Express,* said:

> Johnny Thunders, for one, looks about as well as his guitar is in tune. He staggers around the stage in obvious discomfort, attempting to motivate himself and the band simultaneously and succeeding only in

beating his instrument into an ever-more horrendous state of tune-lessness. The sound reaches its nadir on "Vietnamese Baby," when the guitar interplay is so drastically off-balanced that it becomes quite grotesque to listen to. On the next number Thunders stops half-way through, puts down his guitar and moves behind the amplifiers to throw up for five minutes. "Y'know, in some ways Johnny is just a child," Marty Thau will state later, with a dewy-eyed paternal concern.

There was another disagreement about who would produce the Dolls' second album. David wanted nostalgia and won out with the legendary George "Shadow" Morton, who had written "Leader of the Pack" and produced the Shangri-Las. But Morton had given up teen-girl angst for the Tibetan Book of the Dead. The album, *Too Much Too Soon,* was critically panned. It sold enough for another U.S. tour, however, and since the Dolls were always broke back home, the road was full of excess. "While we were touring, at least we were going to live it up," said Jerry. "Musicians always get chicks, but not like the Dolls. The Dolls took chicks from any other musician, any other band, anybody! If the Dolls were in town, we owned it! I mean we owned it!! Many times there were violent scenes, and I'll tell you why. The way the women felt about us, the men felt the opposite. We totally offended them. We totally put their sexuality at risk. They hated our guts. You see, we threatened guys in two different ways. To lose your girlfriend to a musician was one thing. But to lose your girlfriend to a faggot musician was another thing entirely."

"The Dolls were the most obnoxious creatures ever to enter this country," stated a news editor in Germany after a particularly appalling interview.

PRESS: Did you do much sightseeing?

JOHNNY: Naw.

PRESS: What did you think of our famous beer?

JOHNNY: Tasted like . . . eh . . . it's like junkie's piss or something. . . .

PRESS: I don't have to listen to these pathetic, childish insults.

JERRY: Sure you don't. Fuck off.

SYLVAIN: Why are all Krauts so fuckin' fat?

JOHNNY: It's all them Jew-meat sausages.

Shock value aside, the Dolls' gloss and glam was fading. Arthur Kane had become such a severe alcoholic that one of the roadies hid behind an amp, playing his bass lines, and Jerry and Johnny were dabbling dangerously with hard-core drugs. Marty Thau was desperate and hooked up with Malcolm McLaren (pre–Sex Pistols), who deposited two of the Dolls in rehab before dressing them up in red leather suits and putting them onstage with a communist flag. Johnny and Jerry hated Malcolm and his absurd interference, so when David said, "Anyone in this band can be replaced," the disgruntled musicians got on the first plane back to New York.

True to his threat, David replaced Johnny and Jerry and headed to Japan for a bogus Dolls tour. When the realization hit, Johnny was devastated. "At first Johnny couldn't comprehend the Dolls ending," said Jerry. "I accepted it, though I took it hard. Real fuckin' hard. Johnny just couldn't believe it."

The fake Dolls fell apart while Johnny and Jerry were busy putting together a new band, the Heartbreakers, with Walter Lure and Richard Hell from Television. Gigs came easy with two ex-Dolls in the group, despite some early friction between Johnny and Richard Hell, who wanted to be the front man. Billy Rath soon replaced him.

Posters showed the Heartbreakers covered in blood, clutching bullet-holed chests: "The Heartbreakers—Catch Them While They're Still Alive!" Johnny cut his mad mane into a doo-wop do, trading his Dolls' cross-dressing for *West Side Story*'s leader-of-the-Sharks look. They hired the flamboyant Leee Black Childers as their manager and drew capacity crowds, but record companies balked. When the offer came from Malcolm McLaren to open for the notorious Sex Pistols, the Heartbreakers couldn't resist going to London smack in the middle of Britain's punkmania rage.

"When we hit London we turned it inside out and upside down," said Jerry. "Not only did we bring a lot of excitement, we brought a lot of danger, and well, some tragedy, too. We brought drugs with us—heroin. The groups there didn't know that from nothing. When Johnny and I got to England, everybody became junkies, almost overnight. We partied hard and tough and rough."

The Pistols had more gigs canceled than they played, and by January 1977 the entire tour was off. The Heartbreakers decided to stay, quickly becoming regulars at the Roxy club and the darlings of the speed-freak leather-and-chain set. One reviewer called Johnny "a junk-sick transvestite Eddie Cochran." It's true that Johnny was deep into his addiction by this time, and despite the arrival of his wife and kids from New York, he continued to proudly wage war with the needle. Johnny had broken the "no girlfriends or wives on the road" rule, and Jerry refused to live with Johnny's wife, Julie, and the kids, leaving Walter and Billy to trip over toys. Said Leee, "They all fought constantly . . . threw things around and broke things. . . . Walter and Billy weren't allowed to have girlfriends in because it would make Julie crazy to have groupies around. . . ." Leee finally conned the Heartbreakers a deal with Kit Lambert's new label, Track Records, and the Heartbreakers' *L.A.M.F.* (Like a Mother Fucker) album—including Johnny's junkie lament centerpiece and first single, "Chinese Rocks"—was recorded all over England. The single reached number one on the alternative chart and at one point outsold the Pistols' "God Save the Queen." The European tour, though fraught with the usual madness, garnered rave reviews.

When Tom Petty dared to call his new band the Heartbreakers, Johnny had this to say: "I think we should change our name to the Junkies." Jerry Nolan claims that he turned the Pistols on to heroin: "One time I shot Sid up backwards, pointing the needle down the vein rather than up, and he didn't know you could do that. Scared the shit out of him, but he didn't want to say nothing. That was the whole trip about the Pistols. Everything was a fuckin' act. . . . They were kids. We were a lot older. When it came down to the real nitty-gritty shit, throwing works on the table and cooking up some junk, they got scared."

The Heartbreakers were deported due to trouble with their visas, and when the problem was finally worked out, Jerry went back to London ahead of the others to remix the *L.A.M.F.* album. When Johnny arrived at Heathrow Airport with *two* passports, Leee had to cry real tears to convince the immigration people not to throw his bad boy in jail. Gigs were well received, reviews were mixed. *Sounds,* October: "The Heartbreakers are great, hot and anybody's. All you need is a pair of ears and an open mind." *Sounds,* December: "Why is Johnny Thunders the most arrogant slob ever to stumble across a stage? Sure, we love the New York Dolls, but . . ." Jerry had already threatened to quit the band several times, and had actually been replaced twice, but he knew it was over when Johnny told *Melody Maker* that Jerry "started screwing up all the mixes." Jerry retaliated in *Record Mirror:* "There's one guy in this band I don't like. I've discovered he's a coward, and I can't work with cowards. He's done things behind my back. . . . He gave in to allow the album to be released. He's only interested about reading about himself in the papers. . . . The whole thing's a joke and I want out." Years later Jerry had this to say: "Johnny and I still got together for the odd gig, but he could still be such a pain. . . . He'd get cocky and try to push people around, but if he could push you around, he'd hate you. If you pushed him back, he'd love you for it. If you could smack him down, he'd be your best friend. He needed me for that. He was a little bit of a masochist."

At twenty-four, Johnny had two kids to feed. He formed a short-lived band called the Living Dead, playing a few nights at the Speakeasy before landing a solo deal on Dave Hill's (the Pretenders' manager) Real Records. The single "Dead or Alive" was released in May 1978 and died a quick death. Johnny briefly played with the Pistols' Steve Jones and Paul Cook, calling the venture "Johnny Thunders' Rebels," while he continued recording his solo album, *So Alone,* backed by Jones and Cook as well as a long list of other punk "knowns." Released in October to grudgingly good reviews, it reached number seven on the alternative charts. Johnny was feeling optimistic and told *Sounds* that his dream was about to come true. "I've got someone to finance me to go to New Orleans and I'm gonna try and find a bunch of old black musicians and start a band with them." But it would be over a decade before Johnny made it to Louisiana.

His big heroin habit putting all big dreams on hold, Johnny put the Heartbreakers back together more than once and played some solo gigs, dubbed the "So Alone Revue." Once the rock press's darling, Johnny was now crucified in print whenever he staggered onto a stage. February 1979 found the Pistols' Sid Vicious dead from an overdose, which encouraged Johnny to write one of his most poignant odes, "Sad Vacation." But Sid's OD didn't do a thing for Johnny's deep-down junkie soul. He was starting to resemble a propped-up, blue-hued skeleton with spiky black hair. In July a small label released a live Heartbreakers set recorded at Max's Kansas City. *Sounds:* "As people these guys are odious creeps . . . but plugged in they are MAGIC." Nick Kent at the *N.M.E.* disagreed: "The whole enterprise stinks and there is absolutely no reason for even the most rabid Heartbreakers fan to purchase this piece of shit."

At a gig in Detroit Johnny came across an old hero, Wayne Kramer from the MC5, and they decided to start a band together, calling it Gang War. Johnny's family soon followed and for eight months tried to set up housekeeping in Dexter, Michigan. "One time I was comin' into Detroit Airport," Johnny told a journalist, "right? . . . and I had these red leather trousers on, and they make you look real big . . . they make your balls look real big . . . and . . . uh . . . the cops are lookin' at me real weird . . . and we get picked up by a Rolls-Royce and we get about three miles down the highway when *five* cop cars pull us over, and say to me, 'What's that stashed down your trousers?' . . . and I say . . . 'Well, what do you think it is? . . . and this is goin' on for twenty minutes, so in the end I hadda wind up whippin' it out in the middle of the highway."

Gang War was another short-lived project that lasted one tour, and the Thunders party landed back in Manhattan, where Johnny soon found himself the topic of a nightlife documentary produced by Christopher Giercke (who also became Johnny's manager). The

Johnny Thunders—a defiant mask of decadence. (MARCIA RESNICK)

camera shadowed Johnny into seedy, danger-driven areas on his constant search for a fix, which had become his reason for waking up every day. The Trouser Press Rock Predictions for 1981 insisted that Johnny Thunders was "legally dead" (though still playing in a band) next to a cartoon of the guitarist surrounded by drug paraphernalia, holding a syringe, with several more hanging out of his arm. Audiences didn't expect Johnny to show up at all, and when he did, they hoped for the worst and usually got it. If he forgot all the words or didn't bother to plug in, they cheered. For a while Patti Palladin performed with Johnny. People always asked her if he had died. She said, "He's got a lot to live up to, y'know, he always will. The Dolls were so fucking brilliant, it must create a constant pressure—plus the obsession with his death plays such a major role in his career now, it seems his success is gauged by it. I suppose the value of his catalog would soar." Fed up with the junk life, Julie took the kids and disappeared, and Johnny never saw his wife or sons again. It tore him apart. Little Dino was only three months old.

When Johnny took yet another new band to Sweden, rampant headlines followed him all over the country. The mania started when he arrived (very late) for a television show so blasted he literally couldn't stand up. The show didn't air but the newspapers had a ball: BURNT OUT, WASTED—A DRUGGED HUMAN WRECK—"He looks terribly wasted as he walks over to his guitar. He sat shivering in a black dressing gown. No photos are allowed. When we are about to leave, he mentions tonight's show in Sundsville. 'I can't do it. I can't do it,' says Johnny." And no wonder. The show in question was for an "anti-heroin cause." Within minutes after taking the stage, Johnny hurtled headlong into the audience and was promptly arrested. During another TV appearance, Johnny was surprisingly forthcoming when asked why he started taking drugs: "Like a lot of kids start because they're bored and lonely, y'know? It makes them feel like they're alive, I guess. I would *never* turn anyone on to drugs. It's a hard thing to handle and once you get into it, it's *really* hard to get out of." At the end of the interview he asked people to "have a heart, y'know I'm still a human being." Somehow he made it to London, where he stayed with a friend, Tony James. "He stayed here for two weeks, but it seemed like three years. Things kind of fall apart all around Johnny. . . . It was like the chaos in that scene from *E.T.,* when he's pissed. It's just extraterrestrial Thunders." One night Johnny was joined by ex-Doll Sylvain Sylvain, who told the *N.M.E.* that there was "a certain charisma about a guy that everybody thinks is about to drop dead." As usual, Johnny was stopped at Heathrow Airport on his way back home and was arrested when they found his works and heroin supply. He spent a few days in prison and was fined fifty pounds.

A flurry of Thunders's material was released early in 1982—old demos, bootlegs, and a cool single on the New Rose label, "In Cold Blood." After another tour of Europe with his band, Cosa Nostra, Johnny wound up in Paris, filming another low-budget epic entitled *Personality Crisis* about a guy addicted to heroin. It was never completed. Johnny recorded an acoustic song, "Hurt Me," for New Rose, which came out in late 1983. And despite all the flagrant bad press in Sweden (or because of it), Johnny made it to number twenty-two on the Swedish charts. He also fell in love with a Swedish girl, Susanne, who started traveling with him. He even cut down his drug intake.

Then, one more time, Johnny re-formed the Heartbreakers and played to a sold-out crowd at London's Lyceum after drinking eight double vodkas when his dealer didn't show up. "Hey," he yelled to his howling fans, "any of you kids in the audience old enough to get a hard-on yet?" Johnny played ninety-five concerts in 1984, from Russia to Japan, but was still after that elusive big record deal. Chris Geircke remained Johnny's manager and the two had become close friends. He still had the hope that he might be able to teach Johnny "leadership, standards, and certain rules." When Johnny's biographer, Nina Antonio, asked Chris if Johnny was "very ill" when he met him, he responded, "Well . . . a while back I took Johnny to *corrida* . . . a bullfight, you know . . . and it sickened him so much he almost passed out. Every thrust from the matador's sword was more wounding, more terrible to the animal. It was in great pain, but it would not fall. Does that answer your question?" He hoped Johnny might finally lose the "junk-sick rock star" label. "I mean three years ago, out of twenty-four hours, he would sleep twenty-two. . . . All that has changed now. His level of methadone is down now to fifteen milligrams. . . . It's all up to Johnny. . . ."

In 1985, during an interview for Nina Antonio's book, Johnny admitted to her that heroin addiction had wreaked havoc with his life. "I was very young when I started using heroin, young an' innocent and I thought I knew it all, right? But I didn't know it all and I wouldn't have conformed to it even if I did. . . . I had nobody to warn me off . . . to tell me I wasn't right. . . . I loved taking drugs, right? I thought I was havin' a real good time, takin' drugs and playin' rock and roll . . . but I wasn't. . . . It's easy to start, right? It's when you come to stop you find you got problems. Like, I've been on all sorts of methadone programs an' it's, well, it's horrible. You find that you get to kinda depend on drugs in certain situations, an' it's much harder having to deal with them straight; but really drugs just cocoon you . . . cut you off from the real world . . . alienate you from the entire fuckin' world; but the problems are still around, y'know? After the drugs you always still got the same problems."

The drugs, the illness, and the problems followed Johnny to Paris and then back to London, where he and his band struggled through some new demos at Tin Pan Alley studios. On hand were Mike Monroe from Hanoi Rocks and the Dead Boys' Stiv Bators. "Johnny Thunders is very important," Stiv said. "People should respect that. I mean, I never told him because he's big-headed enough, but a lot of time when you just seem to be spending your whole life slogging around bars and cheap dives, you need an inspiration . . . you need a dream or an image, and Johnny gave it. . . . It was just his general attitude. . . . Nobody else was like him. . . . I guess the last time I saw Johnny was in a bar in New York. He was attacking the drummer out of Tom Petty's Heartbreakers because they'd stolen his name. Johnny Thunders is a rare breed. A very rare breed."

There was another American jaunt, a successful trip to Japan, then Johnny wanted to clean up (one more time, again) so he could present himself to Susanne's parents as the model man. But on the long trip to Stockholm, Johnny ingested too many Valiums and the meeting at the airport was a predictable mess. After only one night with the Sundqvists, Susanne angrily bid him adieu. Soon Johnny was ruining friends' apartments all over New York, Paris, and London before hooking up with a fellow he called "Chief" who became his newest manager. The gigs started up again, and another solo album, *Que Sera Sera,* was recorded before Johnny flew to Stockholm to attempt a reconciliation with Susanne. While he was there, his hand got fractured in a car door, and the American tour had to be postponed.

Johnny convinced Susanne to take him back and, for a time, seemed content living with her in Stockholm. He did another well-received tour of Europe, got together with Jerry Nolan for another record, *Trouble Traveler,* and once again took Japan by storm. More live bootlegs were released. There were more sessions with various motley musicians. Everybody wanted to work with Johnny, even though he didn't show up sometimes, stole clothes and jewelry, not to mention drugs, and raked people through the rock-and-roll coals. It was expected. It was almost cool. Susanne got pregnant, and in 1988 their daughter, Jamie, was born. She stuck by Johnny till the end. The story remained the same. Junk was always a problem. It's amazing he made it as long as he did.

His sister, Marion, tells me Johnny tried several times to clean up. "Yeah, he went away about six months before he died. His biggest problem was this: At the beginning it was his own father, and then the breakup when his wife left him, taking the children and him never seeing them again. That had a lot to do with his continuing drug problem. Julie was pregnant by another man when Johnny met her; he stayed with her and took care of her son, and they had Vito and Dino after that. When she left, he never saw or heard from them again. He had no idea where she was; he even had a private investigator looking for her. He never knew if they were dead or alive." Dino is now sixteen years old. I remark that it seems very unfair to Johnny's sons that they were deprived of their father. "Oh, it's left a tremendous strain on them," she agrees. "They found out he had died from the TV. And the only reason they knew about me was that Julie called and asked if they were in Johnny's will." She laughs bitterly. "Of course, there was no will."

In April 1991, following a tour of Germany, Johnny fulfilled his longtime dream, checking into a motel in New Orleans, hoping to finally hook up with "a bunch of old black musicians" and start a band. He arrived with a cluster of colorful new suits and his pockets full of deutsche marks. The next morning he was dead. "He had always talked about New Orleans, it was just a place he wanted to go. He was very happy to be in New Orleans the night I spoke to him," Marion asserts. "He was so happy to see the street musicians." I ask Marion what Johnny's state of mind was that night. "My son Danny was going to meet him there, and he kept calling Danny, telling him what to get. 'Make sure you get the truck, bring everything down.' That's all he wanted to do, he wanted to leave. He felt that getting out of New York would help his drug problem."

"When the police called," Marion continues, "they just more or less said, 'The junkie OD'd, and that's it. They didn't even rope off the area. We have the feeling that somebody slipped him something. I heard several stories that there was some bad acid going around, and that's one thing Johnny would never do, ever! He would mostly take any drug, but never hallucinogens. I don't know if you could say there's anything like a smart junkie, but Johnny didn't live all those years not being smart. He knew what to do, and what to do it with. The way he was found, the way the room was, it was a mess. His suits were missing, the money, his passport, all his stage makeup, everything. Nothing was recovered."

When I ask Marion about the coroner's report, I am stunned by what she has to say. "Johnny had leukemia," she admits sadly. "He never knew it. A lot of leukemia, from what I understand from my physician, can be similar to withdrawals from drugs, and I guess Johnny just took it all for granted." How far along was the leukemia? I want to know. "It was pretty extensive. According to my physician, he only had six weeks to live." Was the leukemia listed as his cause of death? "They didn't put down a cause," she marvels. "What they said was that he had leukemia, and there were traces of methadone. No alcohol either. Nothing adds up. He had just flown, and John did not fly without drinking on the plane, because he hated flying." Marion then tells me that she's trying to find someone to redo the toxicology report but is running into a lot of dead ends. Finally I ask Marion how Johnny was found. "On the floor, alone."

Nick Kent, who called Johnny "a fearless little motherfucker" who was "never boring," saw him a few weeks before his death. "Jesus Christ, I could hardly stand to look at John. You know in a bullfight how when the decisive dagger has been plunged into the neck of the bull and basically it's all over for the poor creature and it goes limp and cross-eyed before sinking into the sawdust? Well, that's how Thunders looked . . . being ushered in: limp and cross-eyed from all the torments he'd been visiting upon himself in the pursuit of maintaining his righteous rock-and-roll identity. A few weeks later he died in New Orleans in a lonely hotel room with only some bad cocaine [and] some prescription methadone. . . . *Que sera sera.*"

In a *Village Voice* article, Jerry Nolan wrote about losing his friend: "I have a rough time getting through the days. I get real lonely, and I miss Johnny terribly. I don't like the idea of living without him. . . . He never had a father. I was like a father to him, a brother to him. It's just not fair. Everywhere I look I see Johnny's clones. Poison, Mötley Crüe, I could name a hundred bands that had a Johnny Thunders clone in them." A few weeks later Jerry told the *Village Voice* about bumping into Keith Richards, walking down Broadway: "He gave me the typical limp handshake and says, 'Look, Jerry, I'm sorry. I know what it's like. I don't know what to say. I wish I had a poetic answer. But I will say one thing. Somehow, I don't know, but somehow, hang in there. Stick to it. Don't give up.' Keith really picked up my spirits."

A year later Jerry Nolan died of a drug-related stroke.

STEVIE RAY VAUGHAN

■

The

Sky

Is

Crying

■

In an era when MTV had image-conscious rock and rollers decked out in Duran Duran doll clothes, Stevie Ray Vaughan climbed to the top armed only with his beloved guitar. Nobody could say he was good-looking, but he had magic in his big bony fingers, and his Texas boy's heart was crammed full of the blues.

He was just a little guy the local Oak Cliff kids called "Tomato Nose," but when he secretly plugged in his brother's guitar, shy Stevie Vaughan became king of the closet. The scrawny kid with the itty-bitty teeth knew his handsome older brother, Jimmie, would pound him when he found him wrapped around his precious guitar, hiding out in his closet, but it was more than worth it.

Jimmie Vaughan had been a child prodigy, and the family thought young Stevie was copycatting, but it was soon apparent that he, too, had the musical gift. When he was ten years old, mother Martha and daddy Jim bought their youngest son a Masonite toy guitar from Sears. "After he started playing," said

Martha, "he just never quit." By listening to his brother's influences, young Stevie was already imitating Muddy Waters, Howlin' Wolf, and Bobby "Blue" Bland, but his main hero was his brother, Jimmie. Instead of trading baseball cards or shooting hoops, Stevie hunkered down with Albert King records, determined to copy the master note for blistering note.

Jimmie's first band, the Swinging Pendulums, got gigs all over Dallas, and sometimes twelve-year-old Stevie got to sit in and jam, fortified by a few secret swigs of his daddy's beer. Though Big Jim had a killer of a temper and a penchant for boozing, for a while he allowed his sons to play their music and maybe get a chance at the big time. But when Jimmie went on to join a successful Texas rock band, the Chessmen, and started staggering home bombed at four in the morning, the Vaughans vowed to keep their youngest away from the music business. Fat chance. After Stevie had flipped burgers at the local Dairy Queen for a while, making seventy cents an hour, he realized all he wanted to do was play guitar. His parents would just have to understand.

By the time Stevie entered high school, his band had already played several local gigs. He had a black singer, which irked Big Jim no end. The first time Stevie's dad met Christian Plicque, he had asked him to shine his shoes, but nothing would deter Stevie from his music. When the Chessmen opened for a new mind-boggling guitarist, Jimi Hendrix, Stevie was front and center, gobbling it up, mixing the bold new sound into his burgeoning bowl of blues.

The Chessmen fell apart due to heavy drug and alcohol action, but it wasn't long before Jimmie put Texas Storm together and asked Stevie to play bass until they could round up a permanent member. Finally Stevie felt like his brother's equal, albeit a temporary equal, and as soon as a bass player was found, Stevie joined another band, Liberation, with singer Christian Plicque. At fifteen Stevie Vaughan was playing seedy, sleazy cellars every night, driving hundreds of miles, making almost no money, missing school, messing around with girls, and doing a whole lot of speed. He tried to hide the high life from his folks, but it showed in his face. After the 1971 Christmas holidays, Stevie really pissed off his parents by announcing he wasn't going to finish his senior year at high school. Instead, he and his newly named group, Blackbird, were hitting the high road to Austin, where all the groovy people were pursuing their passions. The little redhead with the John Lennon glasses wielding a guitar would fit right in. Big brother Jimmie was already there—how could it not be the coolest place on earth?

After hanging out in San Francisco with Janis Joplin and taking way too many amphetamines, Jimmie had rediscovered his blues mojo during a Muddy Waters gig and took it to Austin, where he was ripping up the club scene. When Stevie wasn't playing with his own band, he was always in the audience, hooting for his brother. If Jimmie's playing could soothe a savage beast, Stevie's could create one.

After a disappointing whirlwind trip to Los Angeles with a well-connected musician, Marc Benno, who promised Stevie stardom, the nineteen-year-old was back in Austin, stealing steaks from Safeway for his dinner. Not even twenty, Stevie felt like a washed-up nobody until he found a beat-up 1959 Stratocaster at an Austin instrument store, Heart of Texas Music. "I love this old thing," he told the owner. "This feels like what I've been looking for all these years." He traded a newer Strat for the funky older one, telling the store owner that it was the only guitar he had ever played that said what he wanted it to say.

Stevie's dedication proved to be too much for the members of his band, and in less than a year Blackbird was over and Stevie briefly joined Krackerjack. One of the clubs on the band's regular circuit was the Abraxis in Waco, Texas, where the musicians were furnished with cocaine, and Stevie fell right through the sparkling trap door. But the kid felt good about himself. Coke was better for you than speed, right?

Austin's answer to the Fillmore, the Armadillo, became Stevie's headquarters for the next two years. He played until he dropped, developing his flaming bluesy style to kick-ass perfection, eventually joining another R&B band, the Cobras, on New Year's Eve 1974. The band had a lot of camp followers, eager to shove cocaine up Stevie's flattened nose, and he was always flying, wired to the hilt. When the band did some demos, Stevie not only did some ferocious solos, he sang for the first time, and started singing live soon afterward, his voice nearly as soulful as his picking.

Lindi Bethel, Stevie's main squeeze, cooked for him, sewed his clothes, and supported him when he was low on cash, but she couldn't keep him faithful, and Stevie Vaughan was a double-standard kind of guy. He demanded that she be "good" whenever he was on the road, and when Lindi bitched, Stevie said that it was the music, not the devil, that made him do it. The music could take the blame.

Cobra band members called Stevie "Little Nigger" because he loved black music so hard, but mainly because he was such a fuck-up. They were tired of driving the kid around, holding his hand. When Stevie gave his notice, the Cobras heaved a combined sigh of relief.

When the landmark club Antone's opened in Austin, Jimmie Vaughan's Fabulous Thunderbirds were the unofficial house band, opening

Stevie Ray tearing it up. "I have been blessed with something," he said, "and if I don't take it to its fullest extent, I might as well be farting in the ashes." (JAMES FRAHER/MICHAEL OCHS ARCHIVES/VENICE, CALIF.)

for heavy-duty legends like Muddy Waters and Otis Rush. When Albert King came to town, Clifford Antone asked the blues great if Little Stevie Vaughan could sit in, and King begrudgingly obliged. Stevie was so charged up to be playing with the master that he owned the stage, keeping up with King the entire night. King tipped his hat to the kid. It was time for Stevie Vaughan to start his own band.

Rounding up Austin's finest, Stevie put together the Triple Threat Revue and started a fourteen-year road stint. Often waking up in strange houses in strange towns, Stevie wondered where the fuck he was, and where were the drugs? Girls were mad for the shy guitarist, following him from gig to gig, but when he laid eyes on Lenny Bailey, he knew he had to get her away from his friend Diamond Joe. A week later Joe was hurling darts at Stevie's picture, and Lenny was his. The couple had a skewed domestic scene, preferring to score a bag of ice each day instead of springing for a refrigerator. Though Lenny was able to provide the household with drugs, they were both into the spiritual sphere, consulting their horoscopes and throwing stones. Crystals or crystal meth, what was the difference? Above anything else, Stevie valued his musical gift, never really understanding why he was chosen to be so blessed.

Less than a year after their debut, Triple Threat lost a couple of members due to Stevie's jacked-up demands and became Double Trouble, the new name taken from an Otis Rush song. Stevie was playing like a motherfucker, but shooting a lot of speed and downing a fifth of Chivas Regal a day. His fingers bled, but he didn't seem to notice unless it got in the way of his playing. At a show in Lubbock he pulled a bloody callus down to the quick and reattached it with Superglue so he could do a third set. One night, when Jimmie did his usual heckling job from the audience, Stevie jumped offstage and punched his big brother in the jaw, then broke down into remorseful tears. When Stevie talked about Hendrix dying so young and how maybe he was in for the same fate, his friends started to worry about him.

Stevie and Lenny were busted for cocaine possession after Double Trouble opened for Muddy Waters in Houston, and in a state of confusion—after asking former girlfriend Lindi Bethel to come back to him—Stevie proposed to Lenny. They tied the knot between sets in the office of the Rome Inn nightclub, pledging their way-out adoration by creating rings out of wire found on the floor. They were probably guitar-string wedding bands. When the newlyweds went to court for the cocaine bust, Stevie was ordered to undergo drug abuse treatment. It didn't take.

When Double Trouble signed with Chesley Millikin at Classic Management, the new manager liked the sound of the guitarist's middle name, and Stevie became Stevie Ray Vaughan—Stevie Rave On!—the new guitar Wunderkind. "I have been gifted with something," Stevie said, "and if I don't take it to its fullest extent, I might as well be farting in the bushes."

Through Chesley, Double Trouble played a howlingly successful showcase at Danceteria in New York for the Rolling Stones, and the following week the grinning faces of Stevie and Mick Jagger graced the "Random Notes" page of *Rolling Stone*. Mick made noises about getting Stevie on the Stones' new label. It didn't happen, but the word was out.

A friend of Chesley's, Claude Nobs, extended an invitation for Double Trouble to play at the prestigious Montreux Jazz Festival, and after a raunchy, dazzling display of virtuosity from Stevie, audience member David Bowie came backstage to hand out some praise. He also asked if Stevie might be interested in appearing in his new music video. The second night of the festival Double Trouble jammed with Jackson Browne, who offered the band his studio back in L.A. free of charge. Things were looking way, way up for the kid who had hid in the closet with his brother's guitar.

The band took Jackson Browne up on his offer, recording ten songs in three days. While Double Trouble was in the studio, David Bowie called to see if Stevie would like to come to New York and play on his new album, asking what he was doing for the rest of next year. Good question.

Bowie and Stevie Ray were an odd pairing—Mr. Glam Sophistication and a no-frills blues guitarist who was called "Stinky" because he worked and slept in the same clothes for so long. But Stinky tore it up in the studio, completing six songs for the *Let's Dance* album in two and a half hours, and Bowie asked Stevie Ray to join the Serious Moonlight Tour. It was a sticky offer, tearing Stevie up, but he decided it just might jack him into the big time, so when rehearsals began in March 1983, Stevie Ray showed up.

Bowie hadn't planned on Stevie's coke habit or his starstruck wife, Lenny, as part of the package, and quickly laid down the *Let's Dance* law. Stevie's manager thought his client was worth more than three hundred dollars a night, and when Chesley Millikin was asked to cease managing Stevie for the Moonlight Tour, Stevie shocked the rock world by quitting the Bowie tour before it started. The bold move heightened his "working-class guitar hero" image.

After working on music industry icon John Hammond for two years, Chesley was overjoyed when the producer called after hearing a live tape of Double Trouble from Montreux. When he heard the rough mixes from Jackson Browne's studio, he was determined to put out Stevie Ray Vaughan's first album. The Bowie record helped the cause, and after some remixing, Epic released Double Trouble's *Texas Flood* in June 1983. By the end of the year Stevie had gone gold.

Stevie no longer had to worry about paying the bills and always carried five grand in one boot and a gram of coke in the other. He indulged his passion for guitars, buying the best of the best and giving them all names. Onstage he kept his head down and attacked his instrument like a hell-bent lover on a rampage, torturing the strings into adoring submission while his fans went into a frenzy. With the fame came the drug-toting sycophants, and even after a loving yet stern warning from mentor Albert King, Stevie continued daily to down a bottle of Chivas and inhale seven grams of coke.

Texas Flood was nominated for four Grammy awards, winning Best Traditional Blues Category, and the second album from Double Trouble, *Couldn't Stand the Weather,* sold like Texas hotcakes. After a packed date at Carnegie Hall, Stevie found his parents in the glad-handing backstage crowd and hugged Big Jim until they both had tears running down their faces.

Stevie Ray (right) and brother Jimmie Vaughan. Stevie died a few hours later. (ROBERT KNIGHT)

The routine went on and on. Only now there were bigger venues, more money, grander parties, more eager women, jet planes, and never-ending, heaping mounds of cocaine.

Lenny was always pissed off about something. She didn't see Stevie enough. He didn't know how to handle his money. She didn't get enough of it. It was all going up his nose. He was barely coherent half the time. He gave her some kind of venereal infection. He appeared to be having a long-distance infatuation with a seventeen-year-old model, Janna Lapidus. Really it seemed like he was too fucked up to care about anything but the music. But even the music was starting to suffer. The third album, *Soul to Soul,* was a pain in the ass to record, and though his fans flipped over it, the album didn't satisfy Stevie Ray Vaughan.

His addiction got so bad that before and after gigs wasn't enough—Stevie started dissolving a gram of coke into his Crown Royal, imbibing throughout the set. But nobody could help him. He was everybody's meal ticket and too damn stubborn to listen. Brother Jimmie wasn't any help. He was fucked up, too.

A fourth album was due, but Stevie was in no shape to deliver it. The easiest way out was to do a live record, and *Live Alive* is full of some pretty jacked-up, meandering tracks. The guitar solos are ragged, tragic, and full of tears that Stevie needed to cry. He was a total wreck. When Big Jim had a heart attack and died, Stevie still didn't weep. He played the blues instead. On tour in Germany Stevie threw up bloody vomit and was rushed to the hospital, saying all he needed was a drink. His diagnosis was severe internal bleeding. The alcohol laced with coke had been tearing Stevie's guts apart and in another month he would have been dead. On September 29, 1986, Stevie went to the London Clinic to take the cure with the same doctor who had helped Eric Clapton get healthy. He reached out to his mother and she came to her son's side. Eric Clapton came to visit, encouraging his friend in recovery.

After 242 dates with Double Trouble that year, the rest of the tour had to be canceled. On the plane to Charter Hospital in Atlanta, Stevie had his last double Chivas, then collapsed sobbing in his mother's arms.

Stevie grabbed hold of recovery the way he did his music, with every ounce of his being, holding the Twelve Steps of Alcoholics Anonymous in the same esteem as Albert King's guitar playing. The program forced him to stop running, stop hiding behind his Strat, and be brutally honest with himself and the other recovering addicts. "There were a lot of things I was running from," he told a writer. ". . . I was scared that somebody would find out I was scared. And now I'm realizing that fear is the opposite of love."

Out of Charter, Stevie lived one day at a time. He filed for divorce from Lenny, which turned out to be a long and bitter experience. He moved eighteen-year-old Janna Lapidus in with him, and attended several AA meetings a week. He got healthy and stopped eating red meat. Stevie Ray was happy to be sober but nervous about picking up a guitar and playing the blues—after all, the term came from "blue devils," a description of the hallucinations caused by getting too high—but the music didn't fail him. Stevie started embracing people, saying with a huge, goofy grin, "Hugs, not drugs." When old coke buddies swore Stevie's passion had disappeared with his habit, he proved them ragingly wrong with his fifth album, *In Step,* a passionate mixture of hard-learned lessons and solid steamy riffs, which went gold, then platinum, earning him another Grammy, for Best Contemporary Blues Recording of 1989.

Big brother Jimmie was still getting way too high and his career had started to backslide after the Fabulous Thunderbirds' Top Ten hit, "Tuff Enuff." There had always been underlying rivalry, but surrounding it was a deep brotherly love. More than anything, Stevie wanted to get his brother straight and suggested that the two of them finally record an album together, which intrigued Jimmie enough to enter rehab. When he completed the program, the brothers Vaughan went into the studio to make the record of their lives. They played from their hearts and got closer than they had ever been.

When Stevie collected a crate full of honors at the Austin Music Awards, he thanked God he was alive, adding, "I want to thank all the people that loved me back to life so that I could be here with you today."

Some of Stevie's fans swore he had a healing gift. "I've seen that kind of sound heal me and other people," Stevie once remarked. "I'm not saying that I am a healer; I'm saying that wherever those kinds of feelings and emotions come from, or through, music is a healer. If I hadn't had the music to play, I probably would have been dead a long time ago." Stevie seemed grateful and surprised to have made it through his addictions. Onstage in Kansas City he told his audience, "Every day I live now, it's kind of like borrowed time." He was going to make every day count. To a journalist at *Guitar World,* Stevie pointed out the Hendrix pin on his lapel. "See this? You know there's a big lie in this business. The lie is that it's okay to go down in flames. Some of us can be examples about going ahead and growing. And some of us, unfortunately, don't make it there and end up being examples because they had to die. I hit rock bottom, but thank God my bottom wasn't my death."

Stevie and Double Trouble were added to Eric Clapton's lineup for a gigantic gig at Alpine Valley resort in Wisconsin on Labor Day weekend 1990. The first night Stevie stole everybody's thunder, causing Eric Clapton to say the following night, "How am I going to follow this guy?" Opening with "The House Is Rockin'" from *In Step,* Stevie got the audience jumping and gyrating, and when brother Jimmie came onstage for the last three numbers, the entire house was on its feet. At the end of Clapton's set, he made an announcement: "I'd like to bring out to join me here, a big treat, the best guitar players in the entire world: Buddy Guy, Stevie Ray Vaughan, Robert Cray, Jimmie Vaughan." A monster jam ensued, in which Stevie Ray lifted off the stage. "He just sort of kicked everybody's ass and nobody seemed to fight back," Jimmie later recalled. "Stevie was on a cloud or something."

After the set Stevie was in a hurry to get on a helicopter, get back to his hotel, and call Janna. There was a single seat left on one of the Bell 206B JetRangers, and Stevie fastened himself in along with Clapton's agent, Bobby Brooks, tour manager Colin Smythe, and Nigel Browne, Clapton's bodyguard.

The helicopter lifted up through the thick fog and seconds later crashed into a three-hundred-foot-high hill. Nobody heard a thing. All the passengers on board died instantly. It was August 27, 1990, the fourth anniversary of Big Jim Vaughan's death.

At 6:50 A.M. two sheriff's deputies discovered the wreckage, judging the crash site as "a high-energy, high-velocity impact at a low angle." In the chilly morning sun, Jimmie Vaughan and Eric Clapton quietly identified the bodies. Somebody found Stevie's cross necklace, and his big brother put it around his own neck.

A few days later several thousand people mourned the loss of Stevie Ray Vaughan at the Laurel Land Memorial Park in south Oak Cliff. Dr. John played piano while Stevie Wonder sang the Lord's Prayer. Bonnie Raitt and Jackson Browne joined Stevie Wonder in an aching a cappella version of "Amazing Grace," then the local preacher read the Serenity prayer, concluding with the

The ruins of Stevie Ray Vaughan's helicopter—"a high-energy, high-velocity impact at a low angle." (AP/WIDE WORLD PHOTOS)

Prayer of St. Francis, which was found folded up in Stevie's pocket. (". . . For it is in giving that we receive, it is in pardoning that we are pardoned, and it is in dying that we are born to eternal life.")

The Vaughan brothers' album, *Family Style,* released after Stevie's death, shot straight into the *Billboard* Top Ten and won two Grammy awards.

As always, rumors were whispered that there were drugs on the helicopter, that Stevie Ray had been getting high again, but the coroner's report told the truth: Stevie's aorta had been severed. There was no evidence of drug use. Stevie had been clean and sober for three years, 317 days, and forty minutes.

SID VICIOUS

■

Hit

Me

with a

Flower

■

Sid woke up in a blood-soaked bed. Staggering through the chaotic mess to the bathroom, he was horrified to see his precious Nancy in her black lacy underwear, curled into a fetal position under the sink, white as a ghost, which is what she was. Except for all the blood. A hunting knife was sticking out of her side, the same knife she bought for Sid in Times Square the day before. Sid Vicious stood there slack-jawed, in a state of stun-eyed shock from which he would never, ever recover. The only person who gave a shit about him was dead on the floor, killed with his own knife. Though he couldn't remember how it had happened, when the cops arrived Sid admitted to stabbing Nancy. "I did it because I'm a dirty dog," he announced in a tragic monotone before being handcuffed and taken away to prison.

Born John Simon Ritchie on May 10, 1957, Sid Vicious left home—such as it was—at fifteen. His air force father disappeared when Sid was two, and his mum, Anne Beverley, shuttled him from place to place, barely making ends meet, sometimes rolling joints for a living, dragging her son through the drug-torn hippie haze of London's flower power. Later Sid would pick fights with aging hippies, harassing them with, "Do you remember the magical summer of '68?"

During a brief stint at Hackney Technical College, Sid met John Lydon, a like-minded, pissed-off, scrawny young outcast who had suffered with meningitis as a child. Together they went "squatting" in abandoned London dwellings, took fleeting odd jobs, and wandered up and down the King's Road in Chelsea—the trendiest street for fashion in the universe—often hanging out at Sex, a hard-edged fetishwear shop owned by Malcolm McLaren.

Sid Vicious and Nancy Spungen on the set of the documentary *DOA*, nodding out and barely coherent. (COURTESY OF LECH KOWALSKI)

McLaren sold his naughty-sloganed, studded T-shirts, rubberwear, leather knickers, and brightly colored zoot suits to the likes of Jimmy Page and the Kinks but, always on the lookout for something to snazz up his world and make some cash, the frizzy redhead started managing a fledgling band, led by a thieving young street kid, Steve Jones. Almost all of the band's equipment had been stolen: most of the PA from a parked van, the drum kit from BBC studios, a strobe tuner from a Roxy Music concert, two guitars from Rod Stewart's mansion, and—the biggest coup—almost all of David Bowie's equipment from a Hammersmith Odeon gig.

Contrary to the myth that McLaren was the band's Svengali creator, it was in fact Steve Jones who approached Malcolm when he and drummer Paul Cook and bassist Glen Matlock needed a place for their band to audition and rehearse. When Jones realized he needed a front man, Malcolm invited Johnny Lydon down to try out. Decked out in full punk safety-pin fashion, Lydon, hiding his fears with snarling attitude, caterwauled and croaked his way through Alice Cooper's "Eighteen." "We knew he couldn't sing," McLaren said, "but he had this charm of a boy in pain, trying to pretend he's cool." He was hired. The rest of the band were suspicious of Lydon, but Malcolm believed that the antagonism would create just the right combustion. "They're like young assassins," he stated with pride. The newest member had a disgusting habit of picking at and inspecting his rotting teeth. Steve found this nauseating and used to say to Johnny, "Your teeth are rotten, you look rotten," and the name was obnoxious enough to stick.

England was in a recession, with unemployment at its worst since World War II. Sullen and brooding, coming from the working class, the teenagers in Britain weren't able to get jobs, many of them squatting in central London on the dole. And music was nowhere. Glam had faded fast—Marc Bolan had his own chat show. Synthesized and heavily marketed, rock had turned into streamlined, promotable pop or insipid nostalgic rehash. It was the end of 1975, and Steve Jones's band had decided to call themselves the Sex Pistols.

The Pistols started playing out to immediately charged crowds. It became clear right away that the band was acting out the angst for their pent-up audience. When they opened for a band called the Hot-Rods, the headliners weren't even mentioned in the *New Musical Express* review, which warned, "Don't look over your shoulder, but the Sex Pistols are coming." "Actually, we're not into music," Steve Jones had growled at the reporter. "We're into chaos."

Since their rejection of values was mutual, these dangerous urchins weren't out to make their audience like them. Quite the reverse. There was spitting, "gobbing" (the reaction to Rotten's constant stream of snotty phlegm), "slamming" (butting heads, inflicting pain on each other), and "pogoing" (a stiff upward pogo-stick leap, to get a better view of the band). Punks in the know say that this action was started by the Pistols' number-one fan, John Simon Ritchie—newly named "Sid Vicious" by Johnny Rotten (some say the moniker was taken from Lou Reed's "You're So Vicious," but Sid was actually christened after Johnny's evil pet hamster)—for his chain-wielding attacks on unsuspecting audience members.

Malcolm McLaren was in his element, grabbing hold of the novelty-geared British press, determined to stir up a sensation where one was direly needed—

The Sex Pistols—anarchists, anti-Christs, "foul-mouthed yobs."
(ROBERTA BAYLEY)

and make a few pounds in the process. He took his band into the studio, where they recorded seven explosive original songs, one of which, "Anarchy in the U.K.," broke two taboos at once: "I am an anti-Christ/I am an anarchist." With these tapes Malcolm attacked the record industry, finally convincing EMI to take a chance on his menacing brute boys. Nobody bothered to read the contract. "At that age you're naive, you don't think of these things," said Lydon years later. "You just see: contract, the big time. You think of the hundred pounds you're going to get out of it, not how it'll be an albatross for the rest of your life." There would be years of lawsuits with Malcolm before the Pistols finally got their fair share.

"Anarchy" came out to very mixed reviews, but after appearing live on Bill Grundy's TV chat show, on which Steve Jones called the host "a dirty bastard" and a "fucking rotter," the Pistols' publicity storm turned into a tornado. Headlines blazed FURY AT FILTHY TV CHAT, THE BIZARRE FACE OF PUNK ROCK, THE FOUL-MOUTHED YOBS. Chaos ensued, but that's what the Pistols had asked for. Gigs were canceled. The entire country was aghast and afraid. "Anarchy" reached number twenty-seven on the charts before plummeting. But hopping-mad punk bands were springing up everywhere.

Twenty-year-old Sid Vicious had been singing in a band called Flowers of Romance, and when bassist Glen Matlock received his Pistols walking papers, Johnny Rotten insisted that the Pistols' number-one fan take his place. At almost exactly the same time, Sid met Nancy. Already into pill popping, Sid joined nineteen-year-old Nancy Spungen in her heroin haze, where he remained ensnared for the rest of his life.

A highly hyperactive child, Nancy had all but toppled her suburban family back in Philadelphia, entering the first of several psychiatric institutions at the age of eleven. Diagnosed as a schizophrenic, she was into drugs very early, turning both of her siblings on to the joys of pot smoking when they were barely twelve. Two suicide attempts later, Nancy was shooting smack at fifteen, constantly claiming that she would go out in a headlining blaze of glory before she hit twenty-one. All she wanted was to grab hold of a famous guy in a band and fly along for the ride. She claimed to have had sex with every member of Aerosmith, every member of Bad Company, some of the Who, a few of the Allman Brothers. Once her mother found all of the Pretty Things in Nancy's childhood bedroom. When she met the New York Dolls in Manhattan, Nancy followed them to London, where she met her prize, the infamous Sex Pistol, Sid Vicious, glomming on to him hard and fast (though she was originally

Sid and his beloved Nancy. He promised to join her if she happened to die first. He killed her by accident and kept his promise. (LONDON FEATURES INTERNATIONAL)

looking to score top gun Johnny Rotten). From then on, Nancy called him "my Sid." The rest of the band vilified Nancy as a strung-out tramp and a scumbag, calling her "Nauseating Nancy," which made Sid want her all the more.

Sid drops his leather trousers . . . (ROBERTA BAYLEY)

The Pistols signed their second record deal with A&M in front of Buckingham Palace, wreaking havoc, before disappearing to the offices for a meeting about the single "God Save the Queen." In the limo Sid and Paul had a fistfight about who was more "Sex Pistol," and by the time they arrived at

. . . then sheepishly pulls them back up. (ROBERTA BAYLEY)

A&M, Paul was cut up and Sid, scuffed and shoeless, passed out comatose on the couch. Somebody threw wine in his face, and when Sid discovered his feet were bleeding, he proceeded to the bathroom, where he smashed the toilet and crashed through the window, finally bathing his battered feet in the shattered toilet bowl. Sid was already trying to prove he was more "Sex Pistol."

They were supposed to be bad boys, but after a row at a nightclub in which an insulted Sid charged somebody with a broken bottle, and a friend of Rotten's made death threats, A&M dropped the Pistols, destroying all the newly pressed "God Save the Queen" singles. At that point the group was given nothing more than a fifteen-pound weekly wage raise, and while the obstinate Malcolm tried to round up another record deal, Sid was on the loose, scoring bags of heroin with Nancy. When he wound up in the hospital for a month, sick with hepatitis, nobody came to visit except for "his Nancy." The loving couple were creating their own insulated, private junkie world where everybody else was a trespasser. Sid signed the Virgin recording contract from his hospital bed, and "God Save the Queen" sold an amazing 150,000 copies in five days. "There is no future!" Rotten squalled murderously. "No future for you, no future for me, no future for you!"

PUNISH THE PUNKS! raged the headline in the *Sunday Mirror.* Shocking, disturbing, and subversive—accused of everything from conspiracy to communism—the Pistol boys were treated as though they weren't even human beings. Both Johnny and Paul had been accosted on the street and beaten up badly, but despite the national vitriolic dissension, newly bred punks thronged the King's Road wearing their leather jackets, bondage trousers, and shredded, graffiti'd T-shirts, leaking amphetamine violence with every step of their heavy black boots and agreeing with the Pistols that everything was indeed "pretty vacant" and "no fun." The album *Never Mind the Bollocks (Here's the Sex Pistols),* which came out in October of 1977, went straight to number one in the U.K. despite being banned by Boots, Woolworth's, and W. H. Smith. Raging success aside, the Sex Pistols would never record together again.

Discomania was sweeping the States. John Travolta's white suit was copied in polyester and sold at shopping malls from coast to coast. The Bee Gees topped the U.S. charts with the croony ballad "How Deep Is Your Love." Still, Malcolm was determined to overthrow America with his band of terrifying punks and, after signing the Pistols to Warner Bros. Records in the United States, booked a tour excluding Los Angeles and New York, cities he loathed, choosing Atlanta, Georgia, for the Pistols' first show. Nancy wasn't allowed on the trip, and Sid wasn't amused, disappearing into the deep South underworld after the opening gig, searching for a fix. He missed the plane to Memphis, but was rounded up by a roadie the next afternoon, only to get promptly lost in the city where Elvis sleeps. When he finally turned up, just in time to make the show (on what would have been Elvis's forty-third birthday), his bloody chest newly carved with the words "I Wanna Fix," Sid was greeted with open hostility by his three band mates. By the third U.S. date, nobody was speaking to the naughty bass player, who was half-kicking his habit, nodding on Valiums. In the bus en route to Austin, he cut a seven-inch gash into his left arm, saying, "Do you want to see what I do when I'm happy?" The wound got infected, he wouldn't bathe, and the bus was crawling with Sid's crabs.

At the next show in San Antonio, after a hunchbacked Johnny berated his audience ("All you cowboys are fuckin' faggots"), Sid smashed his bass over a photographer's head, bled all over the stage, and made a halfhearted attempt to dodge the barrage of hurtling cans and bottles. In Baton Rouge he had sex on top of the bar with a fleshy, Spandex-clad babe while flashbulbs popped. In Dallas Sid punched holes in the hotel wall with a set of brass knuckles. In the middle of the night somewhere in Middle America, as Sid sat in a coffee shop having his usual rare steak and runny eggs, a big ol' trucker taunted him, "If you're so vicious, can you do this?," putting a cigarette out on his hand. Barely glancing at the man, Sid said, "Yeah," and cut his own hand so badly that blood poured into his plate of food as he ate it. In another version of the story, Malcolm says that Sid bled on the *trucker's* steak and was hurled twenty-five yards into the side of the tour bus. In Tulsa roadies had to rescue a girl from Sid's room after he vomited on her and had a diarrhea attack during a romantic blow job. Things were very grave. In San Francisco Rotten sang, "I'm an abortion," then, slipping into his speaking voice, said, "What does that make you!" He announced he was quitting the Sex Pistols that same night.

Sid turned blue and collapsed on the corner of Haight and Ashbury after mainlining on a scummy mattress on somebody's floor. He slipped into a drug-induced coma on a plane headed for New York and spent a few days in Jamaica Hospital, where photographer Roberta Bayley called him. He told her it was his basic nature to fuck up badly. She told him that his basic nature would get him in a lot of trouble, to which he responded, "My basic nature is going to kill me in six months." He wasn't far off.

In less than two years the Sex Pistols, the most influential band in over a decade, were over. Even though Malcolm was busy finishing a film about the group, John Lydon became a recluse, only appearing briefly in *The Great Rock 'n' Roll Swindle* before starting another band, PiL—Public Image, Ltd.— where he continued to vent his unique brand of wretchedness. Steve and Paul worked on *Swindle* in Rio de Janeiro, eventually forming their own band, the Professionals. Malcolm flew Sid to Paris, where he did his bits for the film, including his pathetic and ferocious thrash bleating of "My Way," soon to become a punk classic. (He refused to record the song unless some of his own lyrics could be used: "I ducked the blows / I shot it up / and killed a cat."

Holed up in London's heroin hell, Sid and Nancy bickered constantly, becoming sicker and more dependent on each other daily. It was during this time that Lech Kowalski filmed the couple for his appropriately titled documentary, *DOA.* Lying in bed, entirely stoned, the two are attempting an interview, but Sid keeps nodding off in mid-word. Nancy tries to arouse him repeatedly, whining and yowling, but he's nodding hard. He continually fondles a hunting knife, and actually burns her with a cigarette at one point. Nancy seems oddly proud of who they are. "Sid and Nancy," she moons as if they were already dead. "We were partners in crime, we helped each other out." The partners went on short-term methadone cures but were mostly adrift and pitiful. Determined to live up to his name at the Speakeasy club one frantic night, Sid got into another fight, this time with a marine who severed a nerve in Sid's right eye so severely that he could no longer open it fully. The droopy eye went well with his sneering pirate's leer.

After burning bridge after bridge in London, the pair moved to New York, checking into the infamous Chelsea Hotel, where they planned on getting clean and maybe even getting married, but the couple's fatal reputation preceded them. Nancy, always bruised and battered because she provoked Sid into beating on her, egged him into confrontations. Sid got into constant fights, even at the Spring Street methadone clinic. But he still wanted to be a star. With Nancy as his "manager," Sid played a few gigs with some of the New York Dolls and even had meager hopes of a solo record deal. But the American music industry wasn't interested in a broken-down Pistol with a habit. It was a bad time. That September Sid said, "The world has put us under house arrest."

To recuperate one more time, Sid and Nancy went to spend a week with Nancy's parents in Philadelphia. In Deborah Spungen's harrowing account about her daughter's sad, short life, *And I Don't Want to Live This Life,* she describes the couple's arrival at the train station: "She looked like a Holocaust victim. . . . Her skin was a translucent bluish-white. Her eyes had sunk deep into their sockets and had black circles under them. Her hair was bleached white and along the hairline there were yellowish bruises and sores and scabs. . . . Behind her lurked Sid . . . his spiky hair stood straight up on his head. He, too, was bluish-white and painfully thin. . . . There was a total absence of life to them. It was as if the rest of the world were in color and they were in black and white." Oblivious to the gaping stares, Nancy ran to embrace her mother, proudly introducing her to Sid. "He stuck out his hand," Deborah reported. "I shook it. It was wet and limp, a boy's hand. He was a boy, shy and more than a little confused by the strange surroundings. 'Allo, Mum,' he said quietly." Thus began a traumatic week in suburbia. The lovebirds constantly swigged out of their methadone bottle, popped heavy downers like Tuinals and Dilaudids (Elvis's drug of choice), and watched cartoons, groping each other and dropping lit cigarettes on the family sofa. Deborah plucked stitches out of her daughter's ear to avoid a scene at the local hospital. In one of their fights, Sid had actually torn off Nancy's ear, but she kept that information from her tragically concerned mother. He had also dangled Nancy out a seventh-story window by her ankles, but she didn't tell her mother about that episode, either. When a forlorn Sid asked Deborah if she could help him find a plastic surgeon for his eye, she said she would try. "Thank you," he said, "that'd be very nice of you. I don't like my eye, you know. I got it in a fight. People always want to fight with me. Teachers. Policemen. Teddys. Everybody. I don't want to, but they do." Before she left for New York, Nancy once again told her mother that she was going to die very soon, before her twenty-first birthday, "in a blaze of glory."

Back in the Chelsea, Sid and Nancy set their bed on fire and were moved to Room 100.

On October 11, 1979, Sid got some Pistols money and Nancy wanted Dilaudid, ordering forty of the pills from dealer Rockets Redglare at about 1:30 A.M., which he was unable to get. He brought the couple a small amount of the drug, and Nancy gave him a few hundred dollars to find more. The pair then went to see a guitarist down the hall, Neon Leon, looking for pot. According to Leon, Sid showed him a five-inch knife that Nancy had bought him that day for protection. Then another dealer, Steve Cincotti, arrived at Room 100 between four and five A.M. with Tuinal.

The next morning Sid woke up to find his bloody valentine under the sink.

But what had actually happened? Had Sid killed Nancy in another one of their violent stoned-out fights? Could it have been an angry young dealer? Drugged-out thieves? Rockets Redglare told police that after Nancy gave him the money for Dilaudid, she still had several hundred left. Where was the money? Perhaps it was a screwed-up suicide pact gone awry? Said a friend at the Chelsea, "They were both really depressed and talked about dying the last few weeks." Another friend said the couple had a longstanding agreement that if one died, the other would follow.

Somehow Malcolm McLaren raised Sid's fifty thousand dollars' bail, and after a grim, nightmarish few days, kicking cold turkey on Rikers Island, Sid was cut loose and hidden from the press at a welfare hotel, the Saville. To raise funds for Sid's defense (and stir up some more controversy), McLaren sold T-shirts with Sid wearing G.I. Joe clothes, shouting the words "I'm Alive, She's Dead, I'm Yours." Sid's mother, Anne Beverley, arrived in New York to provide some comfort for her little boy, reportedly selling her story to the *New York Post* for ten thousand dollars.

October 17, the same day Sid was released, Deborah Spungen buried her daughter Nancy, wearing her green prom dress. Sid was released too late to attend Nancy's funeral, and he was mortified. On the twenty-second, Sid, almost catatonic, attempted suicide during unbearable withdrawal symptoms. Anguished over the death of Nancy, he butchered himself so badly that he was taken to Bellevue psychiatric hospital for observation.

That night, right after Sid's slash fest, Anne called Malcolm, and he arrived with a friend, Joe Stevens, who happened to have a tape recorder in his bag. Malcolm called an ambulance, and while they waited, Stevens turned on the recorder and asked Sid what had happened in Room 100. He answered, "You know how the Dead Boys [Stiv Bators's band] poke each other with the knives through the leather jackets? Nancy slapped me in the nose just after I'd been punched out by the bellhop . . . and I took out the knife and said, 'Do that again and I'm going to take your fucking head off.' And she stuck her belly right in front of my knife. She didn't know. I didn't know that we'd done anything really bad. She crashed out on one bed, I crashed out on the other."

In his guilty torment, Sid began to write to Deborah Spungen. In one of his letters he enclosed a poem he had written for his Nancy.

With genuine wide-eyed innocence, Sid describes Nancy as "just a poor baby, desperate for love," and tells how he was faithful to her. Sid touchingly asks Nancy's mom if he could see her before he dies, since she was "the only one who understood." The poem Sid enclosed is entitled "Nancy" and begins "You were my little baby girl." His life without her is now nothing but pain, Sid laments in the poem, and if he can't live it for Nancy, Sid insists, "I don't want to live this life."

Sid plunged deeper into drugs and despair, awaiting his court date, set for February 1, 1979. There would be another scrape with the law, when Todd Smith, singer Patti Smith's brother, threw a few punches at Sid for allegedly molesting his girlfriend. Sid retaliated with a broken bottle. Todd had to get stitches for a head wound, and Sid wound up kicking junk again, spending Christmas on Rikers Island.

On February 1, Sid's lawyer, James Merberg, made such a convincing plea that Sid was out a day ahead of schedule. Waiting for him was his adoring mother, who had already purchased some heroin for her adored son. After his mum prepared spaghetti for Sid and a few others, he went into the bedroom to shoot up. Already warned by the dealer that the heroin was "close to 100 percent pure," Sid flushed pink and floated around precariously, but survived. Ma Vicious tucked the rest of the junk in her back pocket for safekeeping, but when everybody crashed out, Sid found the packet and, according to friend Joe Stevens, "shot a whole load" and died.

Nobody really knows if Sid OD'd on purpose, but I'm sure his Nancy was waiting for him.

Three weeks later Sid's spitfire version of Eddie Cochran's "Something Else" was released and sold 328,000 copies—nearly double the sales of "God Save the Queen."

On February 2, 1980, in honor of the first anniversary of Sid's death, one thousand punks marched from London's Sloane Square in Chelsea to Hyde Park. Ma Vicious, Anne Beverley, was supposed to have taken part in the proceedings—instead she was taken to a hospital due to a drug overdose.

DENNIS WILSON

■

Pacific Ocean Blues:

A Beach

Boy's Burial

at Sea

■

The Wilson family of Hawthorne, California, by all appearances epitomized the American Dream. To neighbors, the three Wilson brothers seemed to be well-behaved, obedient boys who doted on their overbearing father, Murry, and loving mother, Audree. But what may have been regarded as strict discipline back in 1960 is now considered child abuse. Murry punched, beat, and kicked his sons, tied them to trees, and whacked them with two-by-fours when they got out of line, once burning Dennis's hands after he found him playing with matches. Several years earlier Murry had lost his eye in a freak industrial accident and, to scare the boys, would take his prosthetic eye out at the dinner table and wink at them with his scarred, contorted socket. While this horrified Brian and Carl, it amused Murry's mischievous middle son, Dennis, who took the eye out of its container one early morning to share at school for Show and Tell.

Egotistical, fearless, and athletic, Dennis paced the suburban house with nervous energy, pulling pranks even though he knew his father would punish him unmercifully. "That asshole beat the shit out of us," Dennis said. "Instead of saying, 'Son, you shouldn't shoot a BB gun at the streetlight,' he'd go 'BOOOOOM!' I got the blunt end of a broom. CRACK! One minute late, just one minute late! BOOM! He treated us like shit and his punishments were sick, but you played a tune for him and he was a marshmallow. This mean motherfucker would cry with bliss like the lion in *The Wizard of Oz* when he heard the music."

It's no wonder the Wilson boys learned to make music at an early age, forming a group with cousin Mike Love and pal Al Jardine before they were even out of high school. Dennis, as the only surfer in the brand-new band, had the blazing idea to write a song about the California surfing craze, which resulted in the Beach Boys' first release, "Surfin'," reaching number seventy-five on the charts. Despite its success, frustrated songwriter Murry complained that the song was amateurish and took over as producer. He also formed his own publishing company, writing the contracts giving him controlling interest in Sea of Tunes, which allowed him tremendous control over the Beach Boys' career while his oldest boy, Brian, churned out song after song after song, hit after staggering hit.

Fun-loving, upbeat, and full of sunshine, fast cars, and surfboards, the Beach Boys' songs came to embody wholesome teenage California living. I used to spread cocoa butter all over my budding body and bake at the beach while my transistor blasted "Let's go surfin' now / Everybody's learnin' how . . ." It felt so good to be a teenager on the brink of life's sparkling possibilities.

Even though the boys had hot new cars and a lot of female attention, especially eighteen-year-old Dennis, who was balancing several girlfriends at once, Murry continued to exert his domineering pressure on the band, once slapping Dennis across the face for cursing in front of a group of fans. The final affront came in April 1964 as Brian was working

Dennis Wilson—before. (MICHAEL OCHS ARCHIVES/VENICE, CALIF.)

on the catchy anthem "I Get Around" in the studio. Murry told Brian that he was a loser, that the music was second rate, that *he,* Murry, had the real talent in the family. Brian picked his father up out of the chair, threw him up against a wall, and fired him. But Murry would get his revenge.

While Brian overworked himself to the point of exhaustion, coming up with new songs for his ever-demanding record company, his handsome younger brother Dennis was enjoying the rock-god high life. Calling himself "The Wood," because he was always "hard and ready," Dennis had thick, sandy hair and a chiseled surfer body. By the time the fifth single, "Little Deuce Coupe," hit the charts, Dennis rarely played drums on the sessions, too busy spending money and hanging out with an ever-changing assortment of motley humanity, only too happy to indulge in his rebellious generosity of spirit. He married his sweetheart, Carol Freedman, adopting her toddler, Scott, but cheated on her consistently without apology or remorse.

Desperately wanting to be part of the burgeoning hip Hollywood scene, despite his wife, Marilyn's, protests, Brian took his first tab of LSD in early 1965, made by a San Francisco chemist named Owsley Stanley—acid that was so strong, the dosage would later be cut to one-tenth the amount. Already smoking grass, and precariously overtaxed and on the outer edge of reality, Brian decided to stop touring with the Beach Boys. Eventually he had a gigantic tented sandbox built in his bedroom, where he placed his baby grand piano so he could wiggle his toes in the sand while he composed.

Dennis Wilson—after. (COPYRIGHT ©1994 MICHAEL JACOBS/MJP)

In late 1966 Brian's psychedelic masterpiece, "Good Vibrations," was high on the charts, and even without him on the road, the Beach Boys' tours were earning two million dollars a year, and Dennis was having one wild-ass time. He loved the spotlight, the limousines, the ever-ready females, the crazed adulation from the crowds, and despite his underlying desire to please his father by staying sober, Dennis also began to indulge heavily in drugs and alcohol. Even after Mike Love took him to meet the Beatles' Indian savior, the Maharishi Mahesh Yogi, Dennis continued to spin further out of control.

Dennis picked up two hippie girls in Malibu one spring afternoon in 1968, took them home to show off his gold records, and had sex with both of them.

(He would soon discover he had gotten gonorrhea for the pleasure.) At three A.M. that same night he came home from a recording session to find his house on Sunset Boulevard overrun with a dozen half-naked girls, including that afternoon's double duo, who introduced Dennis to their prophet—a slight, untidy, hunchbacked fellow with malevolent eyes. "This is the guy we were telling you about. This is Charles Manson."

Dennis was easy prey for Manson, an illiterate, long-haired ex-con who took full advantage of the sixties peace-and-love philosophy by offering his passel of women in exchange for whatever he could get. Charlie and the oddly subservient girls moved in with Dennis and stayed the entire summer, helping themselves to his cars, clothes, food, and money, having nightly orgies, weirdly choreographed by the ever-watchful Manson.

Charlie wanted to be a rock star and thought Dennis was his surefire ticket into the recording studio. But after extolling the musical virtues of "the Wizard," Dennis couldn't convince anyone at his record company to give Charlie a break. Dennis introduced Manson to his friend Gregg Jakobson, who was impressed enough to bring producer Terry Melcher to the Sunset Boulevard house to hear him sing. On one occasion Dennis drove Melcher home to Melcher's house at 10050 Cielo Drive while Charlie strummed his guitar in the backseat. Finally Dennis took Charlie and several of his girls to the new studio Brian had built in his house and a few songs got recorded. Brian's wife, Marilyn, was so freaked out by Manson that she disinfected her sinks and toilets whenever "the Family" left. Brian stayed in his sandbox.

After the sessions Charlie expected that Terry Melcher would help him get a contract with a major label, but it never happened. Melcher also promised Charlie that he would listen to his new songs, but on the appointed day he didn't show up.

By the end of the summer, Dennis wanted the Manson Family out of his house. They had relieved him of over a hundred thousand dollars—money spent on food, clothes, a wrecked Mercedes, and constant doctor's bills for the recurring bouts of the clap. And Charlie's true nature had started to reveal itself. He pulled a knife on Dennis, and a couple of weeks later, while the Beach Boys were on the road, Dennis let his lease expire and the Family were thrown out.

In March 1969 Manson went back to Cielo Drive looking for Terry Melcher, only to find that he had rented the place to director Roman Polanski and his wife, Sharon Tate. On August 9, while Roman was working in Europe, five people were brutally massacred on Cielo Drive, including Sharon Tate, who was eight months pregnant.

Not long afterward Manson showed up at Gregg Jakobson's house, looking for Dennis. Told he was out of town, Manson raged, "Oh yeah? Well, when you see Dennis, tell him this is for him," and pulling a .45 from his waistband, threw a bullet onto the floor. "And I've got one for Scott [his stepson], too."

On November 19 Manson and the Family were arrested for the gruesome murders on Cielo Drive. Though reporters often queried Dennis about this period in his life, he usually refused to discuss it. But during an interview in 1976, he said, "I don't talk about Manson, I think he's a sick fuck. I think of Roman and those wonderful people who had a beautiful family and they fucking had their tits cut off. I want to benefit from *that*?"

Later that same year Murry got his revenge, selling Sea of Tunes—*all* of Brian's songs, up to *Pet Sounds*—for one lump sum, which he kept. "It killed him," Brian's wife, Marilyn, said. "It *killed* him, he was tortured. He couldn't believe his father had done that to his songs." The total worth of that catalog is inestimable. (Murry died in 1973, and Brian recently went to court and reclaimed his catalog along with ten million dollars. Mike Love then sued Brian, saying he contributed to the songs, and Brian agreed that Mike would receive five million and split future royalties on 3 songs.)

Dennis remarried in 1970, and his relationship with waitress Barbara Charren started out full of promise. They had two sons, Michael and Carl, but by 1972 had moved fourteen chaotic times. His temper started creeping out of control and during one argument with Barbara, Dennis put his fist through a plate-glass window, cutting his hand so severely that he had to be replaced on tour for over a year. He went into therapy, suffering from guilt over his "undeserved" fame and money and the fear that he would always live in the shadow of his brothers. Dennis later laughingly admitted that the only reason he went to therapy week after week was to see if he could talk the female doctor into sleeping with him.

Dennis deeply desired to communicate with his father, but when Murry died of a heart attack, the only son to attend the funeral was Carl. To make sure his father was really dead, Dennis took Barbara with him to the morgue,

A Beach Boy on the beach in his birthday suit. (BOOM! ARCHIVES)

but the day of the funeral he flew to Europe with one of Barbara's best friends. Dennis's second marriage was over.

Wife number three (and four) was actress Karen Lamm. A volatile blond beauty, she seemed to be a flawless match for the impulsive, self-destructive drummer. "Dennis taught me that you treat a person in the gutter the same way you treat people in the White House. He was the same with everybody," Karen recalled. "But Dennis was in a lot of pain because of his hellish relationship with his father. Murry was the all-time tyrant son of a bitch, and Dennis never received the kind of love, admiration, and respect that Brian got, so he vied for attention by pulling antics and being a practical joker." Then she added sadly, "He was a bit lost."

Dennis bought himself a beautiful Japanese sailing ship, calling it the *Harmony,* and the world seemed good for the couple. "Dennis didn't do drugs when we were first married, he was the best guy. He'd get up in the morning and catch halibut for our breakfast, he'd go out and dive and surf, we'd run on the beach every morning. It was so good, he didn't think he deserved it. He was an angel, he didn't mess around. I had a great three-year stint. The other five years I got my butt kicked!!"

Karen seemed to be able to accept the rock-and-roll infidelities after her singing stint on the road with the Beach Boys. "I know Dennis loved me with all his heart. Guys will be guys, boys will be boys. It's all about the male ego and has nothing to do with the woman in their life. I'm not saying I applauded it, but I understood it. When you perform in front of two hundred and fifty thousand people, you get it. When you come offstage, you think you can go to the hotel, call your wife, and go to bed? The energy, the adrenaline is pumpin', people are telling you how great you are, and it's lonely on tour. But he was jealous—when I'd say hello to someone on the street, it was, 'Did you fuck him? Did you fuck him?'" But Dennis's drug taking threatened the marriage. Once Karen found a bottle of cocaine at the studio and spilled it all over the carpet. Upon returning the next day and finding the locks had been changed, she hurled a brick through the front window. Another time she shot up the Mercedes 450SL Dennis bought her. "We were both dynamos. When you put two dynamos together, you get dynamite!" she said with a wicked smile. "It was as tempestuous as it gets." During this turbulent period Dennis recorded a solo album, *Pacific Ocean Blue,* which sold a respectable two hundred thousand copies, earned excellent reviews, and created jealous resentment within the band. Despite the beautiful music they made together, Dennis and Karen got their first divorce in 1976—but didn't stop seeing each other.

For fifteen years the Beach Boys had remained a viable, money-making band, and after some very controversial therapy with Dr. Eugene Landy, Brian resumed touring in the summer of 1976. In spite of serious inner turmoil, road-stoned madness, and backstabbing, the Beach Boy machine continued to make millions.

Though Dennis had beaten Karen up pretty brutally on a road trip to New Zealand, fracturing her sternum in three places, and had been caught with a sixteen-year-old girl in Arizona and arrested for "contributing to the delinquency of a minor," Karen Lamm remarried Dennis in Las Vegas in the summer of 1978. "When I tell you he was the greatest man I've ever known, I don't say it lightly," Karen told me. "I say it with all my heart." Dennis went into a detox center, and the two dynamos hoped for another new start. A few months later, however, while recording songs at Village Studios for his second solo album, Dennis met Christine McVie, keyboardist and singer for Fleetwood Mac. Just before Christmas 1978, Dennis moved into Christine's house, where he lived for two years, driving her mad with his severe drug and alcohol addiction and vast array of personal problems.

Brian had been fairly drug-free since his therapy with Dr. Landy, but after he did some heroin on a tour of Australia, Dennis was blamed for the incident, and the internal rift between band members escalated to the breaking point. In front of a sold-out crowd at the Universal Amphitheater, Dennis mumbled into the microphone something about "cocaine and Quaaludes," knocked his drums over, and leapt ferociously at Mike Love. Eventually a mutual restraining order was obtained to keep Dennis and Mike apart. So much for the Maharishi. Then Dennis was asked to leave the band "for his own good." "The band kicked him out when they threw up their hands and said, 'We can't do anything'" Karen told me. "They got all this advice, tough-love shit." By this time Dennis was so heavily in debt that he was forced to sell his beloved sailing ship, the *Harmony*.

Dennis almost destroyed Christine McVie's life before he finally moved out and got his own place in Venice, which was soon filled up with vagrants, pushers, and hangers-on. One day a blond teenage girl showed up with a friend. Sixteen-year-old Shawn was Mike Love's shunned illegitimate daughter, and Dennis set out to make her his own. "Mike Love was a total asshole," Karen Lamm said. "Dennis came offstage one night, and the light was in his eyes and Mike kicked him square in the balls. Dennis stole shows. He was a heartthrob. He married Shawn as a "fuck you" to Mike." Shawn became one of the many people who crashed at Dennis's pad, and when their son, Gage, was born, Dennis married her. Shawn had hoped that her close proximity to the Beach Boys would endear her to her father, but the ploy didn't work. Neither did the marriage. Less than four months after the wedding, Shawn drove her silver BMW right into the front door of Dennis's rented Trancas beach house, scrawling "No love" and "No respect" on the walls with crayons. Dennis filed for divorce, and Shawn moved into the Santa Monica Bay Inn with baby Gage.

When the lease was up on the beach house, Dennis's manager, Bob Levine, made him an offer—Dennis could spend some time in rehab, and when he finished the program Bob would get him a new home. Dennis was half a million dollars in debt, with no real place to live and no money in his pockets. He was overweight and bloated, his bearded faced heavily lined, his eyes blood-shot. He spoke in a hard, rasping voice, made worse by several operations to remove polyps from his vocal cords, and still smoked two packs of unfiltered Camels a day. Over the past few years many people who cared for Dennis had tried to get him some help. At one point the Beach Boys put a private jet at his disposal to take him to the rehab center of his choice, but Dennis never set foot on the plane. They offered to pay him one-fifth of the touring money—even though he wasn't on tour—as long as he was in a clinic. He had tremors and had started to have seizures, but Dennis always had an excuse not to go to rehab, and his latest excuse was Gage.

On December 4, 1983, his thirty-ninth birthday, Dennis went to Room 353 at the Bay Inn to pick up his son Gage, and found Shawn asleep in bed with two men (all of them fully clothed), his son wandering around the room unattended. He went wild, screaming and ripping the room apart. Threatening to call police and have them all arrested for drugs, Dennis suddenly bolted with the baby and wandered into traffic on Ocean Avenue. When he saw the BMW he had bought for Shawn in the parking lot, he smashed the windows in with a baseball bat. Eventually Dennis dropped Gage off with friends and resumed his frenzied downhill roaming.

During the month of December, Dennis was adrift and disoriented, crashing in cheap motels and at friends' apartments. Two days before Christmas, Bob Levine drove Dennis to St. John's Hospital for a twenty-one-day detox program. He was given Librium to relieve the wretched withdrawal symptoms and, though he tried to reach Carl and Brian several times, seemed determined to stick out the three-week program. Then Shawn called to tell him that she and Gage were being thrown out of the Bay Inn for nonpayment of rent. Determined to help, Dennis left the clinic on Christmas Day and, arriving at the Bay Inn, found Shawn with a boyfriend. A shoving match ensued, and Dennis, doped up with Librium, got beaten very badly. St. John's Hospital refused to readmit him, so Dennis checked into Marina Hospital, where he spent one night before making yet another escape. A sometime girlfriend, former Playboy Bunny Crystal McGovern, picked him up and they went to see an old friend of Dennis's, Bill Oster, on his boat, the *Emerald,* right next to the empty slip where the *Harmony* had been docked. Bill and his girlfriend, Brenda, were happy to see Dennis but were concerned about the condition he was in, hiding his bottle of vodka several times. Oster told Dennis, "It wasn't six months ago that I said to Brenda, 'I hope the next time we see Dennis it's not at his funeral.'" To which Dennis replied, "Don't you worry about that." The foursome slept that night on the *Emerald,* and Dennis was up at nine A.M. drinking screwdrivers. He called Bob Levine and agreed to spend thirty days in a detox program in New Mexico if Levine would buy back the *Harmony* for him, swearing over and over that he would complete the program—for Gage's sake. He would pull his life together for Gage.

After lunch Dennis decided to take a swim in the icy water, diving down thirteen feet where the *Harmony* had been berthed, recovering small pieces of metal fittings, an old rotted piece of rope. After about twenty minutes he came in for another turkey sandwich and his friends tried to convince him to stay out of the freezing water. He got the shivers, his teeth were chattering, and he was knocking back the screwdrivers. Swearing there was a treasure chest below, Dennis insisted on diving again, this time returning with a large rectangular object covered with mud that turned out to be a wedding picture of Dennis and Karen Lamm in a sterling silver frame. The glass was shattered, but the water-bleached photo showed the confident young couple, laughing at the world. Then Dennis went down into the dark waters again, and never came up.

Dennis was found forty-five minutes later. A four-man team located his body on the muddy floor of the marina, directly under the spot where his precious *Harmony* had been berthed. The only surfer in the Beach Boys had drowned.

Since the divorce hadn't come through, Shawn was still legally Dennis's widow, and the family had to go along with her wishes that Dennis be buried at sea. It turned out that there was a federal law prohibiting burial at sea, but a personal request was made to President Reagan, and special permission was granted. Dennis's body was put in a body bag and dropped into the ocean.

"I've always had this deep-seated thing in me that I've never talked about,"

DEPARTMENT OF TRANSPORTATION
UNITED STATES COAST GUARD

MAILING ADDRESS:
COMMANDER (dpt)
ELEVENTH COAST GUARD DISTRICT
UNION BANK BLDG.
400 OCEANGATE
LONG BEACH, CA. 90822

09 January 1984

Regional Director
Environmental Protection Agency
Region IX Office
100 California Street
San Francisco, California 94111

Dear Sir:

Pursuant to Title 40 CFR, Part 229, the remains of DENNIS WILSON were buried at sea by USCGC POINT JUDITH (WPB 82345) at 1711 local time (5:11 Pm) 04 January 1984, in location 33-53.9°N, 118-38.8°W. This position is greater than three nautical miles from land and the water depth in excess of 100 fathoms.

Sincerely,

J. F. STUMPFF
Commander, U. S. Coast Guard
Chief, Planning Staff
By direction of the District Commander

Karen Lamm later told me. "I know he was on one hundred milligrams of Librium a day to get off alcohol, he was in rehab at St. John's, and within forty-eight hours he was dead. He had a huge gash in his head, and they called it hypothermia, and I've talked to several detectives and doctors—the water temperature was fifty-eight degrees, and his body was not even near that, so it wasn't hypothermia." Karen says she's not convinced by any of the explanations of how Dennis died.

"The killer for me was he had just found our wedding frame. He'd pitched it over the boat when he was mad at me. The last words he spoke were about that picture." Karen's eyes brimmed with tears. "Dennis had the deepest, most caring heart. He was in a lot of pain because he was so supersensitive. There's a medical terminology for someone who is so hypersensitive. I can find it out for you."

Said big brother Brian Wilson in his heartfelt book, *Wouldn't It Be Nice:*

> I thought of the last time I'd seen him. Where? A concert. He'd stumbled out from behind his drums and wobbled to the microphone. He smiled. That never changed. Then, in a voice ruined by cigarettes and alcohol, he sang, "You Are So Beautiful." As he sang, tears ran down his face as if he was singing for the last time. After the show, I'd stood backstage and watched Dennis sip from a can of soda. He wasn't much different from when we were kids, still angry and restless. . . . I was riveted in the front of the [television] set through the five, six and seven o'clock local broadcasts. They provided me with a glimpse of my middle brother. They showed Dennis lying on the cement, covered by a large body sack. His arm and leg stuck out. I knew the picture was real, but I still hoped, expected, Dennis to get up and yell "Surprise!" He didn't. He couldn't. I thought, My God, that's the last time I'll ever see Dennis.

FINAL CHAPTER

■

■

JIM GORDON

■

Mother, I Want to . . .

As one of the finest drummers in rock and roll, Jim Gordon played with John Lennon, George Harrison, the Beach Boys, and Frank Zappa, and was a member of Eric Clapton's Derek and the Dominoes, Traffic, and one of my faves, the Souther, Hillman, Furay Band. Brought up in the San Fernando Valley by hardworking parents who appreciated his musical talent, by the age of twelve Jim had his own drums and a music room to practice in. Jim's dad coached his Little League team, and even though Jim was a shy teenager, he was voted class president in junior high. But something was wrong. As a little boy, Jim felt isolated and alone, turning at first to food for solace, until his weight became a problem, and then to the voices. Inside his head the voices cheered Jim, made him feel worthwhile. But in high school, the voices gradually took a backseat to his music, which had become all-important.

His first band, Frankie and the Jesters, played Hollywood clubs, and when UCLA offered Jim a music scholarship, he turned it down, ready to pursue a career in rock and roll. Spotted by the Everly Brothers' bass player, Jim landed a gig touring Europe, which led to more gigs, and pretty soon he was an in-demand session drummer, charging double time for his services. In 1964 Jim married a lively go-go dancer, and the couple both worked on the TV show "Shindig," buying themselves a house near Jim's parents. Jim continued to do well as a session drummer, briefly forming his own band before joining the bluesy duo Delaney and Bonnie in 1969, which led to a stoned-out stint with Joe Cocker's Mad Dogs and Englishmen. He had only piddled around with pot, but on the road Jim discovered psychedelics and found he had a huge appetite for all kinds of drugs. Having divorced his wife, Jim took up with singer Rita Coolidge—also on the Cocker tour—but the romance ended when, for no apparent reason, Jim gave Rita a black eye. Called to England by George Harrison, who wanted him to play on *All Things Must Pass,* Jim was asked to become a part of Eric Clapton's Derek and the Dominoes. Jim's creativity was at full force when he cowrote "Layla" with Eric, but the group broke up in 1972. "The producers wouldn't pay me for 'Layla,'" Jim told *Rolling Stone,* "because they said I would be dead in six months anyway." Despite the warning, Jim went from heavy cocaine use to shooting heroin, continuing to play drums behind the greats.

After working on John Lennon's *Imagine* album, Jim recorded and toured with Traffic, and back in L.A., he was more in demand than ever. He bought a house, a new Mercedes, and got married again. His reputation was solid, and Jim thought he was happy. The voices had all but faded, kept at bay by his addiction to speedballs (cocaine mixed with heroin). But out of the black they started coming back. Jim's pleasant, outgoing manner was replaced by a brewing paranoia. Even as a new member of Souther, Hillman, Furay, he hid out in hotels, worried about younger drummers stealing his place. Arriving home from the market one afternoon, his wife, Renée, was confronted by a wild-eyed Jim who pointed at the floor, saying "the magic triangle." He then accused her of bringing evil spirits into the house before knocking her down and cracking her ribs. After six months of marriage, Renée left him, but Jim's voices—an entire family of them, including his mother—were there to keep him company.

"The voices started out friendly," Jim told *Rolling Stone.* "They were giving me little pointers. How to take care of myself and the house. How to shop. I was glad for the help. . . . They said I had some kind of responsibility to God and country. I was king of the universe, they said. I had to make sacrifices, and

I had to do what they said. That's when my mother started making me eat half my food." Jim may have eaten only half the food on his plate, but his alcohol consumption quadrupled. He still managed to play drums. Barely. When Jim accused session guitarist Dean Parks of "moving his hands," word got out that Jim Gordon had become a liability. One after another, women came and went, frightened by Jim's uncontrollable violent streak, and the voices, especially the voice of his mother, tormented him night and day, demanding the impossible.

In the real world, Jim's mother was very concerned, insisting that Jim seek help. He checked into a psychiatric hospital for the first of fourteen times, but the voices continued and he attempted suicide. Ironically, his mother saved his life. Encouraged by an offer from Jackson Browne to tour, Jim made an attempt to bring his life into some kind of order, but was thwarted by the imagined voice of his mother. Dylan asked him to go on the road, but Mother said no. In the middle of a Vegas gig with Paul Anka, Mother made Jim go back to L.A., where he checked back into the hospital and threatened to kill a nurse. By 1980 Jim had given up his music and started moving from place to place, uncomfortable wherever he went. His mother's voice had become the voice of evil, and his mother had *become* that voice. He believed she had killed Karen Carpenter and wanted him to die, too. In October 1982 Jim checked himself into the hospital again, claiming that he was "dying of hate." On June 1, 1983, Jim called his mother, telling her that she was "bugging" him again, threatening to kill her. When Mrs. Gordon called the police, they told her to leave her lights on. She tried to get a restraining order against her son, but got no help and finally had to give up.

The voices told Jim how to silence his mother's voice. He was to hit her with the hammer first, so that she wouldn't suffer when he began stabbing. When Mrs. Gordon opened the door to her son at eleven-thirty the night of June 3, that's exactly what he did, leaving the knife in the seventy-two-year-old woman's chest before heading to a bar and getting beyond blitzed. When the police arrived at his door to tell Jim of his mother's death, he calmly confessed. In the police car Jim sobbed, "I'm sorry, I'm sorry, I'm sorry, but she's tortured me for years." Later he said, "I had no interest in killing her, I wanted to stay away from her. I had no choice. It was so matter-of-fact, like I was being guided like a zombie. She wanted me to kill her, and good riddance to her."

James Beck Gordon was found guilty of second-degree murder and given sixteen years to life, even though five psychiatrists testified that he was an acute paranoid schizophrenic. Even after Mother was gone, the voices didn't stop. In his head Jim was forced to obey his attorney and his brother, who wouldn't let him eat desserts. Jim has served fourteen years and, despite being heavily medicated, has a dim hope of release. In a recent interview with the *Washington Post,* Jim wasn't able to admit to the crime, believing that it just "happened." But he no longer hears the voices. "My mother, she persecuted me a great deal, I felt. And it finally got so bad that I just gave up and got a condominium and just stayed indoors. I didn't ever go anyplace. That's when I started hearing voices and having delusional thoughts and hallucinations, and all of a sudden the crime occurred."

I wrote to Jim in jail, sending him my first book, and received a letter many months later, which began: "You may not remember who I am. I am Jim Gordon the drummer from Hollywood and Sherman Oaks." In closing he told me that he was still playing drums, "and keeping my music up. . . ."

■

KURT STRUEBING

■

On April 7, 1986, a Seattle 911 operator received a call regarding a "problem." When asked the nature of the problem, the caller referred to it as a "God job." Asked what a "God job" was, the caller replied "insanity," adding that he had just killed his mother with a pair of scissors and a hatchet. When the police arrived on the scene, they discovered a young nude male standing in the parking lot. Kurt Struebing, age twenty, approached the officer, saying, "I killed my mother and then I killed myself." The officer then went inside the house and made a report: "I took a preliminary walk through the apartment, a white victim approximately fifty years is naked on her back in the master bedroom . . . partially clothed with her nightclothes pulled up above her hips. . . . The victim's head has numerous hatchet-type wounds. There are numerous stab wounds to the left breast and neck as well as defense type wounds to both arms. There is a bloodied hatchet and a pair of scissors on a wall chest of drawers. . . . The walls are bloodspattered." A search warrant revealed various books on "the occult and Satan," as well as photos of Kurt in "staged death scenes."

N.M.E. (spelled with swastikas instead of periods) were/are a doomy death-metal band from Federal Way, Washington, and guitarist Kurt Struebing was/is the driving force. Their first album, *Unholy Death,* came out on a small label, Pentagram Records. In a 1985 blurb in *Subway* magazine, N.M.E. placed an ad that read:

> N.M.E. are of Hell—or is it more? We, young as we may be, have taken a responsibility . . . have declared war on the world, be it a peaceful or violent war. I, Kurt have taken the responsibility of New Messiah Emerging. Spewing forth from the New Metal Energy capi-

tol [sic] of Seattle, we N.M.E. are very intent on getting our message across. . . . If doubt is evil, then evil we are. Take this only as serious as it is meant, but don't bet against us. . . . respectively, N.M.E.—Kurt Struebing—The New Messiah.

In the police car, Kurt said that his mother, Darlene Struebing, was a data processor for Pacific Northwest Bell, and when asked to describe events leading to the murder, Kurt replied, "It's been a long night, I just got off from reality, can I still be an artist?" The police wondered why Kurt felt his mother had to die and he answered, "I just got caught up in everything, I couldn't cry. I learned too late that I could be whatever I want to be."

According to Kurt's friends, although he didn't get along with his father, his relationship with his mother was one of mutual respect and support. (His parents were divorced.) They also said that Kurt was not a heavy drug user but had gotten "weird" right before committing the heinous crime, cutting off his waist-length hair and admitting to one friend that he had recently realized he was gay. The day before the murder Kurt had been practicing with N.M.E. and acting strangely, saying that he was reading people's minds and felt "psychotic." The band rented a rug shampooer to clean the rugs, and unbeknownst to the rest of N.M.E., Kurt drank an entire bottle of rug shampoo, later telling police he had wanted to "clean himself out." He became violently ill and stripped naked before heading back home.

"Kurt says that during this confusing time he was thinking that all people were robots," his psychiatric evaluation reveals. "He had paranoid thoughts such as that people were stealing things from him. He was unable to sleep and very hyperactive. He felt his friends were going to kill him when they took him home. He grabbed a baseball bat . . . and hit one of his friends in the chin. He indicated that his mind was 'racing'. . . . He kept having recurring thoughts that he was really an alien cleaning up after humans. He felt that he was a robot placed here in order to build up the planet for some other force. He remembers killing his mother with the ax and scissors, but denies any sexual activity of any kind. However, at Western State Hospital he did tell one orderly attendant that something sexual had gone on. Apparently he felt that if he killed himself and his mother, he would be killing robots who would be replaced by the other force. . . . This was an experiment for him to determine whether or not they were actually robots."

Kurt Struebing was charged with first-degree murder as well as rape and sent to Western State Hospital for evaluation, where he tried to kill himself by leaping from his bed and landing on his head on the cement floor. He pleaded guilty to second-degree murder when several mental-health experts found that he was psychotic at the time of the crime. He was then sentenced to twelve years in the mentally ill offenders' unit of the reformatory at Monroe,

Washington. The prosecutor's office recommended that Kurt serve eight years, and the judge agreed. "We believe that at the time of the crime Struebing suffered from mental disability. His capacity to appreciate the wrongfulness of his conduct or to conform his conduct to the requirements of the law was significantly impaired." When Kurt was released in April 1994, he got himself a job making pizzas, re-formed N.M.E. with most of the original members, and started playing clubs and looking for a record deal. N.M.E.'s album, *Unholy Death,* has recently been rereleased.

■

CHUCK BERRY

■

My Ding-a-Ling

It's pretty scary that one of rock's premier forces is seventy years old. But for an old guy Chuck Berry still seems to have plenty of sex drive.

When he was honored at the Twenty-seventh Annual Grammy Awards show with a Lifetime Achievement Award, Chuck Berry was heralded as "one of the most influential and creative innovators in the history of American popular music, a composer and performer whose talents inspired the elevation of rock and roll to one of music's major art forms." No doubt about it. But Chuck Berry isn't a very nice guy. I saw him in a Vegas bar a few years back; I was very excited and went over to thank him for being so brilliant. He gave me an evil look, then just stared straight ahead as if I didn't exist. I can understand that he might not want to be bugged, but that was just plain mean.

Charles Edward Anderson Berry was born in San Jose, California, in 1926, though in his autobiography he claims to be from St. Louis, Missouri. After spending three years in reform school for robbery, Chuck got his cosmetology degree, then formed a trio, playing clubs at night while working at St. Louis's Poro School of Beauty Culture by day. He married Themetta Suggs and would eventually have four children with her. In 1955, at age twenty-eight, Chuck met the great Muddy Waters, who put him in touch with Chess Records, where he cut his first single, "Maybellene," which went straight into the Top Ten. The legendary guitar-driven bluesy-country-rockabilly three minutes would influence rock-and-roll artists right up to right now. "The big beat, cars, and young love," said Leonard Chess, "it was a trend and we jumped on it." Next came "Roll Over Beethoven" and a part in the movie *Rock, Rock,*

Rock. Chuck continued to record smash after influential smash, selling multi-millions of records, taking his famous duckwalk around the world.

In December 1959 Chuck was arrested and charged with violating the Mann Act after "transporting a minor across a State Line for immoral purposes." He had hired a fourteen-year-old Apache Indian as a hatcheck girl in his nightclub, but didn't know she had been working as a prostitute. When he found out, Chuck fired her and she called the cops on him. Convicted and sentenced to five years, Chuck eventually served two years in the Indiana Federal Penitentiary.

A boost from the Beatles, who recorded "Roll Over Beethoven," brought Chuck back into the mainstream spotlight and he had another spate of success with "Nadine" and "No Particular Place to Go." In 1972 he recorded his biggest-selling album, *The London Chuck Berry Sessions,* and the naughty "My Ding-a-Ling" became his most successful single.

In June 1978 Chuck performed for President Jimmy Carter at the White House. A month later he was sentenced to five months in prison for tax evasion. Although no more hits were forthcoming, Chuck traveled the world, successfully making the rounds on the oldies circuit. In 1986 he was inducted into the Rock and Roll Hall of Fame by Keith Richards, got his star on the Hollywood Walk of Fame, and was featured in the movie *Hail! Hail! Rock 'n' Roll*. In 1988 Chuck released his autobiography, in which he proudly hints at the shadowy side of his nature: "Now that I know much more about the writing of a book, strangely enough I intend to go for another. One that I will enjoy, the true story of my sex life. It shall not infringe on anyone or thing but me and my excessive desire to continue melting the ice of American hypocrisy regarding behavior and beliefs that are now 'in the closet' and only surface in court, crime, or comical conversation."

In the early seventies my friend Mercy melted some ice with Chuck Berry at Disneyland, of all places. A huge fan of his for years, she was waiting in the backstage area for his arrival. "The whole area was foggy. I was all by myself back there, and an old black Cadillac drives up, something like Mae West ran around in, something from another dimension, and out pops Chuck Berry, and I said, 'I've been waiting for you.' He said, 'Come with me,' and we went into his trailer. I was so high I don't remember if I had sexual intercourse with him," Mercy admits, "but I know he asked me to go to the bathroom in a bucket . . . number two. He wanted to watch me in the act." He then took a photo of her for "his book." "I was naked with a big rainbow wig." When I ask Mercy how she was able to perform on cue, she laughs. "I don't know. I probably had to go to the bathroom and he got lucky!"

On December 27, 1989, it was reported in the *St. Louis Post Dispatch* that a civil suit for invasion of privacy had been filed in St. Charles County Circuit Court by Hosana A. Huck—a former cook at Southern Air, a Wentzville, Missouri, eatery owned by Chuck Berry—alleging that Berry had installed video cameras in the women's restrooms, secretly taping her as well as many other women. The confiscated tapes revealed quick cuts of hundreds of women, all white, in the act of relieving themselves. One of the cameras must have been built right into the toilet, because it captured, close up, the moment of defecation and urination, while overhead cameras displayed the toilet's contents before they were flushed. Most of the women seemed to be of legal age, but some were little girls.

A class-action suit was later filed by ten women, who were representing at least two hundred others who were videotaped while using a bathroom at Chuck's restaurant or Berry Park. Other women claiming they had been secretly videotaped filed separate suits.

Tapes also were found by police during a raid on Berry's home after a tip led to suspicion that Chuck was trafficking in cocaine. One informant quoted in the affidavit police filed to obtain the search warrant had told police that Chuck had carried twenty-five kilos of the drug in his guitar case. According to the affidavit, Chuck had allegedly netted nine million dollars over the years from drug trafficking. But no cocaine was discovered in the raid and no charges of drug trafficking were ever filed by authorities against Berry. Some marijuana was found in the police raid and money was seized, along with pornographic slides and fifty-nine videotapes. Chuck was charged with one count of marijuana possession and three counts of child abuse—Missouri law states that the filming of nude children under the age of seventeen for sexual gratification constitutes child abuse. When he arrived back from a tour of Sweden, Chuck turned himself in, but denied making the tapes, using or selling any cocaine.

Three months after the raid, the U.S. Attorney's Office returned Chuck's money, and on November 3, 1990, Chuck sued county prosecutor Bill Hannah, calling the criminal charges against him "maliciously baseless and politically motivated." After the child abuse charges were dropped, Chuck dropped his suit against the prosecutor, agreeing to two years' probation for the misdemeanor marijuana charge and a five-thousand-dollar contribution to local substance abuse programs.

Chuck later settled the suits brought by the women claiming to have been secretly videotaped. According to his lawyer, Chuck paid $1.2 million altogether in settlement, but has continued to deny any involvement in the videotaping.

Somehow one of Chuck's personal X-rated tapes surfaced, and after scrounging around underground I was able to buy the thing for twenty dollars. I watched it between my fingers, like I was seven years old at a horror movie. There's a whole lot of what Mercy doesn't remember doing with Chuck, and then as his buxom blond partner is having a bubble bath, Chuck steps into the tub, holding his ding-a-ling. "See this here? This is what you're gonna bathe in." "It is?" she queries, wide-eyed, before he demands that she "kiss it." "Do you love me?" he asks as he begins to urinate. "Put your hands down!" he demands. "Take it! Take it! Open your mouth!" Pulling her hair off her face, she does as Chuck says. He passes a long blow of gas before the last drop falls. The blonde starts to weep, but Chuck doesn't seem to notice, asking her, "How's that piss taste? Salty, ain't it?" He wants to know if she loves him. She wants a kiss. "Baby, I can't kiss you. You smell like piss. Stand up and take a shower." After the shower, cameraman Chuck says, "Now it's time for my breakfast." Then they're back in the tub, the blonde straddling Chuck's beaming face, doing what Mercy did in the bucket at Disneyland.

■

G.G. ALLIN

■

Public Animal Number One

"To me comfort and conformity are the two biggest enemies. I want to die in tragedy. That really excites me." G.G.'s big plan was to off himself onstage, but he died in an all-too-common OD on June 28, 1993, after being chased out of another one of his outer-limits performance at the Gas Station club in New York.

When asked what kind of music he played, G.G. responded, "Mud, rot, cunt-suckin' sleaze trash. It can't be described at all. We don't fit in with anybody and nobody wants anything to do with us." Answering the question why he started a band, G.G. said, "Just to fuckin' bother people, for revenge. I don't give a fuck what you think of me. I wanted total destruction and I didn't and don't care if everyone hates it. Fuck you. I wanted to be the total self-destructive animal, and I am. I don't like or trust anybody really. When I'm onstage nothin' fuckin' matters. You could fuckin' shoot me, but I might fuck you up first, and I'll definitely rape some bitches." Arrested over fifty times for attempted murder, assault and battery, public lewdness, inciting a riot, indecent exposure, endangering lives, etc., G.G. made sure his audience knew how much he hated himself and all of them through nudity, assault, defecation, urination, masturbation (himself and others), oral sex, rape, eating and flinging his feces, sex with dead animals, bashing out his teeth, eating his own flesh, breaking bones (his own and others), setting himself on fire, slicing himself up with broken bottles and ripped aluminum cans, and knocking himself completely unconscious. But G.G. Allin had a surprisingly dedicated following. "You'd have the real fans who knew G.G. and understood, they would stand right there and exchange punches and get covered with blood and love it," G.G.'s brother and band mate Merle tells me. "It was the greatest thing they had ever experienced—'Here I am covered with blood. I love you, G.G.' "

In 1988, G.G. released a song called "Expose Yourself to Kids"—"Let's fuck some kids/They can't say no/Molest them now/Before they grow." Was this guy serious?

Merle is the keeper of his younger brother's flame—a fascinating combo of outrage and charm. He provides G.G.'s devoted fans with an astonishing number of live videos and taped concerts.

I watched one of G.G.'s videos, *Hated,* and was so repulsed when he got down on his knees and ate his own feces that the ghastly image stayed with me for days. I'm sure that would have pleased G.G. no end. I ask Merle when and why G.G. started this charming practice. "It was in '86 that G.G. first defecated onstage. As things progressed, he had to have an answer for it, so his answer was it was a communion to his people. If you were a Christian, you ate the body of Christ. If you're a G.G. Allin worshiper, you ate the body of G.G. Allin. It was a communion to his people. His blood, his piss, all of that was for his people. "How was he able to do it on call?" I inquire sweetly. "That's a talent right there! When he started defecating onstage, he would use Ex-Lax before a show. I don't know what it was. It seemed like he could do it whenever he wanted to! Ha-ha-ha. . . ."

In an article for *Naked Aggression Magazine,* written by a friend of G.G.'s, Joe Coughlin, he describes one of G.G.'s shows:

> G.G. owns the place. The hype, it turns out, was true all along. This is war. . . . He turns his back to them and squats. They seem to've been expecting it. . . . He pumps out a chain of dark, wet turds, spins around, drops to his knees. . . . They know he's gonna do it, but they're praying he won't just the same. . . . He starts gulping down the pile, spits mouthfuls at the crowd, barking out lines of the chorus between bites. The room is choking on its own dread. Then of all things, *a fucking guitar solo.* G.G. scoops his poop, grunts, drops the mike, takes a whiff and smears it over his face with both hands, down his chest, around his cock, and runs back into the crowd. He gets up and smacks his head into the nearest wall a few times. . . .

It took a lot of digging, but when I finally located G.G.'s brother, Merle, he invited me to his wicked New York loft (his kitchen is painted blood red, decorated with skulls and severed body parts made of some scary, unrecognizable substance), where he reflected on the mad/tragic life he shared with his little brother. "We had a really strange childhood. We lived in a log cabin in New

Hampshire, no shower, no bath. You couldn't drink the water or flush the toilet. We didn't socialize with other kids, go to their houses. My dad was . . . a religious fanatic. When G.G. was born my dad named him Jesus Christ Allin." (His mother later changed it to Kevin Michael.) In the sixth grade G.G. started playing drums, graduating to guitar, preferring music to girls or drugs. "The first time G.G. tripped was when I stuck a tab of acid in his French fries at McDonald's," Merle insists. "He wasn't into drugs. He never had girlfriends in high school. The only sex G.G. had when he was a kid was me and him masturbating each other as young teenagers. He was heavily into masturbation."

I'm a bit apprehensive at first, but soon warm to Merle. He's actually quite appealing in a curious way, covered in leather, his beard in braids. He proudly walks me over to a colorful, childlike painting done by mass murderer John Wayne Gacy, who was brother G.G.'s pen pal. It seems the two men shared a perverse kindred spirit. Merle then continues on with G.G.'s life story.

G.G. played in local bands, recorded with small labels, married his only girlfriend in high school, and settled down. "I was totally disgusted with G.G. at that point," Merle says. "Sandy had him pussy-whipped. He was wearing button-down shirts and taking out the garbage." But since G.G. hadn't sown his wacky oats, after five years of marital bliss he was off with a thirteen-year-old ("G.G. liked 'em young," says Merle. "Ha-ha"), living off people, crashing in cheap boardinghouses. Merle moved to Boston and G.G. worked with two different bands, the Jabbers and the Scumfucs, cutting many records on many different labels, teetering closer and closer to the edge.

"G.G.'s big thing was getting women's panties, getting a bottle of their urine and drinking it or having them pee in his mouth and masturbate. He wasn't into sex, not at all," Merle told me.

Merle returned and briefly formed the AIDS Brigade with his brother, but G.G. was arrested in 1989 and spent eighteen months in prison. Merle calls it "the Ann Arbor incident." A woman, who had invited the band to stay with her while they were performing a gig, accused G.G. of having assaulted her when she passed out after drinking with the band. Apparently G.G. went to town on this girl after she woke up, carving her breasts, face, and stomach, dripping hot wax into her wounds, putting cigarettes out on her and choking her for three days. In her statement to investigators, the victim said, "He was cutting at my chest. He said it was beautiful. Like painting a picture. He wanted my breasts to bleed more. He gouged at my left breast . . . and when it began to bleed more he said . . . that my breast looked like crying eyes." "What happened was," Merle recalls, "she had to go to the hospital and the police made her fill out a report. Originally she accused a bunch of black guys." However, the victim says that she was initially afraid of retaliation by G.G., so she didn't name him at first.

After pleading no contest to felonious assault charges, G.G. spent eighteen months in prison. When he was released in 1991, he formed the Murder Junkies with Merle and continued to tour. Joe Coughlin recalls a show in Atlanta: "In a stark moment I saw him standing under a severe white light, his bandanna off, his face knotted in a rage, a trickle of blood running into his eyes. I was sad and drained to think he's endured fifteen years of this. I thought of the million bands I'd seen and suddenly they meant nothing, a fluffy bunch of notes. This was uncool, a threat, what rock and roll was meant to be, but it was more than that. G.G. hit me as everything both right and wrong with being alive all at once: all of the power and all of the sickness working together. There wasn't one possible emotion not being felt in that room. That in itself was dangerous. It was huge, and it was *real*."

"Prison was the best thing to happen to G.G." says Merle. "It made him more angry, stronger, and it made him realize he wanted to go out and fuck other people up. He was much more focused on getting his message out there. The intensity level was multiplied by ten." G.G. wanted to kill himself onstage. "He would have taken many people with him," Merle insists. "He talked about sticking dynamite up his ass and jumping into the crowd, or having a machine gun. He would have killed as many people as he could have while killing himself." In 1992, after being arrested all over the country, G.G. was extradited back to Michigan and had to serve another year in prison. Upon release, the Murder Junkies did another record, G.G. appeared on the Jerry Springer and Jane Whitney talk shows, pissing off America, and went back on the road. The last show of the tour was the Gas Station in New York. Merle tells me G.G. was sick from the blood poisoning he got so often—the hazard of feces getting into fresh wounds. "I don't know if it had anything to do with his death, but G.G. wasn't really healthy when he came off tour. It wasn't a suicide. He would have been angry at himself for dying that way." After the Gas Station mania, G.G. took heroin with some acquaintances and OD'd. "Drugs were something G.G. would do when everything else was taken care of," Merle says. "He had his message to get across, and that was the most important thing to him. The tour was over, we had just done our last show, the record was in the can, he was in New York, so let's get high!"

Merle misses his brother. "G.G. was Kevin and Kevin was G.G. He was a multiple personality. He tried to balance both parts out as much as he could, but G.G. always took over. He could be Kevin in front of me and my mom. . . . He could relax and enjoy without having to prove himself to everyone, without having to be this tough guy that he was ninety percent of the time. He was always trapped. People wanted more all the time and G.G. felt he had to come up with something more to shock them. Every time he would do something, you'd think, 'Wow! How can he top that?' He always would." Merle has so much respect for his brother, it's quite remarkable. "He really did it the hard way," Merle marvels. "G.G. took it ten times more extreme than Sid Vicious. Sid was a pussy. No doubt."

Excerpts from "Childhood Essay" by G.G. Allin

Born: jesus christ allin
august 29, 1956
lancaster, nh

the first five years of my life were infested with sickness and violence
. . . we lived in darkness father hated light . . . i observed the world
around me as a mere movie, a movie of culprits and phonies. i was the
leading man outside of the screen with a hammer just waiting for my
chance to smash it all to oblivion . . . ˜brother and I became partners in
drug dealing and theft. i never felt like i belonged around anyone. i felt
superior. i hated school and all the other students . . . i would pur-
posely piss my pants so the teachers would send me home . . . my
principal once told me i was a penny waiting for change . . . i also had
predetermined very early in life that i obtained a special, very powerful soul that nobody would . . . be able to stop me from achieving
whatever i wanted. an irritating fire was building up inside of me from
a seed that was planted at my birth . . . bizarre personalities were
awakening within . . . i realize now that these personalities were the
demons living inside of me. i welcomed them as my friends. later in
life i would have intercourse with the devil himself. i could always
make anyone believe what i had to make them believe. the bottom line
was, when you turn your back i'll stab you in it. i also enjoyed wearing my mothers clothes . . . i was a wild child who wanted to look
beautifully outrageous and bright, even if i was filled with inner darkness and machine gun thoughts.

sexual abnormalities were awakening. i liked to play under the table
when mother had company . . . to check out the tightly fitted panties
and fantasize. soon fantasy became reality. i got off sucking the crusty
cunt scrapings from mothers panties . . . i would raid hampers, garbage
cans, and toilets for panties, snot rags, piss, shit, bloody rags, etc. if female company came over i would fix the toilet so it wouldn't flush.
that way i could go in later and feast on body fluids while jerking
off . . . i was always masturbating . . . i had a constant erection. the first
sex i had with another human was with brother. but later in life . . .
with the smelliest of prostitutes, living and dead animals would pre-
vail. i always felt like my parents must have found me on the ground
somewhere and that the darkness of night came from an alien storm
leaving me from another galaxy on the back grounds of that broken
down cabin . . .

CONCLUSION—my demons, inner strengths and physical battles
have guided me through life. my demons and i are not compatible. we

never have been and never will be. we invite you to danger and possibly DEATH . . . i guess after all i must be my father's sons, i am the second coming of jesus christ through alm and constant fire . . .

G. G. Allin

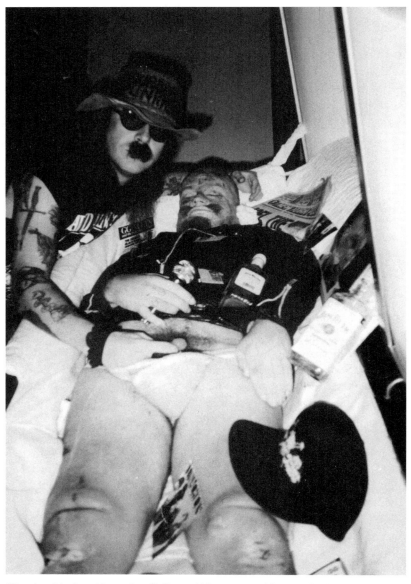

"Brother Merle told me that G.G. would have wanted him to do this last favor for him." (COURTESY MERLE C. ALLIN)

■

AXL ROSE

■

Welcome to the Jungle

At seventeen William Bruce Bailey found out that the man he believed to be his father was in fact his stepfather. When he discovered the shocking truth, Bill Bailey was devastated and enraged, tossing his old name out with the garbage, rechristening himself W. Axl Rose. He once sang in the church choir and taught Sunday school, but Axl said that God had let him down. "If there's somebody up there," he said, "I don't know him. I just don't have a clue about it." The eldest of three children, Axl was raised in Lafayette, Indiana, and had a difficult time in high school, dropping out in his junior year, growing his flaming-red hair long, and singing in rock bands. "When I was in school there were all these stereotypes," Axl said. "If you liked the Stones, you were a faggot because of the time Jagger kissed Keith Richards on 'Saturday Night Live.' If you liked the Grateful Dead, you were a hippie. If you liked the Sex Pistols you were a punker. I guess that would make me a faggot hippie punk rocker." Axl soon escaped the uptight Midwest in favor of the Sunset Strip. Thrown in jail many times, once for an entire summer, Axl finally left Indiana in 1980. Meeting up with another Lafayette boy, Izzy Stradlin, Axl formed various bands, struggling on the local circuit, eventually hooking up with guitarist Slash, drummer Steven Adler, and bassist Duff McKagan. In June 1985 Guns N' Roses played their first gig at the Troubadour. Two people turned up for the show. It was rough going for a long time. The entire band lived and rehearsed in one funky room on Gardner Street. When a dollar could be scrounged up, they would get loaded on wino wine called Nighttrain. By day Axl sold God-knows-what on the telephone, and worked for a while as the night manager at Tower Video. But the buzz was brewing. Guns N' Roses shows were angry and demanding—they created a frenzy, were axed from clubs, pissed off the other bands with their bravado. In March 1986 they signed with Geffen, spending the first half of their advance on clothes and equipment, the second half on drugs. It was right around this time that Axl met nineteen-year-old model Erin Everly, daughter of Don, the Everly Brother. "It was the first relationship I had had," Erin told *People* magazine." I felt like we were two people who didn't have much but who had found each other." According to Erin, police were called later that year by a friend after Axl became violent with Erin. But Erin dismissed it as a "false alarm." She admitted later that her fear had been "bigger than you can imagine."

Appetite for Destruction was released in July 1987, but languished low in the charts. After a cameo by Axl in Clint Eastwood's *The Dead Pool,* "Welcome to the Jungle" made it back on the radio and all hell broke loose. Cowritten with Slash, the song came from an incident Axl had while sleeping in a Bronx schoolyard. "This black guy came up to me and said, 'You know where you are? You in the jungle, baby! You gonna die!'" *Appetite for Destruction* became the biggest-selling (seventeen million) debut album in history.

In January 1989 Axl was arrested for disorderly conduct and public drunkenness after hollering obscenties from Slash's balcony. According to the police report, he asked the arresting officer, "Do you know who we are? I'm a millionaire. I can have your stupid ass!" Police detained Axl for several hours, but no charges were filed.

Erin's friends and family tried to get her to leave Axl. One friend told *People* that she witnessed Axl slap Erin and pull her hair at a barbecue in the Hollywood Hills, saying that he was like a rabid dog. But Erin thought she could ease some of Axl's childhood pain. He had revealed to Erin that he had been sexually abused by his real father at the age of two, and that his stepfather had beat him unmercifully. Erin never knew what might set off Axl's raging temper. "I always thought things would get better," she said, but had to cancel one of her modeling jobs because of the cuts and abrasions she received when Axl dragged her out of their apartment. "There was so much anger in him," Erin told *People.* "Maybe I was this easy person to take it out on."

Erin said that despite her misgivings, when Axl showed up at her door at four A.M. on April 27, 1990, telling her had a gun in the car and threatening to shoot himself if she didn't marry him, she went with him to the Cupid Wedding Chapel in Vegas, where they tied the knot. Axl made solemn promises he would never divorce Erin and never hit her ever again, but according to Erin, he reneged on both counts, beating her so badly that she wound up in the hospital. While she recuperated, Axl brought her things back to his condo, and she gave her marriage another try. But Erin didn't have her own key, and she said Axl wouldn't give her any money. When she had a miscarriage in September, Erin said that she had to sell her Jeep to pay medical expenses. Once again Axl destroyed the house, causing $100,000 worth of damage.

Axl was arrested again in October 1990 for assaulting his female neighbor, supposedly smacking her over the head with a bottle of wine. Axl denied the accusation, claiming his neighbor was an obsessed fan. "She came at me with a wine bottle, she swung it at me, and I grabbed the bottle. I didn't hit her with it—if I had, she wouldn't be walking. She wouldn't be alive." Axl took a lie detector test, which he passed, and the charges were dropped.

In November, Erin told *People,* Axl slapped her around when he didn't like the way she cleaned his CD collection. Erin finally moved out and went into hiding. When Axl tracked her down, she just kept on moving. A year later the marriage was annulled.

In August 1991 Axl was issued a warrant for his arrest after being charged with four counts of misdemeanor assault and one count of property damage in connection with an aborted Guns N' Roses concert in St. Louis that escalated into a riot. In December Axl threatened to sue *Spin* magazine for making "defamatory statements." When asked if he would countersue, publisher Bob Guiccione Jr. replied, "You can't countersue him for being a moron!"

Insisting on releasing two albums at once, Guns N' Roses made history when *Use Your Illusion I* entered the *Billboard* chart at number one while its companion, *Use Your Illusion II*, charted at number two. Axl justified the offensive lyrics in "One in a Million" to *Rolling Stone:* "I used the word 'nigger' because it's a word to describe somebody that is basically a pain in your life, a problem." When asked about the word "faggot," Axl recalled a bad experience he had with a homosexual who attempted to rape him, adding, "I'm not into gay or bisexual experiences. But that's hypocritical of me, because I'd rather see two women together than just about anything else. That happens to be my personal favorite thing." Meanwhile Axl kept missing his court dates in St. Louis while his lawyers negotiated with prosecutors, and was finally arrested in July 1992 at JFK Airport in New York and released on a hundred thousand dollars' bail. In November Axl was fined fifty thousand dollars and placed on two years' probation after being convicted of the assault and property damage charges. When told that his fine would be going to social service groups in the St. Louis area, Axl doubled the payment, saying, "If it's going to a good cause, that's great. We've already given millions to charity, so this is peanuts."

Among his other legal difficulties stemming from the St. Louis concert, Axl was also sued by William Stephenson, a fan who said Axl attacked and injured him during the ruckus that ended the St. Louis concert. That suit was settled although Axl denied attacking the fan.

In August 1993 a twenty-year-old Australian fan hung himself while listening to Guns N' Roses' "Estranged." Said his mother, "I believe this band is inciting kids to do this."

In March 1994 Erin Everly filed suit in L.A., claiming "physical and emotional abuse, assault, sexual battery and false imprisonment" after being subpoenaed by another girlfriend of Axl's, model Stephanie Seymour, who was actually countersuing Axl. Axl sued the supermodel for "kicking and grabbing" him at a 1992 Christmas party in their Malibu home, but it boomeranged on him when she countersued, alleging that Axl had attacked her first, kicking her down a flight of stairs, giving her a black eye and a bloody nose. Eventually, both suits were dropped. In court papers Axl claimed that his actions against Erin were also in self-defense. Erin, at the time of the *People* magazine story, weighed not much more than a hundred pounds.

Erin further accused Axl of "punching her, slapping her, shoving her, kicking her, tying her up, gagging her, spitting on her, striking her with foreign objects, throwing foreign objects at her, picking her up and throwing her and dragging her by her hair." After one beating Erin claimed that she "awoke in a hospital to learn she had been injected with heroin and cocaine and had gone into cardiac arrest." Another time Axl allegedly "caused a friend to break into Everly's house and steal pictures of her dogs who had died, because Rose claimed he needed the pictures to 'transfer the dead dogs' souls to living dogs.'" As of the time of this writing the suit was still pending.

BIBLIOGRAPHY

BOOKS

Antonio, Nina. *Johnny Thunders: In Cold Blood. The Official Biography.* London: Jungle Books, 1987.

Arnold, Gina. *Route 666: On the Road to Nirvana.* New York: St. Martin's Press, 1993.

Azerad, Michael. *The Story of Nirvana: Come As You Are.* New York: Doubleday, 1993.

Bashe, Phillip. *Teenage Idol: The Complete Biography of Rick Nelson.* New York: Hyperion, 1992.

Bockris, Victor. *Keith Richards.* New York: Poseidon, 1991.

Bromberg, Craig. *The Wicked Ways of Malcolm McLaren.* New York: Harper & Row, 1989.

Butler, Dougal. *Full Moon: The Amazing Rock and Roll Life of Keith Moon.* New York: William Morrow, 1981.

Caserta, Peggy. *Going Down with Janis.* Secaucus, N.J.: Lyle Stuart, 1973.

Clark, Alan. *Eddie Cochran: Never to Be Forgotten.* West Covina, Calif.: The National Rock and Roll Archives, 1991.

Cole, Richard. *Stairway to Heaven: Led Zeppelin Uncensored.* New York: Harper & Row, 1992.

Davis, Stephen. *Hammer of the Gods: The Led Zeppelin Saga.* New York: William Morrow, 1985.

Evans, David. *Freddie Mercury: This Is the Real Life.* London: Britannica, 1992.

Fong-Torres, Ben. *Hickory Wind: The Life and Times of Gram Parsons.* New York: Pocket Books, 1991.

Friedman, Myra. *Janis Joplin: Buried Alive.* New York: William Morrow, 1973.

Gaines, Steven. *Heroes and Villains: The True Story of the Beach Boys.* London: Macmillan, 1986.

Green, Jonathon. *The Book of Rock Quotes.* New York: A Delilah Putnam Book, 1982.

Griffin, Sid. *Gram Parsons.* Pasadena, Calif.: Sierra, 1985.

Hopkins, Jerry. *The Lizard King.* New York: Charles Scribner's Sons, 1992.

Hopkins, Jerry, and Danny Sugerman. *No One Here Gets Out Alive.* New York: Warner Books, 1980.

Hotchner, A. E. *Blown Away.* New York: Simon & Schuster, 1990.

Jackson, Laura. *Golden Stone: The Untold Life and Tragic Death of Brian Jones.* New York: St. Martin's Press, 1992.

Joplin, Laura. *Love, Janis.* New York: Viking, 1992.

Kaufman, Phil. *Road Mangler Deluxe.* California: Montrose, 1993.

Kent, Nick. *The Dark Stuff.* London: Penguin, 1994.

Marsh, Dave. *Before I Get Old: The Story of the Who.* New York: St. Martin's Press, 1983.

Mitchell, Mitch. *Jimi Hendrix: Inside the Experience.* New York: St. Martin's Press, 1990.

Monk, Noel, and Jimmy Guterman. *12 Days on the Road with the Sex Pistols.* New York: Quill, 1990.

Patoski, Nick. *Stevie Ray Vaughan: Caught in the Crossroads.* Boston: Little, Brown, 1993.

Paytress, Mark. *Twentieth-Century Boy: The Marc Bolan Story.* London: Sidgwick & Jackson Limited, 1992.

Pike, Jeff. *The Death of Rock and Roll.* Boston: Faber & Faber, 1993.

Prochnicky, Jerry, and James Riordan. *Break On Through.* New York: William Morrow, 1991.

Rawlings, Terry. *Who Killed Christopher Robin? The Truth Behind the Murder of Brian Jones.* London: Merlin, 1994.

Redding, Noel, and Carol Appleby. *Are You Experienced?: The Inside Story Behind the Jimi Hendrix Experience.* London: Picador, 1990.

Rees, Dafydd. *Rock Movers and Shakers.* New York: Billboard, 1991.

Ritz, David. *Divided Soul: The Life of Marvin Gaye.* New York: Da Capo Press, 1995.

Sanchez, Tony. *Up and Down with the Rolling Stones.* New York: William Morrow, 1979.

Savage, Jon. *England's Dreaming: Anarchy, Sex Pistols, Punk Rock and Beyond.* New York: St. Martin's Press, 1992.

Schaffner, Nicholas. *Saucerful of Secrets: The Pink Floyd Odyssey.* New York: Harmony Books, 1991.

Shapiro, Harry, and Caesar Glebbeck. *Jimi Hendrix: Electric Gypsy.* New York: St. Martin's Press, 1990.

Sky, Rick. *The Show Must Go On: The Life of Freddie Mercury.* New York: Citadel Press, 1992.

Spungen, Deborah. *And I Don't Want to Live This Life.* New York: Fawcett, 1983.

Sugerman, Danny. *Appetite for Destruction: The Days of Guns N' Roses.* New York: St. Martin's Press, 1991.

Thompson, Dave. *Never Fade Away: The Kurt Cobain Story.* New York: St. Martin's Press, 1994.

Watkinson, Mike. *Crazy Diamond: Syd Barrett and the Dawn of Pink Floyd.* London: Omnibus, 1991.

Willans, Caron, and John Thomas. *Marc Bolan: Wilderness of the Mind.* London: Xanadu, 1992.

Wolf, Daniel. *You Send Me.* New York: William Morrow, 1994.

NEWSPAPERS AND MAGAZINES

The Clear Lake Mirror Reporter (Iowa)
Entertainment Weekly
Evening Standard (London)
Daily Sketch (London)

The Guardian (London)
Jet
The Los Angeles Times
Melody Maker
New Musical Express
The New York Times
People
The Rocket
Rolling Stone
Seattle Weekly
Spin
Spy
St. Charles Journal (Louisiana)
Vibe
Village Voice
The Washington Post

Pamela Des Barres

INDEX

The Killer backstage at the Palomino Club, shortly before John Belushi's death. (Jasper Dailey)

Red Hot Chili Peppers
In't keep Hillel Slovak
Another heroin OD.
n S. Braun)

Mother Love Bone's supertalented Andrew Wood OD'd on heroin. (Charles Peterson)

N.M.E.'s prophetic album title— before leader Kurt Streubling committed unholy matricide.

NME UNHOLYDEATH

UNHOLY DEATH

Stiv Bators of the Dead Boys with his pants down
while he was still very much alive. (Copyright ©
Chuck Krall Still Photographs)

Tupac Shakur showing his respect for the press. (AP/Wide World Photos)

Two members of Badfinger, Peter Ham (top left) and Tommy Evans (bottom right), hanged themselves eight years apart. (Michael Ochs Archives, Venice, Calif.)

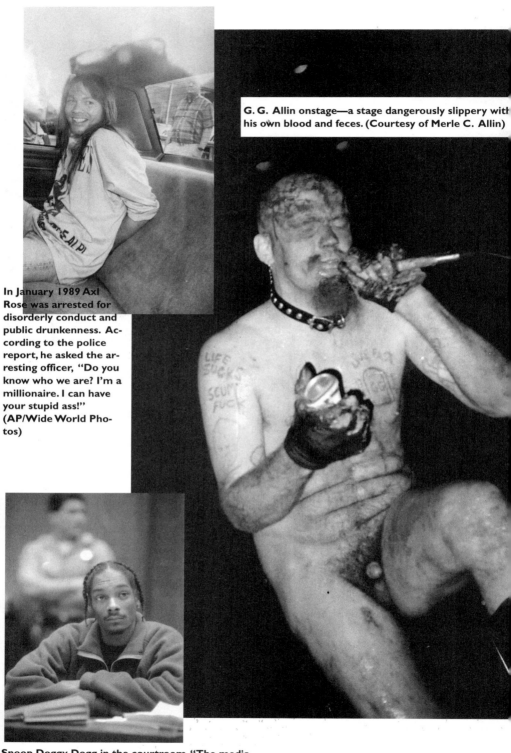

G. G. Allin onstage—a stage dangerously slippery with his own blood and feces. (Courtesy of Merle C. Allin)

In January 1989 Axl Rose was arrested for disorderly conduct and public drunkenness. According to the police report, he asked the arresting officer, "Do you know who we are? I'm a millionaire. I can have your stupid ass!" (AP/Wide World Photos)

Snoop Doggy Dogg in the courtroom. "The media made us guilty, but by the grace of God the jury found us not guilty." (Lisa Rose/Globe Photos)